OUTLINE OF
U.S. HISTORY

Bureau of International Information Programs
U.S. Department of State
2011

OUTLINE OF
U.S. HISTORY

CONTENTS

CHAPTER 1   Early America 4
CHAPTER 2   The Colonial Period. 22
CHAPTER 3   The Road to Independence 50
CHAPTER 4   The Formation of a National Government 66
CHAPTER 5   Westward Expansion and Regional Differences 110
CHAPTER 6   Sectional Conflict. 128
CHAPTER 7   The Civil War and Reconstruction. 140
CHAPTER 8   Growth and Transformation 154
CHAPTER 9   Discontent and Reform. 188
CHAPTER 10   War, Prosperity, and Depression. 202
CHAPTER 11   The New Deal and World War II. 212
CHAPTER 12   Postwar America 256
CHAPTER 13   Decades of Change: 1960-1980 274
CHAPTER 14   The New Conservatism and a New World Order. 304
CHAPTER 15   Bridge to the 21st Century 320
CHAPTER 16   Politics of Hope. 340

PICTURE PROFILES

        Becoming a Nation. 38
        Transforming a Nation 89
        Monuments and Memorials. 161
        Turmoil and Change 229
        21st Century Nation 293

Bibliography 346

Index 349

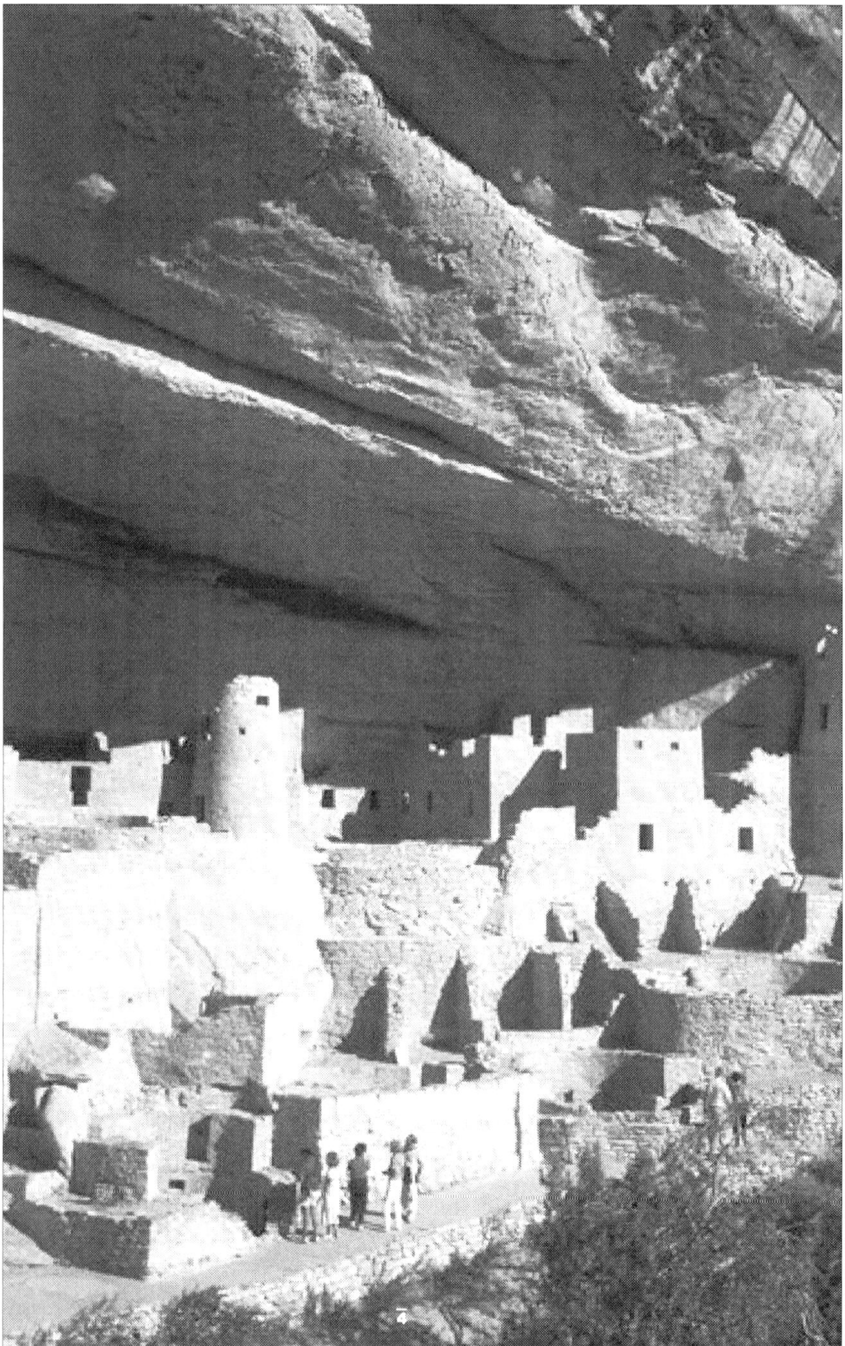

CHAPTER 1

EARLY AMERICA

Mesa Verde settlement in Colorado, 13th century.

CHAPTER 1: EARLY AMERICA

"Heaven and Earth never agreed better to frame a place for man's habitation."

Jamestown founder John Smith, 1607

THE FIRST AMERICANS

At the height of the Ice Age, between 34,000 and 30,000 B.C., much of the world's water was locked up in vast continental ice sheets. As a result, the Bering Sea was hundreds of meters below its current level, and a land bridge, known as Beringia, emerged between Asia and North America. At its peak, Beringia is thought to have been some 1,500 kilometers wide. A moist and treeless tundra, it was covered with grasses and plant life, attracting the large animals that early humans hunted for their survival.

The first people to reach North America almost certainly did so without knowing they had crossed into a new continent. They would have been following game, as their ancestors had for thousands of years, along the Siberian coast and then across the land bridge.

Once in Alaska, it would take these first North Americans thousands of years more to work their way through the openings in great glaciers south to what is now the United States. Evidence of early life in North America continues to be found. Little of it, however, can be reliably dated before 12,000 B.C.; a recent discovery of a hunting lookout in northern Alaska, for example, may date from almost that time. So too may the finely crafted spear points and items found near Clovis, New Mexico.

Similar artifacts have been found at sites throughout North and South America, indicating that life was probably already well established in much of the Western Hemisphere by some time prior to 10,000 B.C.

Around that time the mammoth began to die out and the bison took its place as a principal source of food and hides for these early North Americans. Over time, as more and more species of large game vanished — whether from overhunting or natural causes — plants, berries, and seeds became an increasingly important part of the early American diet. Gradually, foraging and the first attempts at primitive agriculture appeared. Native Americans in what is now central Mexico led the way, cultivating corn, squash, and beans, perhaps as early as 8,000 B.C. Slowly, this knowledge spread northward.

By 3,000 B.C., a primitive type of corn was being grown in the river valleys of New Mexico and Arizona. Then the first signs of irrigation began to appear, and, by 300 B.C., signs of early village life.

By the first centuries A.D., the Hohokam were living in settlements near what is now Phoenix, Arizona, where they built ball courts and pyramid-like mounds reminiscent of those found in Mexico, as well as a canal and irrigation system.

MOUND BUILDERS AND PUEBLOS

The first Native-American group to build mounds in what is now the United States often are called the Adenans. They began constructing earthen burial sites and fortifications around 600 B.C. Some mounds from that era are in the shape of birds or serpents; they probably served religious purposes not yet fully understood.

The Adenans appear to have been absorbed or displaced by various groups collectively known as Hopewellians. One of the most important centers of their culture was found in southern Ohio, where the remains of several thousand of these mounds still can be seen. Believed to be great traders, the Hopewellians used and exchanged tools and materials across a wide region of hundreds of kilometers.

By around 500 A.D., the Hopewellians disappeared, too, gradually giving way to a broad group of tribes generally known as the Mississippians or Temple Mound culture. One city, Cahokia, near Collinsville, Illinois, is thought to have had a population of about 20,000 at its peak in the early 12th century. At the center of the city stood a huge earthen mound, flattened at the top, that was 30 meters high and 37 hectares at the base. Eighty other mounds have been found nearby.

Cities such as Cahokia depended on a combination of hunting, foraging, trading, and agriculture for their food and supplies. Influenced by the thriving societies to the south, they evolved into complex hierarchical societies that took slaves and practiced human sacrifice.

In what is now the southwest United States, the Anasazi, ancestors of the modern Hopi Indians, began building stone and adobe pueblos around the year 900. These unique and amazing apartment-like structures were often built along cliff faces; the most famous, the "cliff palace" of Mesa Verde, Colorado, had more than 200 rooms. Another site, the Pueblo Bonito ruins along New Mexico's Chaco River, once contained more than 800 rooms.

Perhaps the most affluent of the pre-Columbian Native Americans lived in the Pacific Northwest, where the natural abundance of fish and raw materials made food supplies plentiful and permanent villages possible as early as 1,000 B.C. The opulence of their "potlatch" gatherings remains a standard for extravagance and festivity probably unmatched in early American history.

NATIVE-AMERICAN CULTURES

The America that greeted the first Europeans was, thus, far from an empty wilderness. It is now thought that as many people lived in the Western Hemisphere as in Western Europe at that time — about 40 million. Estimates of the number of Native Americans living in what is now the United States at the onset of European colonization range from two to 18 million, with most historians tending toward the lower figure. What is certain is the devastating effect that European disease had on the indigenous population practically from the time of initial contact. Smallpox, in particular, ravaged whole communities and is thought to have been a much more direct cause of the precipitous decline in the Indian population in the 1600s than the numerous wars and skirmishes with European settlers.

Indian customs and culture at the time were extraordinarily diverse, as could be expected, given the expanse of the land and the many different environments to which they had adapted. Some generalizations, however, are possible. Most tribes, particularly in the wooded eastern region and the Midwest, combined aspects of hunting, gathering, and the cultivation of maize and other products for their food supplies. In many cases, the women were responsible for farming and the distribution of food, while the men hunted and participated in war.

By all accounts, Native-American society in North America was closely tied to the land. Identification with nature and the elements was integral to religious beliefs. Their life was essentially clan-oriented and communal, with children allowed more freedom and tolerance than was the European custom of the day.

Although some North American tribes developed a type of hieroglyphics to preserve certain texts, Native-American culture was primarily oral, with a high value placed on the recounting of tales and dreams. Clearly, there was a good deal of trade among various groups and strong evidence exists that neighboring tribes maintained extensive and formal relations — both friendly and hostile.

THE FIRST EUROPEANS

The first Europeans to arrive in North America — at least the first for whom there is solid evidence — were Norse, traveling west from Greenland, where Erik the Red had founded a settlement around the year 985. In 1001 his son Leif is thought to have explored the northeast coast of what is now Canada and spent at least one winter there.

While Norse sagas suggest that Viking sailors explored the Atlantic coast of North America down as far as the Bahamas, such claims remain unproven. In 1963, however, the ruins of some Norse houses dating from that era were discovered at L'Anse-aux-Meadows in northern Newfoundland, thus supporting at least some of the saga claims.

In 1497, just five years after Christopher Columbus landed in the Caribbean looking for a western route to Asia, a Venetian sailor named John Cabot arrived in Newfoundland on a mission for the British king. Although quickly forgotten, Cabot's journey was later to provide the basis for British claims to North America. It also opened the way to the rich fishing grounds off George's Banks, to which European fishermen, particularly the Portuguese, were soon making regular visits.

Columbus never saw the mainland of the future United States, but the first explorations of it were launched from the Spanish possessions that he helped establish. The first of these took place in 1513 when a group of men under Juan Ponce de León landed on the Florida coast near the present city of St. Augustine.

With the conquest of Mexico in 1522, the Spanish further solidified their position in the Western Hemisphere. The ensuing discoveries added to Europe's knowledge of what was now named America — after the Italian Amerigo Vespucci, who wrote a widely popular account of his voyages to a "New World." By 1529 reliable maps of the Atlantic coastline from Labrador to Tierra del Fuego had been drawn up, although it would take more than another century before hope of discovering a "Northwest Passage" to Asia would be completely abandoned.

Among the most significant early Spanish explorations was that of Hernando De Soto, a veteran conquistador who had accompanied Francisco Pizarro in the conquest of Peru. Leaving Havana in 1539, De Soto's expedition landed in Florida and ranged through the southeastern United States as far as the Mississippi River in search of riches.

Another Spaniard, Francisco Vázquez de Coronado, set out from Mexico in 1540 in search of the mythical Seven Cities of Cibola. Coronado's travels took him to the Grand Canyon and Kansas, but failed to reveal the gold or treasure his men sought. However, his party did leave the peoples of the region a remarkable, if unintended, gift: Enough of his horses escaped to transform life on the Great Plains. Within a few generations, the Plains Indians had become masters of horsemanship, greatly expanding the range of their activities.

While the Spanish were pushing up from the south, the northern portion of the present-day United States was slowly being revealed through the journeys of men such as Giovanni da Verrazano. A Florentine who sailed for the French, Verrazano made landfall in North Carolina in 1524, then sailed north along the Atlantic Coast past what is now New York harbor.

A decade later, the Frenchman Jacques Cartier set sail with the hope — like the other Europeans before him — of finding a sea passage to Asia. Cartier's expeditions along the St. Lawrence River laid the foundation for the French claims to North America, which were to last until 1763.

Following the collapse of their first Quebec colony in the 1540s, French Huguenots attempted to settle the northern coast of Florida two decades later. The Spanish, viewing the French as a threat to their trade route along the Gulf Stream, destroyed the colony in 1565. Ironically, the leader of the Spanish forces, Pedro Menéndez, would soon establish a town not far away — St. Augustine. It was the first permanent European settlement in what would become the United States.

The great wealth that poured into Spain from the colonies in Mexico, the Caribbean, and Peru provoked great interest on the part of the other European powers. Emerging maritime nations such as England, drawn in part by Francis Drake's successful raids on Spanish treasure ships, began to take an interest in the New World.

In 1578 Humphrey Gilbert, the author of a treatise on the search for the Northwest Passage, received a patent from Queen Elizabeth to colonize the "heathen and barbarous landes" in the New World that other European nations had not yet claimed. It would be five years before his efforts could begin. When he was lost at sea, his half-brother, Walter Raleigh, took up the mission.

In 1585 Raleigh established the first British colony in North America, on Roanoke Island off the coast of North Carolina. It was later abandoned, and a second effort two years later also proved a failure. It would be 20 years before the British would try again. This time — at Jamestown in 1607 — the colony would succeed, and North America would enter a new era.

EARLY SETTLEMENTS

The early 1600s saw the beginning of a great tide of emigration from Europe to North America. Spanning more than three centuries, this movement grew from a trickle of a few hundred English colonists to a flood of millions of newcomers. Impelled by powerful and diverse motivations, they built a new civilization on the northern part of the continent.

The first English immigrants to what is now the United States crossed the Atlantic long after thriving Spanish colonies had been established in Mexico, the West Indies, and South America. Like all early travelers to the New World, they came in small, overcrowded ships. During their six- to 12-week voyages, they lived on meager rations. Many died of disease, ships were often battered by storms, and some were lost at sea.

Most European emigrants left their homelands to escape political oppression, to seek the freedom to practice their religion, or to find opportunities denied them at home. Between 1620 and 1635, economic difficulties swept England. Many people could not find work. Even skilled artisans could earn little more than a bare living. Poor crop yields added to the distress. In addition, the Commercial Revolution had created a burgeoning textile industry, which demanded an ever-increasing supply of wool to keep the looms running. Landlords enclosed farmlands and evicted the peasants in favor of sheep cultivation. Colonial expansion became an outlet for this displaced peasant population.

The colonists' first glimpse of the new land was a vista of dense woods. The settlers might not have survived had it not been for the help of friendly Indians, who taught them how to grow native plants — pumpkin, squash, beans, and corn. In addition, the vast, virgin forests, extending nearly 2,100 kilometers along the Eastern seaboard, proved a rich source of game and firewood. They also provided abundant raw materials used to build houses, furniture, ships, and profitable items for export.

Although the new continent was remarkably endowed by nature, trade with Europe was vital for articles the settlers could not produce. The coast served the immigrants well. The whole length of shore provided many inlets and harbors. Only two areas — North Carolina and southern New Jersey — lacked harbors for ocean-going vessels.

Majestic rivers — the Kennebec, Hudson, Delaware, Susquehanna, Potomac, and numerous others — linked lands between the coast and the Appalachian Mountains with the sea. Only one river, however, the St. Lawrence — dominated by the French in Canada — offered a water passage to the Great Lakes and the heart of the continent. Dense forests, the resistance of some Indian tribes, and the formidable barrier of the Appalachian Mountains discouraged settlement beyond the coastal plain. Only trappers and traders ventured into the wilderness. For the first hundred years the colonists built their settlements compactly along the coast.

Political considerations influenced many people to move to America. In the 1630s, arbitrary rule by England's Charles I gave impetus to the migration. The subsequent revolt and triumph of Charles' opponents under Oliver Cromwell in the 1640s led many cavaliers — "king's men" — to cast their lot in Virginia. In the German-speaking regions of Europe, the oppressive policies of various petty princes — particularly with regard to religion — and the devastation caused by a long series of wars helped swell the movement to America in the late 17th and 18th centuries.

The journey entailed careful planning and management, as well as considerable expense and risk. Settlers had to be transported nearly 5,000 kilometers across the sea. They needed utensils, clothing, seed, tools, building materials, livestock, arms, and ammunition. In contrast to the colonization policies of other countries and other periods, the emigration from England was not directly sponsored by the government but by private groups of individuals whose chief motive was profit.

JAMESTOWN

The first of the British colonies to take hold in North America was Jamestown. On the basis of a charter which King James I granted to the Virginia (or London) Company, a group of about 100 men set out for the Chesapeake Bay in 1607. Seeking to avoid conflict with the Spanish, they chose a site about 60 kilometers up the James River from the bay.

Made up of townsmen and adventurers more interested in finding gold than farming, the group was unequipped by temperament or ability to embark upon a completely new life in the wilderness. Among them, Captain John Smith emerged as the dominant figure. Despite quarrels, starvation, and Native-American attacks, his ability to enforce discipline held the little colony together through its first year.

In 1609 Smith returned to England, and in his absence, the colony descended into anarchy. During the winter of 1609-1610, the majority of the colonists succumbed to disease. Only 60 of the original 300 settlers were still alive by May 1610. That same year, the town of Henrico (now Richmond) was established farther up the James River.

It was not long, however, before a development occurred that revolutionized Virginia's economy. In 1612 John Rolfe began cross-breeding imported tobacco seed from the West Indies with native plants and produced a new variety that was pleasing to European taste. The first shipment of this tobacco reached London in 1614. Within a decade it had become Virginia's chief source of revenue.

Prosperity did not come quickly, however, and the death rate from disease and Indian attacks remained extraordinarily high. Between 1607 and 1624 approximately 14,000 people migrated to the colony, yet only

1,132 were living there in 1624. On recommendation of a royal commission, the king dissolved the Virginia Company, and made it a royal colony that year.

MASSACHUSETTS

During the religious upheavals of the 16th century, a body of men and women called Puritans sought to reform the Established Church of England from within. Essentially, they demanded that the rituals and structures associated with Roman Catholicism be replaced by simpler Calvinist Protestant forms of faith and worship. Their reformist ideas, by destroying the unity of the state church, threatened to divide the people and to undermine royal authority.

In 1607 a small group of Separatists — a radical sect of Puritans who did not believe the Established Church could ever be reformed — departed for Leyden, Holland, where the Dutch granted them asylum. However, the Calvinist Dutch restricted them mainly to low-paid laboring jobs. Some members of the congregation grew dissatisfied with this discrimination and resolved to emigrate to the New World.

In 1620, a group of Leyden Puritans secured a land patent from the Virginia Company. Numbering 101, they set out for Virginia on the *Mayflower*. A storm sent them far north and they landed in New England on Cape Cod. Believing themselves outside the jurisdiction of any organized government, the men drafted a formal agreement to abide by "just and equal laws" drafted by leaders of their own choosing. This was the Mayflower Compact.

In December the *Mayflower* reached Plymouth harbor; the Pilgrims began to build their settlement during the winter. Nearly half the colonists died of exposure and disease, but neighboring Wampanoag Indians provided the information that would sustain them: how to grow maize. By the next fall, the Pilgrims had a plentiful crop of corn, and a growing trade based on furs and lumber.

A new wave of immigrants arrived on the shores of Massachusetts Bay in 1630 bearing a grant from King Charles I to establish a colony. Many of them were Puritans whose religious practices were increasingly prohibited in England. Their leader, John Winthrop, urged them to create a "city upon a hill" in the New World — a place where they would live in strict accordance with their religious beliefs and set an example for all of Christendom.

The Massachusetts Bay Colony was to play a significant role in the development of the entire New England region, in part because Winthrop and his Puritan colleagues were able to bring their charter with them. Thus the authority for the colony's government resided in Massachusetts, not in England.

Under the charter's provisions, power rested with the General Court, which was made up of "freemen" required to be members of the Puritan, or Congregational, Church. This guaranteed that the Puritans would be the dominant political as well as religious force in the colony. The General Court elected the governor, who for most of the next generation would be John Winthrop.

The rigid orthodoxy of the Puritan rule was not to everyone's liking. One of the first to challenge the General Court openly was a young clergyman named Roger Williams, who objected to the colony's seizure of Indian lands and advocated separation of church and state. Another dissenter, Anne Hutchinson, challenged key doctrines of Puritan theology. Both they and their followers were banished.

Williams purchased land from the Narragansett Indians in what is now Providence, Rhode Island, in 1636. In 1644, a sympathetic Puritan-controlled English Parliament gave him the charter that established Rhode Island as a distinct colony where complete separation of church and state as well as freedom of religion was practiced.

So-called heretics like Williams were not the only ones who left Massachusetts. Orthodox Puritans, seeking better lands and opportunities, soon began leaving Massachusetts Bay Colony. News of the fertility of the Connecticut River Valley, for instance, attracted the interest of farmers having a difficult time with poor land. By the early 1630s, many were ready to brave the danger of Indian attack to obtain level ground and deep, rich soil. These new communities often eliminated church membership as a prerequisite for voting, thereby extending the franchise to ever larger numbers of men.

At the same time, other settlements began cropping up along the New Hampshire and Maine coasts, as more and more immigrants sought the land and liberty the New World seemed to offer.

NEW NETHERLAND AND MARYLAND

Hired by the Dutch East India Company, Henry Hudson in 1609 explored the area around what is now New York City and the river that bears his name, to a point probably north of present-day Albany, New York. Subsequent Dutch voyages laid the basis for their claims and early settlements in the area.

As with the French to the north, the first interest of the Dutch was the fur trade. To this end, they cultivated close relations with the Five Nations of the Iroquois, who were the key to the heartland from which the furs came. In 1617 Dutch settlers built a fort at the junction of the Hudson and the Mohawk Rivers, where Albany now stands.

Settlement on the island of Manhattan began in the early 1620s. In 1624, the island was purchased from local Native Americans for the reported price of $24. It was promptly renamed New Amsterdam.

In order to attract settlers to the Hudson River region, the Dutch encouraged a type of feudal aristocracy, known as the "patroon" system. The first of these huge estates were established in 1630 along the Hudson River. Under the patroon system, any stockholder, or patroon, who could bring 50 adults to his estate over a four-year period was given a 25-kilometer river-front plot, exclusive fishing and hunting privileges, and civil and criminal jurisdiction over his lands. In turn, he provided livestock, tools, and buildings. The tenants paid the patroon rent and gave him first option on surplus crops.

Further to the south, a Swedish trading company with ties to the Dutch attempted to set up its first settlement along the Delaware River three years later. Without the resources to consolidate its position, New Sweden was gradually absorbed into New Netherland, and later, Pennsylvania and Delaware.

In 1632 the Catholic Calvert family obtained a charter for land north of the Potomac River from King Charles I in what became known as Maryland. As the charter did not expressly prohibit the establishment of non-Protestant churches, the colony became a haven for Catholics. Maryland's first town, St. Mary's, was established in 1634 near where the Potomac River flows into the Chesapeake Bay.

While establishing a refuge for Catholics, who faced increasing persecution in Anglican England, the Calverts were also interested in creating profitable estates. To this end, and to avoid trouble with the British government, they also encouraged Protestant immigration.

Maryland's royal charter had a mixture of feudal and modern elements. On the one hand the Calvert family had the power to create manorial estates. On the other, they could only make laws with the consent of freemen (property holders). They found that in order to attract settlers — and make a profit from their holdings — they had to offer people farms, not just tenancy on manorial estates. The number of independent farms grew in consequence. Their owners demanded a voice in the affairs of the colony. Maryland's first legislature met in 1635.

COLONIAL-INDIAN RELATIONS

By 1640 the British had solid colonies established along the New England coast and the Chesapeake Bay. In between were the Dutch and the tiny Swedish community. To the west were the original Americans, then called Indians.

Sometimes friendly, sometimes hostile, the Eastern tribes were no longer strangers to the Europeans. Although Native Americans benefited from access to new technology and trade, the disease and thirst for land that the early settlers also brought posed a serious challenge to their long-established way of life.

At first, trade with the European settlers brought advantages: knives, axes, weapons, cooking utensils, fishhooks, and a host of other goods. Those Indians who traded initially had significant advantage over rivals who did not. In response to European demand, tribes such as the Iroquois began to devote more attention to fur trapping during the 17th century. Furs and pelts provided tribes the means to purchase colonial goods until late into the 18th century.

Early colonial-Native-American relations were an uneasy mix of cooperation and conflict. On the one hand, there were the exemplary relations that prevailed during the first half century of Pennsylvania's existence. On the other were a long series of setbacks, skirmishes, and wars, which almost invariably resulted in an Indian defeat and further loss of land.

The first of the important Native-American uprisings occurred in Virginia in 1622, when some 347 whites were killed, including a number of missionaries who had just recently come to Jamestown.

White settlement of the Connecticut River region touched off the Pequot War in 1637. In 1675 King Philip, the son of the native chief who had made the original peace with the Pilgrims in 1621, attempted to unite the tribes of southern New England against further European encroachment of their lands. In the struggle, however, Philip lost his life and many Indians were sold into servitude.

The steady influx of settlers into the backwoods regions of the Eastern colonies disrupted Native-American life. As more and more game was killed off, tribes were faced with the difficult choice of going hungry, going to war, or moving and coming into conflict with other tribes to the west.

The Iroquois, who inhabited the area below lakes Ontario and Erie in northern New York and Pennsylvania, were more successful in resisting European advances. In 1570 five tribes joined to form the most complex Native-American nation of its time, the "Ho-De-No-Sau-Nee," or League of the Iroquois. The league was run by a council made up of 50 representatives from each of the five member tribes. The council dealt with matters common to all the tribes, but it had no say in how the free and equal tribes ran their day-to-day affairs. No tribe was allowed to make war by itself. The council passed laws to deal with crimes such as murder.

The Iroquois League was a strong power in the 1600s and 1700s. It traded furs with the British and sided with them against the French in the war for the dominance of America between 1754 and 1763. The British might not have won that war otherwise.

The Iroquois League stayed strong until the American Revolution. Then, for the first time, the council could not reach a unanimous decision on whom to support. Member tribes made their own decisions, some fighting with the British, some with the colonists, some remaining neutral. As a result, everyone fought against the Iroquois. Their losses were great and the league never recovered.

SECOND GENERATION OF BRITISH COLONIES

The religious and civil conflict in England in the mid-17th century limited immigration, as well as the attention the mother country paid the fledgling American colonies.

In part to provide for the defense measures England was neglecting, the Massachusetts Bay, Plymouth, Connecticut, and New Haven colonies formed the New England Confederation in 1643. It was the European colonists' first attempt at regional unity.

The early history of the British settlers reveals a good deal of contention — religious and political — as groups vied for power and position among themselves and their neighbors. Maryland, in particular, suffered from the bitter religious rivalries that afflicted England during the era of Oliver Cromwell. One of the casualties was the state's Toleration Act, which was revoked in the 1650s. It was soon reinstated, however, along with the religious freedom it guaranteed.

With the restoration of King Charles II in 1660, the British once again turned their attention to North America. Within a brief span, the first European settlements were established in the Carolinas and the Dutch driven out of New Netherland. New proprietary colonies were established in New York, New Jersey, Delaware, and Pennsylvania.

The Dutch settlements had been ruled by autocratic governors appointed in Europe. Over the years, the local population had become estranged from them. As a result, when the British colonists began encroaching on Dutch claims in Long Island and Manhattan, the unpopular governor was unable to rally the population to their defense. New Netherland fell in 1664. The terms of the capitulation, however, were mild: The Dutch settlers were able to retain their property and worship as they pleased.

As early as the 1650s, the Albemarle Sound region off the coast of what is now northern North Carolina was inhabited by settlers trickling down from Virginia. The first proprietary governor arrived in 1664. The first town in Albemarle, a remote area even today, was not established until the arrival of a group of French Huguenots in 1704.

In 1670 the first settlers, drawn from New England and the Caribbean island of Barbados, arrived in what is now Charleston, South Carolina. An elaborate system of government, to which the British philosopher John Locke contributed, was prepared for the new colony. One of its prominent features was a failed attempt to create a hereditary nobility. One of the colony's least appealing aspects was the early trade in

Indian slaves. With time, however, timber, rice, and indigo gave the colony a worthier economic base.

In 1681 William Penn, a wealthy Quaker and friend of Charles II, received a large tract of land west of the Delaware River, which became known as Pennsylvania. To help populate it, Penn actively recruited a host of religious dissenters from England and the continent — Quakers, Mennonites, Amish, Moravians, and Baptists.

When Penn arrived the following year, there were already Dutch, Swedish, and English settlers living along the Delaware River. It was there he founded Philadelphia, the "City of Brotherly Love."

In keeping with his faith, Penn was motivated by a sense of equality not often found in other American colonies at the time. Thus, women in Pennsylvania had rights long before they did in other parts of America. Penn and his deputies also paid considerable attention to the colony's relations with the Delaware Indians, ensuring that they were paid for land on which the Europeans settled.

Georgia was settled in 1732, the last of the 13 colonies to be established. Lying close to, if not actually inside the boundaries of Spanish Florida, the region was viewed as a buffer against Spanish incursion. But it had another unique quality: The man charged with Georgia's fortifications, General James Oglethorpe, was a reformer who deliberately set out to create a refuge where the poor and former prisoners would be given new opportunities.

SETTLERS, SLAVES, AND SERVANTS

Men and women with little active interest in a new life in America were often induced to make the move to the New World by the skillful persuasion of promoters. William Penn, for example, publicized the opportunities awaiting newcomers to the Pennsylvania colony. Judges and prison authorities offered convicts a chance to migrate to colonies like Georgia instead of serving prison sentences.

But few colonists could finance the cost of passage for themselves and their families to make a start in the new land. In some cases, ships' captains received large rewards from the sale of service contracts for poor migrants, called indentured servants, and every method from extravagant promises to actual kidnapping was used to take on as many passengers as their vessels could hold.

In other cases, the expenses of transportation and maintenance were paid by colonizing agencies like the Virginia or Massachusetts Bay Companies. In return, indentured servants agreed to work for the agencies as contract laborers, usually for four to seven years. Free at the end of this term, they would be given "freedom dues," sometimes including a small tract of land.

Perhaps half the settlers living in the colonies south of New England came to America under this system. Although most of them fulfilled their obligations faithfully, some ran away from their employers. Nevertheless, many of them were eventually able to secure land and set up homesteads, either in the colonies in which they had originally settled or in neighboring ones. No social stigma was attached to a family that had its beginning in America under this semi-bondage. Every colony had its share of leaders who were former indentured servants.

There was one very important exception to this pattern: African slaves. The first black Africans were brought to Virginia in 1619, just 12 years after the founding of Jamestown. Initially, many were regarded as indentured servants who could earn their freedom. By the 1660s, however, as the demand for plantation labor in the Southern colonies grew, the institution of slavery began to harden around them, and Africans were brought to America in shackles for a lifetime of involuntary servitude. ◊

THE ENDURING MYSTERY OF THE ANASAZI

Time-worn pueblos and dramatic cliff towns, set amid the stark, rugged mesas and canyons of Colorado and New Mexico, mark the settlements of some of the earliest inhabitants of North America, the Anasazi (a Navajo word meaning "ancient ones").

By 500 A.D. the Anasazi had established some of the first villages in the American Southwest, where they hunted and grew crops of corn, squash, and beans. The Anasazi flourished over the centuries, developing sophisticated dams and irrigation systems; creating a masterful, distinctive pottery tradition; and carving multiroom dwellings into the sheer sides of cliffs that remain among the most striking archaeological sites in the United States today.

Yet by the year 1300, they had abandoned their settlements, leaving their pottery, implements, even clothing — as though they intended to return — and seemingly vanished into history. Their homeland remained empty of human beings for more than a century — until the arrival of new tribes, such as the Navajo and the Ute, followed by the Spanish and other European settlers.

The story of the Anasazi is tied inextricably to the beautiful but harsh environment in which they chose to live. Early settlements, consisting of simple pithouses scooped out of the ground, evolved into sunken kivas (underground rooms) that served as meeting and religious sites. Later generations developed the masonry techniques for building square, stone pueblos. But the most dramatic change in Anasazi living was the move to the cliff sides below the flat-topped mesas, where the Anasazi carved their amazing, multilevel dwellings.

The Anasazi lived in a communal society. They traded with other peoples in the region, but signs of warfare are few and isolated. And although the Anasazi certainly had religious and other leaders, as well as skilled artisans, social or class distinctions were virtually nonexistent.

Religious and social motives undoubtedly played a part in the building of the cliff communities and their final abandonment. But the struggle to raise food in an increasingly difficult environment was probably the paramount factor. As populations grew, farmers planted larger areas on the mesas, causing some communities to farm marginal lands, while others left the mesa tops for the cliffs. But the Anasazi couldn't halt the steady loss of the land's fertility from constant use, nor withstand the region's cyclical droughts. Analysis of tree rings, for example, shows that a drought lasting 23 years, from 1276 to 1299, finally forced the last groups of Anasazi to leave permanently.

Although the Anasazi dispersed from their ancestral homeland, their legacy remains in the remarkable archaeological record that they left behind, and in the Hopi, Zuni, and other Pueblo peoples who are their descendants. ◆

OUTLINE OF U.S. HISTORY

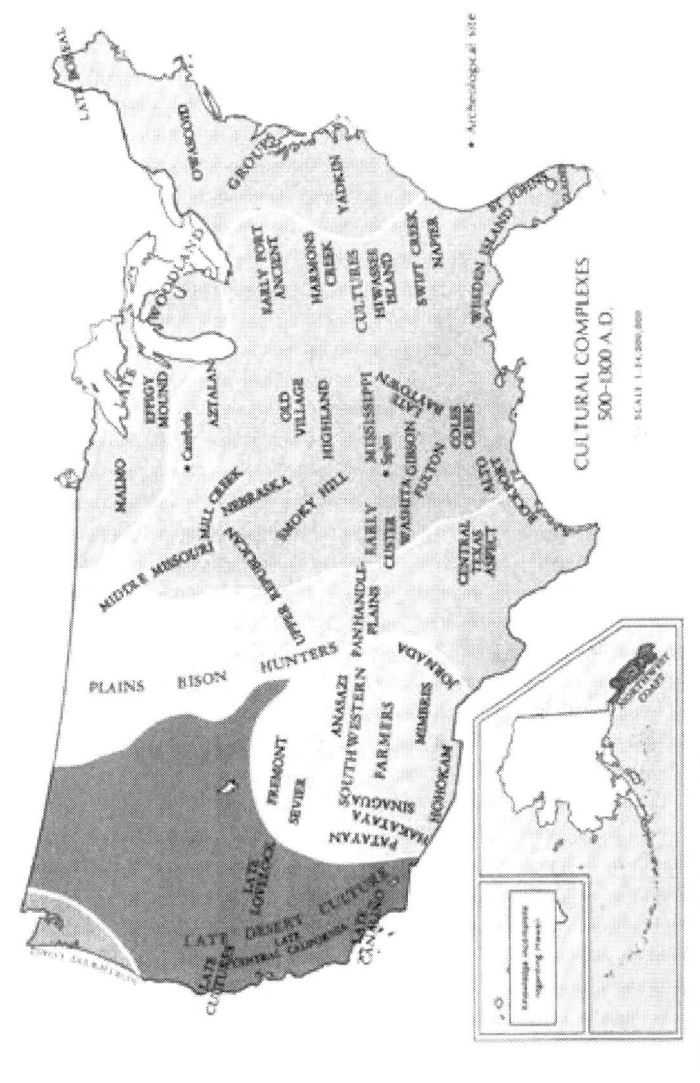

Major Native American cultural groupings, A.D. 500–1300.

22

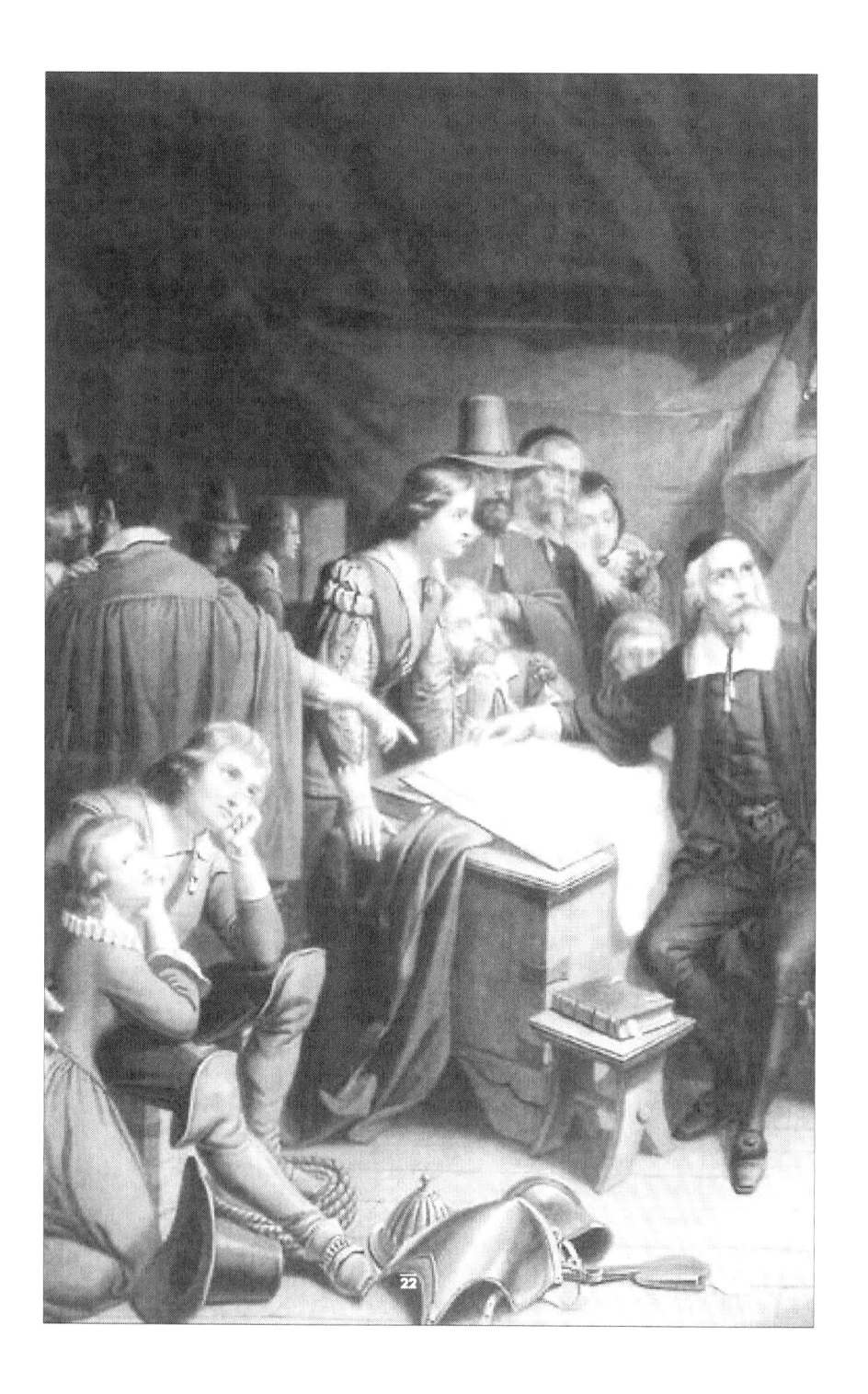

CHAPTER

2

THE COLONIAL PERIOD

Pilgrims signing the Mayflower Compact aboard ship, 1620.

"What then is the American, this new man?"

American author and agriculturist
J. Hector St. John de Crèvecoeur, 1782

NEW PEOPLES

Most settlers who came to America in the 17th century were English, but there were also Dutch, Swedes, and Germans in the middle region, a few French Huguenots in South Carolina and elsewhere, slaves from Africa, primarily in the South, and a scattering of Spaniards, Italians, and Portuguese throughout the colonies. After 1680 England ceased to be the chief source of immigration, supplanted by Scots and "Scots-Irish" (Protestants from Northern Ireland). In addition, tens of thousands of refugees fled northwestern Europe to escape war, oppression, and absentee-landlordism. By 1690 the American population had risen to a quarter of a million. From then on, it doubled every 25 years until, in 1775, it numbered more than 2.5 million. Although families occasionally moved from one colony to another, distinctions between individual colonies were marked. They were even more so among the three regional groupings of colonies.

NEW ENGLAND

The northeastern New England colonies had generally thin, stony soil, relatively little level land, and long winters, making it difficult to make a living from farming. Turning to other pursuits, the New Englanders harnessed waterpower and established grain mills and sawmills. Good stands of timber encouraged shipbuilding. Excellent harbors promoted trade, and the sea became a source of great wealth. In Massachusetts, the cod industry alone quickly furnished a basis for prosperity.

With the bulk of the early settlers living in villages and towns around the harbors, many New Englanders carried on some kind of trade or business. Common pastureland and woodlots served the needs of townspeople, who worked small farms nearby. Compactness made possible the village school, the village church, and the village or town hall, where citizens met to discuss matters of common interest.

The Massachusetts Bay Colony continued to expand its commerce. From the middle of the 17th century onward it grew prosperous, so that Boston became one of America's greatest ports.

Oak timber for ships' hulls, tall pines for spars and masts, and pitch for the seams of ships came from the Northeastern forests. Building their own vessels and sailing them to ports all over the world, the shipmasters of Massachusetts Bay laid the foundation for a trade that was to grow steadily in importance. By the end of the colonial period, one-third of all vessels under the British flag were built in New England. Fish, ship's stores, and woodenware swelled the exports. New England merchants and shippers soon discovered that rum and slaves were profitable commodities. One of their most enterprising — if unsavory — trading practices of the time was the "triangular trade." Traders would purchase slaves off the coast of Africa for New England rum, then sell the slaves in the West Indies where they would buy molasses to bring home for sale to the local rum producers.

THE MIDDLE COLONIES

Society in the middle colonies was far more varied, cosmopolitan, and tolerant than in New England. Under William Penn, Pennsylvania functioned smoothly and grew rapidly. By 1685, its population was almost 9,000. The heart of the colony was Philadelphia, a city of broad, tree-shaded streets, substantial brick and stone houses, and busy docks. By the end of the colonial period, nearly a century later, 30,000 people lived there, representing many languages, creeds, and trades. Their talent for successful business enterprise made the city one of the thriving centers of the British Empire.

Though the Quakers dominated in Philadelphia, elsewhere in Pennsylvania others were well represented. Germans became the colony's most skillful farmers. Important, too, were cottage industries such as weaving, shoemaking, cabinetmaking, and other crafts. Pennsylvania was also the principal gateway into the New World for the Scots-Irish, who moved into the colony in the early 18th century. "Bold and indigent strangers," as one Pennsylvania official called them, they hated the English and were suspicious of all government. The Scots-Irish tended to settle in the backcountry, where they cleared land and lived by hunting and subsistence farming.

New York best illustrated the polyglot nature of America. By 1646 the population along the Hudson River included Dutch, French, Danes, Norwegians, Swedes, English, Scots, Irish, Germans, Poles, Bohemians, Portuguese, and Italians. The Dutch continued to exercise an important social and economic influence on the New York region long after the fall of New Netherland and their integration into the British colonial system. Their sharp-stepped gable roofs became a permanent part of the city's architecture, and their merchants gave Manhattan much of its original bustling, commercial atmosphere.

THE SOUTHERN COLONIES

In contrast to New England and the middle colonies, the Southern colonies were predominantly rural settlements.

By the late 17th century, Virginia's and Maryland's economic and social structure rested on the great planters and the yeoman farmers. The planters of the Tidewater region, supported by slave labor, held most of the political power and the best land. They built great houses, adopted an aristocratic way of life, and kept in touch as best they could with the world of culture overseas.

The yeoman farmers, who worked smaller tracts, sat in popular assemblies and found their way into political office. Their outspoken independence was a constant warning to the oligarchy of planters not to encroach too far upon the rights of free men.

The settlers of the Carolinas quickly learned to combine agriculture and commerce, and the marketplace became a major source of prosperity. Dense forests brought revenue: Lumber, tar, and resin from the longleaf pine provided some of the best shipbuilding materials in the world. Not bound to a single crop as was Virginia, North and South Carolina also produced and exported rice and indigo, a blue dye obtained from native plants that was used in coloring fabric. By 1750 more than 100,000 people lived in the two colonies of North and South Carolina. Charleston, South Carolina, was the region's leading port and trading center.

In the southernmost colonies, as everywhere else, population growth in the backcountry had special significance. German immigrants and Scots-Irish, unwilling to live in the original Tidewater settlements where English influence was strong, pushed inland. Those who could not secure fertile land along the coast, or who had exhausted the lands they held, found the hills farther west a bountiful refuge. Although their hardships were enormous, restless settlers kept coming; by the 1730s they were pouring into the Shenandoah Valley of Virginia. Soon the interior was dotted with farms.

Living on the edge of Native American country, frontier families built cabins, cleared the wilderness, and cultivated maize and wheat. The men wore leather made from the skin of deer or sheep, known as buckskin; the women wore garments of cloth they spun at home. Their food consisted of venison, wild turkey, and fish. They had their own amusements: great barbecues, dances, housewarmings for newly married couples, shooting matches, and contests for making quilted blankets. Quilt-making remains an American tradition today.

SOCIETY, SCHOOLS, AND CULTURE

A significant factor deterring the emergence of a powerful aristocratic or gentry class in the colonies was the ability of anyone in an established colony to find a new home on the frontier. Time after time, dominant Tidewater figures were obliged to liberalize political policies, land-grant requirements, and religious practices by the threat of a mass exodus to the frontier.

Of equal significance for the future were the foundations of American education and culture established during the colonial period. Harvard College was founded in 1636 in Cambridge, Massachusetts. Near the end of the century, the College of William and Mary was established in Virginia. A few years later, the Collegiate School of Connecticut, later to become Yale University, was chartered.

Even more noteworthy was the growth of a school system maintained by governmental authority. The Puritan emphasis on reading directly from the Scriptures underscored the importance of literacy. In 1647 the Massachusetts Bay Colony enacted the "ye olde deluder Satan" Act, requiring every town having more than 50 families to establish a grammar school (a Latin school to prepare students for college). Shortly thereafter, all the other New England colonies, except for Rhode Island, followed its example.

The Pilgrims and Puritans had brought their own little libraries and continued to import books from London. And as early as the 1680s, Boston booksellers were doing a thriving business in works of classical literature, history, politics, philosophy, science, theology, and belles-lettres. In 1638 the first printing press in the English colonies and the second in North America was installed at Harvard College.

The first school in Pennsylvania was begun in 1683. It taught reading, writing, and keeping of accounts. Thereafter, in some fashion, every Quaker community provided for the elementary teaching of its children. More advanced training — in classical languages, history, and literature — was offered at the Friends Public School, which still operates in Philadelphia as the William Penn Charter School. The school was free to the poor, but parents were required to pay tuition if they were able.

In Philadelphia, numerous private schools with no religious affiliation taught languages, mathematics, and natural science; there were also night schools for adults. Women were not entirely overlooked, but their educational opportunities were limited to training in activities that could be conducted in the home. Private teachers instructed the daughters of prosperous Philadelphians in French, music, dancing, painting, singing, grammar, and sometimes bookkeeping.

In the 18th century, the intellectual and cultural development of Pennsylvania reflected, in large measure, the vigorous personalities of two men: James Logan and Benjamin Franklin. Logan was secretary of the colony, and it was in his fine library that young Franklin found the latest scientific works. In 1745 Logan erected a building for his collection and bequeathed both building and books to the city.

Franklin contributed even more to the intellectual activity of Philadelphia. He formed a debating club that became the embryo of the American Philosophical Society. His endeavors also led to the founding of a public academy that later developed into the University of Pennsylvania. He was a prime mover in the establishment of a subscription library, which he called "the mother of all North American subscription libraries."

In the Southern colonies, wealthy planters and merchants imported private tutors from Ireland or Scotland to teach their children. Some sent their children to school in England. Having these other opportunities, the upper classes in the Tidewater were not interested in supporting public education. In addition, the diffusion of farms and plantations made the formation of community schools difficult. There were only a few free schools in Virginia.

The desire for learning did not stop at the borders of established communities, however. On the frontier, the Scots-Irish, though living in primitive cabins, were firm devotees of scholarship, and they made great efforts to attract learned ministers to their settlements.

Literary production in the colonies was largely confined to New England. Here attention concentrated on religious subjects. Sermons were the most common products of the press. A famous Puritan minister, the Reverend Cotton Mather, wrote some 400 works. His masterpiece, *Magnalia Christi Americana*, presented the pageant of New England's history. The most popular single work of the day was the Reverend Michael Wigglesworth's long poem, "The Day of Doom," which described the Last Judgment in terrifying terms.

In 1704 Cambridge, Massachusetts, launched the colonies' first successful newspaper. By 1745 there were 22 newspapers being published in British North America.

In New York, an important step in establishing the principle of freedom of the press took place with the case of John Peter Zenger, whose *New York Weekly Journal*, begun in 1733, represented the opposition to the government. After two years of publication, the colonial governor could no longer tolerate Zenger's satirical barbs, and had him thrown into prison on a charge of seditious libel. Zenger continued to edit his paper from jail during his nine-month trial, which excited intense interest throughout the colonies. Andrew Hamilton, the prominent lawyer who defended Zenger, argued that the charges printed by Zenger were true and hence not libelous. The jury returned a verdict of not guilty, and Zenger went free.

The increasing prosperity of the towns prompted fears that the devil was luring society into pursuit of worldly gain and may have contributed to the religious reaction of the 1730s, known as the Great Awakening. Its two immediate sources were George Whitefield, a Wesleyan revivalist who arrived from England in 1739, and Jonathan Edwards, who served the Congregational Church in Northampton, Massachusetts.

Whitefield began a religious revival in Philadelphia and then moved on to New England. He enthralled audiences of up to 20,000 people at a time with histrionic displays, gestures, and emotional oratory. Religious turmoil swept throughout New England and the middle colonies as ministers left established churches to preach the revival.

Edwards was the most prominent of those influenced by Whitefield and the Great Awakening. His most memorable contribution was his 1741 sermon, "Sinners in the Hands of an Angry God." Rejecting theatrics, he delivered his message in a quiet, thoughtful manner, arguing that the established churches sought to deprive Christianity of its function of redemption from sin. His magnum opus, *Of Freedom of Will* (1754), attempted to reconcile Calvinism with the Enlightenment.

The Great Awakening gave rise to evangelical denominations (those Christian churches that believe in personal conversion and the inerrancy of the Bible) and the spirit of revivalism, which continue to play significant roles in American religious and cultural life. It weakened the status of the established clergy and provoked believers to rely on their own conscience. Perhaps most important, it led to the proliferation of sects and denominations, which in turn encouraged general acceptance of the principle of religious toleration.

EMERGENCE OF COLONIAL GOVERNMENT

In the early phases of colonial development, a striking feature was the lack of controlling influence by the English government. All colonies except Georgia emerged as companies of shareholders, or as feudal proprietorships stemming from charters granted by the Crown. The fact that the king had transferred his immediate sovereignty over the New World settlements to stock companies and proprietors did not, of course, mean that the colonists in America were necessarily free of outside control. Under the terms of the Virginia Company charter, for example, full governmental authority was vested in the company itself. Nevertheless, the crown expected that the company would be resident in England. Inhabitants of Virginia, then, would have no more voice in their government than if the king himself had retained absolute rule.

Still, the colonies considered themselves chiefly as commonwealths or states, much like England itself, having only a loose association with the authorities in London. In one way or another, exclusive rule from the outside withered away. The colonists — inheritors of the long English tradition of the struggle for political liberty — incorporated concepts of freedom into Virginia's first charter. It provided that English colonists were to exercise all liberties, franchises, and immunities "as if they had been abiding and born within this our Realm of England." They were, then, to enjoy the benefits of the Magna Carta — the charter of English political and civil liberties granted by King John in 1215 — and the common law — the English system of law based on legal precedents or tradition, not statutory law. In 1618 the Virginia Company issued instructions to its appointed governor providing that free inhabitants of the plantations should elect representatives to join with the governor and an appointive council in passing ordinances for the welfare of the colony.

These measures proved to be some of the most far-reaching in the entire colonial period. From then on, it was generally accepted that the colonists had a right to participate in their own government. In most instances, the king, in making future grants, provided in the charter that the free men of the colony should have a voice in legislation affecting them. Thus, charters awarded to the Calverts in Maryland, William Penn in Pennsylvania, the proprietors in North and South Carolina, and the proprietors in New Jersey specified that legislation should be enacted with "the consent of the freemen."

In New England, for many years, there was even more complete self-government than in the other colonies. Aboard the *Mayflower*, the Pilgrims adopted an instrument for government called the "Mayflower Compact," to "combine ourselves together into a civil body politic for our better ordering and preservation ... and by virtue hereof [to] enact, constitute, and frame such just and equal laws, ordinances, acts, constitutions, and offices ... as shall be thought most meet and convenient for the general good of the colony. ..."

Although there was no legal basis for the Pilgrims to establish a system of self-government, the action was not contested, and, under the compact, the Plymouth settlers were able for many years to conduct their own affairs without outside interference.

A similar situation developed in the Massachusetts Bay Company, which had been given the right to govern itself. Thus, full authority rested in the hands of persons residing in the colony. At first, the dozen or so original members of the company who had come to America attempted to rule autocratically. But the other colonists soon demanded a voice in public affairs and indicated that refusal would lead to a mass migration.

The company members yielded, and control of the government passed to elected representatives. Subsequently, other New England colonies — such as Connecticut and Rhode Island — also succeeded in becoming self-governing simply by asserting that they were beyond any governmental authority, and then setting up their own political system modeled after that of the Pilgrims at Plymouth.

In only two cases was the self-government provision omitted. These were New York, which was granted to Charles II's brother, the Duke of York (later to become King James II), and Georgia, which was granted to a group of "trustees." In both instances the provisions for governance were short-lived, for the colonists demanded legislative representation so insistently that the authorities soon yielded.

In the mid-17th century, the English were too distracted by their Civil War (1642-49) and Oliver Cromwell's Puritan Commonwealth to pursue an effective colonial policy. After the restoration of Charles II and the Stuart dynasty in 1660, England had more opportunity to attend to colonial administration. Even then, however, it was inefficient and lacked a coherent plan. The colonies were left largely to their own devices.

The remoteness afforded by a vast ocean also made control of the colonies difficult. Added to this was the character of life itself in early America. From countries limited in space and dotted with populous towns, the settlers had come to a land of seemingly unending reach. On such a continent, natural conditions promoted a tough individualism, as people became used to making their own decisions. Government penetrated the backcountry only slowly, and conditions of anarchy often prevailed on the frontier.

Yet the assumption of self-government in the colonies did not go entirely unchallenged. In the 1670s, the Lords of Trade and Plantations, a royal committee established to enforce the mercantile system in the colonies, moved to annul the Massachusetts Bay charter because the colony was resisting the government's economic policy. James II in 1685 approved a proposal to create a Dominion of New England and place colonies south through New Jersey under its jurisdiction, thereby tightening the Crown's control over the whole region. A royal governor, Sir Edmund Andros, levied taxes by executive order, implemented a number of other harsh measures, and jailed those who resisted.

When news of the Glorious Revolution (1688-89), which deposed James II in England, reached Boston, the population rebelled and imprisoned Andros. Under a new charter, Massachusetts and Plymouth were united for the first time in 1691 as the royal colony of Massachusetts Bay. The other New England colonies quickly reinstalled their previous governments.

The English Bill of Rights and the Toleration Act of 1689 affirmed freedom of worship for Christians in the colonies as well as in England and enforced limits on the Crown. Equally important, John Locke's *Second Treatise on Government* (1690), the Glorious Revolution's major theoretical justification, set forth a theory of government based not on divine right but on contract. It contended that the people, endowed with natural rights of life, liberty, and property, had the right to rebel when governments violated their rights.

By the early 18th century, almost all the colonies had been brought under the direct jurisdiction of the British Crown, but under the rules established by the Glorious Revolution. Colonial governors sought to exercise powers that the king had lost in England, but the colonial assemblies, aware of events there, attempted to assert their "rights" and "liberties." Their leverage rested on two significant powers similar to those held by the English Parliament: the right to vote on taxes and expenditures, and the right to initiate legislation rather than merely react to proposals of the governor.

The legislatures used these rights to check the power of royal governors and to pass other measures to expand their power and influence. The recurring clashes between governor and assembly made colonial politics tumultuous and worked increasingly to awaken the colonists to the divergence between American and English interests. In many cases, the royal authorities did not understand the importance of what the colonial assemblies were doing and simply neglected them. Nonetheless, the precedents and principles established in the conflicts between assemblies and governors eventually became part of the unwritten "constitution" of the colonies. In this way, the colonial legislatures asserted the right of self-government.

THE FRENCH AND INDIAN WAR

France and Britain engaged in a succession of wars in Europe and the Caribbean throughout the 18th century. Though Britain secured certain advantages — primarily in the sugar-rich islands of the Caribbean — the struggles were generally indecisive, and France remained in a powerful position in North America. By 1754, France still had a strong relationship with a number of Native American tribes in Canada and along the Great Lakes. It controlled the Mississippi River and, by establishing a line of forts and trading posts, had marked out a great crescent-shaped empire stretching from Quebec to New Orleans. The British remained confined to the narrow belt east of the Appalachian Mountains. Thus the French threatened not only the British Empire but also the American colonists themselves, for in holding the Mississippi Valley, France could limit their westward expansion.

An armed clash took place in 1754 at Fort Duquesne, the site where

Pittsburgh, Pennsylvania, is now located, between a band of French regulars and Virginia militiamen under the command of 22-year-old George Washington, a Virginia planter and surveyor. The British government attempted to deal with the conflict by calling a meeting of representatives from New York, Pennsylvania, Maryland, and the New England colonies. From June 19 to July 10, 1754, the Albany Congress, as it came to be known, met with the Iroquois in Albany, New York, in order to improve relations with them and secure their loyalty to the British.

But the delegates also declared a union of the American colonies "absolutely necessary for their preservation" and adopted a proposal drafted by Benjamin Franklin. The Albany Plan of Union provided for a president appointed by the king and a grand council of delegates chosen by the assemblies, with each colony to be represented in proportion to its financial contributions to the general treasury. This body would have charge of defense, Native American relations, and trade and settlement of the west. Most importantly, it would have independent authority to levy taxes. But none of the colonies accepted the plan, since they were not prepared to surrender either the power of taxation or control over the development of the western lands to a central authority.

England's superior strategic position and her competent leadership ultimately brought victory in the conflict with France, known as the French and Indian War in America and the Seven Years' War in Europe. Only a modest portion of it was fought in the Western Hemisphere.

In the Peace of Paris (1763), France relinquished all of Canada, the Great Lakes, and the territory east of the Mississippi to the British. The dream of a French empire in North America was over.

Having triumphed over France, Britain was now compelled to face a problem that it had hitherto neglected, the governance of its empire. London thought it essential to organize its now vast possessions to facilitate defense, reconcile the divergent interests of different areas and peoples, and distribute more evenly the cost of imperial administration.

In North America alone, British territories had more than doubled. A population that had been predominantly Protestant and English now included French-speaking Catholics from Quebec, and large numbers of partly Christianized Native Americans. Defense and administration of the new territories, as well as of the old, would require huge sums of money and increased personnel. The old colonial system was obviously inadequate to these tasks. Measures to establish a new one, however, would rouse the latent suspicions of colonials who increasingly would see Britain as no longer a protector of their rights, but rather a danger to them.

AN EXCEPTIONAL NATION?

The United States of America did not emerge as a nation until about 175 years after its establishment as a group of mostly British colonies. Yet from the beginning it was a different society in the eyes of many Europeans who viewed it from afar, whether with hope or apprehension. Most of its settlers — whether the younger sons of aristocrats, religious dissenters, or impoverished indentured servants — came there lured by a promise of opportunity or freedom not available in the Old World. The first Americans were reborn free, establishing themselves in a wilderness unencumbered by any social order other than that of the primitive aboriginal peoples they displaced. Having left the baggage of a feudal order behind them, they faced few obstacles to the development of a society built on the principles of political and social liberalism that emerged with difficulty in 17th- and 18th-century Europe. Based on the thinking of the philosopher John Locke, this sort of liberalism emphasized the rights of the individual and constraints on government power.

Most immigrants to America came from the British Isles, the most liberal of the European polities along with The Netherlands. In religion, the majority adhered to various forms of Calvinism with its emphasis on both divine and secular contractual relationships. These greatly facilitated the emergence of a social order built on individual rights and social mobility. The development of a more complex and highly structured commercial society in coastal cities by the mid-18th century did not stunt this trend; it was in these cities that the American Revolution was made. The constant reconstruction of society along an ever-receding Western frontier equally contributed to a liberal-democratic spirit.

In Europe, ideals of individual rights advanced slowly and unevenly; the concept of democracy was even more alien. The attempt to establish both in continental Europe's oldest nation led to the French Revolution. The effort to destroy a neofeudal society while establishing the rights of man and democratic fraternity generated terror, dictatorship, and Napoleonic despotism. In the end, it led to reaction and gave legitimacy to a decadent old order. In America, the European past was overwhelmed by ideals that sprang naturally from the process of building a new society on virgin land. The principles of liberalism and democracy were strong from the beginning. A society that had thrown off the burdens of European history would naturally give birth to a nation that saw itself as exceptional. ◆

THE WITCHES OF SALEM

In 1692 a group of adolescent girls in Salem Village, Massachusetts, became subject to strange fits after hearing tales told by a West Indian slave. They accused several women of being witches. The townspeople were appalled but not surprised: Belief in witchcraft was widespread throughout 17th-century America and Europe. Town officials convened a court to hear the charges of witchcraft. Within a month, six women were convicted and hanged.

The hysteria grew, in large measure because the court permitted witnesses to testify that they had seen the accused as spirits or in visions. Such "spectral evidence" could neither be verified nor made subject to objective examination. By the fall of 1692, 20 victims, including several men, had been executed, and more than 100 others were in jail (where another five victims died) — among them some of the town's most prominent citizens. When the charges threatened to spread beyond Salem, ministers throughout the colony called for an end to the trials. The governor of the colony agreed. Those still in jail were later acquitted or given reprieves.

Although an isolated incident, the Salem episode has long fascinated Americans. Most historians agree that Salem Village in 1692 experienced a kind of public hysteria, fueled by a genuine belief in the existence of witchcraft. While some of the girls may have been acting, many responsible adults became caught up in the frenzy as well.

Even more revealing is a closer analysis of the identities of the accused and the accusers. Salem Village, as much of colonial New England, was undergoing an economic and political transition from a largely agrarian, Puritan-dominated community to a more commercial, secular society. Many of the accusers were representatives of a traditional way of life tied to farming and the church, whereas a number of the accused witches were members of a rising commercial class of small shopkeepers and tradesmen. Salem's obscure struggle for social and political power between older traditional groups and a newer commercial class was one repeated in communities throughout American history. It took a bizarre and deadly detour when its citizens were swept up by the conviction that the devil was loose in their homes.

The Salem witch trials also serve as a dramatic parable of the deadly consequences of making sensational, but false, charges. Three hundred years later, we still call false accusations against a large number of people a "witch hunt." ◆

CHAPTER 2: THE COLONIAL PERIOD

Map depicting the English colonies and western territories, 1763-1775.

ENGLISH COLONIES
1763–1775.

John Smith, the stalwart English explorer and settler whose leadership helped save Jamestown from collapse during its critical early years.

BECOMING A
NATION
A PICTURE PROFILE

The United States of America was transformed in the two centuries from the first English settlement at Jamestown in 1607 to the beginning of the 19th century. From a series of isolated colonial settlements hugging the Atlantic Coast, the United States evolved into a new nation, born in revolution, and guided by a Constitution embodying the principles of democratic self-government.

Detail from a painting by American artist Benjamin West (1738-1820), which depicts William Penn's treaty with the Native Americans living where he founded the colony of Pennsylvania as a haven for Quakers and others seeking religious freedom. Penn's fair treatment of the Delaware Indians led to long-term, friendly relations, unlike the conflicts between European settlers and Indian tribes in other colonies.

A devout Puritan elder (right) confronts patrons drinking ale outside a tavern. Tensions between the strictly religious Puritans, who first settled the region, and the more secular population were characteristic of the colonial era in New England.

Cotton Mather was one of the leading Puritan figures of the late 17th and early 18th centuries. His massive *Ecclesiastical History of New England* (1702) is an exhaustive chronicle of the settlement of New England and the Puritan effort to establish a kingdom of God in the wilderness of the New World.

Statue of Roger Williams, early champion of religious freedom and the separation of church and state. Williams founded the colony of Rhode Island after leaving Massachusetts because of his disapproval of its religious ties to the Church of England.

Drawing of revolutionary firebrand Patrick Henry (standing to the left) uttering perhaps the most famous words of the American Revolution — "Give me liberty or give me death!" — in a debate before the Virginia Assembly in 1775.

Benjamin Franklin: scientist, inventor, writer, newspaper publisher, city father of Philadelphia, diplomat, and signer of both the Declaration of Independence and the Constitution. Franklin embodied the virtues of shrewd practicality and the optimistic belief in self-improvement often associated with America itself.

James Madison, fourth president of the United States, is often regarded as the "Father of the Constitution." His essays in the debate over ratification of the Constitution were collected with those of Alexander Hamilton and John Jay as *The Federalist Papers*. Today, they are regarded as a classic defense of republican government, in which the executive, legislative, and judicial branches check and balance each other to protect the rights and freedoms of the people.

Artist's depiction of the first shots of the American Revolution, fired at Lexington, Massachusetts, on April 19, 1775. Local militia confronted British troops marching to seize colonial armaments in the nearby town of Concord.

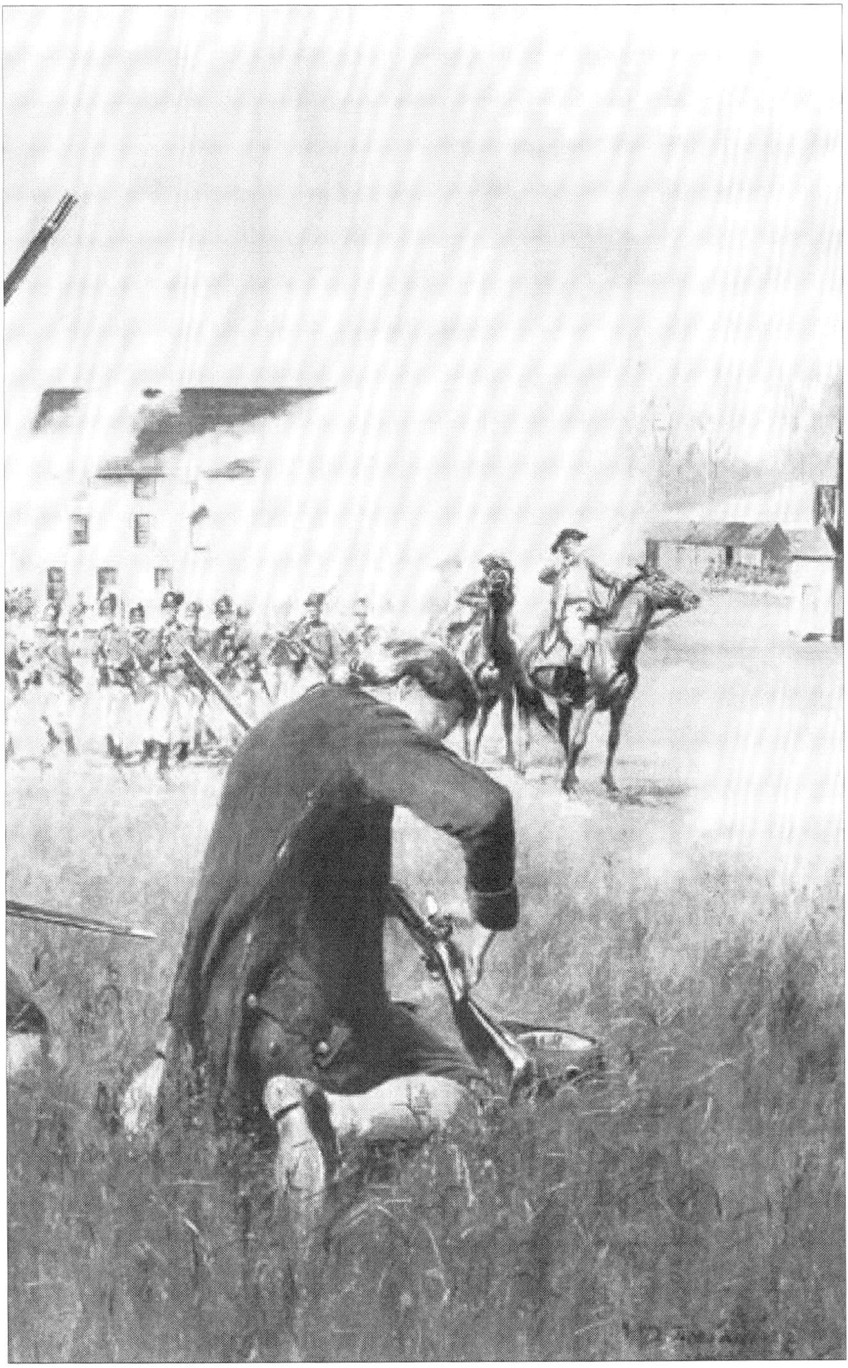

Thomas Jefferson, author of the Declaration of Independence and third president of the United States. Jefferson also founded the University of Virginia and built one of America's most celebrated houses, Monticello, in Charlottesville, Virginia.

Above: Surrender of Lord Cornwallis and the British army to American and French forces commanded by George Washington at Yorktown, Virginia, on October 19, 1781. The battle of Yorktown led to the end of the war and American independence, secured in the 1783 Treaty of Paris.

Left: U.S. postage stamp commemorating the bicentennial of the Lewis and Clark expedition, one of Thomas Jefferson's visionary projects. Meriwether Lewis, Jefferson's secretary, and his friend, William Clark, accompanied by a party of more than 30 persons, set out on a journey into the uncharted West that lasted four years. They traveled thousands of miles, from Camp Wood, Illinois, to Oregon, through lands that eventually became 11 American states.

Alexander Hamilton, secretary of the treasury in the administration of President George Washington. Hamilton advocated a strong federal government and the encouragement of industry. He was opposed by Thomas Jefferson, a believer in decentralized government, states' rights, and the virtues of the independent farmers and land owners.

John Marshall, chief justice of the U.S. Supreme Court from 1801 to 1835, in a portrait by Alonzo Chappel. In a series of landmark cases, Marshall established the principle of judicial review – the right of the courts to determine if any act of Congress or the executive branch is constitutional, and therefore valid and legal.

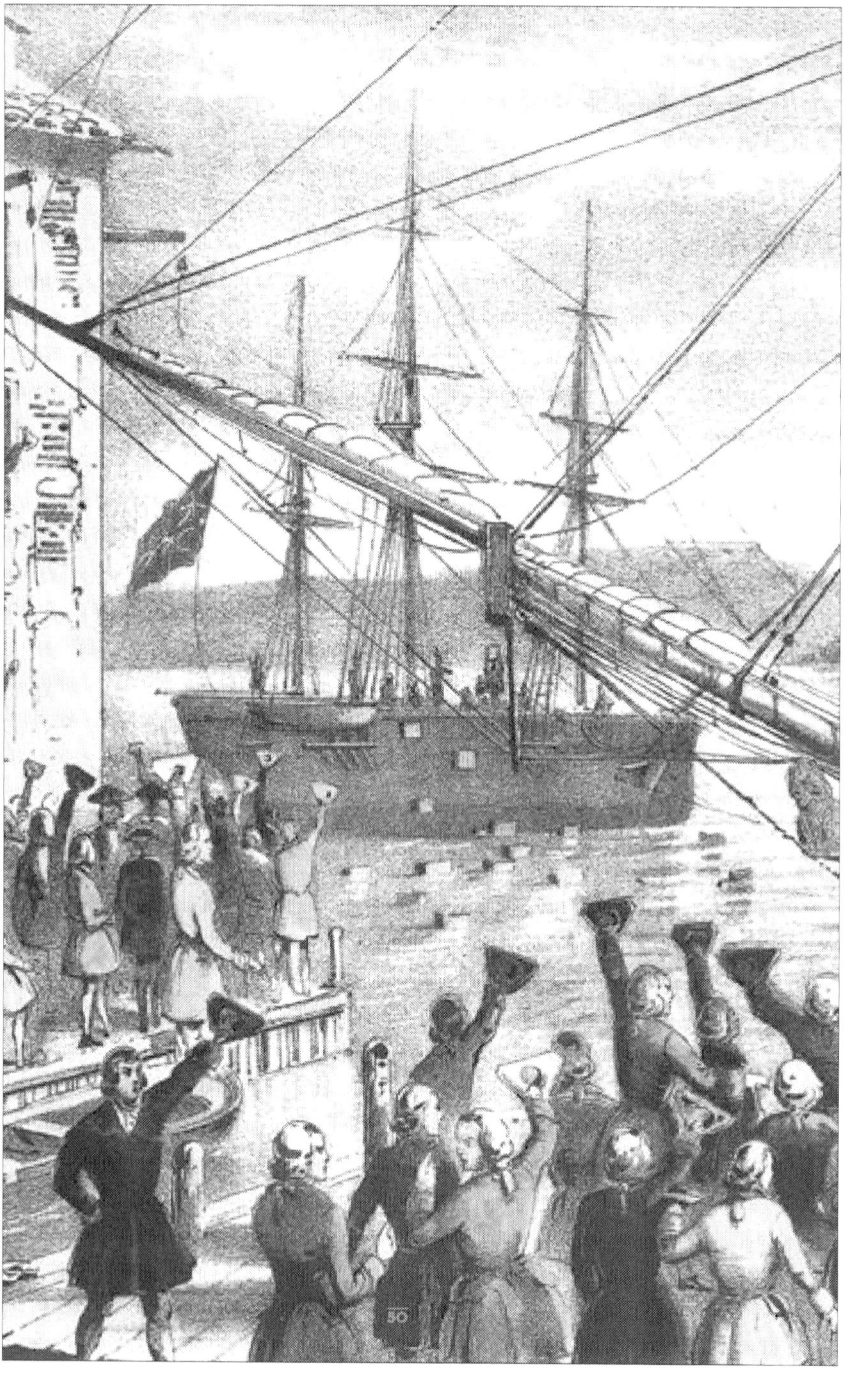

CHAPTER 3

THE ROAD TO INDEPENDENCE

The protest against British taxes known as the "Boston Tea Party," 1773.

CHAPTER 3: THE ROAD TO INDEPENDENCE

> "The Revolution was effected before the war commenced. The Revolution was in the hearts and minds of the people."
>
> Former President John Adams, 1818

Throughout the 18th century, the maturing British North American colonies inevitably forged a distinct identity. They grew vastly in economic strength and cultural attainment; virtually all had long years of self-government behind them. In the 1760s their combined population exceeded 1,500,000 — a six-fold increase since 1700. Nonetheless, England and America did not begin an overt parting of ways until 1763, more than a century and a half after the founding of the first permanent settlement at Jamestown, Virginia.

A NEW COLONIAL SYSTEM

In the aftermath of the French and Indian War, London saw a need for a new imperial design that would involve more centralized control, spread the costs of empire more equitably, and speak to the interests of both French Canadians and North American Indians. The colonies, on the other hand, long accustomed to a large measure of independence, expected more, not less, freedom. And, with the French menace eliminated, they felt far less need for a strong British presence. A scarcely comprehending Crown and Parliament on the other side of the Atlantic found itself contending with colonists trained in self-government and impatient with interference.

The organization of Canada and of the Ohio Valley necessitated policies that would not alienate the French and Indian inhabitants. Here London was in fundamental conflict with the interests of the colonies. Fast increasing in population, and needing more land for settlement, they claimed the right to extend their boundaries as far west as the Mississippi River.

The British government, fearing a series of Indian wars, believed that the lands should be opened on a more gradual basis. Restricting movement was also a way of ensuring royal control over existing settlements before allowing the formation of new ones. The Royal Proclamation of 1763 reserved all the western territory between the Allegheny Mountains, Florida, the Mississippi River, and Quebec for use by Native Americans. Thus the Crown attempted to sweep away every western land claim of the 13 colonies and to stop westward expansion. Although never effectively enforced, this measure, in the eyes of the colonists, constituted a high-handed disregard of their fundamental right to occupy and settle western lands.

More serious in its repercussions was the new British revenue policy. London needed more money to support its growing empire and faced growing taxpayer discontent at home. It seemed reasonable enough that the colonies should pay for their own defense. That would involve new taxes, levied by Parliament — at the expense of colonial self-government.

The first step was the replacement of the Molasses Act of 1733, which placed a prohibitive duty, or tax, on the import of rum and molasses from non-English areas, with the Sugar Act of 1764. This act outlawed the importation of foreign rum; it also put a modest duty on molasses from all sources and levied taxes on wines, silks, coffee, and a number of other luxury items. The hope was that lowering the duty on molasses would reduce the temptation to smuggle the commodity from the Dutch and French West Indies for the rum distilleries of New England. The British government enforced the Sugar Act energetically. Customs officials were ordered to show more effectiveness. British warships in American waters were instructed to seize smugglers, and "writs of assistance," or warrants, authorized the king's officers to search suspected premises.

Both the duty imposed by the Sugar Act and the measures to enforce it caused consternation among New England merchants. They contended that payment of even the small duty imposed would be ruinous to their businesses. Merchants, legislatures, and town meetings protested the law. Colonial lawyers protested "taxation without representation," a slogan that was to persuade many Americans they were being oppressed by the mother country.

Later in 1764, Parliament enacted a Currency Act "to prevent paper bills of credit hereafter issued in any of His Majesty's colonies from being made legal tender." Since the colonies were a deficit trade area and were constantly short of hard currency, this measure added a serious burden to the colonial economy. Equally objectionable from the colonial viewpoint was the Quartering Act, passed in 1765, which required colonies to provide royal troops with provisions and barracks.

THE STAMP ACT

A general tax measure sparked the greatest organized resistance. Known as the "Stamp Act," it required all newspapers, broadsides, pamphlets, licenses, leases, and other legal documents to bear revenue stamps. The proceeds, collected by American customs agents, would be used for "defending, protecting, and securing" the colonies.

Bearing equally on people who did any kind of business, the Stamp Act aroused the hostility of the most powerful and articulate groups in the American population: journalists, lawyers, clergymen, merchants and businessmen, North and South, East and West. Leading merchants organized for resistance and formed nonimportation associations.

Trade with the mother country fell off sharply in the summer of 1765, as prominent men organized themselves into the "Sons of Liberty" — secret organizations formed to protest the Stamp Act — often through violent means. From Massachusetts to South Carolina, mobs, forcing luckless customs agents to resign their offices, destroyed the hated stamps. Militant resistance effectively nullified the Act.

Spurred by delegate Patrick Henry, the Virginia House of Burgesses passed a set of resolutions in May denouncing taxation without representation as a threat to colonial liberties. It asserted that Virginians, enjoying the rights of Englishmen, could be taxed only by their own representatives. The Massachusetts Assembly invited all the colonies to appoint delegates to a "Stamp Act Congress" in New York, held in October 1765, to consider appeals for relief to the Crown and Parliament. Twenty-seven representatives from nine colonies seized the opportunity to mobilize colonial opinion. After much debate, the congress adopted a set of resolutions asserting that "no taxes ever have been or can be constitutionally imposed on them, but by their respective legislatures," and that the Stamp Act had a "manifest tendency to subvert the rights and liberties of the colonists."

TAXATION WITHOUT REPRESENTATION

The issue thus drawn centered on the question of representation. The colonists believed they could not be represented unless they actually elected members to the House of Commons. But this idea conflicted with the English principle of "virtual representation," according to which each member of Parliament represented the interests of the whole country and the empire — even if his electoral base consisted of only a tiny minority of property owners from a given district. This theory assumed that all British subjects shared the same interests as the property owners who elected members of Parliament.

The American leaders argued that their only legal relations were with the Crown. It was the king who had agreed to establish colonies beyond the sea and the king who provided them with governments. They asserted that he was equally a king of England and a king of the colonies, but they insisted that the English Parliament had no more right to pass laws for the colonies than any colonial legislature had the right to pass laws for England. In fact, however, their struggle was equally with King George III and Parliament. Factions aligned with the Crown generally controlled Parliament and reflected the king's determination to be a strong monarch.

The British Parliament rejected the colonial contentions. British merchants, however, feeling the effects of the American boycott, threw their weight behind a repeal movement. In 1766 Parliament yielded, repealing the Stamp Act and modifying the Sugar Act. However, to mollify the supporters of central control over the colonies, Parliament followed these actions with passage of the Declaratory Act, which asserted the authority of Parliament to make laws binding the colonies "in all cases whatsoever." The colonists had won only a temporary respite from an impending crisis.

THE TOWNSHEND ACTS

The year 1767 brought another series of measures that stirred anew all the elements of discord. Charles Townshend, British chancellor of the exchequer, attempted a new fiscal program in the face of continued discontent over high taxes at home. Intent upon reducing British taxes by making more efficient the collection of duties levied on American trade, he tightened customs administration and enacted duties on colonial imports of paper, glass, lead, and tea from Britain. The "Townshend Acts" were based on the premise that taxes imposed on goods imported by the colonies were legal while internal taxes (like the Stamp Act) were not.

The Townshend Acts were designed to raise revenue that would be used in part to support colonial officials and maintain the British army in America. In response, Philadelphia lawyer John Dickinson, in *Letters of a Pennsylvania Farmer*, argued that Parliament had the right to control imperial commerce but did not have the right to tax the colonies, whether the duties were external or internal.

The agitation following enactment of the Townshend duties was less violent than that stirred by the Stamp Act, but it was nevertheless strong, particularly in the cities of the Eastern seaboard. Merchants once again resorted to non-importation agreements, and people made do with local products. Colonists, for example, dressed in homespun clothing and found substitutes for tea. They used homemade paper and their houses went unpainted. In Boston, enforcement of the new regulations provoked violence.

When customs officials sought to collect duties, they were set upon by the populace and roughly handled. For this infraction, two British regiments were dispatched to protect the customs commissioners.

The presence of British troops in Boston was a standing invitation to disorder. On March 5, 1770, antagonism between citizens and British soldiers again flared into violence. What began as a harmless snowballing of British soldiers degenerated into a mob attack. Someone gave the order to fire. When the smoke had cleared, three Bostonians lay dead in the snow. Dubbed the "Boston Massacre," the incident was dramatically pictured as proof of British heartlessness and tyranny.

Faced with such opposition, Parliament in 1770 opted for a strategic retreat and repealed all the Townshend duties except that on tea, which was a luxury item in the colonies, imbibed only by a very small minority. To most, the action of Parliament signified that the colonists had won a major concession, and the campaign against England was largely dropped. A colonial embargo on "English tea" continued but was not too scrupulously observed. Prosperity was increasing and most colonial leaders were willing to let the future take care of itself.

SAMUEL ADAMS

During a three-year interval of calm, a relatively small number of radicals strove energetically to keep the controversy alive. They contended that payment of the tax constituted an acceptance of the principle that Parliament had the right to rule over the colonies. They feared that at any time in the future, the principle of parliamentary rule might be applied with devastating effect on all colonial liberties.

The radicals' most effective leader was Samuel Adams of Massachusetts, who toiled tirelessly for a single end: independence. From the time he graduated from Harvard College in 1743, Adams was a public servant in some capacity — inspector of chimneys, tax-collector, and moderator of town meetings. A consistent failure in business, he was shrewd and able in politics, with the New England town meeting his theater of action.

Adams wanted to free people from their awe of social and political superiors, make them aware of their own power and importance, and thus arouse them to action. Toward these objectives, he published articles in newspapers and made speeches in town meetings, instigating resolutions that appealed to the colonists' democratic impulses.

In 1772 he induced the Boston town meeting to select a "Committee of Correspondence" to state the rights and grievances of the colonists. The committee opposed a British decision to pay the salaries of judges from customs revenues; it feared that the judges would no longer be dependent on the legislature for their incomes and thus no longer accountable to it, thereby leading to the emergence of "a despotic form of government." The committee communicated with other towns on this matter and requested them to draft replies. Committees were set up in virtually all the colonies, and out of them grew a base of effective revolutionary organizations. Still, Adams did not have enough fuel to set a fire.

THE BOSTON "TEA PARTY"

In 1773, however, Britain furnished Adams and his allies with an incendiary issue. The powerful East India Company, finding itself in critical financial straits, appealed to the British government, which granted it a monopoly on all tea exported to the colonies. The government also permitted the East India Company to supply retailers directly, bypassing colonial wholesalers. By then, most of the tea consumed in America was imported illegally, duty-free. By selling its tea through its own agents at a price well under the customary one, the East India Company made smuggling unprofitable and threatened to eliminate the independent colonial merchants. Aroused not only by the loss of the tea trade but also by the monopolistic practice involved, colonial traders joined the radicals agitating for independence.

In ports up and down the Atlantic coast, agents of the East India Company were forced to resign. New shipments of tea were either returned to England or warehoused. In Boston, however, the agents defied the colonists; with the support of the royal governor, they made preparations to land incoming cargoes regardless of opposition. On the night of December 16, 1773, a band of men disguised as Mohawk Indians and led by Samuel Adams boarded three British ships lying at anchor and dumped their tea cargo into Boston harbor. Doubting their countrymen's commitment to principle, they feared that if the tea were landed, colonists would actually purchase the tea and pay the tax.

A crisis now confronted Britain. The East India Company had carried out a parliamentary statute. If the destruction of the tea went unpunished, Parliament would admit to the world that it had no control over the colonies. Official opinion in Britain almost unanimously condemned the Boston Tea Party as an act of vandalism and advocated legal measures to bring the insurgent colonists into line.

THE COERCIVE ACTS

Parliament responded with new laws that the colonists called the "Coercive" or "Intolerable Acts." The first, the Boston Port Bill, closed the port of Boston until the tea was paid for. The action threatened the very life of the city, for to prevent Boston from having access to the sea meant economic disaster. Other enactments restricted local authority and banned most town meetings held without the governor's consent.

A Quartering Act required local authorities to find suitable quarters for British troops, in private homes if necessary. Instead of subduing and isolating Massachusetts, as Parliament intended, these acts rallied its sister colonies to its aid. The Quebec Act, passed at nearly the same time, extended the boundaries of the province of Quebec south to the Ohio River. In conformity with previous French practice, it provided for trials without jury, did not establish a representative assembly, and gave the Catholic Church semi-established status. By disregarding old charter claims to western lands, it threatened to block colonial expansion to the North and Northwest; its recognition of the Roman Catholic Church outraged the Protestant sects that dominated every colony. Though the Quebec Act had not been passed as a punitive measure, Americans associated it with the Coercive Acts, and all became known as the "Five Intolerable Acts."

At the suggestion of the Virginia House of Burgesses, colonial representatives met in Philadelphia on September 5, 1774, "to consult upon the present unhappy state of the Colonies." Delegates to this meeting, known as the First Continental Congress, were chosen by provincial congresses or popular conventions. Only Georgia failed to send a delegate; the total number of 55 was large enough for diversity of opinion, but small enough for genuine debate and effective action. The division of opinion in the colonies posed a genuine dilemma for the delegates. They would have to give an appearance of firm unanimity to induce the British government to make concessions. But they also would have to avoid any show of radicalism or spirit of independence that would alarm more moderate Americans.

A cautious keynote speech, followed by a "resolve" that no obedience was due the Coercive Acts, ended with adoption of a set of resolutions affirming the right of the colonists to "life, liberty, and property," and the right of provincial legislatures to set "all cases of taxation and internal polity." The most important action taken by the Congress, however, was the formation of a "Continental Association" to reestablish the trade boycott. It set up a system of committees to inspect customs entries, publish the names of merchants who violated the agreements, confiscate their imports, and encourage frugality, economy, and industry.

The Continental Association immediately assumed the leadership in the colonies, spurring new local organizations to end what remained of royal authority. Led by the pro-independence leaders, they drew their support not only from the less well-to-do, but from many members of the professional class (especially lawyers), most of the planters of the Southern colonies, and a number of merchants. They intimidated the hesitant into joining the popular movement and punished the hostile;

began the collection of military supplies and the mobilization of troops; and fanned public opinion into revolutionary ardor.

Many of those opposed to British encroachment on American rights nonetheless favored discussion and compromise as the proper solution. This group included Crown-appointed officers, Quakers, and members of other religious sects opposed to the use of violence, numerous merchants (especially in the middle colonies), and some discontented farmers and frontiersmen in the Southern colonies.

The king might well have effected an alliance with these moderates and, by timely concessions, so strengthened their position that the revolutionaries would have found it difficult to proceed with hostilities. But George III had no intention of making concessions. In September 1774, scorning a petition by Philadelphia Quakers, he wrote, "The die is now cast, the Colonies must either submit or triumph." This action isolated Loyalists who were appalled and frightened by the course of events following the Coercive Acts.

THE REVOLUTION BEGINS

General Thomas Gage, an amiable English gentleman with an American-born wife, commanded the garrison at Boston, where political activity had almost wholly replaced trade. Gage's main duty in the colonies had been to enforce the Coercive Acts. When news reached him that the Massachusetts colonists were collecting powder and military stores at the town of Concord, 32 kilometers away, Gage sent a strong detail to confiscate these munitions.

After a night of marching, the British troops reached the village of Lexington on April 19, 1775, and saw a grim band of 77 Minutemen — so named because they were said to be ready to fight in a minute — through the early morning mist. The Minutemen intended only a silent protest, but Marine Major John Pitcairn, the leader of the British troops, yelled, "Disperse, you damned rebels! You dogs, run!" The leader of the Minutemen, Captain John Parker, told his troops not to fire unless fired at first. The Americans were withdrawing when someone fired a shot, which led the British troops to fire at the Minutemen. The British then charged with bayonets, leaving eight dead and 10 wounded. In the often-quoted phrase of 19th century poet Ralph Waldo Emerson, this was "the shot heard round the world."

The British pushed on to Concord. The Americans had taken away most of the munitions, but they destroyed whatever was left. In the meantime, American forces in the countryside had mobilized to harass the British on their long return to Boston. All along the road, behind stone walls, hillocks, and houses, militiamen from "every Middlesex village and farm" made targets of the bright red coats of the British soldiers. By the time Gage's weary detachment stumbled into Boston, it had suffered more than 250 killed and wounded. The Americans lost 93 men.

The Second Continental Congress met in Philadelphia, Pennsylvania, on May 10. The Congress voted to go to war, inducting the colonial militias into continental service. It appointed Colonel George Washington of Virginia as their commander-in-chief on June 15. Within two days, the Americans had incurred high casualties at Bunker Hill just outside Boston. Congress also ordered American expeditions to march northward into Canada by fall. Capturing Montreal, they failed in a winter assault on Quebec, and eventually retreated to New York.

Despite the outbreak of armed conflict, the idea of complete separation from England was still repugnant to many members of the Continental Congress. In July, it adopted the Olive Branch Petition, begging the king to prevent further hostile actions until some sort of agreement could be worked out. King George rejected it; instead, on August 23, 1775, he issued a proclamation declaring the colonies to be in a state of rebellion.

Britain had expected the Southern colonies to remain loyal, in part because of their reliance on slavery. Many in the Southern colonies feared that a rebellion against the mother country would also trigger a slave uprising. In November 1775, Lord Dunmore, the governor of Virginia, tried to capitalize on that fear by offering freedom to all slaves who would fight for the British. Instead, his proclamation drove to the rebel side many Virginians who would otherwise have remained Loyalist.

The governor of North Carolina, Josiah Martin, also urged North Carolinians to remain loyal to the Crown. When 1,500 men answered Martin's call, they were defeated by revolutionary armies before British troops could arrive to help.

British warships continued down the coast to Charleston, South Carolina, and opened fire on the city in early June 1776. But South Carolinians had time to prepare, and repulsed the British by the end of the month. They would not return South for more than two years.

COMMON SENSE AND INDEPENDENCE

In January 1776, Thomas Paine, a radical political theorist and writer who had come to America from England in 1774, published a 50-page pamphlet, *Common Sense*. Within three months, it sold 100,000 copies. Paine attacked the idea of a hereditary monarchy, declaring that one honest man was worth more to society than "all the crowned ruffians that ever lived." He presented the alternatives — continued submission to a tyrannical king and an outworn government, or liberty and happiness as a self-sufficient, independent republic. Circulated throughout the colonies, *Common Sense* helped to crystallize a decision for separation.

There still remained the task, however, of gaining each colony's approval of a formal declaration. On June 7, Richard Henry Lee of Virginia introduced a resolution in the Second Continental Congress, declaring, "That these United Colonies are, and of right ought to be, free and independent states. ..." Immediately, a committee of five, headed by Thomas Jefferson of Virginia, was appointed to draft a document for a vote.

Largely Jefferson's work, the Declaration of Independence, adopted July 4, 1776, not only announced the birth of a new nation, but also set forth a philosophy of human freedom that would become a dynamic force throughout the entire world. The Declaration drew upon French and English Enlightenment political philosophy, but one influence in particular stands out: John Locke's *Second Treatise on Government*. Locke took conceptions of the traditional rights of Englishmen and universalized them into the natural rights of all humankind. The Declaration's familiar opening passage echoes Locke's social-contract theory of government:

> *We hold these truths to be self-evident, that all men are created equal, that they are endowed by their Creator with certain unalienable Rights, that among these are Life, Liberty and the pursuit of Happiness. — That to secure these rights, Governments are instituted among Men, deriving their just powers from the consent of the governed, — That whenever any Form of Government becomes destructive of these ends, it is the Right of the People to alter or to abolish it, and to institute new Government, laying its foundation on such principles and organizing its powers in such form, as to them shall seem most likely to effect their Safety and Happiness.*

Jefferson linked Locke's principles directly to the situation in the colonies. To fight for American independence was to fight for a government based on popular consent in place of a government by a king who had "combined with others to subject us to a jurisdiction foreign to our constitution, and unacknowledged by our laws. ..." Only a government based on popular consent could secure natural rights to life, liberty, and the pursuit of happiness. Thus, to fight for American independence was to fight on behalf of one's own natural rights.

DEFEATS AND VICTORIES

Although the Americans suffered severe setbacks for months after independence was declared, their tenacity and perseverance eventually paid off. During August 1776, in the Battle of Long Island in New York, Washington's position became untenable, and he executed a masterly retreat in small boats from Brooklyn to the Manhattan shore. British General William Howe twice hesitated and allowed the Americans to escape. By November, however, Howe had captured Fort Washington on Manhattan Island. New York City would remain under British control until the end of the war.

That December, Washington's forces were near collapse, as supplies and promised aid failed to materialize. Howe again missed his chance to crush the Americans by deciding to wait until spring to resume fighting. On Christmas Day, December 25, 1776, Washington crossed the Delaware River, north of Trenton, New Jersey. In the early-morning hours of December 26, his troops surprised the British garrison there, taking more than 900 prisoners. A week later, on January 3, 1777, Washington attacked the British at Princeton, regaining most of the territory formally occupied by the British. The victories at Trenton and Princeton revived flagging American spirits.

In September 1777, however, Howe defeated the American army at Brandywine in Pennsylvania and occupied Philadelphia, forcing the Continental Congress to flee. Washington had to endure the bitterly cold winter of 1777-1778 at Valley Forge, Pennsylvania, lacking adequate food, clothing, and supplies. Farmers and merchants exchanged their goods for British gold and silver rather than for dubious paper money issued by the Continental Congress and the states.

Valley Forge was the lowest ebb for Washington's Continental Army, but elsewhere 1777 proved to be the turning point in the war. British General John Burgoyne, moving south from Canada, attempted to invade New York and New England via Lake Champlain and the Hudson River. He had too much heavy equipment to negotiate the wooded and marshy terrain. On August 6, at Oriskany, New York, a band of Loyalists and Native Americans under Burgoyne's command ran into a mobile and seasoned American force that managed to halt their advance. A few days later at Bennington, Vermont, more of Burgoyne's forces, seeking much-needed supplies, were pushed back by American troops.

Moving to the west side of the Hudson River, Burgoyne's army advanced on Albany. The Americans were waiting for him. Led by Benedict Arnold — who would later betray the Americans at West Point, New York — the colonials twice repulsed the British. Having by this time incurred heavy losses, Burgoyne fell back to Saratoga, New York, where a vastly superior American force under General Horatio Gates surrounded the British troops. On October 17, 1777, Burgoyne surrendered his entire army — six generals, 300 other officers, and 5,500 enlisted personnel.

FRANCO-AMERICAN ALLIANCE

In France, enthusiasm for the American cause was high: The French intellectual world was itself stirring against feudalism and privilege. However, the Crown lent its support to the colonies for geopolitical rather than ideological reasons: The French government had been eager for reprisal against Britain ever since France's defeat in 1763. To further the American cause, Benjamin Franklin was sent to Paris in 1776. His wit, guile, and intellect soon made their presence felt in the French capital, and played a major role in winning French assistance.

France began providing aid to the colonies in May 1776, when it sent 14 ships with war supplies to America. In fact, most of the gunpowder used by the American armies came from France. After Britain's defeat at Saratoga, France saw an opportunity to seriously weaken its ancient enemy and restore the balance of power that had been upset by the Seven Years' War (called the French and Indian War in the American colonies). On February 6, 1778, the colonies and France signed a Treaty of Amity and Commerce, in which France recognized the United States and offered trade concessions. They also signed a Treaty of Alliance, which stipulated that if France entered the war, neither country would lay down its arms until the colonies won their independence, that neither would conclude peace with Britain without the consent of the other, and that each guaranteed the other's possessions in America. This was the only bilateral defense treaty signed by the United States or its predecessors until 1949.

The Franco-American alliance soon broadened the conflict. In June 1778 British ships fired on French vessels, and the two countries went to war. In 1779 Spain, hoping to reacquire territories taken by Britain in the Seven Years' War, entered the conflict on the side of France, but not as an ally of the Americans. In 1780 Britain declared war on the Dutch, who had continued to trade with the Americans. The combination of these European powers, with France in the lead, was a far greater threat to Britain than the American colonies standing alone.

THE BRITISH MOVE SOUTH

With the French now involved, the British, still believing that most Southerners were Loyalists, stepped up their efforts in the Southern colonies. A campaign began in late 1778, with the capture of Savannah, Georgia. Shortly thereafter, British troops and naval forces converged on Charleston, South Carolina, the principal Southern port. They managed to bottle up American forces on the Charleston peninsula. On May 12, 1780, General Benjamin Lincoln surrendered the city and its 5,000 troops, in the greatest American defeat of the war.

But the reversal in fortune only emboldened the American rebels. South Carolinians began roaming the countryside, attacking British supply lines. In July, American General Horatio Gates, who had assembled a replacement force of untrained militiamen, rushed to Camden,

South Carolina, to confront British forces led by General Charles Cornwallis. But Gates's makeshift army panicked and ran when confronted by the British regulars. Cornwallis's troops met the Americans several more times, but the most significant battle took place at Cowpens, South Carolina, in early 1781, where the Americans soundly defeated the British. After an exhausting but unproductive chase through North Carolina, Cornwallis set his sights on Virginia.

VICTORY AND INDEPENDENCE

In July 1780 France's King Louis XVI had sent to America an expeditionary force of 6,000 men under the Comte Jean de Rochambeau. In addition, the French fleet harassed British shipping and blocked reinforcement and resupply of British forces in Virginia. French and American armies and navies, totaling 18,000 men, parried with Cornwallis all through the summer and into the fall. Finally, on October 19, 1781, after being trapped at Yorktown near the mouth of Chesapeake Bay, Cornwallis surrendered his army of 8,000 British soldiers.

Although Cornwallis's defeat did not immediately end the war — which would drag on inconclusively for almost two more years — a new British government decided to pursue peace negotiations in Paris in early 1782, with the American side represented by Benjamin Franklin, John Adams, and John Jay. On April 15, 1783, Congress approved the final treaty. Signed on September 3, the Treaty of Paris acknowledged the independence, freedom, and sovereignty of the 13 former colonies, now states. The new United States stretched west to the Mississippi River, north to Canada, and south to Florida, which was returned to Spain. The fledgling colonies that Richard Henry Lee had spoken of more than seven years before had finally become "free and independent states."

The task of knitting together a nation remained. >

THE SIGNIFICANCE OF THE AMERICAN REVOLUTION

The American Revolution had a significance far beyond the North American continent. It attracted the attention of a political intelligentsia throughout the European continent. Idealistic notables such as Thaddeus Kosciusko, Friedrich von Steuben, and the Marquis de Lafayette joined its ranks to affirm liberal ideas they hoped to transfer to their own nations. Its success strengthened the concept of natural rights throughout the Western world and furthered the Enlightenment rationalist critique of an old order built around hereditary monarchy and an established church. In a very real sense, it was a precursor to the French Revolution, but it lacked the French Revolution's violence and chaos because it had occurred in a society that was already fundamentally liberal.

The ideas of the Revolution have been most often depicted as a triumph of the social contract/natural rights theories of John Locke. Correct so far as it goes, this characterization passes too quickly over the continuing importance of Calvinist-dissenting Protestantism, which from the Pilgrims and Puritans on had also stood for the ideals of the social contract and the self-governing community. Lockean intellectuals and the Protestant clergy were both important advocates of compatible strains of liberalism that had flourished in the British North American colonies.

Scholars have also argued that another persuasion contributed to the Revolution: "republicanism." Republicanism, they assert, did not deny the existence of natural rights but subordinated them to the belief that the maintenance of a free republic required a strong sense of communal responsibility and the cultivation of self-denying virtue among its leaders. The assertion of individual rights, even the pursuit of individual happiness, seemed egoistic by contrast. For a time republicanism threatened to displace natural rights as the major theme of the Revolution. Most historians today, however, concede that the distinction was much overdrawn. Most individuals who thought about such things in the 18th century envisioned the two ideas more as different sides of the same intellectual coin.

Revolution usually entails social upheaval and violence on a wide scale. By these criteria, the American Revolution was relatively mild. About 100,000 Loyalists left the new United States. Some thousands were members of old elites who had suffered expropriation of their property and been expelled; others were simply common people faithful to their King. The majority of those who went into exile did so voluntarily. The Revolution did open up and further liberalize an already liberal society. In New York and the Carolinas, large Loyalist estates were divided among small farmers. Liberal assumptions became the official norm of American political culture — whether in the disestablishment of the Anglican Church, the principle of elected national and state executives, or the wide dissemination of the idea of individual freedom. Yet the structure of society changed little. Revolution or not, most people remained secure in their life, liberty, and property. ◆

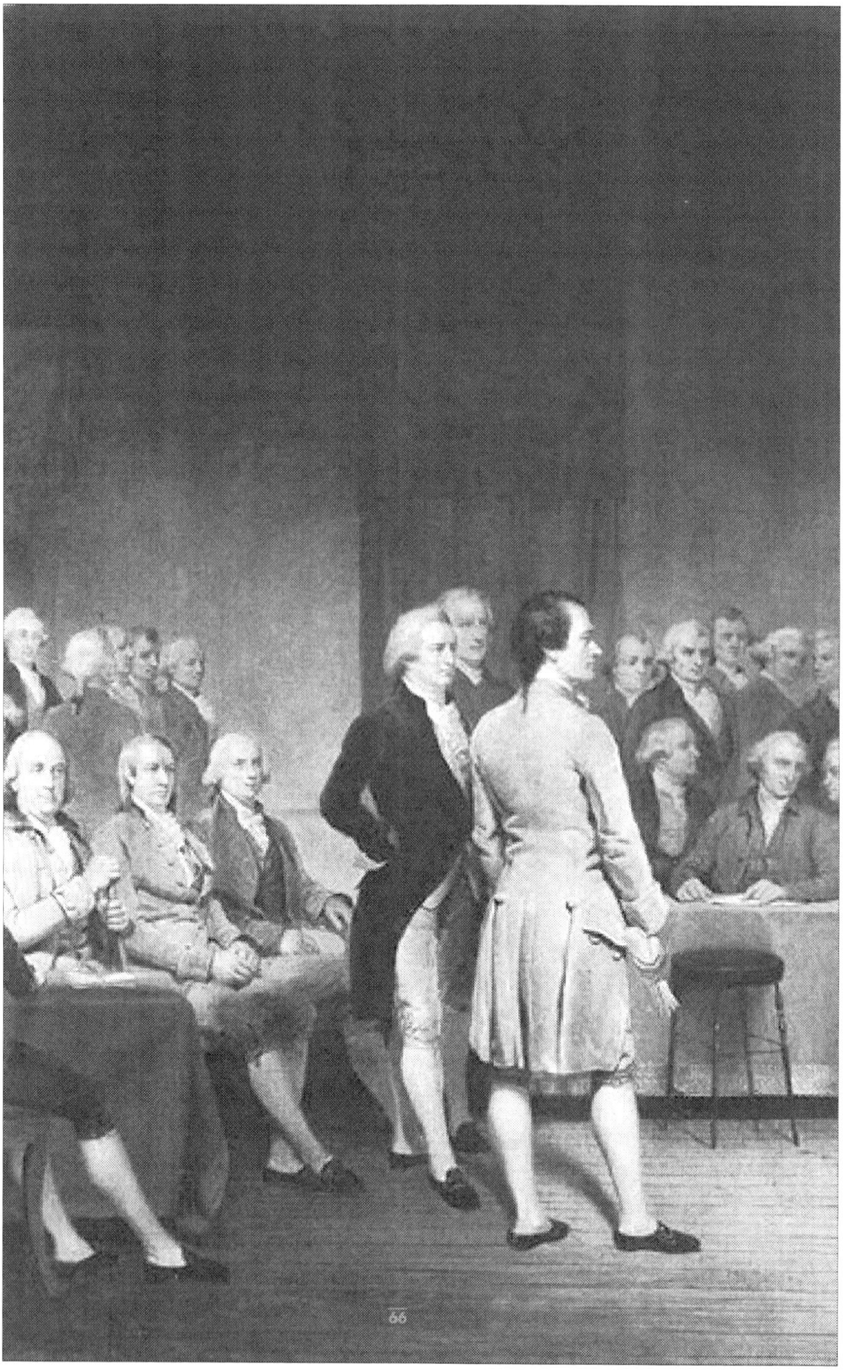

CHAPTER 4

THE FORMATION OF A NATIONAL GOVERNMENT

George Washington addressing the Constitutional Convention in Philadelphia, 1787.

> "Every man, and every body of men on Earth, possesses the right of self-government."
>
> Drafter of the Declaration of Independence
> Thomas Jefferson, 1790

STATE CONSTITUTIONS

The success of the Revolution gave Americans the opportunity to give legal form to their ideals as expressed in the Declaration of Independence, and to remedy some of their grievances through state constitutions. As early as May 10, 1776, Congress had passed a resolution advising the colonies to form new governments "such as shall best conduce to the happiness and safety of their constituents." Some of them had already done so, and within a year after the Declaration of Independence, all but three had drawn up constitutions.

The new constitutions showed the impact of democratic ideas. None made any drastic break with the past, since all were built on the solid foundation of colonial experience and English practice. But each was also animated by the spirit of republicanism, an ideal that had long been praised by Enlightenment philosophers.

Naturally, the first objective of the framers of the state constitutions was to secure those "unalienable rights" whose violation had caused the former colonies to repudiate their connection with Britain. Thus, each constitution began with a declaration or bill of rights. Virginia's, which served as a model for all the others, included a declaration of principles: popular sovereignty, rotation in office, freedom of elections, and an enumeration of fundamental liberties: moderate bail and humane punishment, speedy trial by jury, freedom of the press and of conscience, and the right of the majority to reform or alter the government.

Other states enlarged the list of liberties to freedom of speech, of assembly, and of petition. Their constitutions frequently included such provisions as the right to bear arms, to a writ of habeas corpus, to inviolability of domicile, and to equal protection under the law. Moreover, all prescribed a three-branch structure of government — executive, legislative, and judiciary — each checked and balanced by the others.

Pennsylvania's constitution was the most radical. In that state, Philadelphia artisans, Scots-Irish frontiersmen, and German-speaking farmers had taken control. The provincial congress adopted a constitution that permitted every male taxpayer and his sons to vote, required rotation in office (no one could serve as a representative more than four years out of every seven), and set up a single-chamber legislature.

The state constitutions had some glaring limitations, particularly by more recent standards. Constitutions established to guarantee people their natural rights did not secure for everyone the most fundamental natural right — equality. The colonies south of Pennsylvania excluded their slave populations from their inalienable rights as human beings. Women had no political rights. No state went so far as to permit universal male suffrage, and even in those states that permitted all taxpayers to vote (Delaware, North Carolina, and Georgia, in addition to Pennsylvania), office-holders were required to own a certain amount of property.

THE ARTICLES OF CONFEDERATION

The struggle with England had done much to change colonial attitudes. Local assemblies had rejected the Albany Plan of Union in 1754, refusing to surrender even the smallest part of their autonomy to any other body, even one they themselves had elected. But in the course of the Revolution, mutual aid had proved effective, and the fear of relinquishing individual authority had lessened to a large degree.

John Dickinson produced the "Articles of Confederation and Perpetual Union" in 1776. The Continental Congress adopted them in November 1777, and they went into effect in 1781, having been ratified by all the states. Reflecting the fragility of a nascent sense of nationhood, the Articles provided only for a very loose union. The national government lacked the authority to set up tariffs, to regulate commerce, and to levy taxes. It possessed scant control of international relations: A number of states had begun their own negotiations with foreign countries. Nine states had their own armies, several their own navies. In the absence of a sound common currency, the new nation conducted its commerce with a curious hodgepodge of coins and a bewildering variety of state and national paper bills, all fast depreciating in value.

Economic difficulties after the war prompted calls for change. The end of the war had a severe effect on merchants who supplied the armies of both sides and who had lost the advantages deriving from participation in the British mercantile system. The states gave preference to American goods in their tariff policies, but these were inconsistent, leading to the demand for a stronger central government to implement a uniform policy.

Farmers probably suffered the most from economic difficulties following the Revolution. The supply of farm produce exceeded demand; unrest centered chiefly among farmer-debtors who wanted strong remedies to avoid foreclosure on their property and imprisonment for debt. Courts were clogged with suits for payment filed by their creditors. All through the summer of 1786, popular conventions and informal gatherings in several states demanded reform in the state administrations.

That autumn, mobs of farmers in Massachusetts under the leadership of a former army captain, Daniel Shays, began forcibly to prevent the county courts from sitting and passing further judgments for debt, pending the next state election. In January 1787 a ragtag army of 1,200 farmers moved toward the federal arsenal at Springfield. The rebels, armed chiefly with staves and pitchforks, were repulsed by a small state militia force; General Benjamin Lincoln then arrived with reinforcements from Boston and routed the remaining Shaysites, whose leader escaped to Vermont. The government captured 14 rebels and sentenced them to death, but ultimately pardoned some and let the others off with short prison terms. After the defeat of the rebellion, a newly elected legislature, whose majority sympathized with the rebels, met some of their demands for debt relief.

THE PROBLEM OF EXPANSION

With the end of the Revolution, the United States again had to face the old unsolved Western question, the problem of expansion, with its complications of land, fur trade, Indians, settlement, and local government. Lured by the richest land yet found in the country, pioneers poured over the Appalachian Mountains and beyond. By 1775 the far-flung outposts scattered along the waterways had tens of thousands of settlers. Separated by mountain ranges and hundreds of kilometers from the centers of political authority in the East, the inhabitants established their own governments. Settlers from all the Tidewater states pressed on into the fertile river valleys, hardwood forests, and rolling prairies of the interior. By 1790 the population of the trans-Appalachian region numbered well over 120,000.

Before the war, several colonies had laid extensive and often overlapping claims to land beyond the

Appalachians. To those without such claims this rich territorial prize seemed unfairly apportioned. Maryland, speaking for the latter group, introduced a resolution that the western lands be considered common property to be parceled by the Congress into free and independent governments. This idea was not received enthusiastically. Nonetheless, in 1780 New York led the way by ceding its claims. In 1784 Virginia, which held the grandest claims, relinquished all land north of the Ohio River. Other states ceded their claims, and it became apparent that Congress would come into possession of all the lands north of the Ohio River and west of the Allegheny Mountains. This common possession of millions of hectares was the most tangible evidence yet of nationality and unity, and gave a certain substance to the idea of national sovereignty. At the same time, these vast territories were a problem that required solution.

The Confederation Congress established a system of limited self-government for this new national Northwest Territory. The Northwest Ordinance of 1787 provided for its organization, initially as a single district, ruled by a governor and judges appointed by the Congress. When this territory had 5,000 free male inhabitants of voting age, it was to be entitled to a legislature of two chambers, itself electing the lower house. In addition, it could at that time send a nonvoting delegate to Congress. Three to five states would be formed as the territory was settled. Whenever any one of them had 60,000 free inhabitants, it was to be admitted to the Union "on an equal footing with the original states in all respects." The ordinance guaranteed civil rights and liberties, encouraged education, and prohibited slavery or other forms of involuntary servitude.

The new policy repudiated the time-honored concept that colonies existed for the benefit of the mother country, were politically subordinate, and peopled by social inferiors. Instead, it established the principle that colonies ("territories") were an extension of the nation and entitled, not as a privilege but as a right, to all the benefits of equality.

CONSTITUTIONAL CONVENTION

By the time the Northwest Ordinance was enacted, American leaders were in the midst of drafting a new and stronger constitution to replace the Articles of Confederation. Their presiding officer, George Washington, had written accurately that the states were united only by a "rope of sand." Disputes between Maryland and Virginia over navigation on the Potomac River led to a conference of representatives of five states at Annapolis, Maryland, in 1786. One of the delegates, Alexander Hamilton of New York, convinced his colleagues that commerce was bound up with large political and economic questions. What was required was a fundamental rethinking of the Confederation.

The Annapolis conference issued a call for all the states to appoint representatives to a convention to be held the following spring in Philadelphia. The Continental Congress was at first indignant over this bold step, but it acquiesced after Washington gave the project his backing and was elected a delegate. During the next fall and winter, elections were held in all states but Rhode Island.

A remarkable gathering of notables assembled at the Federal Convention in May 1787. The state legislatures sent leaders with experience in colonial and state governments, in Congress, on the bench, and in the army. Washington, regarded as the country's first citizen because of his integrity and his military leadership during the Revolution, was chosen as presiding officer.

Prominent among the more active members were two Pennsylvanians: Gouverneur Morris, who clearly saw the need for national government, and James Wilson, who labored indefatigably for the national idea. Also elected by Pennsylvania was Benjamin Franklin, nearing the end of an extraordinary career of public service and scientific achievement. From Virginia came James Madison, a practical young statesman, a thorough student of politics and history, and, according to a colleague, "from a spirit of industry and application ... the best-informed man on any point in debate." He would be recognized as the "Father of the Constitution."

Massachusetts sent Rufus King and Elbridge Gerry, young men of ability and experience. Roger Sherman, shoemaker turned judge, was one of the representatives from Connecticut. From New York came Alexander Hamilton, who had proposed the meeting. Absent from the Convention were Thomas Jefferson, who was serving as minister representing the United States in France, and John Adams, serving in the same capacity in Great Britain. Youth predominated among the 55 delegates — the average age was 42.

Congress had authorized the Convention merely to draft amendments to the Articles of Confederation but, as Madison later wrote, the delegates, "with a manly confidence in their country," simply threw the Articles aside and went ahead with the building of a wholly new form of government.

They recognized that the paramount need was to reconcile two different powers — the power of local control, which was already being exercised by the 13 semi-independent states, and the power of a central government. They adopted the principle that the functions and powers of the national government — being new, general, and inclusive — had to be carefully defined and stated, while all other functions and powers were to be understood as belonging to the states. But realizing that the central government had to have real power, the delegates also generally accepted the fact that the government should be authorized, among other things, to coin money, to regulate commerce, to declare war, and to make peace.

DEBATE AND COMPROMISE

The 18th-century statesmen who met in Philadelphia were adherents of Montesquieu's concept of the balance of power in politics. This principle was supported by colonial experience and strengthened by the writings of John Locke, with which most of the delegates were familiar. These influences led to the conviction that three equal and coordinate branches of government should be established. Legislative, executive, and judicial powers were to be so harmoniously balanced that no one could ever gain control. The delegates agreed that the legislative branch, like the colonial legislatures and the British Parliament, should consist of two houses.

On these points there was unanimity within the assembly. But sharp differences also arose. Representatives of the small states — New Jersey, for instance — objected to changes that would reduce their influence in the national government by basing representation upon population rather than upon statehood, as was the case under the Articles of Confederation.

On the other hand, representatives of large states, like Virginia, argued for proportionate representation. This debate threatened to go on endlessly until Roger Sherman came forward with arguments for representation in proportion to the population of the states in one house of Congress, the House of Representatives, and equal representation in the other, the Senate.

The alignment of large against small states then dissolved. But almost every succeeding question raised new divisions, to be resolved only by new compromises. Northerners wanted slaves counted when determining each state's tax share, but not in determining the number of seats a state would have in the House of Representatives. Under a compromise reached with little dissent, tax levies and House membership would be apportioned according to the number of free inhabitants plus three-fifths of the slaves.

Certain members, such as Sherman and Elbridge Gerry, still smarting from Shays's Rebellion, feared that the mass of people lacked sufficient wisdom to govern themselves and thus wished no branch of the federal government to be elected directly by the people. Others thought the national government should be given as broad a popular base as possible. Some delegates wished to exclude the growing West from the opportunity of statehood; others championed the equality principle established in the Northwest Ordinance of 1787.

There was no serious difference on such national economic questions as paper money, laws concerning contract obligations, or the role of women, who were excluded from politics. But there was a need for balancing sectional economic interests; for settling arguments as to the powers, term, and selection of the chief executive; and for solving problems involving the tenure of judges and the kind of courts to be established.

Laboring through a hot Philadelphia summer, the convention finally achieved a draft incorporating in a brief document the organization of the most complex government yet devised, one that would be supreme within a clearly defined and limited sphere. It would have full power to levy taxes, borrow money, establish uniform duties and excise taxes, coin money, regulate interstate commerce, fix weights and measures, grant patents and copyrights, set up post offices, and build post roads. It also was authorized to raise and maintain an army and navy, manage Native American affairs, conduct foreign policy, and wage war. It could pass laws for naturalizing foreigners and controlling public lands; it could admit new states on a basis of absolute equality with the old. The power to pass all necessary and proper laws for executing these clearly defined powers rendered the federal government able to meet the needs of later generations and of a greatly expanded body politic.

The principle of separation of powers had already been given a fair trial in most state constitutions and had proved sound. Accordingly, the convention set up a governmental system with separate legislative, executive, and judiciary branches, each checked by the others. Thus congressional enactments were not to become law until approved by the president. And the president was to submit the most important of his appointments and all his treaties to the Senate for confirmation. The president, in turn, could be impeached and removed by Congress. The judiciary was to hear all cases arising under federal laws and the Constitution; in effect, the courts were empowered to interpret both the fundamental and the statute law. But members of the judiciary, appointed by the president and confirmed by the Senate, could also be impeached by Congress.

To protect the Constitution from hasty alteration, Article V stipulated that amendments to the Constitution be proposed either by two-thirds of both houses of Congress or by two-thirds of the states, meeting in convention. The proposals were to be ratified by one of two methods: either by the legislatures of three-fourths of the states, or by convention in three-fourths of the states, with the Congress proposing the method to be used.

Finally, the convention faced the most important problem of all: How should the powers given to the new government be enforced? Under the Articles of Confederation, the national government had possessed — on paper — significant powers, which, in practice, had come to naught, for the states paid no attention to them. What was to save the new government from the same fate?

At the outset, most delegates furnished a single answer — the use of force. But it was quickly seen that the application of force upon the states would destroy the Union. The decision was that the government should not act upon the states but upon the people within the states, and should legislate for and upon all the individual residents of the country. As the keystone of the Constitution, the convention adopted two brief but highly significant statements:

> *Congress shall have power ... to make all Laws which shall be necessary and proper for carrying into Execution the ... Powers vested by this Constitution in the Government of the United States.* ... (Article I, Section 7)

> *This Constitution, and the Laws of the United States which shall be made in Pursuance thereof; and all Treaties made, or which shall be made, under the Authority of the United States, shall be the supreme Law of the Land; and the Judges in every State shall be bound thereby, any Thing in the Constitution or Laws of any State to the Contrary notwithstanding.* (Article VI)

Thus the laws of the United States became enforceable in its own national courts, through its own judges and marshals, as well as in the state courts through the state judges and state law officers.

Debate continues to this day about the motives of those who wrote the Constitution. In 1913 historian Charles Beard, in *An Economic Interpretation of the Constitution*, argued that the Founding Fathers represented emerging commercial-capitalist interests that needed a strong national government. He also believed many may have been motivated by personal holdings of large amounts of depreciated government securities. However, James Madison, principal drafter of the Constitution, held no bonds and was a Virginia planter. Conversely, some opponents of the Constitution owned large amounts of bonds and securities. Economic interests influenced the course of the debate, but so did state, sectional, and ideological interests. Equally important was the idealism of the framers. Products of the Enlightenment, the Founding Fathers designed a government that they believed would promote individual liberty and public virtue. The ideals embodied in the U.S. Constitution remain an essential element of the American national identity.

RATIFICATION AND THE BILL OF RIGHTS

On September 17, 1787, after 16 weeks of deliberation, the finished Constitution was signed by 39 of the 42 delegates present. Franklin, pointing to the half-sun painted in brilliant gold on the back of Washington's chair, said:

I have often in the course of the session ... looked at that [chair] behind the president, without being able to tell whether it was rising or setting; but now, at length, I have the happiness to know that it is a rising, and not a setting, sun.

The convention was over; the members "adjourned to the City Tavern, dined together, and took a cordial leave of each other." Yet a crucial part of the struggle for a more perfect union remained to be faced. The consent of popularly elected state conventions was still required before the document could become effective.

The convention had decided that the Constitution would take effect upon ratification by conventions in nine of the 13 states. By June 1788 the required nine states had ratified the Constitution, but the large states of Virginia and New York had not. Most people felt that without their support the Constitution would never be honored. To many, the document seemed full of dangers: Would not the strong central government that it established tyrannize them, oppress them with heavy taxes, and drag them into wars?

Differing views on these questions brought into existence two parties, the Federalists, who favored a strong central government, and the Antifederalists, who preferred a loose association of separate states. Impassioned arguments on both sides were voiced by the press, the legislatures, and the state conventions.

In Virginia, the Antifederalists attacked the proposed new government by challenging the opening phrase of the Constitution: "We the People of the United States." Without using the individual state names in the Constitution, the delegates argued, the states would not retain their separate rights or powers. Virginia Antifederalists were led by Patrick Henry, who became the chief spokesman for back-country farmers who feared the powers of the new central government. Wavering delegates were persuaded by a proposal that the Virginia convention recommend a bill of rights, and Antifederalists joined with the Federalists to ratify the Constitution on June 25.

In New York, Alexander Hamilton, John Jay, and James Madison pushed for the ratification of the Constitution in a series of essays known as *The Federalist Papers*. The essays, published in New York newspapers, provided a now-classic argument for a central federal government, with separate executive, legislative, and judicial branches that checked and balanced one another. With *The Federalist Papers* influencing the New York delegates, the Constitution was ratified on July 26.

Antipathy toward a strong central government was only one concern among those opposed to the Constitution; of equal concern to many was the fear that the Constitution did not protect individual rights and freedoms sufficiently. Virginian George Mason, author of Virginia's Declaration of Rights of 1776, was one of three delegates to the Constitutional Convention who had refused to sign the final document because it did not enumerate individual rights. Together with Patrick Henry, he campaigned vigorously against ratification of the Constitution by Virginia. Indeed, five states, including Massachusetts, ratified the Constitution on the condition that such amendments be added immediately.

When the first Congress convened in New York City in September 1789, the calls for amendments protecting individual rights were virtually unanimous. Congress quickly adopted 12 such amendments; by December 1791, enough states had ratified 10 amendments to make them part of the Constitution. Collectively, they are known as the Bill of Rights. Among their provisions: freedom of speech, press, religion, and the right to assemble peacefully, protest, and demand changes (First Amendment); protection against unreasonable searches, seizures of property, and arrest (Fourth Amendment); due process of law in all criminal cases (Fifth Amendment); right to a fair and speedy trial (Sixth Amendment); protection against cruel and unusual punishment (Eighth Amendment); and provision that the people retain additional rights not listed in the Constitution (Ninth Amendment).

Since the adoption of the Bill of Rights, only 17 more amendments have been added to the Constitution. Although a number of the subsequent amendments revised the federal government's structure and operations, most followed the precedent established by the Bill of Rights and expanded individual rights and freedoms.

PRESIDENT WASHINGTON

One of the last acts of the Congress of the Confederation was to arrange for the first presidential election, setting March 4, 1789, as the date that the new government would come into being. One name was on everyone's lips for the new chief of state, George Washington. He was unanimously chosen president and took the oath of office at his inauguration on April 30, 1789. In words spoken by every president since, Washington pledged to execute the duties of the presidency faithfully and, to the best of his ability, to "preserve, protect, and defend the Constitution of the United States."

When Washington took office, the new Constitution enjoyed neither tradition nor the full backing of organized public opinion. The new government had to create its own machinery and legislate a system of taxation that would support it. Until a judiciary could be established, laws could not be enforced. The army was small. The navy had ceased to exist.

Congress quickly created the departments of State and Treasury, with Thomas Jefferson and Alexander Hamilton as their respective secretaries. Departments of War and Justice were also created. Since Washington preferred to make decisions only after consulting those men whose judgment he valued, the American presidential Cabinet came into existence, consisting of the heads of all the departments that Congress might create. Simultaneously, Congress provided for a federal judiciary — a Supreme Court, with one chief justice and five associate justices, three circuit courts, and 13 district courts.

Meanwhile, the country was growing steadily and immigration from Europe was increasing. Americans were moving westward: New Englanders and Pennsylvanians into Ohio; Virginians and Carolinians into Kentucky and Tennessee. Good farms were to be had for small sums; labor was in strong demand. The rich valley stretches of upper New York, Pennsylvania, and Virginia soon became great wheat-growing areas.

Although many items were still homemade, the Industrial Revolution was dawning in the United States. Massachusetts and Rhode Island were laying the foundation of important textile industries; Connecticut was beginning to turn out tinware and clocks; New York, New Jersey, and Pennsylvania were producing paper, glass, and iron. Shipping had grown to such an extent that on the seas the United States was second only to Britain. Even before 1790, American ships were traveling to China to sell furs and bring back tea, spices, and silk.

At this critical juncture in the country's growth, Washington's wise leadership was crucial. He organized a national government, developed policies for settlement of territories previously held by Britain and Spain, stabilized the northwestern frontier, and oversaw the admission of three new states: Vermont (1791), Kentucky (1792), and Tennessee (1796). Finally, in his Farewell Address, he warned the nation to "steer clear of permanent alliances with any portion of the foreign world." This advice influenced American attitudes toward the rest of the world for generations to come.

HAMILTON VS. JEFFERSON

A conflict took shape in the 1790s between America's first political parties. Indeed, the Federalists, led by Alexander Hamilton, and the Republicans (also called Democratic-Republicans), led by Thomas Jefferson, were the first political parties in the Western world. Unlike loose political groupings in the British House of Commons or in the American colonies before the Revolution, both had reasonably consistent and principled platforms, relatively stable popular followings, and continuing organizations.

The Federalists in the main represented the interests of trade and manufacturing, which they saw as forces of progress in the world. They believed these could be advanced only by a strong central government capable of establishing sound public credit and a stable currency. Openly distrustful of the latent radicalism of the masses, they could nonetheless credibly appeal to workers and artisans. Their political stronghold was in the New England states. Seeing England as in many respects an example the United States should try to emulate, they favored good relations with their mother country.

Although Alexander Hamilton was never able to muster the popular appeal to stand successfully for elective office, he was far and away the Federalists' main generator of ideology and public policy. He brought to public life a love of efficiency, order, and organization. In response to the call of the House of Representatives for a plan for the "adequate support of public credit," he laid down and supported principles not only of the public economy, but of effective government. Hamilton pointed out that the United States must have credit for industrial development, commercial activity, and the operations of government, and that its obligations must have the complete faith and support of the people.

There were many who wished to repudiate the Confederation's national debt or pay only part of it. Hamilton insisted upon full payment and also upon a plan by which the federal government took over the unpaid debts of the states incurred during the Revolution. He also secured congressional legislation for a Bank of the United States. Modeled after the Bank of England, it acted as the nation's central financial institution and operated branches in different parts of the country. Hamilton sponsored a national mint, and argued in favor of tariffs, saying that temporary protection of new firms could help foster the development of competitive national industries. These measures — placing the credit of the federal government on a firm foundation and giving it all the revenues it needed — encouraged commerce and industry, and created a solid phalanx of interests firmly behind the national government.

The Republicans, led by Thomas Jefferson, spoke primarily for agricultural interests and values. They distrusted bankers, cared little for commerce and manufacturing, and believed that freedom and democracy flourished best in a rural society composed of self-sufficient farmers. They felt little need for a strong central government; in fact, they tended to see it as a potential source of oppression. Thus they favored states' rights. They were strongest in the South.

Hamilton's great aim was more efficient organization, whereas Jefferson once said, "I am not a friend to a very energetic government." Hamilton feared anarchy and thought in terms of order; Jefferson feared tyranny and thought in terms of freedom. Where Hamilton saw England as an example, Jefferson, who had been minister to France in the early stages of the French Revolution, looked to the overthrow of the French monarchy as vindication of the liberal ideals of the Enlightenment. Against Hamilton's instinctive conservatism, he projected an eloquent democratic radicalism.

An early clash between them, which occurred shortly after Jefferson took office as secretary of state, led to a new and profoundly important interpretation of the Constitution. When Hamilton introduced his bill to establish a national bank, Jefferson, speaking for those who believed in states' rights, argued that the Constitution expressly enumerated all the powers belonging to the federal government and reserved all other powers to the states. Nowhere was the federal government empowered to set up a bank.

Hamilton responded that because of the mass of necessary detail, a vast body of powers had to be implied by general clauses, and one of these authorized Congress to "make all laws which shall be necessary and proper" for carrying out other powers specifically granted. The Constitution authorized the national government to levy and collect taxes, pay debts, and borrow money. A national bank would materially help in performing these functions efficiently. Congress, therefore, was entitled, under its implied powers, to create such a bank. Washington and the Congress accepted Hamilton's view — and set an important precedent for an expansive interpretation of the federal government's authority.

CITIZEN GENET AND FOREIGN POLICY

Although one of the first tasks of the new government was to strengthen the domestic economy and make the nation financially secure, the United States could not ignore foreign affairs. The cornerstones of Washington's foreign policy were to preserve peace, to give the country time to recover from its wounds, and to permit the slow work of national integration to continue. Events in Europe threatened these goals. Many Americans watched the French Revolution with keen interest and sympathy. In April 1793, news came that France had declared war on Great Britain and Spain, and that a new French envoy, Edmond Charles Genet — Citizen Genet — was coming to the United States.

When the revolution in France led to the execution of King Louis XVI in January 1793, Britain, Spain, and Holland became involved in war with France. According to the Franco-American Treaty of Alliance of 1778, the United States and France were perpetual allies, and the United States was obliged to help France defend the West Indies. However, the United States, militarily and economically a very weak country, was in no position to become involved in another war with major European powers.

On April 22, 1793, Washington effectively abrogated the terms of the

1778 treaty that had made American independence possible by proclaiming the United States to be "friendly and impartial toward the belligerent powers." When Genet arrived, he was cheered by many citizens, but treated with cool formality by the government. Angered, he violated a promise not to outfit a captured British ship as a privateer (privately owned warships commissioned to prey on ships of enemy nations). Genet then threatened to take his cause directly to the American people, over the head of the government. Shortly afterward, the United States requested his recall by the French government.

The Genet incident strained American relations with France at a time when those with Great Britain were far from satisfactory. British troops still occupied forts in the West, property carried off by British soldiers during the Revolution had not been restored or paid for, and the British Navy was seizing American ships bound for French ports. The two countries seemed to be drifting toward war. Washington sent John Jay, first chief justice of the Supreme Court, to London as a special envoy. Jay negotiated a treaty that secured withdrawal of British soldiers from western forts but allowed the British to continue the fur trade with the Indians in the Northwest. London agreed to pay damages for American ships and cargoes seized in 1793 and 1794, but made no commitments on possible future seizures. Moreover, the treaty failed to address the festering issue of British "impressment" of American sailors into the Royal Navy, placed severe limitations on American trade with the West Indies, and accepted the British view that food and naval stores, as well as war materiel, were contraband subject to seizure if bound for enemy ports on neutral ships.

American diplomat Charles Pinckney was more successful in dealing with Spain. In 1795, he negotiated an important treaty settling the Florida border on American terms and giving Americans access to the port of New Orleans. All the same, the Jay Treaty with the British reflected a continuing American weakness vis-a-vis a world superpower. Deeply unpopular, it was vocally supported only by Federalists who valued cultural and economic ties with Britain. Washington backed it as the best bargain available, and, after a heated debate, the Senate approved it.

Citizen Genet's antics and Jay's Treaty demonstrated both the difficulties faced by a small weak nation caught between two great powers and the wide gap in outlook between Federalists and Republicans. To the Federalists, Republican backers of the increasingly violent and radical French Revolution were dangerous radicals ("Jacobins"); to the Republicans, advocates of amity with England were monarchists who would subvert the natural rights of Americans. The Federalists connected virtue and national development with commerce; the Republicans saw

America's destiny as that of a vast agrarian republic. The politics of their conflicting positions became increasingly vehement.

ADAMS AND JEFFERSON

Washington retired in 1797, firmly declining to serve for more than eight years as the nation's head. Thomas Jefferson of Virginia (Republican) and John Adams (Federalist) vied to succeed him. Adams won a narrow election victory. From the beginning, however, he was at the head of a party and an administration divided between his backers and those of his rival, Hamilton.

Adams faced serious international difficulties. France, angered by Jay's treaty with Britain, adopted its definition of contraband and began to seize American ships headed for Britain. By 1797 France had snatched 300 American ships and broken off diplomatic relations with the United States. When Adams sent three commissioners to Paris to negotiate, agents of Foreign Minister Charles Maurice de Talleyrand (whom Adams labeled X, Y, and Z in his report to Congress) informed the Americans that negotiations could only begin if the United States loaned France $12 million and bribed officials of the French government. American hostility to France rose to an excited pitch. The so-called XYZ Affair led to the enlistment of troops and the strengthening of the fledgling U.S. Navy.

In 1799, after a series of sea battles with the French, war seemed inevitable. In this crisis, Adams rejected the guidance of Hamilton, who wanted war, and reopened negotiations with France. Napoleon, who had just come to power, received them cordially. The danger of conflict subsided with the negotiation of the Convention of 1800, which formally released the United States from its 1778 defense alliance with France. However, reflecting American weakness, France refused to pay $20 million in compensation for American ships taken by the French Navy.

Hostility to France had led Congress to pass the Alien and Sedition Acts, which had severe repercussions for American civil liberties. The Naturalization Act, which changed the requirement for citizenship from five to 14 years, was targeted at Irish and French immigrants suspected of supporting the Republicans. The Alien Act, operative for two years only, gave the president the power to expel or imprison aliens in time of war. The Sedition Act proscribed writing, speaking, or publishing anything of "a false, scandalous, and malicious" nature against the president or Congress. The few convictions won under it created martyrs to the cause of civil liberties and aroused support for the Republicans.

The acts met with resistance. Jefferson and Madison sponsored the passage of the Kentucky and Virginia Resolutions by the legislatures of these two states in November and

December 1798. Extreme declaration of states' rights, the resolutions asserted that states could "interpose" their views on federal actions and "nullify" them. The doctrine of nullification would be used later for the Southern states' resistance to protective tariffs, and, more ominously, slavery.

By 1800 the American people were ready for a change. Under Washington and Adams, the Federalists had established a strong government, but sometimes failing to honor the principle that the American government must be responsive to the will of the people, they had followed policies that alienated large groups. For example, in 1798 they had enacted a tax on houses, land, and slaves, affecting every property owner in the country.

Jefferson had steadily gathered behind him a great mass of small farmers, shopkeepers, and other workers. He won a close victory in a contested election. Jefferson enjoyed extraordinary favor because of his appeal to American idealism. In his inaugural address, the first such speech in the new capital of Washington, D.C., he promised "a wise and frugal government" that would preserve order among the inhabitants but leave people "otherwise free to regulate their own pursuits of industry, and improvement."

Jefferson's mere presence in the White House encouraged democratic procedures. He preached and practiced democratic simplicity, eschewing much of the pomp and ceremony of the presidency. In line with Republican ideology, he sharply cut military expenditures. Believing America to be a haven for the oppressed, he secured a liberal naturalization law. By the end of his second term, his far-sighted secretary of the treasury, Albert Gallatin, had reduced the national debt to less than $560 million. Widely popular, Jefferson won reelection as president easily.

LOUISIANA AND BRITAIN

One of Jefferson's acts doubled the area of the country. At the end of the Seven Years' War, France had ceded its territory west of the Mississippi River to Spain. Access to the port of New Orleans near its mouth was vital for the shipment of American products from the Ohio and Mississippi river valleys. Shortly after Jefferson became president, Napoleon forced a weak Spanish government to cede this great tract, the Louisiana Territory, back to France. The move filled Americans with apprehension and indignation. French plans for a huge colonial empire just west of the United States seriously threatened the future development of the United States. Jefferson asserted that if France took possession of Louisiana, "from that moment we must marry ourselves to the British fleet and nation."

Napoleon, however, lost interest after the French were expelled from Haiti by a slave revolt. Knowing that another war with Great Britain was impending, he resolved to fill his treasury and put Louisiana beyond the reach of Britain by selling it to the United States. His offer presented Jefferson with a dilemma: The Constitution conferred no explicit power to purchase territory. At first the president wanted to propose an amendment, but delay might lead Napoleon to change his mind. Advised that the power to purchase territory was inherent in the power to make treaties, Jefferson relented, saying that "the good sense of our country will correct the evil of loose construction when it shall produce ill effects."

The United States obtained the "Louisiana Purchase" for $15 million in 1803. It contained more than 2,600,000 square kilometers as well as the port of New Orleans. The nation had gained a sweep of rich plains, mountains, forests, and river systems that within 80 years would become its heartland — and a breadbasket for the world.

As Jefferson began his second term in 1805, he declared American neutrality in the struggle between Great Britain and France. Although both sides sought to restrict neutral shipping to the other, British control of the seas made its interdiction and seizure much more serious than any actions by Napoleonic France. British naval commanders routinely searched American ships, seized vessels and cargoes, and took off sailors believed to be British subjects. They also frequently impressed American seamen into their service.

When Jefferson issued a proclamation ordering British warships to leave U.S. territorial waters, the British reacted by impressing more sailors. Jefferson then decided to rely on economic pressure; in December 1807 Congress passed the Embargo Act, forbidding all foreign commerce. Ironically, the law required strong police authority that vastly increased the powers of the national government. Economically, it was disastrous. In a single year American exports fell to one-fifth of their former volume. Shipping interests were almost ruined by the measure; discontent rose in New England and New York. Agricultural interests suffered heavily also. Prices dropped drastically when the Southern and Western farmers could not export their surplus grain, cotton, meat, and tobacco.

The embargo failed to starve Great Britain into a change of policy. As the grumbling at home increased, Jefferson turned to a milder measure, which partially conciliated domestic shipping interests. In early 1809 he signed the Non-Intercourse Act permitting commerce with all countries except Britain or France and their dependencies.

James Madison succeeded Jefferson as president in 1809. Relations with Great Britain grew worse, and the two countries moved rapidly toward war. The president laid before Congress a detailed report, showing several thousand instances in which the British had impressed American citizens. In addition, northwestern settlers had suffered from attacks by Indians whom they believed had been incited by British agents in Canada. In turn, many Americans favored conquest of Canada and the elimination of British influence in North America, as well as vengeance for impressment and commercial repression. By 1812, war fervor was dominant. On June 18, the United States declared war on Britain.

THE WAR OF 1812

The nation went to war bitterly divided. While the South and West favored the conflict, New York and New England opposed it because it interfered with their commerce. The U.S. military was weak. The army had fewer than 7,000 regular soldiers, distributed in widely scattered posts along the coast, near the Canadian border, and in the remote interior. The state militias were poorly trained and undisciplined.

Hostilities began with an invasion of Canada, which, if properly timed and executed, would have brought united action against Montreal. Instead, the entire campaign miscarried and ended with the British occupation of Detroit. The U.S. Navy, however, scored successes. In addition, American privateers, swarming the Atlantic, captured 500 British vessels during the fall and winter months of 1812 and 1813.

The campaign of 1813 centered on Lake Erie. General William Henry Harrison — who would later become president — led an army of militia, volunteers, and regulars from Kentucky with the object of reconquering Detroit. On September 12, while he was still in upper Ohio, news reached him that Commodore Oliver Hazard Perry had annihilated the British fleet on Lake Erie. Harrison occupied Detroit and pushed into Canada, defeating the fleeing British and their Indian allies on the Thames River. The entire region now came under American control.

A year later Commodore Thomas Macdonough won a point-blank gun duel with a British flotilla on Lake Champlain in upper New York. Deprived of naval support, a British invasion force of 10,000 men retreated to Canada. Nevertheless, the British fleet harassed the Eastern seaboard with orders to "destroy and lay waste." On the night of August 24, 1814, an expeditionary force routed American militia, marched to Washington, D.C., and left the city in flames. President James Madison fled to Virginia.

British and American negotiators conducted talks in Europe. The British envoys decided to concede, however, when they learned of Macdonough's victory on Lake Champlain. Faced with the depletion of the British treasury due in large part to the heavy costs of the Napoleonic Wars, the negotiators for Great Britain accepted the Treaty of Ghent in December 1814. It provided for the cessation of hostilities, the restoration of conquests, and a commission to settle boundary disputes. Unaware that a peace treaty had been signed, the two sides continued fighting into 1815 near New Orleans, Louisiana. Led by General Andrew Jackson, the United States scored the greatest land victory of the war, ending once and for all any British hopes of reestablishing continental influence south of the Canadian border.

While the British and Americans were negotiating a settlement, Federalist delegates selected by the legislatures of Massachusetts, Rhode Island, Connecticut, Vermont, and New Hampshire gathered in Hartford, Connecticut, to express opposition to "Mr. Madison's war." New England had managed to trade with the enemy throughout the conflict, and some areas actually prospered from this commerce. Nevertheless, the Federalists claimed that the war was ruining the economy. With a possibility of secession from the Union in the background, the convention proposed a series of constitutional amendments that would protect New England interests. Instead, the end of the war, punctuated by the smashing victory at New Orleans, stamped the Federalists with a stigma of disloyalty from which they never recovered. >

THE SECOND GREAT AWAKENING

By the end of the 18th century, many educated Americans no longer professed traditional Christian beliefs. In reaction to the secularism of the age, a religious revival spread westward in the first half of the 19th century.

This "Second Great Awakening" consisted of several kinds of activity, distinguished by locale and expression of religious commitment. In New England, the renewed interest in religion inspired a wave of social activism. In western New York, the spirit of revival encouraged the emergence of new denominations. In the Appalachian region of Kentucky and Tennessee, the revival strengthened the Methodists and the Baptists, and spawned a new form of religious expression — the camp meeting.

In contrast to the Great Awakening of the 1730s, the revivals in the East were notable for the absence of hysteria and open emotion. Rather, unbelievers were awed by the "respectful silence" of those bearing witness to their faith. The evangelical enthusiasm in New England gave rise to interdenominational missionary societies, formed to evangelize the West. Members of these societies not only acted as apostles for the faith, but as educators, civic leaders, and exponents of Eastern, urban culture. Publication and education societies promoted Christian education. Most notable among them was the American Bible Society, founded in 1816. Social activism inspired by the revival gave rise to abolition of slavery groups and the Society for the Promotion of Temperance, as well as to efforts to reform prisons and care for the handicapped and mentally ill.

Western New York, from Lake Ontario to the Adirondack Mountains, had been the scene of so many religious revivals in the past that it was known as the "Burned-Over District." Here, the dominant figure was Charles Grandison Finney, a lawyer who had experienced a religious epiphany and set out to preach the Gospel. His revivals were characterized by careful planning, showmanship, and advertising. Finney preached in the Burned-Over District throughout the 1820s and the early 1830s, before moving to Ohio in 1835 to take a chair in theology at Oberlin College, of which he subsequently became president.

Two other important religious denominations in America — the Mormons and the Seventh Day Adventists — also got their start in the Burned-Over District.

In the Appalachian region, the revival took on characteristics similar to the Great Awakening of the previous century. But here, the center of the revival was the camp meeting, a religious service of several days' length, for a group that was obliged to take shelter on the spot because of the distance from home. Pioneers in thinly populated areas looked to the camp meeting as a refuge from the lonely life on the frontier. The sheer exhilaration of participating in a religious revival with hundreds and perhaps thousands of people inspired the dancing, shouting, and singing associated with these events. Probably the largest camp meeting was at Cane Ridge, Kentucky, in August 1801; between 10,000 and 25,000 people attended.

The great revival quickly spread throughout Kentucky, Tennessee, and southern Ohio, with the Methodists and the Baptists its prime beneficiaries. Each denomination had assets that allowed it to thrive on the frontier. The Methodists had a very efficient organization that depended on ministers — known as circuit riders — who sought out people in remote frontier locations. The circuit riders came from among the common people and possessed a rapport with the frontier families they hoped to convert. The Baptists had no formal church organization. Their farmer-preachers were people who received "the call" from God, studied the Bible, and founded a church, which then ordained them. Other candidates for the ministry emerged from these churches, and established a presence farther into the wilderness. Using such methods, the Baptists became dominant throughout the border states and most of the South.

The Second Great Awakening exercised a profound impact on American history. The numerical strength of the Baptists and Methodists rose relative to that of the denominations dominant in the colonial period — Anglicans, Presbyterians, and Congregationalists. The growing differences within American Protestantism reflected the growth and diversity of an expanding nation. ◆

Andrew Jackson, president from 1829 to 1837. Charismatic, forceful, and passionate, Jackson forged an effective political coalition within the Democratic Party with Westerners, farmers, and working people.

TRANSFORMING
A NATION
A PICTURE PROFILE

The United States transformed itself again in the 19th and early 20th centuries. A rural, agricultural nation became an industrial power whose backbone was steel and coal, railroads, and steam power. A young country once bound by the Mississippi River expanded across the North American continent, and on to overseas territories. A nation divided by the issue of slavery and tested by the trauma of civil war became a world power whose global influence was first felt in World War I.

Henry Clay of Kentucky, although never president, was one of the most influential American politicians of the first half of the 19th century. Clay became indispensable for his role in preserving the Union with the Missouri Compromise of 1820 and the Compromise of 1850. Both pieces of legislation resolved, for a time, disputes over slavery in the territories.

The great champions of women's rights in the 19th century: Elizabeth Cady Stanton (seated) and Susan B. Anthony. Stanton helped organize the first women's rights convention in 1848 in Seneca Falls, New York. In later years, she joined Anthony in founding the National Woman Suffrage Association. "I forged the thunderbolts," Stanton said of their partnership, "and she fired them."

William Lloyd Garrison, whose passionate denunciations of slavery and eloquent defense of the rights of enslaved African Americans appeared in his weekly paper, the *Liberator*, from its first issue in 1831 to 1865, when the last issue appeared at the close of the Civil War.

Frederick Douglass, the nation's leading African-American abolitionist of the 19th century, escaped from slavery in 1838. His speech about his sufferings as a slave at the Massachusetts Anti-Slavery Society's annual convention in Nantucket launched his career as an outspoken lecturer, writer, and publisher on the abolition of slavery and racial equality.

Harriet Tubman, a former slave who rescued hundreds from slavery through the Underground Railroad. The Underground Railroad was a vast network of people who helped fugitive slaves escape to the North and to Canada in the first half of the 19th century.

Confederate dead along a stone wall during the Chancellorsville campaign, May 1863. Victorious at Chancellorsville, Southern forces advanced north into Pennsylvania, but were defeated at the three-day battle of Gettysburg, the turning point of the Civil War and the largest battle ever fought in North America. More Americans died in the Civil War (1861-65) than in any other conflict in U.S. history.

93

Encampment of Union troops from New York in Alexandria, Virginia, just across the Potomac River from the capital of Washington.

Union General Ulysses S. Grant, who led Union forces to victory in the Civil War and became the 18th president of the United States. Despite heavy losses in several battles against his opponent, General Lee (below), Grant refused to retreat, leading President Lincoln to say to critics calling for his removal, "I can't spare this general. He fights."

Confederate General Robert E. Lee. Military historians to this day study his tactics and Grant's in battles such as Vicksburg, Chancellorsville, and the Wilderness.

Engraving of the first African-American members elected to the U.S. Congress during the Reconstruction Era, following the Civil War. Seated at left is H.R. Revels, senator from Mississippi. The others were members of the House of Representatives, from the states of Alabama, Florida, South Carolina, and Georgia.

Although practically unknown during her lifetime, Emily Dickinson (1830-1886) is now seen as one of the most brilliant and original poets America has ever produced.

Andrew Carnegie, business tycoon and philanthropist. Born in Scotland of a poor family, Carnegie immigrated to the United States and made his fortune by building the country's largest iron and steel manufacturing corporation. Believing that the wealthy had an obligation to give back to society, he endowed public libraries across the United States.

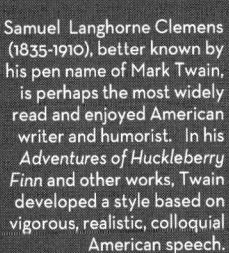

Samuel Langhorne Clemens (1835-1910), better known by his pen name of Mark Twain, is perhaps the most widely read and enjoyed American writer and humorist. In his *Adventures of Huckleberry Finn* and other works, Twain developed a style based on vigorous, realistic, colloquial American speech.

Sitting Bull, Sioux chief who led the last great battle of the Plains Indians against the U.S. Army, when his warriors defeated forces under the command of General George Custer at the Battle of Little Bighorn in 1876.

Custer's army on the march prior to Little Bighorn. The Plains Indians who defeated his army were resisting white intrusions into their sacred lands and U.S. government attempts to force them back onto South Dakota's Great Sioux Reservation.

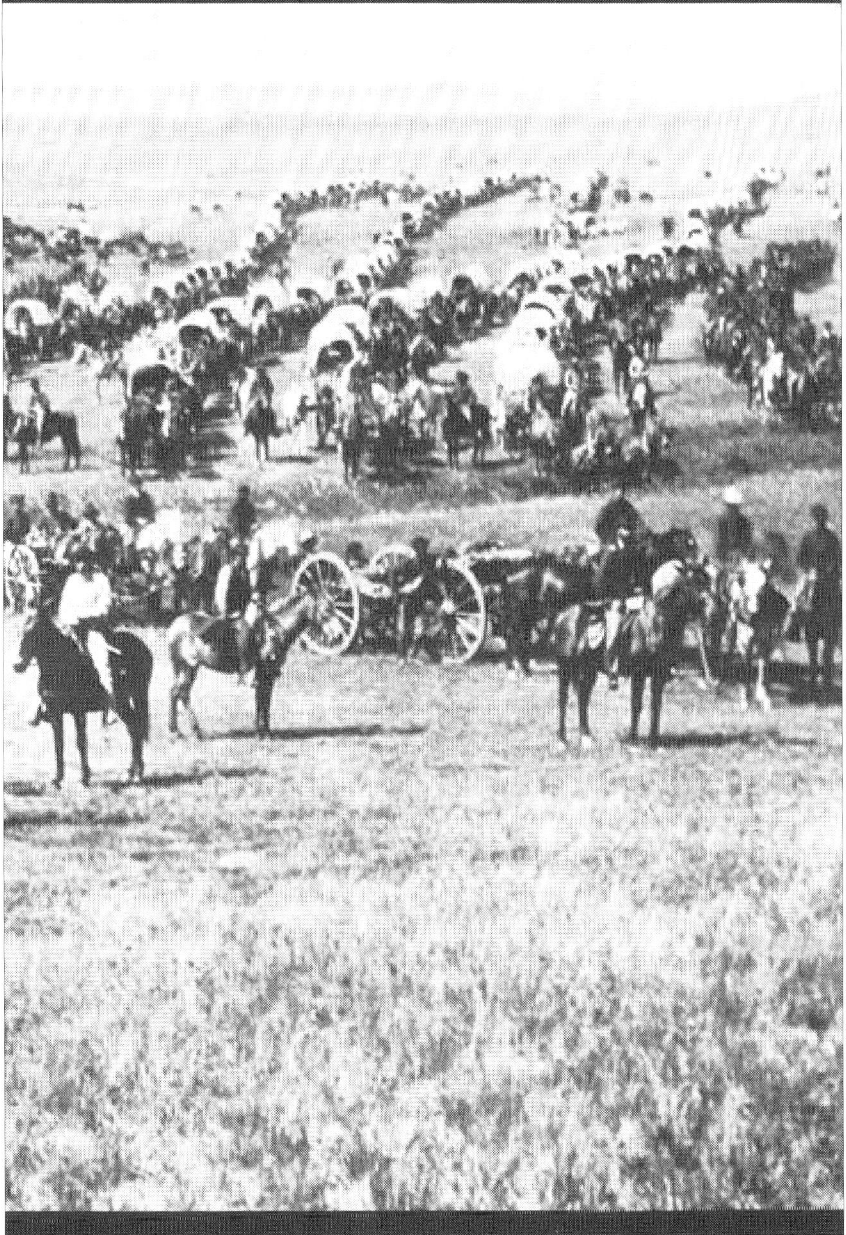

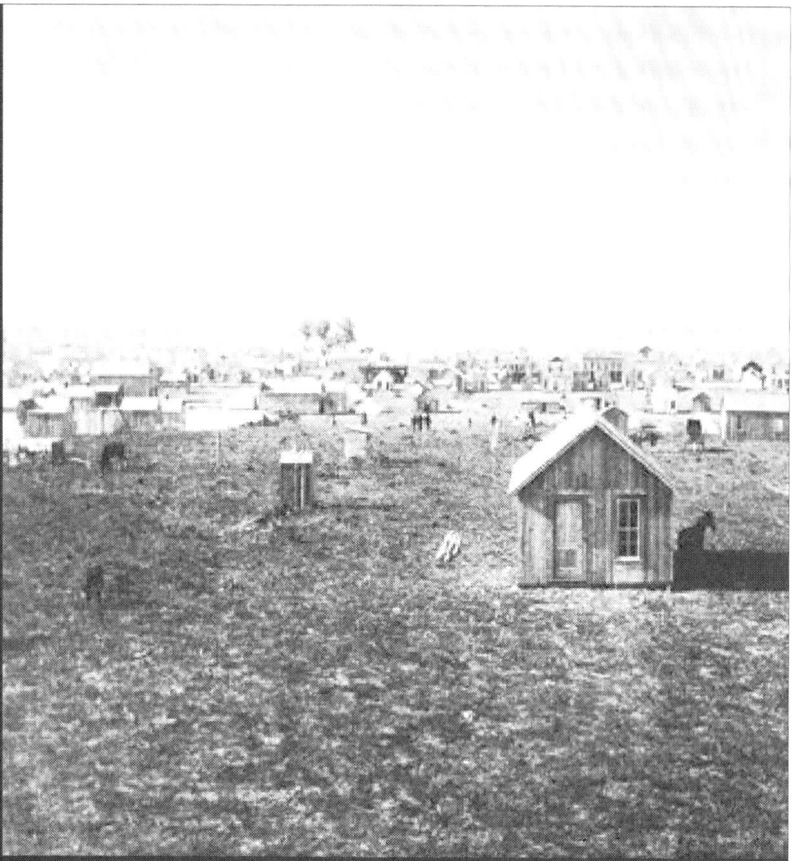

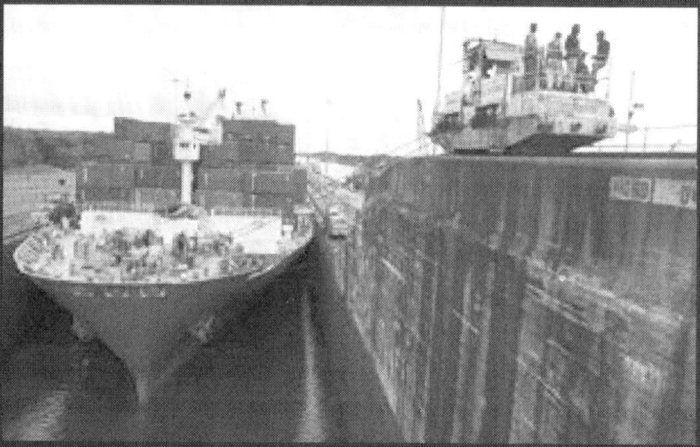

Above, Oklahoma City in 1889, four weeks after the Oklahoma Territory was opened up for settlement. Settlers staked their claim, put up tents, and then swiftly began erecting board shacks and houses — a pattern repeated throughout the West.

Left, a vessel at the Gatun locks of the Panama Canal. The United States acquired the rights to build the canal in 1903 in a treaty with Panama, which had just rebelled and broken away from Colombia. Under the terms of the 1977 treaty, the canal reverted to Panamanian control on December 31, 1999.

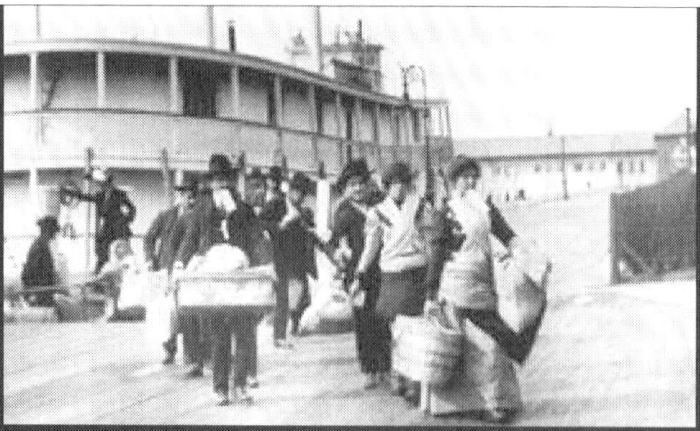

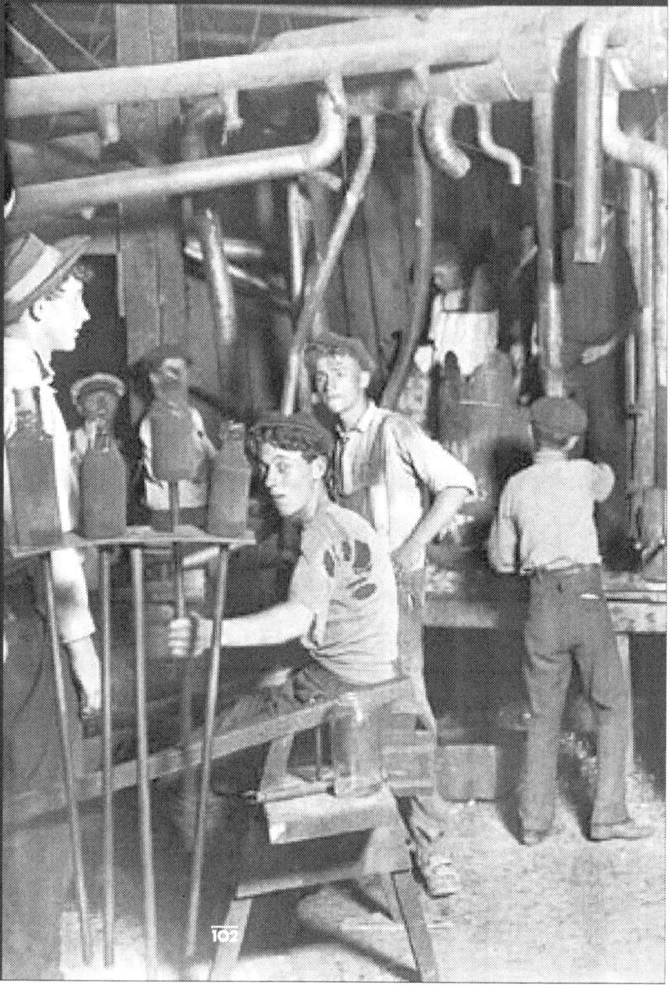

Left, opposite page, immigrants arriving at Ellis Island in New York City, principal gateway to the United States in the late 19th and early 20th centuries. From 1890 to 1921, almost 19 million people entered the United States as immigrants.

Below, children working at the Indiana Glass Works in 1908. Enacting child labor laws was one of the principal goals of the Progressive movement in this era.

Mulberry Street in New York City, also known as "Little Italy," in the early years of the 20th century. Newly arrived immigrant families, largely from Eastern and southern Europe in this period, often settled in densely populated urban enclaves. Typically, their children, or grandchildren, would disperse, moving to other cities or other parts of the country.

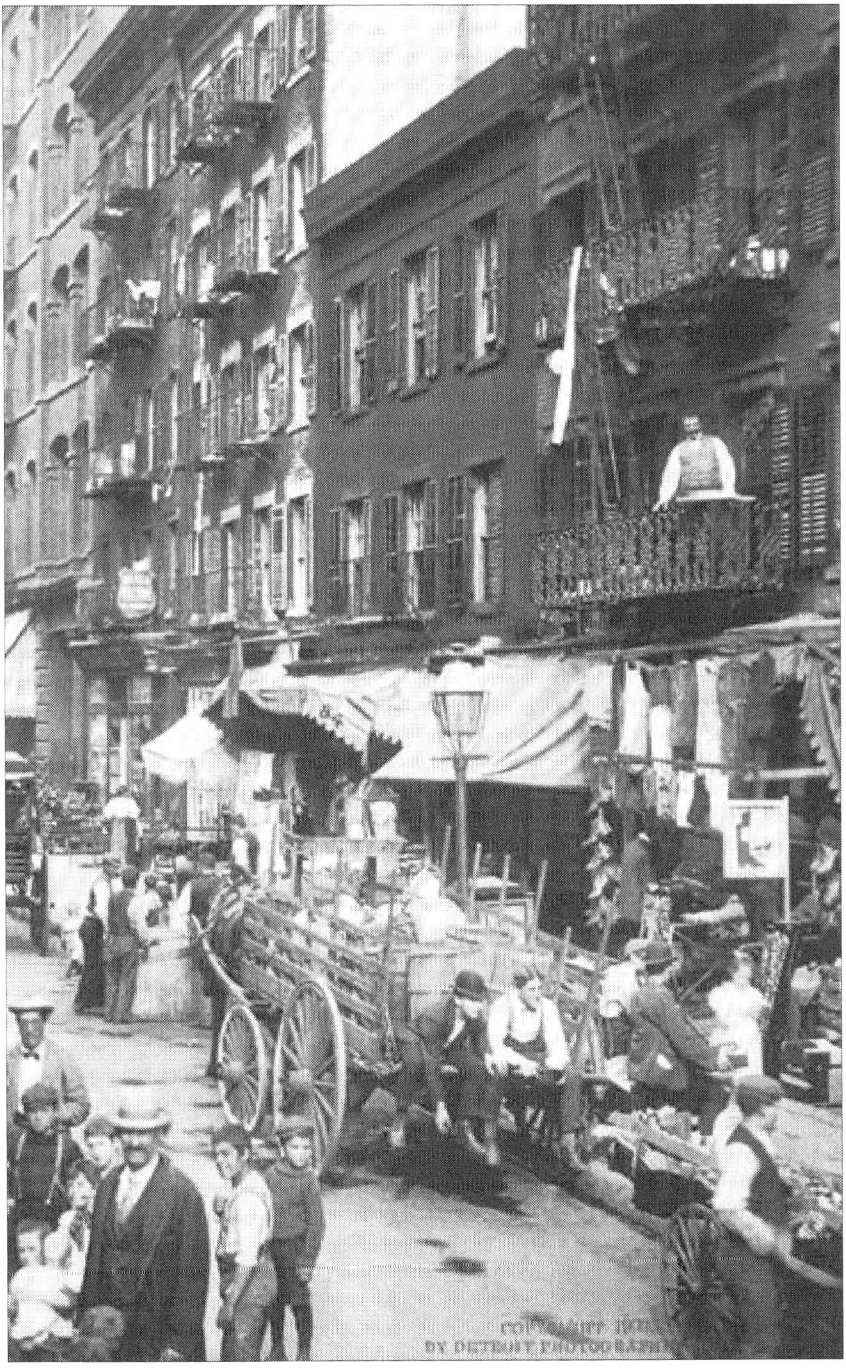

Thomas Edison examines film used in the motion picture projector that he invented with George Eastman. The most celebrated of Edison's hundreds of inventions was the incandescent light bulb.

Orville Wright, who built and flew the first heavier-than-air airplane at Kitty Hawk, North Carolina, in 1903, with his brother Wilbur. Orville is shown here at the controls of a later model plane in 1909.

Alexander Graham Bell makes the first telephone call from New York City to Chicago in 1892. Bell, an immigrant from Scotland who settled in Boston, invented the telephone 16 years earlier, in 1876.

American infantry forces in 1918, firing a 37 mm. gun, advance against German positions in World War I.

The "Big Four" at the Paris Peace Conference in 1919, following the end of World War I. They are, seated from left, Prime Minister Vittorio Orlando of Italy, Prime Minister David Lloyd George of Great Britain, Premier Georges Clemenceau of France, and President Woodrow Wilson of the United States. Despite strenuous efforts, Wilson was unable to persuade the U.S. Senate to agree to American participation in the new League of Nations established in the aftermath of the war.

For the educated and well-to-do, the 1920s was the era of the "Lost Generation," symbolized by writers like Ernest Hemingway, who left the United States for voluntary exile in Paris. It was also the "flapper era" of frivolity and excess in which young people could reject the constraints and traditions of their elders. Top, flappers posing for the camera at a 1920s-era party. Above, Henry Ford and his son stand with one of his early automobiles, and the 10-millionth Ford Model-T. The Model-T was the first car whose price and availability made car ownership possible for large numbers of people.

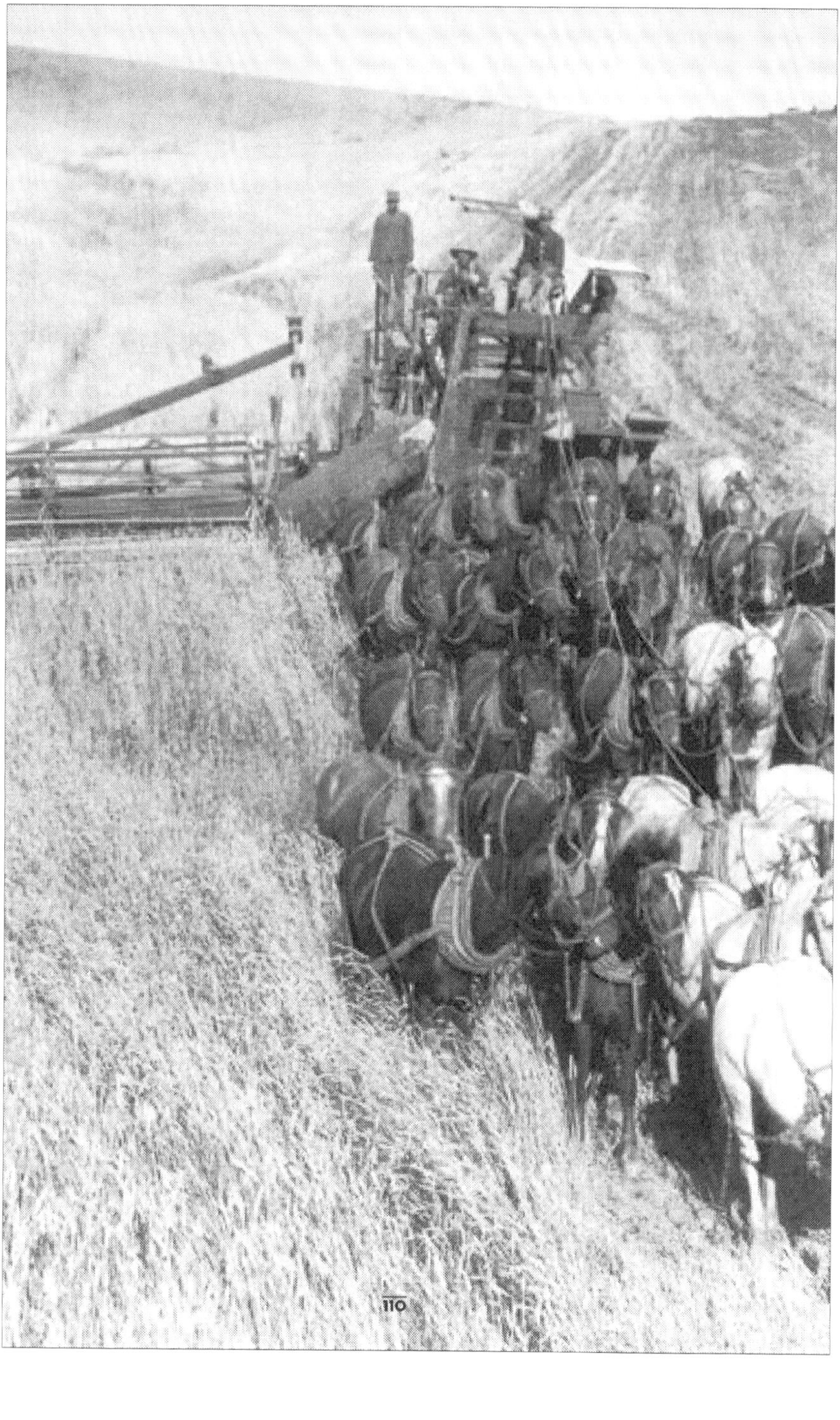

CHAPTER

5

WESTWARD EXPANSION AND REGIONAL DIFFERENCES

Horse-drawn combine harvesting wheat in the Midwest, 19th century.

CHAPTER 5: WESTWARD EXPANSION AND REGIONAL DIFFERENCES

> "Go West, young man,
> and grow up with
> the country."
>
> Newspaper editor **Horace Greeley**, 1851

BUILDING UNITY

The War of 1812 was, in a sense, a second war of independence that confirmed once and for all the American break with England. With its conclusion, many of the serious difficulties that the young republic had faced since the Revolution disappeared. National union under the Constitution brought a balance between liberty and order. With a low national debt and a continent awaiting exploration, the prospect of peace, prosperity, and social progress opened before the nation.

Commerce cemented national unity. The privations of war convinced many of the importance of protecting the manufacturers of America until they could stand alone against foreign competition. Economic independence, many argued, was as essential as political independence. To foster self-sufficiency, congressional leaders Henry Clay of Kentucky and John C. Calhoun of South Carolina urged a policy of protectionism — imposition of restrictions on imported goods to foster the development of American industry.

The time was propitious for raising the customs tariff. The shepherds of Vermont and Ohio wanted protection against an influx of English wool. In Kentucky, a new industry of weaving local hemp into cotton bagging was threatened by the Scottish bagging industry. Pittsburgh, Pennsylvania, already a flourishing center of iron smelting, was eager to challenge British and Swedish iron suppliers. The tariff enacted in 1816 imposed duties high enough to give manufacturers real protection.

In addition, Westerners advocated a national system of roads and canals to link them with Eastern cities and ports, and to open frontier lands for settlement. However, they were unsuccessful in pressing their demands for a federal role in internal improvement because of opposition from New England and the South. Roads and canals remained the province of the states until the passage of the Federal Aid Road Act of 1916.

The position of the federal government at this time was greatly strengthened by several Supreme Court decisions. A committed Federalist, John Marshall of Virginia became chief justice in 1801 and held office until his death in 1835. The court — weak before his administration — was transformed into a powerful tribunal, occupying a position co-equal to the Congress and the president. In a succession of historic decisions, Marshall established the power of the Supreme Court and strengthened the national government.

Marshall was the first in a long line of Supreme Court justices whose decisions have molded the meaning and application of the Constitution. When he finished his long service, the court had decided nearly 50 cases clearly involving constitutional issues. In one of Marshall's most famous opinions — *Marbury v. Madison* (1803) — he decisively established the right of the Supreme Court to review the constitutionality of any law of Congress or of a state legislature. In *McCulloch v. Maryland* (1819), he boldly upheld the Hamiltonian theory that the Constitution by implication gives the government powers beyond those expressly stated.

EXTENSION OF SLAVERY

Slavery, which up to now had received little public attention, began to assume much greater importance as a national issue. In the early years of the republic, when the Northern states were providing for immediate or gradual emancipation of the slaves, many leaders had supposed that slavery would die out. In 1786 George Washington wrote that he devoutly wished some plan might be adopted "by which slavery may be abolished by slow, sure, and imperceptible degrees." Virginians Jefferson, Madison, and Monroe and other leading Southern statesmen made similar statements.

The Northwest Ordinance of 1787 had banned slavery in the Northwest Territory. As late as 1808, when the international slave trade was abolished, there were many Southerners who thought that slavery would soon end. The expectation proved false, for during the next generation, the South became solidly united behind the institution of slavery as new economic factors made slavery far more profitable than it had been before 1790.

Chief among these was the rise of a great cotton-growing industry in the South, stimulated by the introduction of new types of cotton and by Eli Whitney's invention in 1793 of the cotton gin, which separated the seeds from cotton. At the same time, the Industrial Revolution, which made textile manufacturing a large-scale operation, vastly increased the demand for raw cotton. And the opening of new lands in the West after 1812 greatly extended the area available for cotton cultivation. Cotton culture moved rapidly from the Tidewater states on the East Coast through much of the lower South to the delta region of the Mississippi and eventually to Texas.

Sugar cane, another labor-intensive crop, also contributed to slavery's extension in the South. The rich, hot lands of southeastern Louisiana proved ideal for growing sugar cane profitably. By 1830 the state was supplying the nation with about half its sugar supply. Finally, tobacco growers moved westward, taking slavery with them.

As the free society of the North and the slave society of the South spread westward, it seemed politically expedient to maintain a rough equality among the new states carved out of western territories. In 1818, when Illinois was admitted to the Union, 10 states permitted slavery and 11 states prohibited it; but balance was restored after Alabama was admitted as a slave state. Population was growing faster in the North, which permitted Northern states to have a clear majority in the House of Representatives. However, equality between the North and the South was maintained in the Senate.

In 1819 Missouri, which had 10,000 slaves, applied to enter the Union. Northerners rallied to oppose Missouri's entry except as a free state, and a storm of protest swept the country. For a time Congress was deadlocked, but Henry Clay arranged the so-called Missouri Compromise: Missouri was admitted as a slave state at the same time Maine came in as a free state. In addition, Congress banned slavery from the territory acquired by the Louisiana Purchase north of Missouri's southern boundary. At the time, this provision appeared to be a victory for the Southern states because it was thought unlikely that this "Great American Desert" would ever be settled. The controversy was temporarily resolved, but Thomas Jefferson wrote to a friend that "this momentous question, like a fire bell in the night, awakened and filled me with terror. I considered it at once as the knell of the Union."

LATIN AMERICA AND THE MONROE DOCTRINE

During the opening decades of the 19th century, Central and South America turned to revolution. The idea of liberty had stirred the people of Latin America from the time the English colonies gained their freedom. Napoleon's conquest of Spain and Portugal in 1808 provided the signal for Latin Americans to rise in revolt. By 1822, ably led by Simón Bolívar, Francisco Miranda, José de San Martín and Miguel de Hidalgo, most of Hispanic America — from Argentina and Chile in the south to Mexico in the north — had won independence.

The people of the United States took a deep interest in what seemed a repetition of their own experience in breaking away from European rule. The Latin American independence movements confirmed their own belief in self-government. In 1822 President James Monroe, under powerful public pressure, received authority to recognize the new countries of Latin America and soon exchanged ministers with them. He thereby confirmed their status as genuinely independent countries, entirely separated from their former European connections.

At just this point, Russia, Prussia, and Austria formed an association, the Holy Alliance, to protect themselves against revolution. By intervening in countries where popular movements threatened monarchies, the alliance — joined by post-Napoleonic France — hoped to prevent the spread of revolution. This policy was the antithesis of the American principle of self-determination.

As long as the Holy Alliance confined its activities to the Old World, it aroused no anxiety in the United States. But when the alliance announced its intention of restoring to Spain its former colonies, Americans became very concerned. Britain, to which Latin American trade had become of great importance, resolved to block any such action. London urged joint Anglo-American guarantees to Latin America, but Secretary of State John Quincy Adams convinced Monroe to act unilaterally: "It would be more candid, as well as more dignified, to avow our principles explicitly to Russia and France, than to come in as a cock-boat in the wake of the British man-of-war."

In December 1823, with the knowledge that the British navy would defend Latin America from the Holy Alliance and France, President Monroe took the occasion of his annual message to Congress to pronounce what would become known as the Monroe Doctrine — the refusal to tolerate any further extension of European domination in the Americas:

The American continents ... are henceforth not to be considered as subjects for future colonization by any European powers.

We should consider any attempt on their part to extend their [political] system to any portion of this hemisphere, as dangerous to our peace and safety.

With the existing colonies or dependencies of any European power we have not interfered, and shall not interfere. But with the governments who have declared their independence, and maintained it, and whose independence we have ... acknowledged, we could not view any interposition for the purpose of oppressing them, or controlling, in any other manner, their destiny, by any European power in any other light than as the manifestation of an unfriendly disposition towards the United States.

The Monroe Doctrine expressed a spirit of solidarity with the newly independent republics of Latin America. These nations in turn recognized their political affinity with the United States by basing their new constitutions, in many instances, on the North American model.

FACTIONALISM AND POLITICAL PARTIES

Domestically, the presidency of Monroe (1817-1825) was termed the "era of good feelings." The phrase acknowledged the political triumph of the Republican Party over the Federalist Party, which had collapsed as a national force. All the same, this was a period of vigorous factional and regional conflict.

The end of the Federalists led to a brief period of factional politics and brought disarray to the practice of choosing presidential nominees by congressional party caucuses. For a time, state legislatures nominated candidates. In 1824 Tennessee and Pennsylvania chose Andrew Jackson, with South Carolina Senator John C. Calhoun as his running mate. Kentucky selected Speaker of the House Henry Clay; Massachusetts, Secretary of State John Quincy Adams, son of the second president, John Adams. A congressional caucus, widely derided as undemocratic, picked Secretary of the Treasury William Crawford.

Personality and sectional allegiance played important roles in determining the outcome of the election. Adams won the electoral votes from New England and most of New York; Clay won Kentucky, Ohio, and Missouri; Jackson won the Southeast, Illinois, Indiana, the Carolinas, Pennsylvania, Maryland, and New Jersey; and Crawford won Virginia, Georgia, and Delaware. No candidate gained a majority in the Electoral College, so, according to the provisions of the Constitution, the election was thrown into the House of Representatives, where Clay was the most influential figure. He supported Adams, who gained the presidency.

During Adams's administration, new party alignments appeared. Adams's followers, some of whom were former Federalists, took the name of "National Republicans" as emblematic of their support of a federal government that would take a strong role in developing an expanding nation. Though he governed honestly and efficiently, Adams was not a popular president. He failed in his effort to institute a national system of roads and canals. His coldly intellectual temperament did not win friends. Jackson, by contrast, had enormous popular appeal and a strong political organization. His followers coalesced to establish the Democratic Party, claimed direct lineage from the Democratic-Republican Party of Jefferson, and in general advocated the principles of small, decentralized government.

Mounting a strong anti-Adams campaign, they accused the president of a "corrupt bargain" for naming Clay secretary of state. In the election of 1828, Jackson defeated Adams by an overwhelming electoral majority.

Jackson — Tennessee politician, fighter in wars against Native Americans on the Southern frontier, and hero of the Battle of New Orleans during the War of 1812 — drew his support from the "common people." He came to the presidency on a rising tide of enthusiasm for popular democracy. The election of 1828 was a significant benchmark in the trend toward broader voter participation. By then most states had either enacted universal white male suffrage or minimized property requirements. In 1824 members of the Electoral College in six states were still selected by the state legislatures. By 1828 presidential electors were chosen by popular vote in every state but Delaware and South Carolina. These developments were the products of a widespread sense that the people should rule and that government by traditional elites had come to an end.

NULLIFICATION CRISIS

Toward the end of his first term in office, Jackson was forced to confront the state of South Carolina, the most important of the emerging Deep South cotton states, on the issue of the protective tariff. Business and farming interests in the state had hoped that the president would use his power to modify the 1828 act that they called the Tariff of Abominations. In their view, all its benefits of protection went to Northern manufacturers, leaving agricultural South Carolina poorer. In 1828, the state's leading politician — and Jackson's vice president until his resignation in 1832 — John C. Calhoun had declared in his *South Carolina Exposition and Protest* that states had the right to nullify oppressive national legislation.

In 1832, Congress passed and Jackson signed a bill that revised the 1828 tariff downward, but it was not enough to satisfy most South Carolinians. The state adopted an Ordinance of Nullification, which declared both the tariffs of 1828 and 1832 null and void within state borders. Its legislature also passed laws to enforce the ordinance, including authorization for raising a military force and appropriations for arms. Nullification was a long-established theme of protest against perceived excesses by the federal government. Jefferson and Madison had proposed it in the Kentucky and Virginia Resolutions of 1798, to protest the Alien and Sedition Acts. The Hartford Convention of 1814 had invoked it to protest the War of 1812. Never before, however, had a state actually attempted nullification. The young nation faced its most dangerous crisis yet.

In response to South Carolina's threat, Jackson sent seven small naval vessels and a man-of-war to Charleston in November 1832. On

December 10, he issued a resounding proclamation against the nullifiers. South Carolina, the president declared, stood on "the brink of insurrection and treason," and he appealed to the people of the state to reassert their allegiance to the Union. He also let it be known that, if necessary, he personally would lead the U.S. Army to enforce the law.

When the question of tariff duties again came before Congress, Jackson's political rival, Senator Henry Clay, a great advocate of protection but also a devoted Unionist, sponsored a compromise measure. Clay's tariff bill, quickly passed in 1833, specified that all duties in excess of 20 percent of the value of the goods imported were to be reduced year by year, so that by 1842 the duties on all articles would reach the level of the moderate tariff of 1816. At the same time, Congress passed a Force Act, authorizing the president to use military power to enforce the laws.

South Carolina had expected the support of other Southern states, but instead found itself isolated. (Its most likely ally, the state government of Georgia, wanted, and got, U.S. military force to remove Native American tribes from the state.) Eventually, South Carolina rescinded its action. Both sides, nevertheless, claimed victory. Jackson had strongly defended the Union. But South Carolina, by its show of resistance, had obtained many of its demands and had demonstrated that a single state could force its will on Congress.

THE BANK FIGHT

Although the nullification crisis possessed the seeds of civil war, it was not as critical a political issue as a bitter struggle over the continued existence of the nation's central bank, the second Bank of the United States. The first bank, established in 1791 under Alexander Hamilton's guidance, had been chartered for a 20-year period. Though the government held some of its stock, the bank, like the Bank of England and other central banks of the time, was a private corporation with profits passing to its stockholders. Its public functions were to act as a depository for government receipts, to make short-term loans to the government, and above all to establish a sound currency by refusing to accept at face value notes (paper money) issued by state-chartered banks in excess of their ability to redeem.

To the Northeastern financial and commercial establishment, the central bank was a needed enforcer of prudent monetary policy, but from the beginning it was resented by Southerners and Westerners who believed their prosperity and regional development depended upon ample money and credit. The Republican Party of Jefferson and Madison doubted its constitutionality. When its charter expired in 1811, it was not renewed.

For the next few years, the banking business was in the hands of state-chartered banks, which issued currency in excessive amounts, creating great confusion and fueling inflation. It became increasingly clear that state banks could not provide the country with a reliable currency. In 1816 a second Bank of the United States, similar to the first, was again chartered for 20 years. From its inception, the second bank was unpopular in the newer states and territories, especially with state and local bankers who resented its virtual monopoly over the country's credit and currency, but also with less prosperous people everywhere, who believed that it represented the interests of the wealthy few.

On the whole, the bank was well managed and rendered a valuable service; but Jackson had long shared the Republican distrust of the financial establishment. Elected as a tribune of the people, he sensed that the bank's aristocratic manager, Nicholas Biddle, was an easy target. When the bank's supporters in Congress pushed through an early renewal of its charter, Jackson responded with a stinging veto that denounced monopoly and special privilege. The effort to override the veto failed.

In the presidential campaign that followed, the bank question revealed a fundamental division. Established merchant, manufacturing, and financial interests favored sound money. Regional bankers and entrepreneurs on the make wanted an increased money supply and lower interest rates. Other debtor classes, especially farmers, shared those sentiments. Jackson and his supporters called the central bank a "monster" and coasted to an easy election victory over Henry Clay.

The president interpreted his triumph as a popular mandate to crush the central bank irrevocably. In September 1833 he ordered an end to deposits of government money in the bank, and gradual withdrawals of the money already in its custody. The government deposited its funds in selected state banks, characterized as "pet banks" by the opposition.

For the next generation the United States would get by on a relatively unregulated state banking system, which helped fuel westward expansion through cheap credit but kept the nation vulnerable to periodic panics. During the Civil War, the United States initiated a system of national charters for local and regional banks, but the nation returned to a central bank only with the establishment of the Federal Reserve system in 1913.

WHIGS, DEMOCRATS, AND KNOW-NOTHINGS

Jackson's political opponents, united by little more than a common opposition to him, eventually coalesced into a common party called the Whigs, a British term signifying opposition to Jackson's "monarchial rule." Although they organized soon after the election campaign of 1832, it was more than a decade before they reconciled their differences and were able to draw up a platform. Largely through the magnetism of

Henry Clay and Daniel Webster, the Whigs' most brilliant statesmen, the party solidified its membership. But in the 1836 election, the Whigs were still too divided to unite behind a single man. New York's Martin Van Buren, Jackson's vice president, won the contest.

An economic depression and the larger-than-life personality of his predecessor obscured Van Buren's merits. His public acts aroused no enthusiasm, for he lacked the compelling qualities of leadership and the dramatic flair that had attended Jackson's every move. The election of 1840 found the country afflicted with hard times and low wages — and the Democrats on the defensive.

The Whig candidate for president was William Henry Harrison of Ohio, vastly popular as a hero of conflicts with Native Americans and the War of 1812. He was promoted, like Jackson, as a representative of the democratic West. His vice presidential candidate was John Tyler — a Virginian whose views on states' rights and a low tariff were popular in the South. Harrison won a sweeping victory.

Within a month of his inauguration, however, the 68-year-old Harrison died, and Tyler became president. Tyler's beliefs differed sharply from those of Clay and Webster, still the most influential men in Congress. The result was an open break between the new president and the party that had elected him. The Tyler presidency would accomplish little other than to establish definitively that, if a president died, the vice president would assume the office with full powers for the balance of his term.

Americans found themselves divided in other, more complex ways. The large number of Catholic immigrants in the first half of the 19th century, primarily Irish and German, triggered a backlash among native-born Protestant Americans. Immigrants brought strange new customs and religious practices to American shores. They competed with the native-born for jobs in cities along the Eastern seaboard. The coming of universal white male suffrage in the 1820s and 1830s increased their political clout. Displaced patrician politicians blamed the immigrants for their fall from power. The Catholic Church's failure to support the temperance movement gave rise to charges that Rome was trying to subvert the United States through alcohol.

The most important of the nativist organizations that sprang up in this period was a secret society, the Order of the Star-Spangled Banner, founded in 1849. When its members refused to identify themselves, they were swiftly labeled the "Know-Nothings." In a few years, they became a national organization with considerable political power.

The Know-Nothings advocated an extension in the period required for naturalized citizenship from five to 21 years. They sought to exclude the foreign-born and Catholics from public office. In 1855 they won control of legislatures in New York and Massachusetts; by then, about 90 U.S. congressmen were linked to the party. That was its high point. Soon after, the gathering crisis between North and South over the extension of slavery fatally divided the party, consuming it along with the old debates between Whigs and Democrats that had dominated American politics in the second quarter of the 19th century.

STIRRINGS OF REFORM

The democratic upheaval in politics exemplified by Jackson's election was merely one phase of the long American quest for greater rights and opportunities for all citizens. Another was the beginning of labor organization, primarily among skilled and semiskilled workers. In 1835 labor forces in Philadelphia, Pennsylvania, succeeded in reducing the old "dark-to-dark" workday to a 10-hour day. By 1860, the new work day had become law in several of the states and was a generally accepted standard.

The spread of suffrage had already led to a new concept of education. Clear-sighted statesmen everywhere understood that universal suffrage required a tutored, literate electorate. Workingmen's organizations demanded free, tax-supported schools open to all children. Gradually, in one state after another, legislation was enacted to provide for such free instruction. The leadership of Horace Mann in Massachusetts was especially effective. The public school system became common throughout the North. In other parts of the country, however, the battle for public education continued for years.

Another influential social movement that emerged during this period was the opposition to the sale and use of alcohol, or the temperance movement. It stemmed from a variety of concerns and motives: religious beliefs, the effect of alcohol on the work force, the violence and suffering women and children experienced at the hands of heavy drinkers. In 1826 Boston ministers organized the Society for the Promotion of Temperance. Seven years later, in Philadelphia, the society convened a national convention, which formed the American Temperance Union. The union called for the prohibition of all alcoholic beverages, and pressed state legislatures to ban their production and sale. Thirteen states had done so by 1855, although the laws were subsequently challenged in court. They survived only in northern New England, but between 1830 and 1860 the temperance movement reduced Americans' per capita consumption of alcohol.

Other reformers addressed the problems of prisons and care for the insane. Efforts were made to turn prisons, which stressed punishment, into penitentiaries where the guilty would undergo rehabilitation. In Massachusetts, Dorothea Dix led a struggle to improve conditions for insane persons, who were kept confined in wretched almshouses and prisons. After winning improvements in Massachusetts, she took her campaign to the South, where nine states established hospitals for the insane between 1845 and 1852.

WOMEN'S RIGHTS

Such social reforms brought many women to a realization of their own unequal position in society. From colonial times, unmarried women had enjoyed many of the same legal rights as men, although custom required that they marry early. With matrimony, women virtually lost their separate identities in the eyes of the law. Women were not permitted to vote. Their education in the 17th and 18th centuries was limited largely to reading, writing, music, dancing, and needlework.

The awakening of women began with the visit to America of Frances Wright, a Scottish lecturer and journalist, who publicly promoted women's rights throughout the United States during the 1820s. At a time when women were often forbidden to speak in public places, Wright not only spoke out, but shocked audiences by her views advocating the rights of women to seek information on birth control and divorce. By the 1840s an American women's rights movement emerged. Its foremost leader was Elizabeth Cady Stanton.

In 1848 Cady Stanton and her colleague Lucretia Mott organized a women's rights convention — the first in the history of the world — at Seneca Falls, New York. Delegates drew up a "Declaration of Sentiments," demanding equality with men before the law, the right to vote, and equal opportunities in education and employment. The resolutions passed unanimously with the exception of the one for women's suffrage, which won a majority only after an impassioned speech in favor by Frederick Douglass, the black abolitionist.

At Seneca Falls, Cady Stanton gained national prominence as an eloquent writer and speaker for women's rights. She had realized early on that without the right to vote, women would never be equal with men. Taking the abolitionist William Lloyd Garrison as her model, she saw that the key to success lay in changing public opinion, and not in party action. Seneca Falls became the catalyst for future change. Soon other women's rights conventions were held, and other women would come to the forefront of the movement for their political and social equality.

In 1848 also, Ernestine Rose, a Polish immigrant, was instrumental in getting a law passed in the state of New York that allowed married women to keep their property in their own name. Among the first laws in the nation of this kind, the Married Women's Property Act encouraged other state legislatures to enact similar laws.

In 1869 Elizabeth Cady Stanton and another leading women's rights activist, Susan B. Anthony, founded the National Woman Suffrage Association (NWSA) to promote a constitutional amendment for women's right to the vote. These two would become the women's movement's most outspoken advocates. Describing their partnership, Cady Stanton would say, "I forged the thunderbolts and she fired them."

WESTWARD

The frontier did much to shape American life. Conditions along the entire Atlantic seaboard stimulated migration to the newer regions. From New England, where the soil was incapable of producing high yields of grain, came a steady stream of men and women who left their coastal farms and villages to take advantage of the rich interior land of the continent. In the backcountry settlements of the Carolinas and Virginia, people handicapped by the lack of roads and canals giving access to coastal markets and resentful of the political dominance of the Tidewater planters also moved westward. By 1800 the Mississippi and Ohio River valleys were becoming a great frontier region. "Hi-o, away we go, floating down the river on the O-hi-o," became the song of thousands of migrants.

The westward flow of population in the early 19th century led to the division of old territories and the drawing of new boundaries. As new states were admitted, the political map stabilized east of the Mississippi River. From 1816 to 1821, six states were created — Indiana, Illinois, and Maine (which were free states), and Mississippi, Alabama, and Missouri (slave states). The first frontier had been tied closely to Europe, the second to the coastal settlements, but the Mississippi Valley was independent and its people looked west rather than east.

Frontier settlers were a varied group. One English traveler described them as "a daring, hardy race of men, who live in miserable cabins. ... They are unpolished but hospitable, kind to strangers, honest, and trustworthy. They raise a little Indian corn, pumpkins, hogs, and sometimes have a cow or two. ... But the rifle is their principal means of support." Dexterous with the ax, snare, and fishing line, these men blazed the trails, built the first log cabins, and confronted Native American tribes, whose land they occupied.

As more and more settlers penetrated the wilderness, many became farmers as well as hunters. A comfortable log house with glass windows, a chimney, and partitioned rooms replaced the cabin; the well replaced the spring. Industrious settlers would rapidly clear their land of timber, burning the wood for potash and letting the stumps decay. They grew their own grain, vegetables, and fruit; ranged the woods for deer, wild turkeys, and honey; fished the nearby streams; looked after cattle and hogs. Land speculators bought large tracts of the cheap land and, if land values rose, sold their holdings and moved still farther west, making way for others.

Doctors, lawyers, storekeepers, editors, preachers, mechanics, and politicians soon followed the farmers. The farmers were the sturdy base, however. Where they settled, they intended to stay and hoped their children would remain after them. They built large barns and brick or frame houses. They brought improved livestock, plowed the land skillfully, and sowed productive seed. Some erected flour mills, sawmills, and distilleries. They laid out good highways, and built churches and schools. Incredible transformations were accomplished in a few years. In 1830, for example, Chicago, Illinois, was merely an unpromising trading village with a fort; but long before some of its original settlers had died, it had become one of the largest and richest cities in the nation.

Farms were easy to acquire. Government land after 1820 could be bought for $1.25 for about half a hectare, and after the 1862 Homestead Act, could be claimed by merely occupying and improving it. In addition, tools for working the land were easily available. It was a time when, in a phrase coined by Indiana newspaperman John Soule and popularized by *New York Tribune* editor Horace Greeley, young men could "go west and grow with the country."

Except for a migration into Mexican-owned Texas, the westward march of the agricultural frontier did not pass Missouri into the vast Western territory acquired in the Louisiana Purchase until after 1840. In 1819, in return for assuming the claims of American citizens to the amount of $5 million, the United States obtained from Spain both Florida and Spain's rights to the Oregon country in the Far West. In the meantime, the Far West had become a field of great activity in the fur trade, which was to have significance far beyond the value of the skins. As in the first days of French exploration in the Mississippi Valley, the trader was a pathfinder for the settlers beyond the Mississippi. The French and Scots-Irish trappers, exploring the great rivers and their tributaries and discovering the passes through the Rocky and Sierra Mountains, made possible the overland migration of the 1840s and the later occupation of the interior of the nation.

Overall, the growth of the nation was enormous: Population grew from 7.25 million to more than 23 million from 1812 to 1852, and the land available for settlement increased by almost the size of Western Europe — from 4.4 million to 7.8 million square kilometers. Still unresolved, however, were the basic conflicts rooted in sectional differences that, by the decade of the 1860s, would explode into civil war. Inevitably, too, this westward expansion brought settlers into conflict with the original inhabitants of the land: the Native Americans.

In the first part of the 19th century, the most prominent figure associated with these conflicts was Andrew Jackson, the first "Westerner" to occupy the White House. In the midst of the War of 1812, Jackson, then in charge of the Tennessee militia, was sent into southern Alabama, where he ruthlessly put down an uprising of Creek Indians. The Creeks soon ceded two-thirds of their land to the United States. Jackson later routed bands of Seminoles from their sanctuaries in Spanish-owned Florida.

In the 1820s, President Monroe's secretary of war, John C. Calhoun, pursued a policy of removing the remaining tribes from the old Southwest and resettling them beyond the Mississippi. Jackson continued this policy as president. In 1830 Congress passed the Indian Removal Act, providing funds to transport the eastern tribes beyond the Mississippi. In 1834 a special Native American territory was set up in what is now Oklahoma. In all, the tribes signed 94 treaties during Jackson's two terms, ceding millions of hectares to the federal government and removing dozens of tribes from their ancestral homelands.

The most terrible chapter in this unhappy history concerned the Cherokees, whose lands in western North Carolina and Georgia had been guaranteed by treaty since 1791. Among the most progressive of the eastern tribes, the Cherokees nevertheless were sure to be displaced when gold was discovered on their land in 1829. Forced to make a long and cruel trek to Oklahoma in 1838, the tribe lost many of its numbers from disease and privation on what became known as the "Trail of Tears." >

THE FRONTIER, "THE WEST," AND THE AMERICAN EXPERIENCE

The frontier — the point at which settled territory met unoccupied land — began at Jamestown and Plymouth Rock. It moved in a westward direction for nearly 300 years through densely forested wilderness and barren plains until the decennial census of 1890 revealed that at last the United States no longer possessed a discernible line of settlement.

At the time it seemed to many that a long period had come to an end — one in which the country had grown from a few struggling outposts of English civilization to a huge independent nation with an identity of its own. It was easy to believe that the experience of settlement and post-settlement development, constantly repeated as a people conquered a continent, had been the defining factor in the nation's development.

In 1893, the historian Frederick Jackson Turner, expressing a widely held sentiment, declared that the frontier had made the United States more than an extension of Europe. It had created a nation with a culture that was perhaps coarser than Europe's, but also more pragmatic, energetic, individualistic, and democratic. The existence of large areas of "free land" had created a nation of property holders and had provided a "safety valve" for discontent in cities and more settled areas. His analysis implied that an America without a frontier would trend ominously toward what were seen as the European ills of stratified social systems, class conflict, and diminished opportunity.

After more than a hundred years scholars still debate the significance of the frontier in American history. Few believe it was quite as all-important as Turner suggested; its absence does not appear to have led to dire consequences. Some have gone farther, rejecting the Turner argument as a romantic glorification of a bloody, brutal process — marked by a war of conquest against Mexico, near-genocidal treatment of Native American tribes, and environmental despoliation. The common experience of the frontier, they argue, was one of hardship and failure.

Yet it remains hard to believe that three centuries of westward movement had no impact on the national character and suggestive that intelligent foreign observers, such as the French intellectual Alexis de Tocqueville, were fascinated by the American West. Indeed, the last area of frontier settlement, the vast area stretching north from Texas to the Canadian border, which Americans today commonly call "the West," still seems characterized by ideals of individualism, democracy, and opportunity that are more palpable than in the rest of the nation. It is perhaps also revealing that many people in other lands, when hearing the word "American," so often identify it with a symbol of that final frontier — the "cowboy." ◆

Major Acquisitions of Territory by the United States and Dates of Admission of States

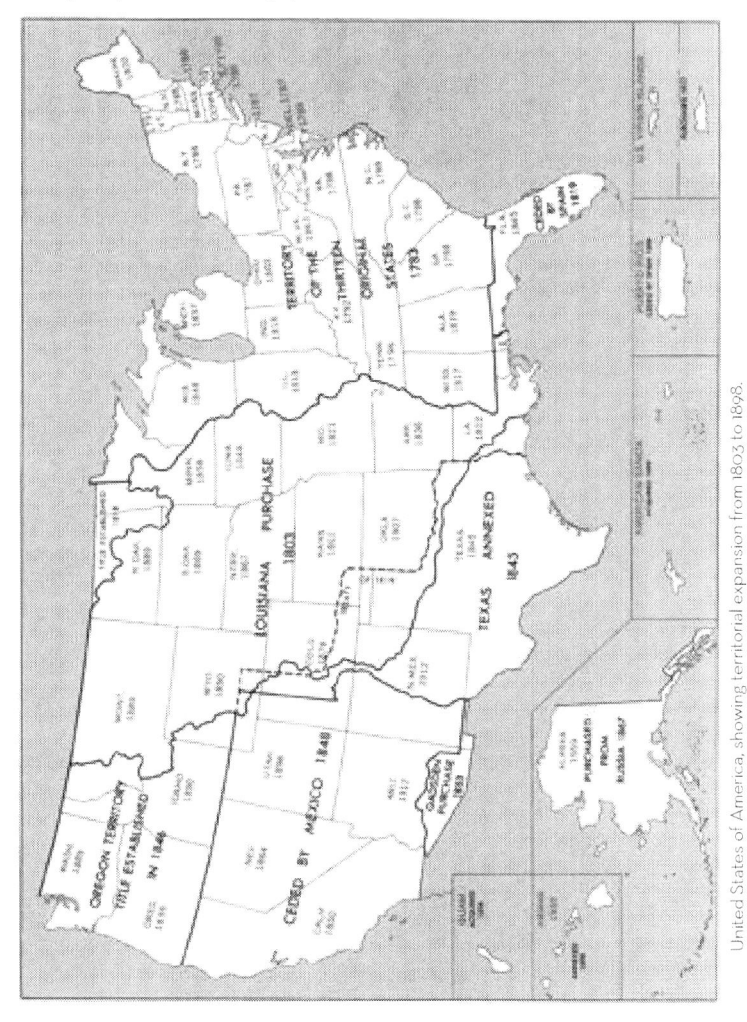

U.S. Department of Commerce
1-6 UNITED STATES SUMMARY

Bureau of Census
NUMBER OF INHABITANTS

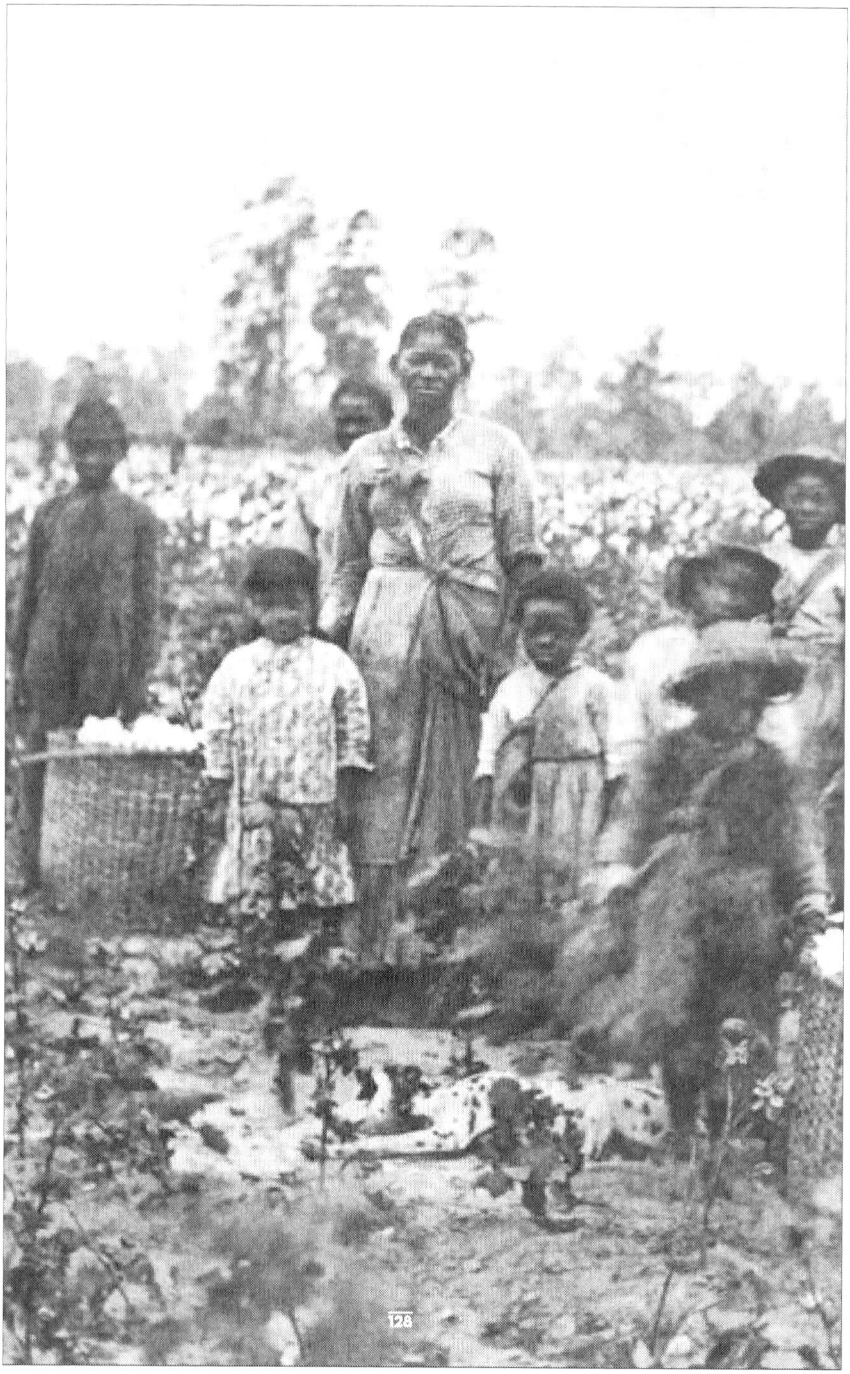

CHAPTER

6

SECTIONAL CONFLICT

Slave family picking cotton near Savannah, Georgia, in the early 1860s.

CHAPTER 6: SECTIONAL CONFLICT

> "A house divided against itself cannot stand. I believe this government cannot endure permanently half-slave and half-free."
>
> Senatorial candidate Abraham Lincoln, 1858

TWO AMERICAS

No visitor to the United States left a more enduring record of his travels and observations than the French writer and political theorist Alexis de Tocqueville, whose *Democracy in America*, first published in 1835, remains one of the most trenchant and insightful analyses of American social and political practices. Tocqueville was far too shrewd an observer to be uncritical about the United States, but his verdict was fundamentally positive. "The government of a democracy brings the notion of political rights to the level of the humblest citizens," he wrote, "just as the dissemination of wealth brings the notion of property within the reach of all men." Nonetheless, Tocqueville was only one in the first of a long line of thinkers to worry whether such rough equality could survive in the face of a growing factory system that threatened to create divisions between industrial workers and a new business elite.

Other travelers marveled at the growth and vitality of the country, where they could see "everywhere the most unequivocal proofs of prosperity and rapid progress in agriculture, commerce, and great public works." But such optimistic views of the American experiment were by no means universal. One skeptic was the English novelist Charles Dickens, who first visited the United States in 1841-42. "This is not the Republic I came to see," he wrote in a letter. "This is not the Republic of my imagination. ... The more I think of its youth and strength, the poorer and more trifling in a thousand respects, it appears in my eyes.

In everything of which it has made a boast — excepting its education of the people, and its care for poor children — it sinks immeasurably below the level I had placed it upon."

Dickens was not alone. America in the 19th century, as throughout its history, generated expectations and passions that often conflicted with a reality at once more mundane and more complex. The young nation's size and diversity defied easy generalization and invited contradiction: America was both a freedom-loving and slave-holding society, a nation of expansive and primitive frontiers, a society with cities built on growing commerce and industrialization.

LANDS OF PROMISE

By 1850 the national territory stretched over forest, plain, and mountain. Within its far-flung limits dwelt 23 million people in a Union comprising 31 states. In the East, industry boomed. In the Midwest and the South, agriculture flourished. After 1849 the gold mines of California poured their precious ore into the channels of trade.

New England and the Middle Atlantic states were the main centers of manufacturing, commerce, and finance. Principal products of these areas were textiles, lumber, clothing, machinery, leather, and woolen goods. The maritime trade had reached the height of its prosperity; vessels flying the American flag plied the oceans, distributing wares of all nations.

The South, from the Atlantic to the Mississippi River and beyond, featured an economy centered on agriculture. Tobacco was important in Virginia, Maryland, and North Carolina. In South Carolina, rice was an abundant crop. The climate and soil of Louisiana encouraged the cultivation of sugar. But cotton eventually became the dominant commodity and the one with which the South was identified. By 1850 the American South grew more than 80 percent of the world's cotton. Slaves cultivated all these crops.

The Midwest, with its boundless prairies and swiftly growing population, flourished. Europe and the older settled parts of America demanded its wheat and meat products. The introduction of labor-saving implements — notably the McCormick reaper (a machine to cut and harvest grain) — made possible an unparalleled increase in grain production. The nation's wheat crops swelled from some 35 million hectoliters in 1850 to nearly 61 million in 1860, more than half grown in the Midwest.

An important stimulus to the country's prosperity was the great improvement in transportation facilities; from 1850 to 1857 the Appalachian Mountain barrier was pierced by five railway trunk lines linking the Midwest and the Northeast. These links established the economic interests that would undergird the political alliance of the Union from 1861 to 1865. The South lagged behind. It was not until the late 1850s that a continuous line ran through the mountains connecting the lower Mississippi River area with the southern Atlantic seaboard.

SLAVERY AND SECTIONALISM

One overriding issue exacerbated the regional and economic differences between North and South: slavery. Resenting the large profits amassed by Northern businessmen from marketing the cotton crop, many Southerners attributed the backwardness of their own section to Northern aggrandizement. Many Northerners, on the other hand, declared that slavery — the "peculiar institution" that the South regarded as essential to its economy — was largely responsible for the region's relative financial and industrial backwardness.

As far back as the Missouri Compromise in 1819, sectional lines had been steadily hardening on the slavery question. In the North, sentiment for outright abolition grew increasingly powerful. Southerners in general felt little guilt about slavery and defended it vehemently. In some seaboard areas, slavery by 1850 was well over 200 years old; it was an integral part of the basic economy of the region.

Although the 1860 census showed that there were nearly four million slaves out of a total population of 12.3 million in the 15 slave states, only a minority of Southern whites owned slaves. There were some 385,000 slave owners out of about 1.5 million white families. Fifty percent of these slave owners owned no more than five slaves. Twelve percent owned 20 or more slaves, the number defined as turning a farmer into a planter. Three-quarters of Southern white families, including the "poor whites," those on the lowest rung of Southern society, owned no slaves.

It is easy to understand the interest of the planters in slave holding. But the yeomen and poor whites supported the institution of slavery as well. They feared that, if freed, blacks would compete with them economically and challenge their higher social status. Southern whites defended slavery not simply on the basis of economic necessity but out of a visceral dedication to white supremacy.

As they fought the weight of Northern opinion, political leaders of the South, the professional classes, and most of the clergy now no longer apologized for slavery but championed it. Southern publicists insisted, for example, that the relationship between capital and labor was more humane under the slavery system than under the wage system of the North.

Before 1830 the old patriarchal system of plantation government, with its personal supervision of the slaves by their owners or masters, was still characteristic. Gradually, however, with the introduction of large-scale cotton production in the lower South, the master gradually ceased to exercise close personal supervision over his slaves, and employed professional overseers charged with exacting from slaves a maximum amount of work. In such circumstances, slavery could become a system of brutality and coercion in which beatings and the breakup of families through the sale of individuals were commonplace. In other settings, however, it could be much milder.

In the end, however, the most trenchant criticism of slavery was not the behavior of individual masters and overseers. Systematically treating African-American laborers as if they were domestic animals, slavery, the abolitionists pointed out, violated every human being's inalienable right to be free.

THE ABOLITIONISTS

In national politics, Southerners chiefly sought protection and enlargement of the interests represented by the cotton/slavery system. They sought territorial expansion because the wastefulness of cultivating a single crop, cotton, rapidly exhausted the soil, increasing the need for new fertile lands. Moreover, new territory would establish a basis for additional slave states to offset the admission of new free states. Antislavery Northerners saw in the Southern view a conspiracy for proslavery aggrandizement. In the 1830s their opposition became fierce.

An earlier antislavery movement, an offshoot of the American Revolution, had won its last victory in 1808 when Congress abolished the slave trade with Africa. Thereafter, opposition came largely from the Quakers, who kept up a mild but ineffectual protest. Meanwhile, the cotton gin and westward expansion into the Mississippi delta region created an increasing demand for slaves.

The abolitionist movement that emerged in the early 1830s was combative, uncompromising, and insistent upon an immediate end to slavery. This approach found a leader in William Lloyd Garrison, a young man from Massachusetts, who combined the heroism of a martyr with the crusading zeal of a demagogue. On January 1, 1831, Garrison produced the first issue of his newspaper, *The Liberator*, which bore the announcement: "I shall strenuously contend for the immediate enfranchisement of our slave population. ... On this subject, I do not wish to think, or speak, or write, with moderation. ... I am in earnest — I will not equivocate — I will not excuse — I will not retreat a single inch — AND I WILL BE HEARD."

Garrison's sensational methods awakened Northerners to the evil in an institution many had long come to regard as unchangeable. He sought to hold up to public gaze the most repulsive aspects of slavery and to castigate slave holders as torturers and traffickers in human life. He recognized no rights of the masters, acknowledged no compromise, tolerated no delay. Other abolitionists, unwilling to subscribe to his law-defying tactics, held that reform should be accomplished by legal and peaceful means. Garrison was joined by another powerful voice, that of Frederick Douglass, an escaped slave who galvanized Northern audiences. Theodore Dwight Weld and many other abolitionists crusaded against slavery in the states of the old Northwest Territory with evangelical zeal.

One activity of the movement involved helping slaves escape to safe refuges in the North or over the border into Canada. The "Underground Railroad," an elaborate network of secret routes, was firmly established in the 1830s in all parts of the North. In Ohio alone, from 1830 to 1860, as many as 40,000 fugitive slaves were helped to freedom. The number of local antislavery societies increased at such a rate that by 1838 there were about 1,350 with a membership of perhaps 250,000.

Most Northerners nonetheless either held themselves aloof from the abolitionist movement or actively opposed it. In 1837, for example, a mob attacked and killed the antislavery editor Elijah P. Lovejoy in Alton, Illinois. Still, Southern repression of free speech allowed the abolitionists to link the slavery issue with the cause of civil liberties for whites. In 1835 an angry mob destroyed abolitionist literature in the Charleston, South Carolina, post office. When the postmaster-general stated he would not enforce delivery of abolitionist material, bitter debates ensued in Congress. Abolitionists flooded Congress with petitions calling for action against slavery. In 1836 the House voted to table such petitions automatically, thus effectively killing them. Former President John Quincy Adams, elected to the House of Representatives in 1830, fought this so-called gag rule as a violation of the First Amendment, finally winning its repeal in 1844.

TEXAS AND WAR WITH MEXICO

Throughout the 1820s, Americans settled in the vast territory of Texas, often with land grants from the Mexican government. However, their numbers soon alarmed the authorities, who prohibited further immigration in 1830. In 1834 General Antonio López de Santa Anna established a dictatorship in Mexico, and the following year Texans revolted. Santa Anna defeated the American rebels at the celebrated siege of the Alamo in early 1836, but Texans under Sam Houston destroyed the Mexican Army and captured Santa Anna a month later at the Battle of San Jacinto, ensuring Texan independence.

For almost a decade, Texas remained an independent republic, largely because its annexation as a huge new slave state would disrupt the increasingly precarious balance of political power in the United States. In 1845, President James K. Polk, narrowly elected on a platform of westward expansion, brought the Republic of Texas into the Union. Polk's move was the first gambit in a larger design. Texas claimed that its border with Mexico was the Rio Grande; Mexico argued that the border stood far to the north along the Nueces River. Meanwhile, settlers were flooding into the territories of New Mexico and California. Many Americans claimed that the United States had a "manifest destiny" to expand westward to the Pacific Ocean.

U.S. attempts to purchase from Mexico the New Mexico and California territories failed. In 1846, after a clash of Mexican and U.S. troops along the Rio Grande, the United States declared war. American troops occupied the lightly populated territory of New Mexico, then supported a revolt of settlers in California. A U.S. force under Zachary Taylor invaded Mexico, winning victories at Monterrey and Buena Vista, but failing to bring the Mexicans to the negotiating table. In March 1847, a U.S. Army commanded by Winfield Scott landed near Veracruz on Mexico's east coast, and fought its way to Mexico City. The United States dictated the Treaty of Guadalupe Hidalgo in which Mexico ceded what would become the American Southwest region and California for $15 million.

The war was a training ground for American officers who would later fight on both sides in the Civil War. It was also politically divisive. Polk, in a simultaneous facedown with Great Britain, had achieved British recognition of American sovereignty in the Pacific Northwest to the 49th parallel. Still, antislavery forces, mainly among the Whigs, attacked Polk's expansion as a proslavery plot.

With the conclusion of the Mexican War, the United States gained a vast new territory of 1.36 million square kilometers encompassing the present-day states of New Mexico, Nevada, California, Utah, most of Arizona, and portions of Colorado and Wyoming. The nation also faced a revival of the most explosive question in American politics of the time: Would the new territories be slave or free?

THE COMPROMISE OF 1850

Until 1845, it had seemed likely that slavery would be confined to the areas where it already existed. It had been given limits by the Missouri Compromise in 1820 and had no opportunity to overstep them. The new territories made renewed expansion of slavery a real likelihood.

Many Northerners believed that if not allowed to spread, slavery would ultimately decline and die. To justify their opposition to adding new slave states, they pointed to the statements of Washington and Jefferson, and to the Ordinance of 1787, which forbade the extension of slavery into the Northwest. Texas, which already permitted slavery, naturally entered the Union as a slave state. But the California, New Mexico, and Utah territories did not have slavery. From the beginning, there were strongly conflicting opinions on whether they should.

Southerners urged that all the lands acquired from Mexico should be thrown open to slave holders. Antislavery Northerners demanded that all the new regions be closed to slavery. One group of moderates suggested that the Missouri Compromise line be extended to the Pacific with free states north of it and slave states to the south. Another group proposed that the question be left to "popular sovereignty." The government should permit settlers to enter the new territory with or without slaves as they pleased. When the time came to organize the region into states, the people themselves could decide.

Despite the vitality of the abolitionist movement, most Northerners were unwilling to challenge the existence of slavery in the South. Many, however, were against its expansion. In 1848 nearly 300,000 men voted for the candidates of a new Free Soil Party, which declared that the best policy was "to limit, localize, and discourage slavery." In the immediate aftermath of the war with Mexico, however, popular sovereignty had considerable appeal.

In January 1848 the discovery of gold in California precipitated a headlong rush of settlers, more than 80,000 in the single year of 1849. Congress had to determine the status of this new region quickly in order to establish an organized government. The venerable Kentucky Senator Henry Clay, who twice before in times of crisis had come forward with compromise arrangements, advanced a complicated and carefully balanced plan. His old Massachusetts rival, Daniel Webster, supported it. Illinois Democratic Senator Stephen A. Douglas, the leading advocate of popular sovereignty, did much of the work in guiding it through Congress.

The Compromise of 1850 contained the following provisions: (1) California was admitted to the Union as a free state; (2) the remainder of the Mexican cession was divided into the two territories of New Mexico and Utah and organized without mention of slavery; (3) the claim of Texas to a portion of New Mexico was satisfied by a payment of $10 million; (4) new legislation (the Fugitive Slave Act) was passed to apprehend runaway slaves and return them to their masters; and (5) the buying and selling of slaves (but not slavery) was abolished in the District of Columbia.

The country breathed a sigh of relief. For the next three years, the compromise seemed to settle nearly all differences. The new Fugitive Slave Law, however, was an immediate source of tension. It deeply offended many Northerners, who refused to have any part in catching slaves. Some actively and violently obstructed its enforcement. The Underground Railroad became more efficient and daring than ever.

A DIVIDED NATION

During the 1850s, the issue of slavery severed the political bonds that had held the United States together.

It ate away at the country's two great political parties, the Whigs and the Democrats, destroying the first and irrevocably dividing the second. It produced weak presidents whose irresolution mirrored that of their parties. It eventually discredited even the Supreme Court.

The moral fervor of abolitionist feeling grew steadily. In 1852, Harriet Beecher Stowe published *Uncle Tom's Cabin*, a novel provoked by the passage of the Fugitive Slave Law. More than 300,000 copies were sold the first year. Presses ran day and night to keep up with the demand. Although sentimental and full of stereotypes, *Uncle Tom's Cabin* portrayed with undeniable force the cruelty of slavery and posited a fundamental conflict between free and slave societies. It inspired widespread enthusiasm for the antislavery cause, appealing as it did to basic human emotions — indignation at injustice and pity for the helpless individuals exposed to ruthless exploitation.

In 1854 the issue of slavery in the territories was renewed and the quarrel became more bitter. The region that now comprises Kansas and Nebraska was being rapidly settled, increasing pressure for the establishment of territorial, and eventually, state governments.

Under terms of the Missouri Compromise of 1820, the entire region was closed to slavery. Dominant slave-holding elements in Missouri objected to letting Kansas become a free territory, for their state would then have three free-soil neighbors (Illinois, Iowa, and Kansas) and might be forced to become a free state as well. Their congressional delegation, backed by Southerners, blocked all efforts to organize the region.

At this point, Stephen A. Douglas enraged all free-soil supporters. Douglas argued that the Compromise of 1850, having left Utah and New Mexico free to resolve the slavery issue for themselves, superseded the Missouri Compromise. His plan called for two territories, Kansas and Nebraska. It permitted settlers to carry slaves into them and eventually to determine whether they should enter the Union as free or slave states.

Douglas's opponents accused him of currying favor with the South in order to gain the presidency in 1856. The free-soil movement, which had seemed to be in decline, reemerged with greater momentum than ever. Yet in May 1854, Douglas's plan in the form of the Kansas-Nebraska Act passed Congress to be signed by President Franklin Pierce. Southern enthusiasts celebrated with cannon fire. But when Douglas subsequently visited Chicago to speak in his own defense, the ships in the harbor lowered their flags to half-mast, the church bells tolled for an hour, and a crowd of 10,000 hooted so loudly that he could not make himself heard.

The immediate results of Douglas's ill-starred measure were momentous. The Whig Party, which had straddled the question of slavery expansion, sank to its death, and in its stead a powerful new organization arose, the Republican Party, whose primary demand was that slavery be excluded from all the territories. In 1856, it nominated John Fremont, whose expeditions into the Far West had won him renown. Fremont lost the election, but the new party swept a great part of the North. Such free-soil leaders as Salmon P. Chase and William Seward exerted greater influence than ever. Along with them appeared a tall, lanky Illinois attorney, Abraham Lincoln.

Meanwhile, the flow of both Southern slave holders and antislavery families into Kansas resulted in armed conflict. Soon the territory was being called "bleeding Kansas." The Supreme Court made things worse with its infamous 1857 Dred Scott decision.

Scott was a Missouri slave who, some 20 years earlier, had been taken by his master to live in Illinois and the Wisconsin Territory; in both places, slavery was banned. Returning to Missouri and becoming discontented with his life there, Scott sued for liberation on the ground of his residence on free soil. A majority of the Supreme Court — dominated by Southerners — decided that Scott lacked standing in court because he was not a citizen; that the laws of a free state (Illinois) had no effect on his status because he was the resident of a slave state (Missouri); and that slave holders had the right to take their "property" anywhere in the federal territories. Thus, Congress could not restrict the expansion of slavery. This last assertion invalidated former compromises on slavery and made new ones impossible to craft.

The Dred Scott decision stirred fierce resentment throughout the North. Never before had the Court been so bitterly condemned. For Southern Democrats, the decision was a great victory, since it gave judicial sanction to their justification of slavery throughout the territories.

LINCOLN, DOUGLAS, AND BROWN

Abraham Lincoln had long regarded slavery as an evil. As early as 1854 in a widely publicized speech, he declared that all national legislation should be framed on the principle that slavery was to be restricted and eventually abolished. He contended also that the principle of popular sovereignty was false, for slavery in the western territories was the concern not only of the local inhabitants but of the United States as a whole.

In 1858 Lincoln opposed Stephen A. Douglas for election to the U.S. Senate from Illinois. In the first paragraph of his opening campaign speech, on June 17, Lincoln struck the keynote of American history for the seven years to follow:

A house divided against itself cannot stand. I believe this government cannot endure permanently half-slave and half-free. I do not expect the Union to be dissolved — I do not expect the house to fall — but I do expect it will cease to be divided.

Lincoln and Douglas engaged in a series of seven debates in the ensuing months of 1858. Senator Douglas, known as the "Little Giant," had an enviable reputation as an orator, but he met his match in Lincoln, who eloquently challenged Douglas's concept of popular sovereignty. In the end, Douglas won the election by a small margin, but Lincoln had achieved stature as a national figure.

By then events were spinning out of control. On the night of October 16, 1859, John Brown, an antislavery fanatic who had captured and killed five proslavery settlers in Kansas three years before, led a band of followers in an attack on the federal arsenal at Harper's Ferry (in what is now West Virginia). Brown's goal was to use the weapons seized to lead a slave uprising. After two days of fighting, Brown and his surviving men were taken prisoner by a force of U.S. Marines commanded by Colonel Robert E. Lee.

Brown's attempt confirmed the worst fears of many Southerners. Antislavery activists, on the other hand, generally hailed Brown as a martyr to a great cause. Virginia put Brown on trial for conspiracy, treason, and murder. On December 2, 1859, he was hanged. Although most Northerners had initially condemned him, increasing numbers were coming to accept his view that he had been an instrument in the hand of God.

THE 1860 ELECTION

In 1860 the Republican Party nominated Abraham Lincoln as its candidate for president. The Republican platform declared that slavery could spread no farther, promised a tariff for the protection of industry, and pledged the enactment of a law granting free homesteads to settlers who would help in the opening of the West. Southern Democrats, unwilling in the wake of the Dred Scott case to accept Douglas's popular sovereignty, split from the party and nominated Vice President John C. Breckenridge of Kentucky for president. Stephen A. Douglas was the nominee of northern Democrats. Diehard Whigs from the border states, formed into the Constitutional Union Party, nominated John C. Bell of Tennessee.

Lincoln and Douglas competed in the North, Breckenridge and Bell in the South. Lincoln won only 39 percent of the popular vote, but had a clear majority of 180 electoral votes, carrying all 18 free states. Bell won Tennessee, Kentucky, and Virginia; Breckenridge took the other slave states except for Missouri, which was won by Douglas. Despite his poor showing, Douglas trailed only Lincoln in the popular vote. >

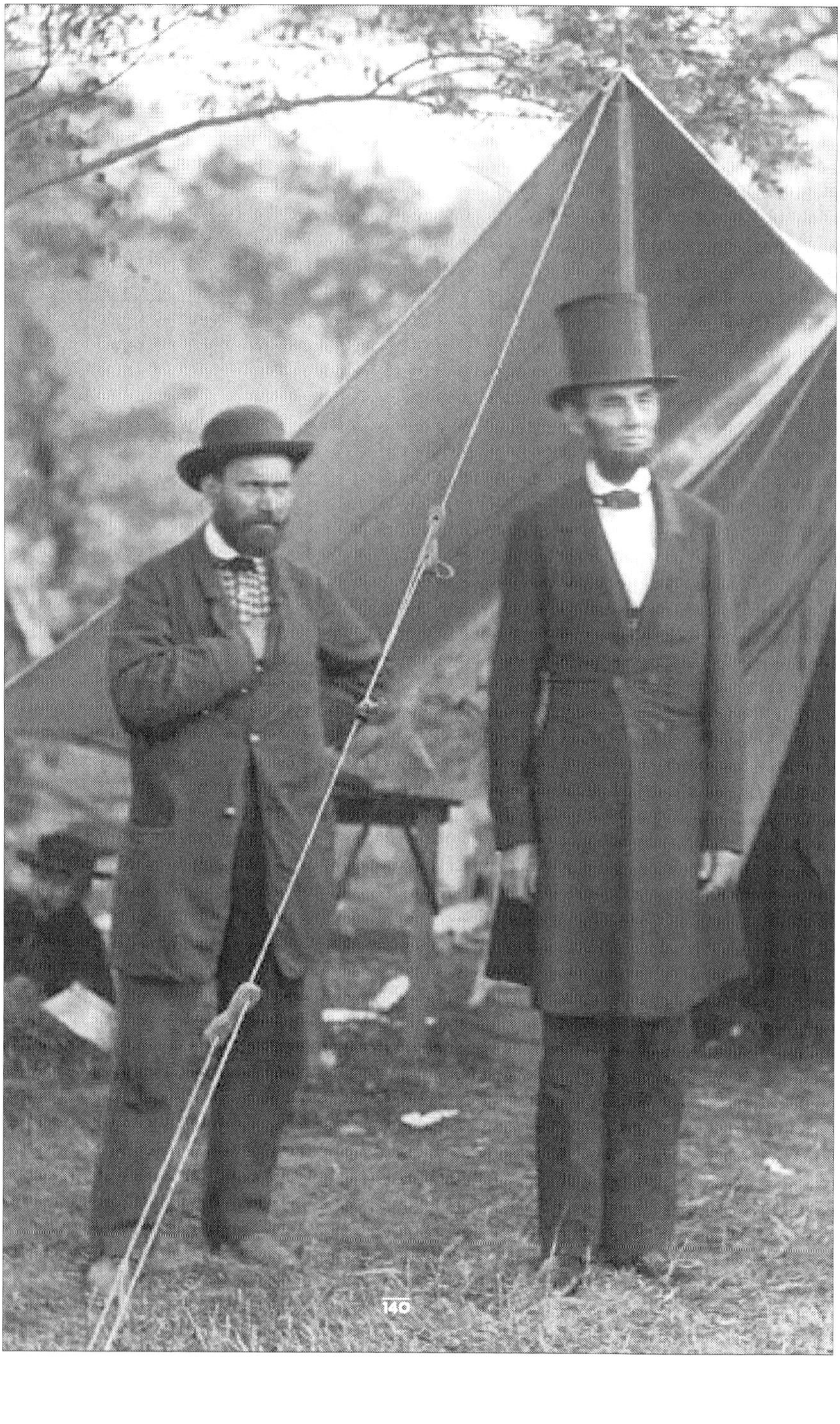

CHAPTER

7

THE CIVIL WAR AND RECONSTRUCTION

President Abraham Lincoln (center) at a Union Army encampment in October 1862, following the battle of Antietam.

CHAPTER 7: THE CIVIL WAR AND RECONSTRUCTION

> "That this nation under God shall have a new birth of freedom."
>
> President Abraham Lincoln, November 19, 1863

SECESSION AND CIVIL WAR

Lincoln's victory in the presidential election of November 1860 made South Carolina's secession from the Union December 20 a foregone conclusion. The state had long been waiting for an event that would unite the South against the antislavery forces. By February 1, 1861, five more Southern states had seceded. On February 8, the six states signed a provisional constitution for the Confederate States of America. The remaining Southern states as yet remained in the Union, although Texas had begun to move on its secession.

Less than a month later, March 4, 1861, Abraham Lincoln was sworn in as president of the United States. In his inaugural address, he declared the Confederacy "legally void." His speech closed with a plea for restoration of the bonds of union, but the South turned a deaf ear. On April 12, Confederate guns opened fire on the federal garrison at Fort Sumter in the Charleston, South Carolina, harbor. A war had begun in which more Americans would die than in any other conflict before or since.

In the seven states that had seceded, the people responded positively to the Confederate action and the leadership of Confederate President Jefferson Davis. Both sides now tensely awaited the action of the slave states that thus far had remained loyal. Virginia seceded on April 17; Arkansas, Tennessee, and North Carolina followed quickly.

No state left the Union with greater reluctance than Virginia. Her statesmen had a leading part in the winning of the Revolution and the framing of the Constitution, and she had provided the nation with five presidents. With Virginia went Colonel Robert E. Lee, who declined the command of the Union Army out of loyalty to his native state.

Between the enlarged Confederacy and the free-soil North lay the border slave states of Delaware, Maryland, Kentucky, and Missouri, which, despite some sympathy with the South, would remain loyal to the Union.

Each side entered the war with high hopes for an early victory. In material resources the North enjoyed a decided advantage. Twenty-three states with a population of 22 million were arrayed against 11 states inhabited by nine million, including slaves. The industrial superiority of the North exceeded even its preponderance in population, providing it with abundant facilities for manufacturing arms and ammunition, clothing, and other supplies. It had a greatly superior railway network.

The South nonetheless had certain advantages. The most important was geography; the South was fighting a defensive war on its own territory. It could establish its independence simply by beating off the Northern armies. The South also had a stronger military tradition, and possessed the more experienced military leaders.

WESTERN ADVANCE, EASTERN STALEMATE

The first large battle of the war, at Bull Run, Virginia (also known as First Manassas) near Washington, stripped away any illusions that victory would be quick or easy. It also established a pattern, at least in the Eastern United States, of bloody Southern victories that never translated into a decisive military advantage for the Confederacy.

In contrast to its military failures in the East, the Union was able to secure battlefield victories in the West and slow strategic success at sea. Most of the Navy, at the war's beginning, was in Union hands, but it was scattered and weak. Secretary of the Navy Gideon Welles took prompt measures to strengthen it. Lincoln then proclaimed a blockade of the Southern coasts. Although the effect of the blockade was negligible at first, by 1863 it almost completely prevented shipments of cotton to Europe and blocked the importation of sorely needed munitions, clothing, and medical supplies to the South.

A brilliant Union naval commander, David Farragut, conducted two remarkable operations. In April 1862, he took a fleet into the mouth of the Mississippi River and forced the surrender of the largest city in the South, New Orleans, Louisiana. In August 1864, with the cry, "Damn the torpedoes! Full speed ahead," he led a force past the fortified entrance of Mobile Bay, Alabama, captured a Confederate ironclad vessel, and sealed off the port.

In the Mississippi Valley, the Union forces won an almost uninterrupted series of victories. They began by breaking a long Confederate line in Tennessee, thus making it possible to occupy almost all the western part of the state. When the important Mississippi River port of Memphis was taken, Union troops advanced some 320 kilometers into the heart of the Confederacy. With the tenacious General Ulysses S. Grant in command, they withstood a sudden Confederate counterattack at Shiloh, on the bluffs overlooking the Tennessee River. Those killed and wounded at Shiloh numbered more than 10,000 on each side, a casualty rate that Americans had never before experienced. But it was only the beginning of the carnage.

In Virginia, by contrast, Union troops continued to meet one defeat after another in a succession of bloody attempts to capture Richmond, the Confederate capital. The Confederates enjoyed strong defense positions afforded by numerous streams cutting the road between Washington and Richmond. Their two best generals, Robert E. Lee and Thomas J. ("Stonewall") Jackson, both far surpassed in ability their early Union counterparts. In 1862 Union commander George McClellan made a slow, excessively cautious attempt to seize Richmond. But in the Seven Days' Battles between June 25 and July 1, the Union troops were driven steadily backward, both sides suffering terrible losses.

After another Confederate victory at the Second Battle of Bull Run (or Second Manassas), Lee crossed the Potomac River and invaded Maryland. McClellan again responded tentatively, despite learning that Lee had split his army and was heavily outnumbered. The Union and Confederate Armies met at Antietam Creek, near Sharpsburg, Maryland, on September 17, 1862, in the bloodiest single day of the war: More than 4,000 died on both sides and 18,000 were wounded. Despite his numerical advantage, however, McClellan failed to break Lee's lines or press the attack, and Lee was able to retreat across the Potomac with his army intact. As a result, Lincoln fired McClellan.

Although Antietam was inconclusive in military terms, its consequences were nonetheless momentous. Great Britain and France, both on the verge of recognizing the Confederacy, delayed their decision, and the South never received the diplomatic recognition and the economic aid from Europe that it desperately sought.

Antietam also gave Lincoln the opening he needed to issue the preliminary Emancipation Proclamation, which declared that as of January 1, 1863, all slaves in states rebelling against the Union were free. In practical terms, the proclamation had little immediate impact; it freed slaves only in the Confederate states, while leaving slavery intact in the border states. Politically, however, it meant that in addition to preserving the Union, the abolition of slavery was now a declared objective of the Union war effort.

The final Emancipation Proclamation, issued January 1, 1863, also authorized the recruitment of African Americans into the Union Army, a move abolitionist leaders such as Frederick Douglass had been urging since the beginning of armed conflict. Union forces already had been sheltering escaped slaves as "contraband of war," but following the Emancipation Proclamation, the Union Army recruited and trained regiments of African-American soldiers that fought with distinction in battles from Virginia to the Mississippi. About 178,000 African Americans served in the U.S. Colored Troops, and 29,500 served in the Union Navy.

Despite the political gains represented by the Emancipation Proclamation, however, the North's military prospects in the East remained bleak as Lee's Army of Northern Virginia continued to maul the Union Army of the Potomac, first at Fredericksburg, Virginia, in December 1862 and then at Chancellorsville in May 1863. But Chancellorsville, although one of Lee's most brilliant military victories, was also one of his most costly. His most valued lieutenant, General "Stonewall" Jackson, was mistakenly shot and killed by his own men.

GETTYSBURG TO APPOMATTOX

Yet none of the Confederate victories was decisive. The Union simply mustered new armies and tried again. Believing that the North's crushing defeat at Chancellorsville gave him his chance, Lee struck northward into Pennsylvania at the beginning of July 1863, almost reaching the state capital at Harrisburg. A strong Union force intercepted him at Gettysburg, where, in a titanic three-day battle — the largest of the Civil War — the Confederates made a valiant effort to break the Union lines. They failed, and on July 4 Lee's army, after crippling losses, retreated behind the Potomac.

More than 3,000 Union soldiers and almost 4,000 Confederates died at Gettysburg; wounded and missing totaled more than 20,000 on each side. On November 19, 1863, Lincoln dedicated a new national cemetery there with perhaps the most famous address in U.S. history. He concluded his brief remarks with these words:

... we here highly resolve that these dead shall not have died in vain — that this nation, under God, shall have a new birth of freedom — and that government of the people, by the people, for the people, shall not perish from the earth.

On the Mississippi, Union control had been blocked at Vicksburg, where the Confederates had strongly fortified themselves on bluffs too high for naval attack. In early 1863 Grant began to move below and around Vicksburg, subjecting it to a six-week siege. On July 4, he captured the town, together with the strongest Confederate Army in the West. The river was now entirely in Union hands. The Confederacy was broken in two, and it became almost impossible to bring supplies from Texas and Arkansas.

The Northern victories at Vicksburg and Gettysburg in July 1863 marked the turning point of the war, although the bloodshed continued unabated for more than a year-and-a-half.

Lincoln brought Grant east and made him commander-in-chief of all Union forces. In May 1864 Grant advanced deep into Virginia and met Lee's Confederate Army in the three-day Battle of the Wilderness. Losses on both sides were heavy, but unlike other Union commanders, Grant refused to retreat. Instead, he attempted to outflank Lee, stretching the Confederate lines and pounding away with artillery and infantry attacks. "I propose to fight it out along this line if it takes all summer," the Union commander said at Spotsylvania, during five days of bloody trench warfare that characterized fighting on the eastern front for almost a year.

In the West, Union forces gained control of Tennessee in the fall of 1863 with victories at Chattanooga and nearby Lookout Mountain, opening the way for General William T. Sherman to invade Georgia. Sherman outmaneuvered several smaller Confederate armies, occupied the state capital of Atlanta, then marched to the Atlantic coast, systematically destroying railroads, factories, warehouses, and other facilities in his path. His men, cut off from their normal supply lines, ravaged the countryside for food. From the coast, Sherman marched northward; by February 1865, he had taken Charleston, South Carolina, where the first shots of the Civil War had been fired. Sherman, more than any other Union general, understood that destroying the will and morale of the South was as important as defeating its armies.

Grant, meanwhile, lay siege to Petersburg, Virginia, for nine months, before Lee, in March 1865, knew that he had to abandon both Petersburg and the Confederate capital of Richmond in an attempt to retreat south. But it was too late. On April 9, 1865, surrounded by huge Union armies, Lee surrendered to Grant at Appomattox Courthouse. Although scattered fighting continued elsewhere for several months, the Civil War was over.

The terms of surrender at Appomattox were magnanimous, and on his return from his meeting with Lee, Grant quieted the noisy demonstrations of his soldiers by reminding them: "The rebels are our countrymen again." The war for Southern independence had become the "lost cause," whose hero, Robert E. Lee, had won wide admiration through the brilliance of his leadership and his greatness in defeat.

WITH MALICE TOWARD NONE

For the North, the war produced a still greater hero in Abraham Lincoln — a man eager, above all else, to weld the Union together again, not by force and repression but by warmth and generosity. In 1864 he had been elected for a second term as president, defeating his Democratic opponent, George McClellan, the general he had dismissed after Antietam. Lincoln's second inaugural address closed with these words:

With malice toward none; with charity for all; with firmness in the right, as God gives us to see the right, let us strive on to finish the work we are in; to bind up the nation's wounds; to care for him who shall have borne the battle, and for his widow, and his orphan — to do all which may achieve and cherish a just, and a lasting peace, among ourselves, and with all nations.

Three weeks later, two days after Lee's surrender, Lincoln delivered his last public address, in which he unfolded a generous reconstruction policy. On April 14, 1865, the president held what was to be his last Cabinet meeting. That evening — with his wife and a young couple who were his guests — he attended a performance at Ford's Theater. There, as he sat in the presidential box, he was assassinated by John Wilkes Booth, a Virginia actor embittered by the South's defeat. Booth was killed in a shootout some days later in a barn in the Virginia countryside. His accomplices were captured and later executed.

Lincoln died in a downstairs bedroom of a house across the street from Ford's Theater on the morning of April 15. Poet James Russell Lowell wrote:

Never before that startled April morning did such multitudes of men shed tears for the death of one they had never seen, as if with him a friendly presence had been taken from their lives, leaving them colder and darker. Never was funeral panegyric so eloquent as the silent look of sympathy which strangers exchanged when they met that day. Their common manhood had lost a kinsman.

The first great task confronting the victorious North — now under the leadership of Lincoln's vice president, Andrew Johnson, a Southerner who remained loyal to the Union — was to determine the status of the states that had seceded. Lincoln had already set the stage. In his view, the people of the Southern states had never legally seceded; they had been misled by some disloyal citizens into a defiance of federal authority. And since the war was the act of individuals, the federal government would have to deal with these individuals and not with the states. Thus, in 1863 Lincoln proclaimed that if in any state 10 percent of the voters of record in 1860 would form a government loyal to the U.S. Constitution and would acknowledge obedience to the laws of the Congress and the proclamations of the president, he would recognize the government so created as the state's legal government.

Congress rejected this plan. Many Republicans feared it would simply entrench former rebels in power; they challenged Lincoln's right to deal with the rebel states without consultation. Some members of Congress advocated severe punishment for all the seceded states; others simply felt the war would have been in vain if the old Southern establishment was restored to power. Yet even before the war was wholly over, new governments had been set up in Virginia, Tennessee, Arkansas, and Louisiana.

To deal with one of its major concerns — the condition of former slaves — Congress established the Freedmen's Bureau in March 1865 to act as guardian over African Americans and guide them toward self-support. And in December of that year, Congress ratified the 13th Amendment to the U.S. Constitution, which abolished slavery.

Throughout the summer of 1865 Johnson proceeded to carry out Lincoln's reconstruction program, with minor modifications. By presidential proclamation he appointed a governor for each of the former Confederate states and freely restored political rights to many Southerners through use of presidential pardons.

In due time conventions were held in each of the former Confederate states to repeal the ordinances of secession, repudiate the war debt, and draft new state constitutions. Eventually a native Unionist became governor in each state with authority to convoke a convention of loyal voters. Johnson called upon each convention to invalidate the secession, abolish slavery, repudiate all debts that went to aid the Confederacy, and ratify the 13th Amendment. By the end of 1865, this process was completed, with a few exceptions.

RADICAL RECONSTRUCTION

Both Lincoln and Johnson had foreseen that the Congress would have the right to deny Southern legislators seats in the U.S. Senate or House of Representatives, under the clause of the Constitution that says, "Each house shall be the judge of the ... qualifications of its own members." This came to pass when, under the leadership of Thaddeus Stevens, those congressmen called "Radical Republicans," who were wary of a quick and easy "reconstruction," refused to seat newly elected Southern senators and representatives. Within the next few months, Congress proceeded to work out a plan for the reconstruction of the South quite different from the one Lincoln had started and Johnson had continued.

Wide public support gradually developed for those members of Congress who believed that African Americans should be given full citizenship. By July 1866, Congress had passed a civil rights bill and set up a new Freedmen's Bureau — both designed to prevent racial discrimination by Southern legislatures. Following this, the Congress passed a 14th Amendment to the Constitution, stating that "all persons born or naturalized in the United States, and subject to the jurisdiction thereof, are citizens of the United States and of the State wherein they reside."

This repudiated the Dred Scott ruling, which had denied slaves their right of citizenship.

All the Southern state legislatures, with the exception of Tennessee, refused to ratify the amendment, some voting against it unanimously. In addition, Southern state legislatures passed "codes" to regulate the African-American freedmen. The codes differed from state to state, but some provisions were common. African Americans were required to enter into annual labor contracts, with penalties imposed in case of violation; dependent children were subject to compulsory apprenticeship and corporal punishments by masters; vagrants could be sold into private service if they could not pay severe fines.

Many Northerners interpreted the Southern response as an attempt to reestablish slavery and repudiate the hard-won Union victory in the Civil War. It did not help that Johnson, although a Unionist, was a Southern Democrat with an addiction to intemperate rhetoric and an aversion to political compromise. Republicans swept the congressional elections of 1866. Firmly in power, the Radicals imposed their own vision of Reconstruction.

In the Reconstruction Act of March 1867, Congress, ignoring the governments that had been established in the Southern states, divided the South into five military districts, each administered by a Union general. Escape from permanent military government was open to those states that established civil governments, ratified the 14th Amendment, and adopted African-American suffrage. Supporters of the Confederacy who had not taken oaths of loyalty to the United States generally could not vote. The 14th Amendment was ratified in 1868. The 15th Amendment, passed by Congress the following year and ratified in 1870 by state legislatures, provided that "The right of citizens of the United States to vote shall not be denied or abridged by the United States or any state on account of race, color, or previous condition of servitude."

The Radical Republicans in Congress were infuriated by President Johnson's vetoes (even though they were overridden) of legislation protecting newly freed African Americans and punishing former Confederate leaders by depriving them of the right to hold office. Congressional antipathy to Johnson was so great that, for the first time in American history, impeachment proceedings were instituted to remove the president from office.

Johnson's main offense was his opposition to punitive congressional policies and the violent language he used in criticizing them. The most serious legal charge his enemies could level against him was that, despite the Tenure of Office Act (which required Senate approval for the removal of any officeholder the Senate had previously confirmed), he had removed from his Cabinet the secretary of war, a staunch supporter of the Congress. When the impeachment trial was held in the Senate, it was proved that Johnson was technically within his rights in removing the Cabinet member. Even more important, it was pointed out that a dangerous precedent would be set if the Congress were to remove a president because he disagreed with the majority of its members. The final vote was one short of the two-thirds required for conviction.

Johnson continued in office until his term expired in 1869, but Congress had established an ascendancy that would endure for the rest of the century. The Republican victor in the presidential election of 1868, former Union general Ulysses S. Grant, would enforce the reconstruction policies the Radicals had initiated.

By June 1868, Congress had re-admitted the majority of the former Confederate states back into the Union. In many of these reconstructed states, the majority of the governors, representatives, and senators were Northern men — so-called carpetbaggers — who had gone South after the war to make their political fortunes, often in alliance with newly freed African Americans. In the legislatures of Louisiana and South Carolina, African Americans actually gained a majority of the seats.

Many Southern whites, their political and social dominance threatened, turned to illegal means to prevent African Americans from gaining equality. Violence against African Americans by such extra-legal organizations as the Ku Klux Klan became more and more frequent. Increasing disorder led to the passage of Enforcement Acts in 1870 and 1871, severely punishing those who attempted to deprive the African-American freedmen of their civil rights.

THE END OF RECONSTRUCTION

As time passed, it became more and more obvious that the problems of the South were not being solved by harsh laws and continuing rancor against former Confederates. Moreover, some Southern Radical state governments with prominent African-American officials appeared corrupt and inefficient. The nation was quickly tiring of the attempt to impose racial democracy and liberal values on the South with Union bayonets. In May 1872, Congress passed a general Amnesty Act, restoring full political rights to all but about 500 former rebels.

Gradually Southern states began electing members of the Democratic Party into office, ousting carpetbagger governments and intimidating African Americans from voting or attempting to hold public office. By 1876 the Republicans remained in power in only three Southern states. As part of the bargaining that resolved the disputed presidential elections that year in favor of Rutherford B. Hayes, the Republicans promised to withdraw federal troops that had propped up the remaining Republican governments. In 1877

Hayes kept his promise, tacitly abandoning federal responsibility for enforcing blacks' civil rights.

The South was still a region devastated by war, burdened by debt caused by misgovernment, and demoralized by a decade of racial warfare. Unfortunately, the pendulum of national racial policy swung from one extreme to the other. A federal government that had supported harsh penalties against Southern white leaders now tolerated new and humiliating kinds of discrimination against African Americans. The last quarter of the 19th century saw a profusion of "Jim Crow" laws in Southern states that segregated public schools, forbade or limited African-American access to many public facilities such as parks, restaurants, and hotels, and denied most blacks the right to vote by imposing poll taxes and arbitrary literacy tests. "Jim Crow" is a term derived from a song in an 1828 minstrel show where a white man first performed in "blackface."

Historians have tended to judge Reconstruction harshly, as a murky period of political conflict, corruption, and regression that failed to achieve its original high-minded goals and collapsed into a sinkhole of virulent racism. Slaves were granted freedom, but the North completely failed to address their economic needs. The Freedmen's Bureau was unable to provide former slaves with political and economic opportunity. Union military occupiers often could not even protect them from violence and intimidation. Indeed, federal army officers and agents of the Freedmen's Bureau were often racists themselves. Without economic resources of their own, many Southern African Americans were forced to become tenant farmers on land owned by their former masters, caught in a cycle of poverty that would continue well into the 20th century.

Reconstruction-era governments did make genuine gains in rebuilding Southern states devastated by the war, and in expanding public services, notably in establishing tax-supported, free public schools for African Americans and whites. However, recalcitrant Southerners seized upon instances of corruption (hardly unique to the South in this era) and exploited them to bring down radical regimes. The failure of Reconstruction meant that the struggle of African Americans for equality and freedom was deferred until the 20th century — when it would become a national, not just a Southern issue. >

THE CIVIL WAR AND NEW PATTERNS OF AMERICAN POLITICS

The controversies of the 1850s had destroyed the Whig Party, created the Republican Party, and divided the Democratic Party along regional lines. The Civil War demonstrated that the Whigs were gone beyond recall and the Republicans on the scene to stay. It also laid the basis for a reunited Democratic Party.

The Republicans could seamlessly replace the Whigs throughout the North and West because they were far more than a free-soil/antislavery force. Most of their leaders had started as Whigs and continued the Whig interest in federally assisted national development. The need to manage a war did not deter them from also enacting a protective tariff (1861) to foster American manufacturing, the Homestead Act (1862) to encourage Western settlement, the Morrill Act (1862) to establish "land grant" agricultural and technical colleges, and a series of Pacific Railway Acts (1862-64) to underwrite a transcontinental railway line. These measures rallied support throughout the Union from groups to whom slavery was a secondary issue and ensured the party's continuance as the latest manifestation of a political creed that had been advanced by Alexander Hamilton and Henry Clay.

The war also laid the basis for Democratic reunification because Northern opposition to it centered in the Democratic Party. As might be expected from the party of "popular sovereignty," some Democrats believed that full-scale war to reinstate the Union was unjustified. This group came to be known as the Peace Democrats. Their more extreme elements were called "Copperheads."

Moreover, few Democrats, whether of the "war" or "peace" faction, believed the emancipation of the slaves was worth Northern blood. Opposition to emancipation had long been party policy. In 1862, for example, virtually every Democrat in Congress voted against eliminating slavery in the District of Columbia and prohibiting it in the territories.

Much of this opposition came from the working poor, particularly Irish and German Catholic immigrants, who feared a massive migration of newly freed African Americans to the North. They also resented the establishment of a military draft (March 1863) that disproportionately affected them. Race riots erupted in several Northern cities. The worst of these occurred in New York, July 13-16, 1863, precipitated by Democratic Governor Horatio Seymour's condemnation of military conscription. Federal troops, who just days earlier had been engaged at Gettysburg, were sent to restore order.

The Republicans prosecuted the war with little regard for civil liberties. In September 1862, Lincoln suspended the writ of habeas corpus and imposed martial law on those who interfered with recruitment or gave aid and comfort to the rebels. This breech of civil law, although constitutionally justified during times of crisis, gave the Democrats another opportunity to criticize Lincoln. Secretary of War Edwin Stanton enforced martial law vigorously, and many thousands — most of them Southern sympathizers or Democrats — were arrested.

Despite the Union victories at Vicksburg and Gettysburg in 1863, Democratic "peace" candidates continued to play on the nation's misfortunes and racial sensitivities. Indeed, the mood of the North was such that Lincoln was convinced he would lose his re-election bid in November 1864. Largely for that reason, the Republican Party renamed itself the Union Party and drafted the Tennessee Democrat Andrew Johnson to be Lincoln's running mate. Sherman's victories in the South sealed the election for them.

Lincoln's assassination, the rise of Radical Republicanism, and Johnson's blundering leadership all played into a postwar pattern of politics in which the Republican Party suffered from overreaching in its efforts to remake the South, while the Democrats, through their criticism of Reconstruction, allied themselves with the neo-Confederate Southern white majority. Ulysses S. Grant's status as a national hero carried the Republicans through two presidential elections, but as the South emerged from Reconstruction, it became apparent that the country was nearly evenly divided between the two parties.

The Republicans would be dominant in the industrial Northeast until the 1930s and strong in most of the rest of the country outside the South. However, their appeal as the party of strong government and national development increasingly would be perceived as one of allegiance to big business and finance.

When President Hayes ended Reconstruction, he hoped it would be possible to build the Republican Party in the South, using the old Whigs as a base and the appeal of regional development as a primary issue. By then, however, Republicanism as the South's white majority perceived it was identified with a hated African-American supremacy. For the next three-quarters of a century, the South would be solidly Democratic. For much of that time, the national Democratic Party would pay solemn deference to states' rights while ignoring civil rights. The group that would suffer the most as a legacy of Reconstruction was the African Americans. ◆

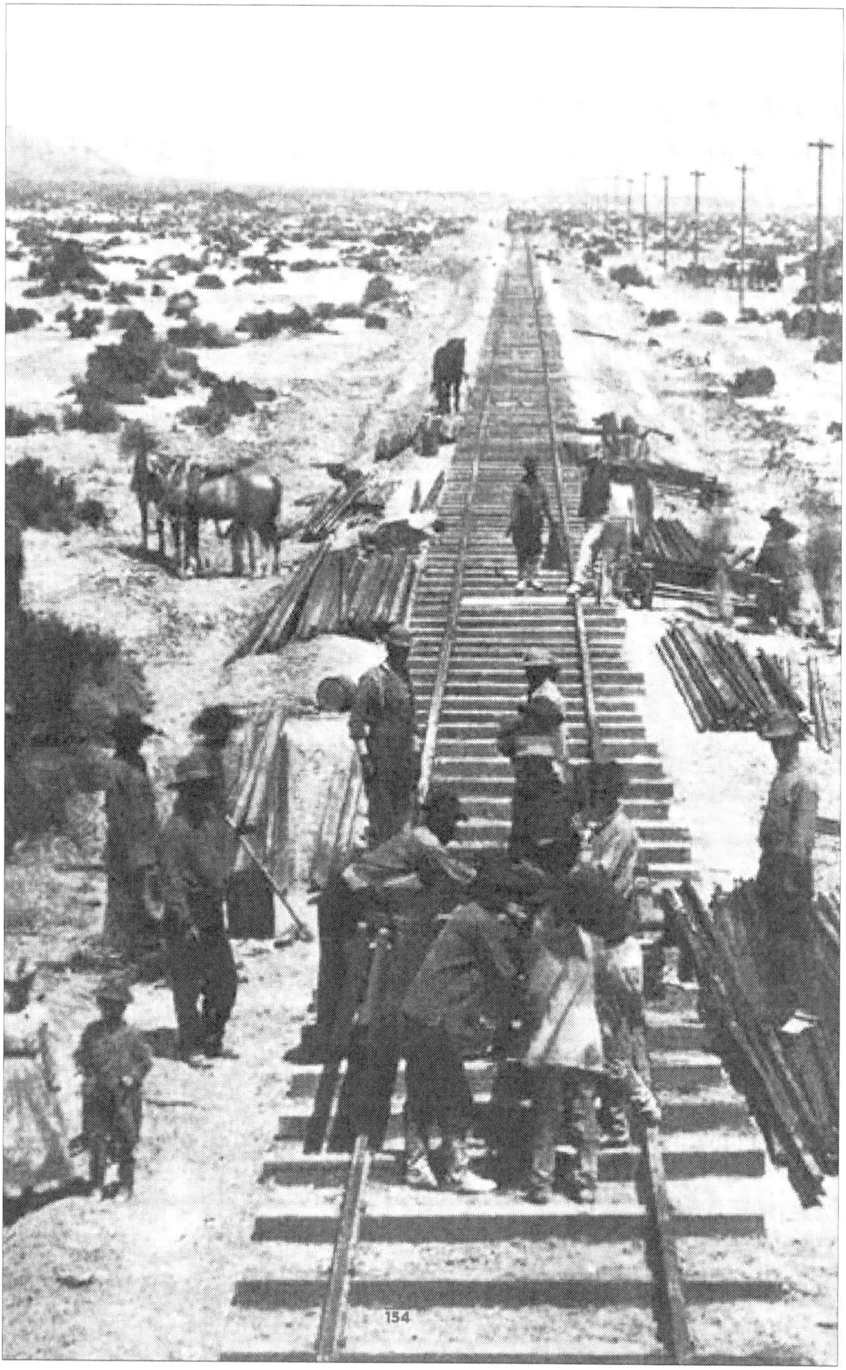

CHAPTER 8

GROWTH AND TRANSFORMATION

Building the transcontinental railroad, 1868.

CHAPTER 8: GROWTH AND TRANSFORMATION

"Upon the sacredness of property, civilization itself depends."

Industrialist and philanthropist Andrew Carnegie, 1889

Between two great wars — the Civil War and the First World War — the United States of America came of age. In a period of less than 50 years it was transformed from a rural republic to an urban nation. The frontier vanished. Great factories and steel mills, transcontinental railroad lines, flourishing cities, and vast agricultural holdings marked the land. With this economic growth and affluence came corresponding problems. Nationwide, a few businesses came to dominate whole industries, either independently or in combination with others. Working conditions were often poor. Cities grew so quickly they could not properly house or govern their growing populations.

TECHNOLOGY AND CHANGE

"The Civil War," says one writer, "cut a wide gash through the history of the country; it dramatized in a stroke the changes that had begun to take place during the preceding 20 or 30 years. ..." War needs had enormously stimulated manufacturing, speeding an economic process based on the exploitation of iron, steam, and electric power, as well as the forward march of science and invention. In the years before 1860, 36,000 patents were granted; in the next 30 years, 440,000 patents were issued, and in the first quarter of the 20th century, the number reached nearly a million.

As early as 1844, Samuel F.B. Morse had perfected electrical telegraphy; soon afterward distant parts of the continent were linked by a network of poles and wires. In 1876 Alexander Graham Bell exhibited a telephone instrument; within half a century, 16 million telephones would quicken the social and economic life of the nation. The growth of business was hastened by the invention of the typewriter in 1867, the adding machine in 1888, and the cash register in 1897. The linotype composing machine, invented in 1886, and rotary press and paper-folding machinery made it possible to print 240,000 eight-page newspapers in an hour. Thomas Edison's incandescent lamp eventually lit millions of homes. The talking machine, or phonograph, was perfected by Edison, who, in conjunction with George Eastman, also helped develop the motion picture. These and many other applications of science and ingenuity resulted in a new level of productivity in almost every field.

Concurrently, the nation's basic industry — iron and steel — forged ahead, protected by a high tariff. The iron industry moved westward as geologists discovered new ore deposits, notably the great Mesabi range at the head of Lake Superior, which became one of the largest producers in the world. Easy and cheap to mine, remarkably free of chemical impurities, Mesabi ore could be processed into steel of superior quality at about one-tenth the previously prevailing cost.

CARNEGIE AND THE ERA OF STEEL

Andrew Carnegie was largely responsible for the great advances in steel production. Carnegie, who came to America from Scotland as a child of 12, progressed from bobbin boy in a cotton factory to a job in a telegraph office, then to one on the Pennsylvania Railroad. Before he was 30 years old he had made shrewd and farsighted investments, which by 1865 were concentrated in iron. Within a few years, he had organized or had stock in companies making iron bridges, rails, and locomotives. Ten years later, he built the nation's largest steel mill on the Monongahela River in Pennsylvania. He acquired control not only of new mills, but also of coke and coal properties, iron ore from Lake Superior, a fleet of steamers on the Great Lakes, a port town on Lake Erie, and a connecting railroad. His business, allied with a dozen others, commanded favorable terms from railroads and shipping lines. Nothing comparable in industrial growth had ever been seen in America before.

Though Carnegie long dominated the industry, he never achieved a complete monopoly over the natural resources, transportation, and industrial plants involved in the making of steel. In the 1890s, new companies challenged his preeminence. He would be persuaded to merge his holdings into a new corporation that would embrace most of the important iron and steel properties in the nation.

CORPORATIONS AND CITIES

The United States Steel Corporation, which resulted from this merger in 1901, illustrated a process under way for 30 years: the combination of independent industrial enterprises into federated or centralized companies. Started during the Civil War, the trend gathered momentum after the 1870s, as businessmen began to fear that overproduction would lead to declining prices and falling profits. They realized that if they could control both production and markets, they could bring competing firms into a single organization. The "corporation" and the "trust" were developed to achieve these ends.

Corporations, making available a deep reservoir of capital and giving business enterprises permanent life and continuity of control, attracted investors both by their anticipated profits and by their limited liability in case of business failure. The trusts were in effect combinations of corporations whereby the stockholders of each placed stocks in the hands of trustees. (The "trust" as a method of corporate consolidation soon gave way to the holding company, but the term stuck.) Trusts made possible large-scale combinations, centralized control and administration, and the pooling of patents. Their larger capital resources provided power to expand, to compete with foreign business organizations, and to drive hard bargains with labor, which was beginning to organize effectively. They could also exact favorable terms from railroads and exercise influence in politics.

The Standard Oil Company, founded by John D. Rockefeller, was one of the earliest and strongest corporations, and was followed rapidly by other combinations — in cottonseed oil, lead, sugar, tobacco, and rubber. Soon aggressive individual businessmen began to mark out industrial domains for themselves. Four great meat packers, chief among them Philip Armour and Gustavus Swift, established a beef trust. Cyrus McCormick achieved preeminence in the reaper business. A 1904 survey showed that more than 5,000 previously independent concerns had been consolidated into some 300 industrial trusts.

The trend toward amalgamation extended to other fields, particularly transportation and communications. Western Union, dominant in telegraphy, was followed by the Bell Telephone System and eventually by the American Telephone and Telegraph Company. In the 1860s, Cornelius Vanderbilt had consolidated 13 separate railroads into a single 800-kilometer line connecting New York City and Buffalo. During the next decade he acquired lines to Chicago, Illinois, and Detroit, Michigan, establishing the New York Central Railroad. Soon the major railroads of the nation were organized into trunk lines and systems directed by a handful of men.

In this new industrial order, the city was the nerve center, bringing to a focus all the nation's dynamic economic forces: vast accumulations of capital, business, and financial institutions, spreading railroad yards, smoky factories, armies of manual and clerical workers. Villages, attracting people from the countryside and from lands across the sea, grew into towns and towns into cities almost overnight. In 1830 only one of every 15 Americans lived in communities of 8,000 or more; in 1860 the ratio was nearly one in every six; and in 1890 three in every 10. No single city had as many as a million inhabitants in 1860; but 30 years later New York had a million and a half; Chicago, Illinois, and Philadelphia, Pennsylvania, each had over a million. In these three decades, Philadelphia and Baltimore, Maryland, doubled in population; Kansas City, Missouri, and Detroit, Michigan, grew fourfold; Cleveland, Ohio, sixfold; Chicago, tenfold. Minneapolis, Minnesota, and Omaha, Nebraska, and many communities like them — hamlets when the Civil War began — increased 50 times or more in population.

RAILROADS, REGULATIONS, AND THE TARIFF

Railroads were especially important to the expanding nation, and their practices were often criticized. Rail lines extended cheaper freight rates to large shippers by rebating a portion of the charge, thus disadvantaging small shippers. Freight rates also frequently were not proportionate to distance traveled; competition usually held down charges between cities with several rail connections. Rates tended to be high between points served by only one line. Thus it cost less to ship goods 1,280 kilometers from Chicago to New York than to places a few hundred kilometers from Chicago. Moreover, to avoid competition rival companies sometimes divided ("pooled") the freight business according to a prearranged scheme that placed the total earnings in a common fund for distribution.

Popular resentment at these practices stimulated state efforts at regulation, but the problem was national in character. Shippers demanded congressional action. In 1887 President Grover Cleveland signed the Interstate Commerce Act, which forbade excessive charges, pools, rebates, and rate discrimination. It created an Interstate Commerce Commission (ICC) to oversee the act, but gave it little enforcement power. In the first decades of its existence, virtually all the ICC's efforts at regulation and rate reductions failed to pass judicial review.

President Cleveland also opposed the protective tariff on foreign goods, which had come to be accepted as permanent national policy under the Republican presidents who dominated the politics of the era. Cleveland, a conservative Democrat, regarded tariff protection as an unwarranted subsidy to big business, giving the trusts pricing power to the disadvantage of ordinary Americans. Reflecting the interests of their Southern base, the Democrats had reverted to their pre Civil War opposition to protection and advocacy of a "tariff for revenue only."

Cleveland, narrowly elected in 1884, was unsuccessful in achieving tariff reform during his first term.

He made the issue the keynote of his campaign for reelection, but Republican candidate Benjamin Harrison, a defender of protectionism, won in a close race. In 1890, the Harrison administration, fulfilling its campaign promises, achieved passage of the McKinley tariff, which increased the already high rates. Blamed for high retail prices, the McKinley duties triggered widespread dissatisfaction, led to Republican losses in the 1890 elections, and paved the way for Cleveland's return to the presidency in the 1892 election.

During this period, public antipathy toward the trusts increased. The nation's gigantic corporations were subjected to bitter attack through the 1880s by reformers such as Henry George and Edward Bellamy. The Sherman Antitrust Act, passed in 1890, forbade all combinations in restraint of interstate trade and provided several methods of enforcement with severe penalties. Couched in vague generalities, the law accomplished little immediately after its passage. But a decade later, President Theodore Roosevelt would use it vigorously.

REVOLUTION IN AGRICULTURE

Despite the great gains in industry, agriculture remained the nation's basic occupation. The revolution in agriculture — paralleling that in manufacturing after the Civil War — involved a shift from hand labor to machine farming, and from subsistence to commercial agriculture. Between 1860 and 1910, the number of farms in the United States tripled, increasing from two million to six million, while the area farmed more than doubled from 160 million to 352 million hectares.

Between 1860 and 1890, the production of such basic commodities as wheat, corn, and cotton outstripped all previous figures in the United States. In the same period, the nation's population more than doubled, with the largest growth in the cities. But the American farmer grew enough grain and cotton, raised enough beef and pork, and clipped enough wool not only to supply American workers and their families but also to create ever-increasing surpluses.

Several factors accounted for this extraordinary achievement. One was the expansion into the West. Another was a technological revolution. The farmer of 1800, using a hand sickle, could hope to cut a fifth of a hectare of wheat a day. With the cradle, 30 years later, he might cut four-fifths. In 1840 Cyrus McCormick performed a miracle by cutting from two to two-and-a-half hectares a day with the reaper, a machine he had been developing for nearly 10 years. He headed west to the young prairie town of Chicago, where he set up a factory — and by 1860 sold a quarter of a million reapers.

Other farm machines were developed in rapid succession: the automatic wire binder, the threshing

(Continued on page 177.)

The silhouette of one of the United States' most revered Founding Fathers, Thomas Jefferson, stands in the shrine dedicated to his memory. "I have sworn upon the altar of God, eternal hostility against every form of tyranny over the mind of man."

MONUMENTS AND
MEMORIALS
A PICTURE PROFILE

The monuments of American history span a continent in distance and centuries in time. They range from a massive serpent-shaped mound created by a long-gone Native-American culture to memorials in contemporary Washington, D.C., and New York City.

The snow-covered Old Granary cemetery in Boston, Massachusetts, is burial ground for, among other leading American patriots, victims of the Boston Massacre, three signers of the Declaration of Independence, and six governors of Massachusetts. Originally founded by religious dissidents from England known as Puritans, Massachusetts was a leader in the struggle for independence against England. It was the setting for the Boston Tea Party and the first battles of the American Revolution — in Lexington and Concord.

163

The historic room in Independence Hall, Philadelphia, where delegates drafted the Constitution of the United States in the summer of 1787. The Constitution is the supreme law of the land. It prescribes the form and authority of the federal government, and ensures the fundamental freedoms and rights of the citizens of the country through the Bill of Rights.

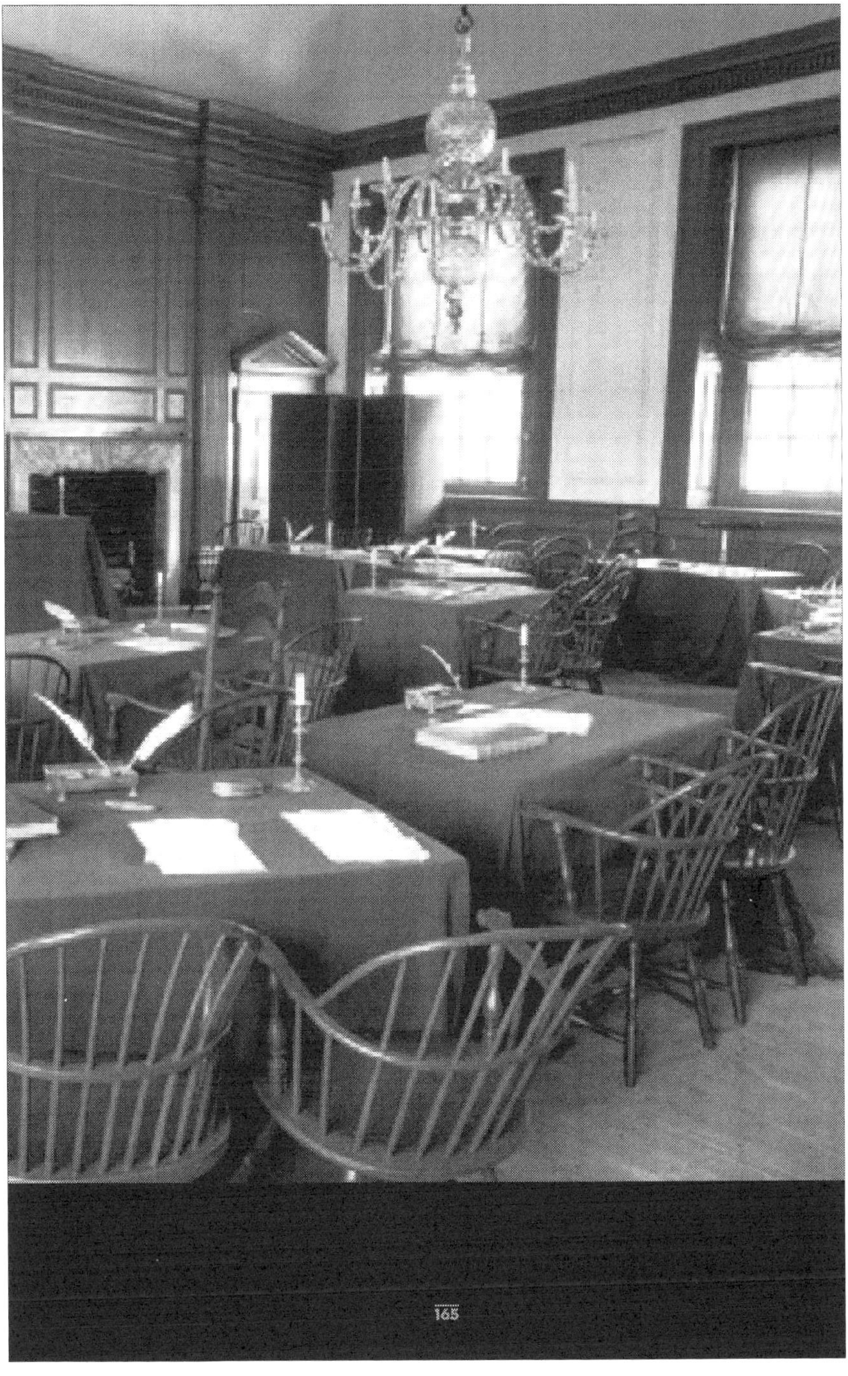

Statues guard the majestic façade of the U.S. Supreme Court, the highest court in the land. The words engraved on the lintel over the Greek pillars embody one of America's founding principles: "Equal Justice Under Law."

The Statue of Liberty, one of the United States' most beloved monuments, stands 151 feet high at the entrance to New York harbor. A gift of friendship from the people of France to the United States, it was intended to be an impressive symbol of human liberty. It was certainly that for the millions of immigrants who came to the United States in the 19th and early 20th centuries, seeking freedom and a better life.

Aerial view of the Great Serpent Mound in Adams County, Ohio. Carbon tests of the effigy revealed that the creators of this 1,330-foot monument were members of the Native-American Fort Ancient Culture (A.D. 1000-1550).

The Liberty Bell in Philadelphia, Pennsylvania, an enduring symbol of American freedom. First rung on July 8, 1776, to celebrate the adoption of the Declaration of Independence, it cracked in 1836 during the funeral of John Marshall, Chief Justice of the U.S. Supreme Court.

Two monuments to the central role Spain played in the exploration of what is now the United States. Top, the Castillo de San Marcos, built 1672-1695 to guard St. Augustine, Florida, the first permanent European settlement in the continental United States. Above, fountain and mission remains of the San Juan Capistrano Mission, California, one of nine missions founded by Spanish Franciscan missionaries led by Fray Junípero Serra in the 1770s. Serra led the Spanish colonization of what is today the state of California.

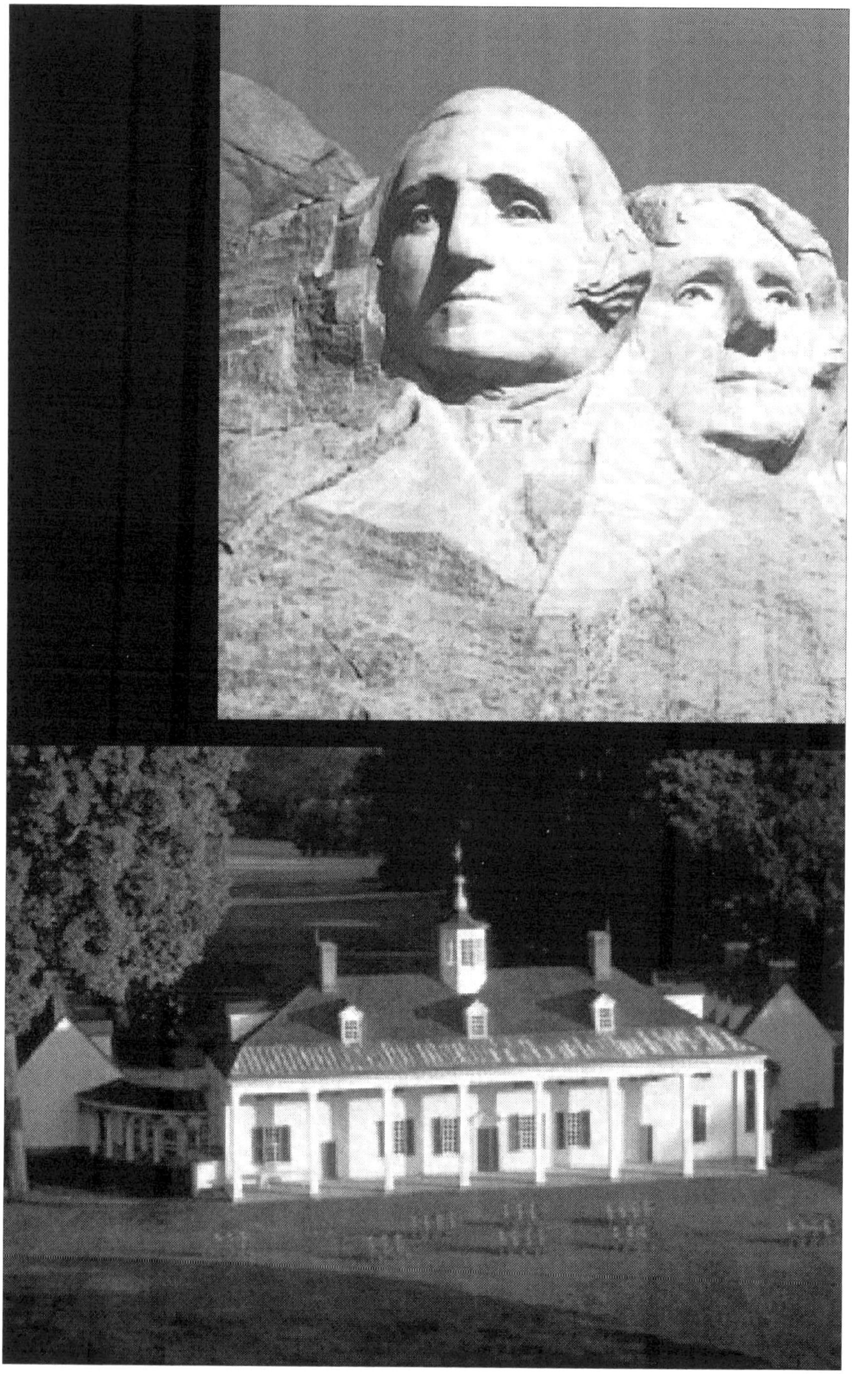

The faces of four of the most admired American presidents were carved by Gutzon Borglum into the southeast face of Mount Rushmore in South Dakota, beginning in 1927. From left to right, they are: George Washington, commander of the Revolutionary Army and first president of the young nation; Thomas Jefferson, author of the Declaration of Independence; Theodore Roosevelt, who led the country toward progressive reforms and a strong foreign policy; and Abraham Lincoln, who led the country through the Civil War and freed the slaves.

George Washington's beloved home, Mount Vernon, by the Potomac River in Virginia, where he died on December 14, 1799, and is buried along with his wife Martha. Among other treasured items owned by the first president on display there, visitors can see one of the keys to the Bastille, a gift to Washington from the Marquis de Lafayette.

Six-year-old Mary Zheng straightens a flower placed at the Vietnam Veterans Memorial in Washington, D.C., April 30, 2000. The names of more than 58,000 servicemen who died in the war or remain missing are etched on the "wall" part of the memorial, pictured here. This portion of the monument was designed by Maya Lin, then a student at Yale University.

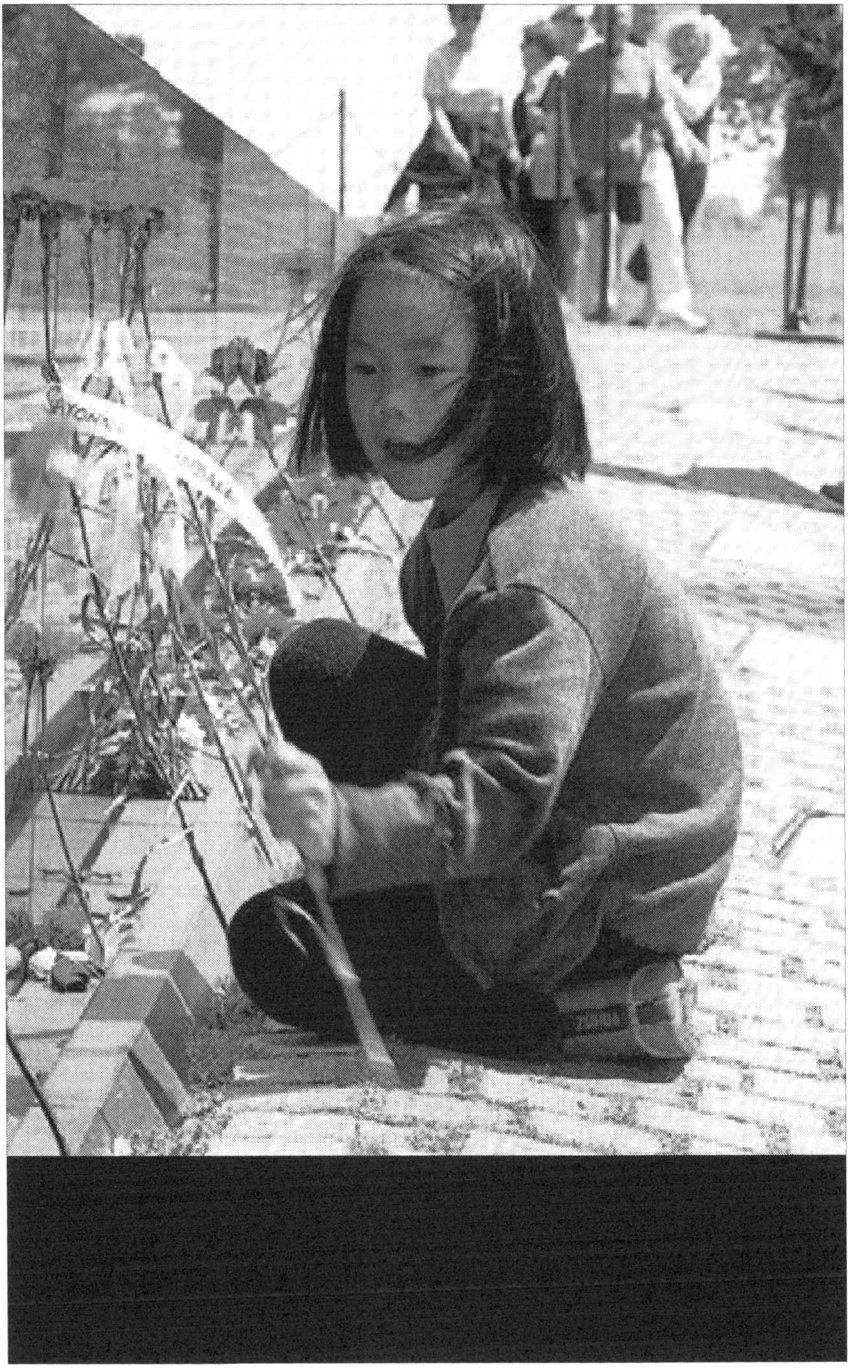

An autumnal view of Arlington Cemetery, Virginia, America's largest and best-known national burial grounds. More than 260,000 people are buried at Arlington Cemetery, including veterans from all the nation's wars.

A mother and daughter viewing documents in the Exhibition Hall of the National Archives. The U.S. Constitution, the Declaration of Independence, and the Bill of Rights are on display in this Washington, D.C., building.

Fireworks celebrating the arrival of the Millennium illuminate two major monuments in Washington, D.C., the Lincoln Memorial on the left and the obelisk-shaped Washington Monument, center. The Lincoln Memorial's north and south side chambers contain carved inscriptions of his Second Inaugural Address and his Gettysburg Address. The tallest structure in the nation's capital, the Washington Monument was dedicated on February 21, 1885.

Top, the World War II Memorial, opened in 2004, is the most recent addition to the many national monuments in Washington, D.C. It honors the 16 million who served in the armed forces of the United States, the more than 400,000 who died, and all who supported the war effort from home. Above, the planned design for the World Trade Center Memorial in New York City is depicted in this photograph of a model unveiled in late 2004. "Reflecting Absence" will preserve not only the memory of those who died in the terrorist attack of September 11, 2001, but the visible remnants of the buildings destroyed that morning, too.

machine, and the reaper-thresher or combine. Mechanical planters, cutters, huskers, and shellers appeared, as did cream separators, manure spreaders, potato planters, hay driers, poultry incubators, and a hundred other inventions.

Scarcely less important than machinery in the agricultural revolution was science. In 1862 the Morrill Land Grant College Act allotted public land to each state for the establishment of agricultural and industrial colleges. These were to serve both as educational institutions and as centers for research in scientific farming. Congress subsequently appropriated funds for the creation of agricultural experiment stations throughout the country and granted funds directly to the Department of Agriculture for research purposes. By the beginning of the new century, scientists throughout the United States were at work on a wide variety of agricultural projects.

One of these scientists, Mark Carleton, traveled for the Department of Agriculture to Russia. There he found and exported to his homeland the rust- and drought-resistant winter wheat that now accounts for more than half the U.S. wheat crop. Another scientist, Marion Dorset, conquered the dreaded hog cholera, while still another, George Mohler, helped prevent hoof-and-mouth disease. From North Africa, one researcher brought back Kaffir corn; from Turkestan, another imported the yellow-flowering alfalfa. Luther Burbank in California produced scores of new fruits and vegetables; in Wisconsin, Stephen Babcock devised a test for determining the butterfat content of milk; at Tuskegee Institute in Alabama, the African-American scientist George Washington Carver found hundreds of new uses for the peanut, sweet potato, and soybean.

In varying degrees, the explosion in agricultural science and technology affected farmers all over the world, raising yields, squeezing out small producers, and driving migration to industrial cities. Railroads and steamships, moreover, began to pull regional markets into one large world market with prices instantly communicated by trans-Atlantic cable as well as ground wires. Good news for urban consumers, falling agricultural prices threatened the livelihood of many American farmers and touched off a wave of agrarian discontent.

THE DIVIDED SOUTH

After Reconstruction, Southern leaders pushed hard to attract industry. States offered large inducements and cheap labor to investors to develop the steel, lumber, tobacco, and textile industries. Yet in 1900 the region's percentage of the nation's industrial base remained about what it had been in 1860. Moreover, the price of this drive for industrialization was high: Disease and child labor proliferated in Southern mill towns. Thirty years after the Civil War, the South was still poor, overwhelmingly agrarian, and economically dependent. Moreover, its race relations reflected not just the legacy of slavery, but what was emerging as the central theme of its history — a determination to enforce white supremacy at any cost.

Intransigent white Southerners found ways to assert state control to maintain white dominance. Several Supreme Court decisions also bolstered their efforts by upholding traditional Southern views of the appropriate balance between national and state power.

In 1873 the Supreme Court found that the 14th Amendment (citizenship rights not to be abridged) conferred no new privileges or immunities to protect African Americans from state power. In 1883, furthermore, it ruled that the 14th Amendment did not prevent individuals, as opposed to states, from practicing discrimination. And in *Plessy v. Ferguson* (1896), the Court found that "separate but equal" public accommodations for African Americans, such as trains and restaurants, did not violate their rights. Soon the principle of segregation by race extended into every area of Southern life, from railroads to restaurants, hotels, hospitals, and schools. Moreover, any area of life that was not segregated by law was segregated by custom and practice. Further curtailment of the right to vote followed. Periodic lynchings by mobs underscored the region's determination to subjugate its African-American population.

Faced with pervasive discrimination, many African Americans followed Booker T. Washington, who counseled them to focus on modest economic goals and to accept temporary social discrimination. Others, led by the African-American intellectual W.E.B. DuBois, wanted to challenge segregation through political action. But with both major parties uninterested in the issue and scientific theory of the time generally accepting black inferiority, calls for racial justice attracted little support.

THE LAST FRONTIER

In 1865 the frontier line generally followed the western limits of the states bordering the Mississippi River, but bulged outward beyond the eastern sections of Texas, Kansas, and Nebraska. Then, running north and south for nearly 1,600 kilometers, loomed huge mountain ranges, many rich in silver, gold, and other metals. To their west, plains and deserts stretched to the wooded coastal ranges and the Pacific Ocean. Apart from the settled districts in California and scattered outposts, the vast inland region was populated by Native Americans: among them the Great Plains tribes — Sioux and Blackfoot, Pawnee and Cheyenne — and the Indian cultures of the Southwest, including Apache, Navajo, and Hopi.

A mere quarter-century later, virtually all this country had been carved into states and territories.

Miners had ranged over the whole of the mountain country, tunneling into the earth, establishing little communities in Nevada, Montana, and Colorado. Cattle ranchers, taking advantage of the enormous grasslands, had laid claim to the huge expanse stretching from Texas to the upper Missouri River. Sheep herders had found their way to the valleys and mountain slopes. Farmers sank their plows into the plains and closed the gap between the East and West. By 1890 the frontier line had disappeared.

Settlement was spurred by the Homestead Act of 1862, which granted free farms of 64 hectares to citizens who would occupy and improve the land. Unfortunately for the would-be farmers, much of the Great Plains was suited more for cattle ranching than farming, and by 1880 nearly 22,400,000 hectares of "free" land were in the hands of cattlemen or the railroads.

In 1862 Congress also voted a charter to the Union Pacific Railroad, which pushed westward from Council Bluffs, Iowa, using mostly the labor of ex-soldiers and Irish immigrants. At the same time, the Central Pacific Railroad began to build eastward from Sacramento, California, relying heavily on Chinese immigrant labor. The whole country was stirred as the two lines steadily approached each other, finally meeting on May 10, 1869, at Promontory Point in Utah. The months of laborious travel hitherto separating the two oceans was now cut to about six days. The continental rail network grew steadily; by 1884 four great lines linked the central Mississippi Valley area with the Pacific.

The first great rush of population to the Far West was drawn to the mountainous regions, where gold was found in California in 1848, in Colorado and Nevada 10 years later, in Montana and Wyoming in the 1860s, and in the Black Hills of the Dakota country in the 1870s. Miners opened up the country, established communities, and laid the foundations for more permanent settlements. Eventually, however, though a few communities continued to be devoted almost exclusively to mining, the real wealth of Montana, Colorado, Wyoming, Idaho, and California proved to be in the grass and soil. Cattle-raising, long an important industry in Texas, flourished after the Civil War, when enterprising men began to drive their Texas longhorn cattle north across the open public land. Feeding as they went, the cattle arrived at railway shipping points in Kansas, larger and fatter than when they started. The annual cattle drive became a regular event; for hundreds of kilometers, trails were dotted with herds moving northward.

Next, immense cattle ranches appeared in Colorado, Wyoming, Kansas, Nebraska, and the Dakota territory. Western cities flourished as centers for the slaughter of cattle and dressing of meat. The cattle boom peaked in the mid-1880s. By then, not far behind the rancher creaked the covered wagons of the farmers bringing their families, their draft horses, cows, and pigs. Under the Homestead Act they staked their claims and fenced them with a new invention, barbed wire. Ranchers were ousted from lands they had roamed without legal title.

Ranching and the cattle drives gave American mythology its last icon of frontier culture — the cowboy. The reality of cowboy life was one of grueling hardship. As depicted by writers like Zane Grey and movie actors such as John Wayne, the cowboy was a powerful mythological figure, a bold, virtuous man of action. Not until the late 20th century did a reaction set in. Historians and filmmakers alike began to depict "the Wild West" as a sordid place, peopled by characters more apt to reflect the worst, rather than the best, in human nature.

THE PLIGHT OF THE NATIVE AMERICANS

As in the East, expansion into the plains and mountains by miners, ranchers, and settlers led to increasing conflicts with the Native Americans of the West. Many tribes of Native Americans — from the Utes of the Great Basin to the Nez Perces of Idaho — fought the whites at one time or another. But the Sioux of the Northern Plains and the Apache of the Southwest provided the most significant opposition to frontier advance. Led by such resourceful leaders as Red Cloud and Crazy Horse, the Sioux were particularly skilled at high-speed mounted warfare. The Apaches were equally adept and highly elusive, fighting in their environs of desert and canyons.

Conflicts with the Plains Indians worsened after an incident where the Dakota (part of the Sioux nation), declaring war against the U.S. government because of long-standing grievances, killed five white settlers. Rebellions and attacks continued through the Civil War. In 1876 the last serious Sioux war erupted, when the Dakota gold rush penetrated the Black Hills. The Army was supposed to keep miners off Sioux hunting grounds, but did little to protect the Sioux lands. When ordered to take action against bands of Sioux hunting on the range according to their treaty rights, however, it moved quickly and vigorously.

In 1876, after several indecisive encounters, Colonel George Custer, leading a small detachment of cavalry encountered a vastly superior force of Sioux and their allies on the Little Bighorn River. Custer and his men were completely annihilated. Nonetheless the Native-American insurgency was soon suppressed. Later, in 1890, a ghost dance ritual on the Northern Sioux reservation at Wounded Knee, South Dakota, led to an uprising and a last, tragic encounter that ended in the death of nearly 300 Sioux men, women, and children.

Long before this, however, the way of life of the Plains Indians had been destroyed by an expanding white population, the coming of the railroads, and the slaughter of the buffalo, almost exterminated in the decade after 1870 by the settlers' indiscriminate hunting.

The Apache wars in the Southwest dragged on until Geronimo, the last important chief, was captured in 1886.

Government policy ever since the Monroe administration had been to move the Native Americans beyond the reach of the white frontier. But inevitably the reservations had become smaller and more crowded. Some Americans began to protest the government's treatment of Native Americans. Helen Hunt Jackson, for example, an Easterner living in the West, wrote *A Century of Dishonor* (1881), which dramatized their plight and struck a chord in the nation's conscience. Most reformers believed the Native American should be assimilated into the dominant culture. The federal government even set up a school in Carlisle, Pennsylvania, in an attempt to impose white values and beliefs on Native-American youths. (It was at this school that Jim Thorpe, often considered the best athlete the United States has produced, gained fame in the early 20th century.)

In 1887 the Dawes (General Allotment) Act reversed U.S. Native-American policy, permitting the president to divide up tribal land and parcel out 65 hectares of land to each head of a family. Such allotments were to be held in trust by the government for 25 years, after which time the owner won full title and citizenship. Lands not thus distributed, however, were offered for sale to settlers. This policy, however well-intentioned, proved disastrous, since it allowed more plundering of Native-American lands. Moreover, its assault on the communal organization of tribes caused further disruption of traditional culture. In 1934 U.S. policy was reversed yet again by the Indian Reorganization Act, which attempted to protect tribal and communal life on the reservations.

AMBIVALENT EMPIRE

The last decades of the 19th century were a period of imperial expansion for the United States. The American story took a different course from that of its European rivals, however, because of the U.S. history of struggle against European empires and its unique democratic development.

The sources of American expansionism in the late 19th century were varied. Internationally, the period was one of imperialist frenzy, as European powers raced to carve up Africa and competed, along with Japan, for influence and trade in Asia. Many Americans, including influential figures such as Theodore Roosevelt, Henry Cabot Lodge, and Elihu Root, felt that to safeguard its own interests, the United States had to stake out spheres of economic influence as well. That view was seconded by a powerful naval lobby, which called for an expanded fleet and network of overseas ports as essential to the economic and political security of the nation. More generally, the doctrine of "manifest destiny," first used to justify America's continental expansion, was now revived to assert that the United States had a right and duty to extend its influence and civilization in the Western Hemisphere and the Caribbean, as well as across the Pacific.

At the same time, voices of anti-imperialism from diverse coalitions of Northern Democrats and reform-minded Republicans remained loud and constant. As a result, the acquisition of a U.S. empire was piecemeal and ambivalent. Colonial-minded administrations were often more concerned with trade and economic issues than political control.

The United States' first venture beyond its continental borders was the purchase of Alaska — sparsely populated by Inuit and other native peoples — from Russia in 1867. Most Americans were either indifferent to or indignant at this action by Secretary of State William Seward, whose critics called Alaska "Seward's Folly" and "Seward's Icebox." But 30 years later, when gold was discovered on Alaska's Klondike River, thousands of Americans headed north, and many of them settled in Alaska permanently. When Alaska became the 49th state in 1959, it replaced Texas as geographically the largest state in the Union.

The Spanish-American War, fought in 1898, marked a turning point in U.S. history. It left the United States exercising control or influence over islands in the Caribbean Sea and the Pacific.

By the 1890s, Cuba and Puerto Rico were the only remnants of Spain's once vast empire in the New World, and the Philippine Islands comprised the core of Spanish power in the Pacific. The outbreak of war had three principal sources: popular hostility to autocratic Spanish rule in Cuba; U.S. sympathy with the Cuban fight for independence; and a new spirit of national assertiveness, stimulated in part by a nationalistic and sensationalist press.

By 1895 Cuba's growing restiveness had become a guerrilla war of independence. Most Americans were sympathetic with the Cubans, but President Cleveland was determined to preserve neutrality. Three years later, however, during the administration of William McKinley, the U.S. warship *Maine*, sent to Havana on a "courtesy visit" designed to remind the Spanish of American concern over the rough handling of the insurrection, blew up in the harbor. More than 250 men were killed. The *Maine* was probably destroyed by an accidental internal explosion, but most Americans believed the Spanish were responsible. Indignation, intensified by sensationalized press coverage, swept across the country. McKinley tried to preserve the peace, but within a few months, believing delay futile, he recommended armed intervention.

The war with Spain was swift and decisive. During the four months it lasted, not a single American reverse of any importance occurred. A week after the declaration of war, Commodore George Dewey, commander of the six-warship Asiatic Squadron then at Hong Kong, steamed to the Philippines. Catching the entire Spanish fleet at anchor in Manila Bay, he destroyed it without losing an American life.

Meanwhile, in Cuba, troops landed near Santiago, where, after winning a rapid series of engagements, they fired on the port. Four armored Spanish cruisers steamed out of Santiago Bay to engage the American navy and were reduced to ruined hulks.

From Boston to San Francisco, whistles blew and flags waved when word came that Santiago had fallen. Newspapers dispatched correspondents to Cuba and the Philippines, who trumpeted the renown of the nation's new heroes. Chief among them were Commodore Dewey and Colonel Theodore Roosevelt, who had resigned as assistant secretary of the navy to lead his volunteer regiment, the "Rough Riders," to service in Cuba. Spain soon sued for an end to the war. The peace treaty signed on December 10, 1898, transferred Cuba to the United States for temporary occupation preliminary to the island's independence. In addition, Spain ceded Puerto Rico and Guam in lieu of war indemnity, and the Philippines for a U.S. payment of $20 million.

Officially, U.S. policy encouraged the new territories to move toward democratic self-government, a political system with which none of them had any previous experience. In fact, the United States found itself in a colonial role. It maintained formal administrative control in Puerto Rico and Guam, gave Cuba only nominal independence, and harshly suppressed an armed independence movement in the Philippines. (The Philippines gained the right to elect both houses of its legislature in 1916. In 1936 a largely autonomous Philippine Commonwealth was established. In 1946, after World War II, the islands finally attained full independence.)

U.S. involvement in the Pacific area was not limited to the Philippines. The year of the Spanish-American War also saw the beginning of a new relationship with the Hawaiian Islands. Earlier contact with Hawaii had been mainly through missionaries and traders. After 1865, however, American investors began to develop the islands' resources — chiefly sugarcane and pineapples.

When the government of Queen Liliuokalani announced its intention to end foreign influence in 1893, American businessmen joined with influential Hawaiians to depose her. Backed by the American ambassador to Hawaii and U.S. troops stationed there, the new government then asked to be annexed to the United States. President Cleveland, just beginning his second term, rejected annexation, leaving Hawaii nominally independent until the Spanish-American War, when, with the backing of President McKinley, Congress ratified an annexation treaty. In 1959 Hawaii would become the 50th state.

To some extent, in Hawaii especially, economic interests had a role in American expansion, but to influential policy makers such as Roosevelt, Senator Henry Cabot Lodge, and Secretary of State John Hay, and to influential strategists such as Admiral Alfred Thayer Mahan, the main impetus was geostrategic. For these people, the major dividend of acquiring Hawaii was Pearl Harbor, which would become the major U.S. naval base in the central Pacific. The Philippines and Guam complemented other Pacific bases — Wake Island, Midway, and American Samoa. Puerto Rico was an important foothold in a Caribbean area that was becoming increasingly important as the United States contemplated a Central American canal.

U.S. colonial policy tended toward democratic self-government. As it had done with the Philippines, in 1917 the U.S. Congress granted Puerto Ricans the right to elect all of their legislators. The same law also made the island officially a U.S. territory and gave its people American citizenship. In 1950 Congress granted Puerto Rico complete freedom to decide its future. In 1952, the citizens voted to reject either statehood or total independence, and chose instead a commonwealth status that has endured despite the efforts of a vocal separatist movement. Large numbers of Puerto Ricans have settled on the mainland, to which they have free access and where they enjoy all the political and civil rights of any other citizen of the United States.

THE CANAL AND THE AMERICAS

The war with Spain revived U.S. interest in building a canal across the isthmus of Panama, uniting the two great oceans. The usefulness of such a canal for sea trade had long been recognized by the major commercial nations of the world; the French had begun digging one in the late 19th century but had been unable to overcome the engineering difficulties. Having become a power in both the Caribbean Sea and the Pacific Ocean, the United States saw a canal as both economically beneficial and a way of providing speedier transfer of warships from one ocean to the other.

At the turn of the century, what is now Panama was the rebellious northern province of Colombia. When the Colombian legislature in 1903 refused to ratify a treaty giving the United States the right to build and manage a canal, a group of impatient Panamanians, with the support of U.S. Marines, rose in rebellion and declared Panamanian independence. The breakaway country was immediately recognized by President Theodore Roosevelt. Under the terms of a treaty signed that November, Panama granted the United States a perpetual lease to a

16-kilometer-wide strip of land (the Panama Canal Zone) between the Atlantic and the Pacific, in return for $10 million and a yearly fee of $250,000. Colombia later received $25 million as partial compensation. Seventy-five years later, Panama and the United States negotiated a new treaty. It provided for Panamanian sovereignty in the Canal Zone and transfer of the canal to Panama on December 31, 1999.

The completion of the Panama Canal in 1914, directed by Colonel George W. Goethals, was a major triumph of engineering. The simultaneous conquest of malaria and yellow fever made it possible and was one of the 20th century's great feats in preventive medicine.

Elsewhere in Latin America, the United States fell into a pattern of fitful intervention. Between 1900 and 1920, the United States carried out sustained interventions in six Western Hemispheric nations — most notably Haiti, the Dominican Republic, and Nicaragua. Washington offered a variety of justifications for these interventions: to establish political stability and democratic government, to provide a favorable environment for U.S. investment (often called dollar diplomacy), to secure the sea lanes leading to the Panama Canal, and even to prevent European countries from forcibly collecting debts. The United States had pressured the French into removing troops from Mexico in 1867. Half a century later, however, as part of an ill-starred campaign to influence the Mexican revolution and stop raids into American territory, President Woodrow Wilson sent 11,000 troops into the northern part of the country in a futile effort to capture the elusive rebel and outlaw Francisco "Pancho" Villa.

Exercising its role as the most powerful — and most liberal — of Western Hemisphere nations, the United States also worked to establish an institutional basis for cooperation among the nations of the Americas. In 1889 Secretary of State James G. Blaine proposed that the 21 independent nations of the Western Hemisphere join in an organization dedicated to the peaceful settlement of disputes and to closer economic bonds. The result was the Pan-American Union, founded in 1890 and known today as the Organization of American States (OAS).

The later administrations of Herbert Hoover (1929-33) and Franklin D. Roosevelt (1933-45) repudiated the right of U.S. intervention in Latin America. In particular, Roosevelt's Good Neighbor Policy of the 1930s, while not ending all tensions between the United States and Latin America, helped dissipate much of the ill-will engendered by earlier U.S. intervention and unilateral actions.

UNITED STATES AND ASIA

Newly established in the Philippines and firmly entrenched in Hawaii at the turn of the century, the United States had high hopes for a vigorous trade with China. However, Japan and various European nations had acquired established spheres of influence there in the form of naval bases, leased territories, monopolistic trade rights, and exclusive concessions for investing in railway construction and mining.

Idealism in American foreign policy existed alongside the desire to compete with Europe's imperial powers in the Far East. The U.S. government thus insisted as a matter of principle upon equality of commercial privileges for all nations. In September 1899, Secretary of State John Hay advocated an "Open Door" for all nations in China — that is, equality of trading opportunities (including equal tariffs, harbor duties, and railway rates) in the areas Europeans controlled. Despite its idealistic component, the Open Door, in essence, was a diplomatic maneuver that sought the advantages of colonialism while avoiding the stigma of its frank practice. It had limited success.

With the Boxer Rebellion of 1900, the Chinese struck out against foreigners. In June, insurgents seized Beijing and attacked the foreign legations there. Hay promptly announced to the European powers and Japan that the United States would oppose any disturbance of Chinese territorial or administrative rights and restated the Open Door policy. Once the rebellion was quelled, Hay protected China from crushing indemnities. Primarily for the sake of American goodwill, Great Britain, Germany, and lesser colonial powers formally affirmed the Open Door policy and Chinese independence. In practice, they consolidated their privileged positions in the country.

A few years later, President Theodore Roosevelt mediated the deadlocked Russo-Japanese War of 1904-05, in many respects a struggle for power and influence in the northern Chinese province of Manchuria. Roosevelt hoped the settlement would provide open-door opportunities for American business, but the former enemies and other imperial powers succeeded in shutting the Americans out. Here as elsewhere, the United States was unwilling to deploy military force in the service of economic imperialism. The president could at least content himself with the award of the Nobel Peace Prize (1906). Despite gains for Japan, moreover, U.S. relations with the proud and newly assertive island nation would be intermittently difficult through the early decades of the 20th century. ▷

J.P. MORGAN AND FINANCE CAPITALISM

The rise of American industry required more than great industrialists. Big industry required big amounts of capital; headlong economic growth required foreign investors. John Pierpont (J.P.) Morgan was the most important of the American financiers who underwrote both requirements.

During the late 19th and early 20th centuries, Morgan headed the nation's largest investment banking firm. It brokered American securities to wealthy elites at home and abroad. Since foreigners needed assurance that their investments were in a stable currency, Morgan had a strong interest in keeping the dollar tied to its legal value in gold. In the absence of an official U.S. central bank, he became the de facto manager of the task.

From the 1880s through the early 20th century, Morgan and Company not only managed the securities that underwrote many important corporate consolidations, it actually originated some of them. The most stunning of these was the U.S. Steel Corporation, which combined Carnegie Steel with several other companies. Its corporate stock and bonds were sold to investors at the then-unprecedented sum of $1.4 billion.

Morgan originated, and made large profits from, numerous other mergers. Acting as primary banker to numerous railroads, moreover, he effectively muted competition among them. His organizational efforts brought stability to American industry by ending price wars to the disadvantage of farmers and small manufacturers, who saw him as an oppressor. In 1901, when he established the Northern Securities Company to control a group of major railroads, President Theodore Roosevelt authorized a successful Sherman Antitrust Act suit to break up the merger.

Acting as an unofficial central banker, Morgan took the lead in supporting the dollar during the economic depression of the mid-1890s by marketing a large government bond issue that raised funds to replenish Treasury gold supplies. At the same time, his firm undertook a short-term guarantee of the nation's gold reserves. In 1907, he took the lead in organizing the New York financial community to prevent a potentially ruinous string of bankruptcies. In the process, his own firm acquired a large independent steel company, which it amalgamated with U.S. Steel. President Roosevelt personally approved the action in order to avert a serious depression.

By then, Morgan's power was so great that most Americans instinctively distrusted and disliked him. With some exaggeration, reformers depicted him as the director of a "money trust" that controlled America. By the time of his death in 1913, the country was in the final stages of at last reestablishing a central bank, the Federal Reserve System, that would assume much of the responsibility he had exercised unofficially. ◆

188

CHAPTER 9

DISCONTENT AND REFORM

Suffragists march on Pennsylvania Avenue, Washington, D.C., March 3, 1913.

CHAPTER 9: DISCONTENT AND REFORM

> "A great democracy will be neither great nor a democracy if it is not progressive."
>
> Former President Theodore Roosevelt, circa 1910

AGRARIAN DISTRESS AND THE RISE OF POPULISM

In spite of their remarkable progress, late-19th century American farmers experienced recurring periods of hardship. Mechanical improvements greatly increased yield per hectare. The amount of land under cultivation grew rapidly throughout the second half of the century, as the railroads and the gradual displacement of the Plains Indians opened up new areas for western settlement. A similar expansion of agricultural lands in countries such as Canada, Argentina, and Australia compounded these problems in the international market, where much of U.S. agricultural production was now sold. Everywhere, heavy supply pushed the price of agricultural commodities downward.

Midwestern farmers were increasingly restive over what they considered excessive railroad freight rates to move their goods to market. They believed that the protective tariff, a subsidy to big business, drove up the price of their increasingly expensive equipment. Squeezed by low market prices and high costs, they resented ever-heavier debt loads and the banks that held their mortgages. Even the weather was hostile. During the late 1880s droughts devastated the western Great Plains and bankrupted thousands of settlers.

In the South, the end of slavery brought major changes. Much agricultural land was now worked by sharecroppers, tenants who gave up to half of their crop to a landowner for rent, seed, and essential supplies. An estimated 80 percent of the South's African-American farmers and 40 percent of its white ones lived under this debilitating system. Most were locked in a cycle of debt, from which the only hope of escape was increased planting. This led to the over-production of cotton and tobacco, and thus to declining prices and the further exhaustion of the soil.

The first organized effort to address general agricultural problems was by the Patrons of Husbandry, a farmer's group popularly known as the Grange Movement. Launched in 1867 by employees of the U.S. Department of Agriculture, the Granges focused initially on social activities to counter the isolation most farm families encountered. Women's participation was actively encouraged. Spurred by the Panic of 1873, the Grange soon grew to 20,000 chapters and one-and-a-half million members.

The Granges set up their own marketing systems, stores, processing plants, factories, and cooperatives, but most ultimately failed. The movement also enjoyed some political success. During the 1870s, a few states passed "Granger laws," limiting railroad and warehouse fees.

By 1880 the Grange was in decline and being replaced by the Farmers' Alliances, which were similar in many respects but more overtly political. By 1890 the alliances, initially autonomous state organizations, had about 1.5 million members from New York to California. A parallel African-American group, the Colored Farmers National Alliance, claimed over a million members. Federating into two large Northern and Southern blocs, the alliances promoted elaborate economic programs to "unite the farmers of America for their protection against class legislation and the encroachments of concentrated capital."

By 1890 the level of agrarian distress, fueled by years of hardship and hostility toward the McKinley tariff, was at an all-time high. Working with sympathetic Democrats in the South or small third parties in the West, the Farmers' Alliances made a push for political power. A third political party, the People's (or Populist) Party, emerged. Never before in American politics had there been anything like the Populist fervor that swept the prairies and cotton lands. The elections of 1890 brought the new party into power in a dozen Southern and Western states, and sent a score of Populist senators and representatives to Congress.

The first Populist convention was in 1892. Delegates from farm, labor, and reform organizations met in Omaha, Nebraska, determined to overturn a U.S. political system they viewed as hopelessly corrupted by the industrial and financial trusts. Their platform stated:

We are met, in the midst of a nation brought to the verge of moral, political, and material ruin. Corruption dominates the ballot-box, the legislatures, the Congress, and touches even the ermine of the bench [courts]. ... From the same prolific womb of governmental injustice we breed the two great classes — tramps and millionaires.

The pragmatic portion of their platform called for the nationalization of the railroads; a low tariff; loans secured by non-perishable crops stored in government-owned warehouses; and, most explosively, currency inflation through Treasury purchase and the unlimited coinage of silver at the "traditional" ratio of 16 ounces of silver to one ounce of gold.

The Populists showed impressive strength in the West and South, and their candidate for president polled more than a million votes. But the currency question soon overshadowed all other issues. Agrarian spokesmen, convinced that their troubles stemmed from a shortage of money in circulation, argued that increasing the volume of money would indirectly raise prices for farm products and drive up industrial wages, thus allowing debts to be paid with inflated currency. Conservative groups and the financial classes, on the other hand, responded that the 16:1 price ratio was nearly twice the market price for silver. A policy of unlimited purchase would denude the U.S. Treasury of all its gold holdings, sharply devalue the dollar, and destroy the purchasing power of the working and middle classes. Only the gold standard, they said, offered stability.

The financial panic of 1893 heightened the tension of this debate. Bank failures abounded in the South and Midwest; unemployment soared and crop prices fell badly. The crisis and President Grover Cleveland's defense of the gold standard sharply divided the Democratic Party. Democrats who were silver supporters went over to the Populists as the presidential elections of 1896 neared.

The Democratic convention that year was swayed by one of the most famous speeches in U.S. political history. Pleading with the convention not to "crucify mankind on a cross of gold," William Jennings Bryan, the young Nebraskan champion of silver, won the Democrats' presidential nomination. The Populists also endorsed Bryan.

In the epic contest that followed, Bryan carried almost all the Southern and Western states. But he lost the more populated, industrial North and East — and the election — to Republican candidate William McKinley.

The following year the country's finances began to improve, in part owing to the discovery of gold in Alaska and the Yukon. This provided a basis for a conservative expansion of the money supply. In 1898 the Spanish-American War drew the nation's attention further from Populist issues. Populism and the silver issue were dead. Many of the movement's other reform ideas, however, lived on.

THE STRUGGLES OF LABOR

The life of a 19th-century American industrial worker was hard. Even in good times wages were low, hours long, and working conditions hazardous. Little of the wealth that the growth of the nation had generated went to its workers. Moreover, women and children made up a high percentage of the work force in some industries and often received but a fraction of the wages a man could earn. Periodic economic crises swept the nation, further eroding industrial wages and producing high levels of unemployment.

At the same time, technological improvements, which added so much to the nation's productivity, continually reduced the demand for skilled labor. Yet the unskilled labor pool was constantly growing, as unprecedented numbers of immigrants — 18 million between 1880 and 1910 — entered the country, eager for work.

Before 1874, when Massachusetts passed the nation's first legislation limiting the number of hours women and child factory workers could perform to 10 hours a day, virtually no labor legislation existed in the country. It was not until the 1930s that the federal government would become actively involved. Until then, the field was left to the state and local authorities, few of whom were as responsive to the workers as they were to wealthy industrialists.

The laissez-faire capitalism that dominated the second half of the 19th century and fostered huge concentrations of wealth and power was backed by a judiciary that time and again ruled against those who challenged the system. In this, they were merely following the prevailing philosophy of the times. Drawing on a simplified understanding of Darwinian science, many social thinkers believed that both the growth of large business at the expense of small enterprise and the wealth of a few alongside the poverty of many was "survival of the fittest," and an unavoidable by-product of progress.

American workers, especially the skilled among them, appear to have lived at least as well as their counterparts in industrial Europe. Still, the social costs were high. As late as the year 1900, the United States had the highest job-related fatality rate of any industrialized nation in the world. Most industrial workers still worked a 10-hour day (12 hours in the steel industry), yet earned less than the minimum deemed necessary for a decent life. The number of children in the work force doubled between 1870 and 1900.

The first major effort to organize workers' groups on a nationwide basis appeared with the Noble Order of the Knights of Labor in 1869. Originally a secret, ritualistic society organized by Philadelphia garment workers and advocating a cooperative program, it was open to all workers, including African Americans, women, and farmers. The Knights grew slowly until its railway workers' unit won a strike against the great railroad baron, Jay Gould, in 1885. Within a year they added 500,000 workers to their rolls, but, not attuned to pragmatic trade unionism and unable to repeat this success, the Knights soon fell into a decline.

Their place in the labor movement was gradually taken by the American Federation of Labor (AFL). Rather than open membership to all, the AFL, under former cigar union official Samuel Gompers, was a group of unions focused on skilled workers. Its objectives were "pure and simple" and apolitical: increasing wages, reducing hours, and improving working conditions. It did much to turn the labor movement away from the socialist views of most European labor movements.

Nonetheless, both before the founding of the AFL and after, American labor history was violent. In the Great Rail Strike of 1877, rail workers across the nation went out in response to a 10-percent pay cut. Attempts to break the strike led to rioting and wide-scale destruction in several cities: Baltimore, Maryland; Chicago, Illinois; Pittsburgh, Pennsylvania; Buffalo, New York; and San Francisco, California. Federal troops had to be sent to several locations before the strike was ended.

Nine years later, in Chicago's Haymarket Square incident, someone threw a bomb at police about to break up an anarchist rally in support of an ongoing strike at the McCormick Harvester Company in Chicago. In the ensuing melee, seven policemen and at least four workers were reported killed. Some 60 police officers were injured.

In 1892, at Carnegie's steel works in Homestead, Pennsylvania, a group of 300 Pinkerton detectives the company had hired to break a bitter strike by the Amalgamated Association of Iron, Steel, and Tin Workers fought a fierce and losing gun battle with strikers. The National Guard was called in to protect non-union workers and the strike was broken. Unions were not let back into the plant until 1937.

In 1894, wage cuts at the Pullman Company just outside Chicago led to a strike, which, with the support of the American Railway Union, soon tied up much of the country's rail system. As the situation deteriorated, U.S. Attorney General Richard Olney, himself a former railroad lawyer, deputized over 3,000 men in an attempt to keep the rails open. This was followed by a federal court injunction against union interference with the trains. When rioting ensued, President Cleveland sent in federal troops, and the strike was eventually broken.

The most militant of the strike-favoring unions was the Industrial Workers of the World (IWW). Formed from an amalgam of unions fighting for better conditions in the West's mining industry, the IWW, or "Wobblies" as they were commonly known, gained particular prominence from the Colorado mine clashes of 1903 and the singularly brutal fashion in which they were put down. Influenced by militant anarchism and openly calling for class warfare, the Wobblies gained many adherents after they won a difficult strike battle in the textile mills of Lawrence, Massachusetts, in 1912. Their call for work stoppages in the midst of World War I, however, led to a government crackdown in 1917 that virtually destroyed them.

THE REFORM IMPULSE

The presidential election of 1900 gave the American people a chance to pass judgment on the Republican administration of President McKinley, especially its foreign policy. Meeting at Philadelphia, the Republicans expressed jubilation over the successful outcome of the war with Spain, the restoration of prosperity, and the effort to obtain new markets through the Open Door policy. McKinley easily defeated his opponent, once again William Jennings Bryan. But the president did not live to enjoy his victory. In September 1901, while attending an exposition in Buffalo, New York, he was shot down by an assassin, the third president to be assassinated since the Civil War.

Theodore Roosevelt, McKinley's vice president, assumed the presidency. Roosevelt's accession coincided with a new epoch in American political life and international relations. The continent was peopled; the frontier was disappearing. A small, formerly struggling republic had become a world power. The country's political foundations had endured the vicissitudes of foreign and civil war, the tides of prosperity and depression. Immense strides had been made in agriculture and industry. Free public education had been largely realized and a free press maintained. The ideal of religious freedom had been sustained. The influence of big business was now more firmly entrenched than ever, however, and local and municipal government often was in the hands of corrupt politicians.

In response to the excesses of 19th-century capitalism and political corruption, a reform movement called "progressivism" arose, which gave American politics and thought its special character from approximately 1890 until the American entry into World War I in 1917. The Progressives had diverse objectives. In general, however, they saw themselves as engaged in a democratic crusade against the abuses of urban political bosses and the corrupt "robber barons" of big business. Their goals were greater democracy and social justice, honest government, more effective regulation of business, and a revived commitment to public service. They believed that expanding the scope of government would ensure the progress of U.S. society and the welfare of its citizens.

The years 1902 to 1908 marked the era of greatest reform activity, as writers and journalists strongly protested practices and principles inherited from the 18th-century rural republic that were proving inadequate for a 20th-century urban state. Years before, in 1873, the celebrated author Mark Twain had exposed American society to critical scrutiny in *The Gilded Age*. Now, trenchant articles dealing with trusts, high finance, impure foods, and abusive railroad practices began to appear in the daily newspapers and in such popular magazines as *McClure's* and *Collier's*. Their authors, such as the journalist Ida M. Tarbell, who crusaded against the Standard Oil Trust, became known as "muckrakers."

In his sensational novel, *The Jungle*, Upton Sinclair exposed unsanitary conditions in the great Chicago meat-packing houses and condemned the grip of the beef trust on the nation's meat supply. Theodore Dreiser, in his novels *The Financier* and *The Titan*, made it easy for laymen to understand the machinations of big business. Frank Norris's *The Octopus* assailed amoral railroad management; his *The Pit* depicted secret manipulations on the Chicago grain market. Lincoln Steffens's *The Shame of the Cities* bared local political corruption. This "literature of exposure" roused people to action.

The hammering impact of uncompromising writers and an increasingly aroused public spurred political leaders to take practical measures. Many states enacted laws to improve the conditions under which people lived and worked. At the urging of such prominent social critics as Jane Addams, child labor laws were strengthened and new ones adopted, raising age limits, shortening work hours, restricting night work, and requiring school attendance.

ROOSEVELT'S REFORMS

By the early 20th century, most of the larger cities and more than half the states had established an eight-hour day on public works. Equally important were the workman's compensation laws, which made employers legally responsible for injuries sustained by employees at work. New revenue laws were also enacted, which, by taxing inheritances, incomes, and the property or earnings of corporations, sought to place the burden of government on those best able to pay.

It was clear to many people — notably President Theodore Roosevelt and Progressive leaders in the Congress (foremost among them Wisconsin Senator Robert La Follette) — that most of the problems reformers were concerned about could be solved only if dealt with on a national scale. Roosevelt declared his determination to give all the American people a "Square Deal."

During his first term, he initiated a policy of increased government supervision through the enforcement of antitrust laws. With his backing, Congress passed the Elkins Act (1903), which greatly restricted the railroad practice of giving rebates to favored shippers. The act made published rates the lawful standard, and shippers equally liable with railroads for rebates. Meanwhile, Congress had created a new Cabinet Department of Commerce and Labor, which included a Bureau of Corporations empowered to investigate the affairs of large business aggregations.

Roosevelt won acclaim as a "trust-buster," but his actual attitude toward big business was complex. Economic concentration, he believed, was inevitable. Some trusts were "good," some "bad." The task of government was to make reasonable distinctions. When, for example, the Bureau of Corporations discovered in 1907 that the American Sugar Refining Company had evaded import duties, subsequent legal actions recovered more than $4 million and convicted several company officials. The Standard Oil Company was indicted for receiving secret rebates from the Chicago and Alton Railroad, convicted, and fined a staggering $29 million.

Roosevelt's striking personality and his trust-busting activities captured the imagination of the ordinary individual; approval of his progressive measures cut across party lines. In addition, the abounding prosperity of the country at this time led people to feel satisfied with the party in office. He won an easy victory in the 1904 presidential election.

Emboldened by a sweeping electoral triumph, Roosevelt called for stronger railroad regulation. In June 1906 Congress passed the Hepburn Act. It gave the Interstate Commerce Commission real authority in regulating rates, extended the commission's jurisdiction, and forced the railroads to surrender their interlocking interests in steamship lines and coal companies.

Other congressional measures carried the principle of federal control still further. The Pure Food and Drug Act of 1906 prohibited the use of any "deleterious drug, chemical, or preservative" in prepared medicines and foods. The Meat Inspection Act of the same year mandated federal inspection of all meat-packing establishments engaged in interstate commerce.

Conservation of the nation's natural resources, managed development of the public domain, and the reclamation of wide stretches of neglected land were among the other major achievements of the Roosevelt era. Roosevelt and his aides were more than conservationists, but given the helter-skelter exploitation of public resources that had preceded them, conservation loomed large on their agenda. Whereas his predecessors had set aside 18,800,000 hectares of timberland for preservation and parks, Roosevelt increased the area to 59,200,000 hectares. They also began systematic efforts to prevent forest fires and to re-timber denuded tracts.

TAFT AND WILSON

Roosevelt's popularity was at its peak as the campaign of 1908 neared, but he was unwilling to break the tradition by which no president had held office for more than two terms. Instead, he supported William Howard Taft, who had served under him as governor of the Philippines and secretary of war. Taft, pledging to continue Roosevelt's programs, defeated Bryan, who was running for the third and last time.

The new president continued the prosecution of trusts with less discrimination than Roosevelt, further strengthened the Interstate Commerce Commission, established a postal savings bank and a parcel post system, expanded the civil service, and sponsored the enactment of two amendments to the Constitution, both adopted in 1913.

The 16th Amendment, ratified just before Taft left office, authorized a federal income tax; the 17th Amendment, approved a few months later, mandated the direct election of senators by the people, instead of state legislatures. Yet balanced against these progressive measures was Taft's acceptance of a new tariff with higher protective schedules; his opposition to the entry of the state of Arizona into the Union because of its liberal constitution; and his growing reliance on the conservative wing of his party.

By 1910 Taft's party was bitterly divided. Democrats gained control of Congress in the midterm elections. Two years later, Woodrow Wilson, the Democratic, progressive governor of the state of New Jersey, campaigned against Taft, the Republican candidate — and also against Roosevelt who ran as the candidate of a new Progressive Party. Wilson, in a spirited campaign, defeated both rivals.

During his first term, Wilson secured one of the most notable legislative programs in American history. The first task was tariff revision. "The tariff duties must be altered," Wilson said. "We must abolish everything that bears any semblance of privilege." The Underwood Tariff, signed on October 3, 1913, provided substantial rate reductions on imported raw materials and foodstuffs, cotton and woolen goods, iron and steel; it removed the duties from more than a hundred other items. Although the act retained many protective features, it was a genuine attempt to lower the cost of living. To compensate for lost revenues, it established a modest income tax.

The second item on the Democratic program was a long overdue, thorough reorganization of the ramshackle banking and currency system. "Control," said Wilson, "must be public, not private, must be vested in the government itself, so that the banks may be the instruments, not the masters, of business and of individual enterprise and initiative."

The Federal Reserve Act of December 23, 1913, was Wilson's most enduring legislative accomplishment. Conservatives had favored establishment of one powerful central bank. The new act, in line with the Democratic Party's Jeffersonian sentiments, divided the country into 12 districts, with a Federal Reserve

Bank in each, all supervised by a national Federal Reserve Board with limited authority to set interest rates. The act assured greater flexibility in the money supply and made provision for issuing federal-reserve notes to meet business demands. Greater centralization of the system would come in the 1930s.

The next important task was trust regulation and investigation of corporate abuses. Congress authorized a Federal Trade Commission to issue orders prohibiting "unfair methods of competition" by business concerns in interstate trade. The Clayton Antitrust Act forbade many corporate practices that had thus far escaped specific condemnation: interlocking directorates, price discrimination among purchasers, use of the injunction in labor disputes, and ownership by one corporation of stock in similar enterprises.

Farmers and other workers were not forgotten. The Smith-Lever Act of 1914 established an "extension system" of county agents to assist farming throughout the country. Subsequent acts made credit available to farmers at low rates of interest. The Seamen's Act of 1915 improved living and working conditions on board ships. The Federal Workingman's Compensation Act in 1916 authorized allowances to civil service employees for disabilities incurred at work and established a model for private enterprise. The Adamson Act of the same year established an eight-hour day for railroad labor.

This record of achievement won Wilson a firm place in American history as one of the nation's foremost progressive reformers. However, his domestic reputation would soon be overshadowed by his record as a wartime president who led his country to victory but could not hold the support of his people for the peace that followed.   >

A NATION OF NATIONS

No country's history has been more closely bound to immigration than that of the United States. During the first 15 years of the 20th century alone, over 13 million people came to the United States, many passing through Ellis Island, the federal immigration center that opened in New York harbor in 1892. (Though no longer in service, Ellis Island reopened in 1992 as a monument to the millions who crossed the nation's threshold there.)

The first official census in 1790 had numbered Americans at 3,929,214. Approximately half of the population of the original 13 states was of English origin; the rest were Scots-Irish, German, Dutch, French, Swedish, Welsh, and Finnish. These white Europeans were mostly Protestants. A fifth of the population was enslaved Africans.

From early on, Americans viewed immigrants as a necessary resource for an expanding country. As a result, few official restrictions were placed upon immigration into the United States until the 1920s. As more and more immigrants arrived, however, some Americans became fearful that their culture was threatened.

The Founding Fathers, especially Thomas Jefferson, had been ambivalent over whether or not the United States ought to welcome arrivals from every corner of the globe. Jefferson wondered whether democracy could ever rest safely in the hands of men from countries that revered monarchs or replaced royalty with mob rule. However, few supported closing the gates to newcomers in a country desperate for labor.

Immigration lagged in the late 18th and early 19th centuries as wars disrupted trans-Atlantic travel and European governments restricted movement to retain young men of military age. Still, as European populations increased, more people on the same land constricted the size of farming lots to a point where families could barely survive. Moreover, cottage industries were falling victim to an Industrial Revolution that was mechanizing production. Thousands of artisans unwilling or unable to find jobs in factories were out of work in Europe.

In the mid-1840s millions more made their way to the United States as a result of a potato blight in Ireland and continual revolution in the German homelands. Meanwhile, a trickle of Chinese immigrants, most from impoverished Southeastern China, began to make their way to the American West Coast.

Almost 19 million people arrived in the United States between 1890 and 1921, the year Congress first passed severe restrictions. Most of these immigrants were from Italy, Russia, Poland, Greece, and the Balkans. Non-Europeans came, too: east from Japan, south from Canada, and north from Mexico.

By the early 1920s, an alliance was forged between wage-conscious organized labor and those who called for restricted immigration on racial or religious grounds, such as the Ku Klux Klan and the Immigration Restriction League. The Johnson-Reed Immigration Act of 1924 permanently curtailed the influx of newcomers with quotas calculated on nation of origin.

The Great Depression of the 1930s dramatically slowed immigration still further. With public opinion generally opposed to immigration, even for persecuted European minorities, relatively few refugees found sanctuary in the United States after Adolf Hitler's ascent to power in 1933.

Throughout the postwar decades, the United States continued to cling to nationally based quotas. Supporters of the McCarran-Walter Act of 1952 argued that quota relaxation might inundate the United States with Marxist subversives from Eastern Europe.

In 1965 Congress replaced national quotas with hemispheric ones. Relatives of U.S. citizens received preference, as did immigrants with job skills in short supply in the United States. In 1978 the hemispheric quotas were replaced by a worldwide ceiling of 290,000, a limit reduced to 270,000 after passage of the Refugee Act of 1980.

Since the mid-1970s, the United States has experienced a fresh wave of immigration, with arrivals from Asia, Africa, and Latin America transforming communities throughout the country. Current estimates suggest a total annual arrival of approximately 600,000 legal newcomers to the United States.

Because immigrant and refugee quotas remain well under demand, however, illegal immigration is still a major problem. Mexicans and other Latin Americans daily cross the Southwestern U.S. borders to find work, higher wages, and improved education and health care for their families. Likewise, there is a substantial illegal migration from countries like China and other Asian nations. Estimates vary, but some suggest that as many as 600,000 illegals per year arrive in the United States.

Large surges of immigration have historically created social strains along with economic and cultural dividends. Deeply ingrained in most Americans, however, is the conviction that the Statue of Liberty does, indeed, stand as a symbol for the United States as she lifts her lamp before the "golden door," welcoming those "yearning to breathe free." This belief, and the sure knowledge that their forebears were once immigrants, has kept the United States a nation of nations. ◆

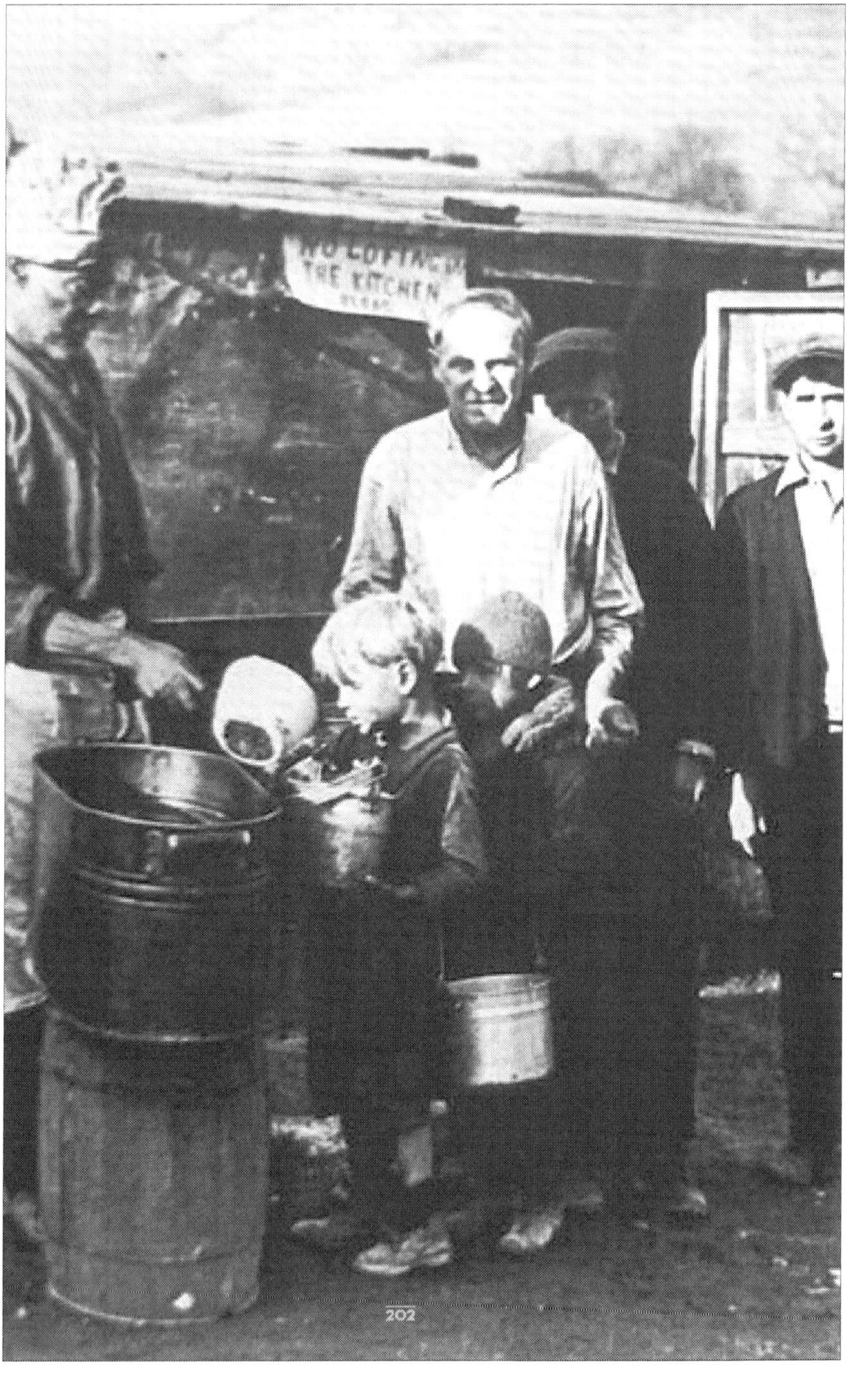
THE KITCHEN

CHAPTER 10

WAR, PROSPERITY, AND DEPRESSION

Depression era soup line, 1930s.

CHAPTER 10: WAR, PROSPERITY, AND DEPRESSION

"The chief business of the American people is business."

President Calvin Coolidge, 1925

WAR AND NEUTRAL RIGHTS

To the American public of 1914, the outbreak of war in Europe — with Germany and Austria-Hungary fighting Britain, France, and Russia — came as a shock. At first the encounter seemed remote, but its economic and political effects were swift and deep. By 1915 U.S. industry, which had been mildly depressed, was prospering again with munitions orders from the Western Allies. Both sides used propaganda to arouse the public passions of Americans — a third of whom were either foreign-born or had one or two foreign-born parents. Moreover, Britain and Germany both acted against U.S. shipping on the high seas, bringing sharp protests from President Woodrow Wilson.

Britain, which controlled the seas, stopped and searched American carriers, confiscating "contraband" bound for Germany. Germany employed its major naval weapon, the submarine, to sink shipping bound for Britain or France. President Wilson warned that the United States would not forsake its traditional right as a neutral to trade with belligerent nations. He also declared that the nation would hold Germany to "strict accountability" for the loss of American vessels or lives. On May 7, 1915, a German submarine sunk the British liner *Lusitania*, killing 1,198 people, 128 of them Americans. Wilson, reflecting American outrage, demanded an immediate halt to attacks on liners and merchant ships.

Anxious to avoid war with the United States, Germany agreed to give warning to commercial vessels — even if they flew the enemy flag — before firing on them. But after two more attacks — the sinking of the British steamer *Arabic* in August 1915, and the torpedoing of the French liner *Sussex* in March 1916 — Wilson issued an ultimatum threatening to break diplomatic relations unless Germany abandoned submarine warfare. Germany agreed and refrained from further attacks through the end of the year.

Wilson won reelection in 1916, partly on the slogan: "He kept us out of war." Feeling he had a mandate to act as a peacemaker, he delivered a speech to the Senate, January 22, 1917, urging the warring nations to accept a "peace without victory."

UNITED STATES ENTERS WORLD WAR I

On January 31, 1917, however, the German government resumed unrestricted submarine warfare. After five U.S. vessels were sunk, Wilson on April 2, 1917, asked for a declaration of war. Congress quickly approved. The government rapidly mobilized military resources, industry, labor, and agriculture. By October 1918, on the eve of Allied victory, a U.S. army of over 1,750,000 had been deployed in France.

In the summer of 1918, fresh American troops under the command of General John J. Pershing played a decisive role in stopping a last-ditch German offensive. That fall, Americans were key participants in the Meuse-Argonne offensive, which cracked Germany's vaunted Hindenburg Line.

President Wilson contributed greatly to an early end to the war by defining American war aims that characterized the struggle as being waged not against the German people but against their autocratic government. His Fourteen Points, submitted to the Senate in January 1918, called for: abandonment of secret international agreements; freedom of the seas; free trade between nations; reductions in national armaments; an adjustment of colonial claims in the interests of the inhabitants affected; self-rule for subjugated European nationalities; and, most importantly, the establishment of an association of nations to afford "mutual guarantees of political independence and territorial integrity to great and small states alike."

In October 1918, the German government, facing certain defeat, appealed to Wilson to negotiate on the basis of the Fourteen Points. After a month of secret negotiations that gave Germany no firm guarantees, an armistice (technically a truce, but actually a surrender) was concluded on November 11.

THE LEAGUE OF NATIONS

It was Wilson's hope that the final treaty, drafted by the victors, would be even-handed, but the passion and material sacrifice of more than four years of war caused the European Allies to make severe demands. Persuaded that his greatest hope for peace, a League of Nations, would never be realized unless he made concessions, Wilson compromised somewhat on the issues of self-determination, open diplomacy, and other specifics. He successfully resisted French demands for the entire Rhineland, and somewhat moderated that country's insistence upon charging Germany the whole cost of the war. The final agreement (the Treaty of Versailles), however, provided for French occupation of the coal- and iron-rich Saar Basin, and a very heavy burden of reparations upon Germany.

In the end, there was little left of Wilson's proposals for a generous and lasting peace but the League of Nations itself, which he had made an integral part of the treaty. Displaying poor judgment, however, the president had failed to involve leading Republicans in the treaty negotiations. Returning with a partisan document, he then refused to make concessions necessary to satisfy Republican concerns about protecting American sovereignty.

With the treaty stalled in a Senate committee, Wilson began a national tour to appeal for support. On September 25, 1919, physically ravaged by the rigors of peacemaking and the pressures of the wartime presidency, he suffered a crippling stroke. Critically ill for weeks, he never fully recovered. In two separate votes — November 1919 and March 1920 — the Senate once again rejected the Versailles Treaty and with it the League of Nations.

The League of Nations would never be capable of maintaining world order. Wilson's defeat showed that the American people were not yet ready to play a commanding role in world affairs. His utopian vision had briefly inspired the nation, but its collision with reality quickly led to widespread disillusion with world affairs. America reverted to its instinctive isolationism.

POSTWAR UNREST

The transition from war to peace was tumultuous. A postwar economic boom coexisted with rapid increases in consumer prices. Labor unions that had refrained from striking during the war engaged in several major job actions. During the summer of 1919, several race riots occurred, reflecting apprehension over the emergence of a "New Negro" who had seen military service or gone north to work in the war industry.

Reaction to these events merged with a widespread national fear of a new international revolutionary movement. In 1917, the Bolsheviks had seized power in Russia; after the war, they attempted revolutions in Germany and Hungary. By 1919, it seemed they had come to America. Excited by the Bolshevik example, large numbers of militants split from the Socialist Party to found what would become the Communist Party of the United States. In April 1919, the postal service intercepted nearly 40 bombs addressed to prominent citizens. Attorney General A. Mitchell Palmer's residence in Washington was bombed. Palmer, in turn, authorized federal roundups of radicals and deported many who were not citizens. Strikes were often blamed on radicals and depicted as the opening shots of a revolution.

Palmer's dire warnings fueled a "Red Scare" that subsided by mid-1920. Even a murderous bombing in Wall Street in September failed to reawaken it. From 1919 on, however, a current of militant hostility toward revolutionary communism would simmer not far beneath the surface of American life.

THE BOOMING 1920s

Wilson, distracted by the war, then laid low by his stroke, had mishandled almost every postwar issue. The booming economy began to collapse in mid-1920. The Republican candidates for president and vice president, Warren G. Harding and Calvin Coolidge, easily defeated their Democratic opponents, James M. Cox and Franklin D. Roosevelt.

Following ratification of the 19th Amendment to the Constitution, women voted in a presidential election for the first time.

The first two years of Harding's administration saw a continuance of the economic recession that had begun under Wilson. By 1923, however, prosperity was back. For the next six years the country enjoyed the strongest economy in its history, at least in urban areas. Governmental economic policy during the 1920s was eminently conservative. It was based upon the belief that if government fostered private business, benefits would radiate out to most of the rest of the population.

Accordingly, the Republicans tried to create the most favorable conditions for U.S. industry. The Fordney-McCumber Tariff of 1922 and the Hawley-Smoot Tariff of 1930 brought American trade barriers to new heights, guaranteeing U.S. manufacturers in one field after another a monopoly of the domestic market, but blocking a healthy trade with Europe that would have reinvigorated the international economy. Occurring at the beginning of the Great Depression, Hawley-Smoot triggered retaliation from other manufacturing nations and contributed greatly to a collapsing cycle of world trade that intensified world economic misery.

The federal government also started a program of tax cuts, reflecting Treasury Secretary Andrew Mellon's belief that high taxes on individual incomes and corporations discouraged investment in new industrial enterprises. Congress, in laws passed between 1921 and 1929, responded favorably to his proposals.

"The chief business of the American people is business," declared Calvin Coolidge, the Vermont-born vice president who succeeded to the presidency in 1923 after Harding's death, and was elected in his own right in 1924. Coolidge hewed to the conservative economic policies of the Republican Party, but he was a much abler administrator than the hapless Harding, whose administration was mired in charges of corruption in the months before his death.

Throughout the 1920s, private business received substantial encouragement, including construction loans, profitable mail-carrying contracts, and other indirect subsidies. The Transportation Act of 1920, for example, had already restored to private management the nation's railways, which had been under government control during the war. The Merchant Marine, which had been owned and largely operated by the government, was sold to private operators.

Republican policies in agriculture, however, faced mounting criticism, for farmers shared least in the prosperity of the 1920s. The period since 1900 had been one of rising farm prices. The unprecedented wartime demand for U.S. farm products had provided a strong stimulus to expansion. But by the close of 1920, with the abrupt end of wartime demand, the commercial agriculture of staple crops such as wheat and corn fell into sharp decline. Many factors accounted for the depression in American agriculture, but foremost was the loss of foreign markets. This was partly in reaction to American tariff policy, but also because excess farm production was a worldwide phenomenon. When the Great Depression struck in the 1930s, it devastated an already fragile farm economy.

The distress of agriculture aside, the Twenties brought the best life ever to most Americans. It was the decade in which the ordinary family purchased its first automobile, obtained refrigerators and vacuum cleaners, listened to the radio for entertainment, and went regularly to motion pictures. Prosperity was real and broadly distributed. The Republicans profited politically, as a result, by claiming credit for it.

TENSIONS OVER IMMIGRATION

During the 1920s, the United States sharply restricted foreign immigration for the first time in its history. Large inflows of foreigners long had created a certain amount of social tension, but most had been of Northern European stock and, if not quickly assimilated, at least possessed a certain commonality with most Americans. By the end of the 19th century, however, the flow was predominantly from southern and Eastern Europe. According to the census of 1900, the population of the United States was just over 76 million. Over the next 15 years, more than 15 million immigrants entered the country.

Around two-thirds of the inflow consisted of "newer" nationalities and ethnic groups — Russian Jews, Poles, Slavic peoples, Greeks, southern Italians. They were non-Protestant, non-"Nordic," and, many Americans feared, nonassimilable. They did hard, often dangerous, low-pay work — but were accused of driving down the wages of native-born Americans. Settling in squalid urban ethnic enclaves, the new immigrants were seen as maintaining Old World customs, getting along with very little English, and supporting unsavory political machines that catered to their needs. Nativists wanted to send them back to Europe; social workers wanted to Americanize them. Both agreed that they were a threat to American identity.

Halted by World War I, mass immigration resumed in 1919, but quickly ran into determined opposition from groups as varied as the American Federation of Labor and the reorganized Ku Klux Klan. Millions of old-stock Americans who belonged to neither organization accepted commonly held assumptions about the inferiority of non-Nordics and backed restrictions. Of course, there were also practical arguments in favor of a maturing nation putting some limits on new arrivals.

In 1921, Congress passed a sharply restrictive emergency immigration act. It was supplanted in 1924 by the Johnson-Reed National Origins Act, which established an immigration quota for each nationality. Those quotas were pointedly based on the census of 1890, a year in which the newer immigration had not yet left its mark. Bitterly resented by southern and Eastern European ethnic groups, the new law reduced immigration to a trickle. After 1929, the economic impact of the Great Depression would reduce the trickle to a reverse flow — until refugees from European fascism began to press for admission to the country.

CLASH OF CULTURES

Some Americans expressed their discontent with the character of modern life in the 1920s by focusing on family and religion, as an increasingly urban, secular society came into conflict with older rural traditions. Fundamentalist preachers such as Billy Sunday provided an outlet for many who yearned for a return to a simpler past.

Perhaps the most dramatic demonstration of this yearning was the religious fundamentalist crusade that pitted Biblical texts against the Darwinian theory of biological evolution. In the 1920s, bills to prohibit the teaching of evolution began appearing in Midwestern and Southern state legislatures. Leading this crusade was the aging William Jennings Bryan, long a spokesman for the values of the countryside as well as a progressive politician. Bryan skillfully reconciled his anti-evolutionary activism with his earlier economic radicalism, declaring that evolution "by denying the need or possibility of spiritual regeneration, discourages all reforms."

The issue came to a head in 1925, when a young high school teacher, John Scopes, was prosecuted for violating a Tennessee law that forbade the teaching of evolution in the public schools. The case became a national spectacle, drawing intense news coverage. The American Civil Liberties Union retained the renowned attorney Clarence Darrow to defend Scopes. Bryan wrangled an appointment as special prosecutor, then foolishly allowed Darrow to call him as a hostile witness. Bryan's confused defense of Biblical passages as literal rather than metaphorical truth drew widespread criticism. Scopes, nearly forgotten in the fuss, was convicted, but his fine was reversed on a technicality. Bryan died shortly after the trial ended. The state wisely declined to retry Scopes. Urban sophisticates ridiculed fundamentalism, but it continued to be a powerful force in rural, small-town America.

Another example of a powerful clash of cultures — one with far greater national consequences — was Prohibition. In 1919, after almost a century of agitation, the 18th Amendment to the Constitution was enacted, prohibiting the manufacture, sale, or transportation of alcoholic beverages. Intended to eliminate the saloon and the drunkard from American society, Prohibition created thousands of illegal drinking places called "speakeasies," made intoxication fashionable, and created a new form of criminal activity — the transportation of illegal liquor, or "bootlegging." Widely observed in rural America, openly evaded in urban America, Prohibition was an emotional issue in the prosperous Twenties. When the Depression hit, it seemed increasingly irrelevant. The 18th Amendment would be repealed in 1933.

Fundamentalism and Prohibition were aspects of a larger reaction to a modernist social and intellectual revolution most visible in changing manners and morals that caused the decade to be called the Jazz Age, the Roaring Twenties, or the era of "flaming youth." World War I had overturned the Victorian social and moral order. Mass prosperity enabled an open and hedonistic life style for the young middle classes.

The leading intellectuals were supportive. H.L. Mencken, the decade's most important social critic, was unsparing in denouncing sham and venality in American life. He usually found these qualities in rural areas and among businessmen. His counterparts of the progressive movement had believed in "the people" and sought to extend democracy. Mencken, an elitist and admirer of Nietzsche, bluntly called democratic man a boob and characterized the American middle class as the "booboisie."

Novelist F. Scott Fitzgerald captured the energy, turmoil, and disillusion of the decade in such works as *The Beautiful and the Damned* (1922) and *The Great Gatsby* (1925). Sinclair Lewis, the first American to win a Nobel Prize for literature, satirized mainstream America in *Main Street* (1920) and *Babbitt* (1922). Ernest Hemingway vividly portrayed the malaise wrought by the war in *The Sun Also Rises* (1926) and *A Farewell to Arms* (1929). Fitzgerald, Hemingway, and many other writers dramatized their alienation from America by spending much of the decade in Paris.

African-American culture flowered. Between 1910 and 1930, huge numbers of African Americans moved from the South to the North in search of jobs and personal freedom. Most settled in urban areas, especially New York City's Harlem, Detroit, and Chicago. In 1910 W.E.B. DuBois and other intellectuals had founded the National Association for the Advancement of Colored People (NAACP), which helped African Americans gain a national voice that would grow in importance with the passing years.

An African-American literary and artistic movement, called the "Harlem Renaissance," emerged. Like the "Lost Generation," its writers, such as the poets Langston Hughes and Countee Cullen, rejected middle-class values and conventional literary forms, even as they addressed the realities of African-American experience. African-American musicians — Duke Ellington, King Oliver, Louis Armstrong — first made jazz a staple of American culture in the 1920s.

THE GREAT DEPRESSION

In October 1929 the booming stock market crashed, wiping out many investors. The collapse did not in itself cause the Great Depression, although it reflected excessively easy credit policies that had allowed the market to get out of hand. It also aggravated fragile economies in Europe that had relied heavily on American loans. Over the next three years, an initial American recession became part of a worldwide depression. Business houses closed their doors, factories shut down, banks failed with the loss of depositors' savings. Farm income fell some 50 percent. By November 1932, approximately one of every five American workers was unemployed.

The presidential campaign of 1932 was chiefly a debate over the causes and possible remedies of the Great Depression. President Herbert Hoover, unlucky in entering the White House only eight months before the stock market crash, had tried harder than any other president before him to deal with economic hard times. He had attempted to organize business, had sped up public works schedules, established the Reconstruction Finance Corporation to support businesses and financial institutions, and had secured from a reluctant Congress an agency to underwrite home mortgages. Nonetheless, his efforts had little impact, and he was a picture of defeat.

His Democratic opponent, Franklin D. Roosevelt, already popular as the governor of New York during the developing crisis, radiated infectious optimism. Prepared to use the federal government's authority for even bolder experimental remedies, he scored a smashing victory — receiving 22,800,000 popular votes to Hoover's 15,700,000. The United States was about to enter a new era of economic and political change.

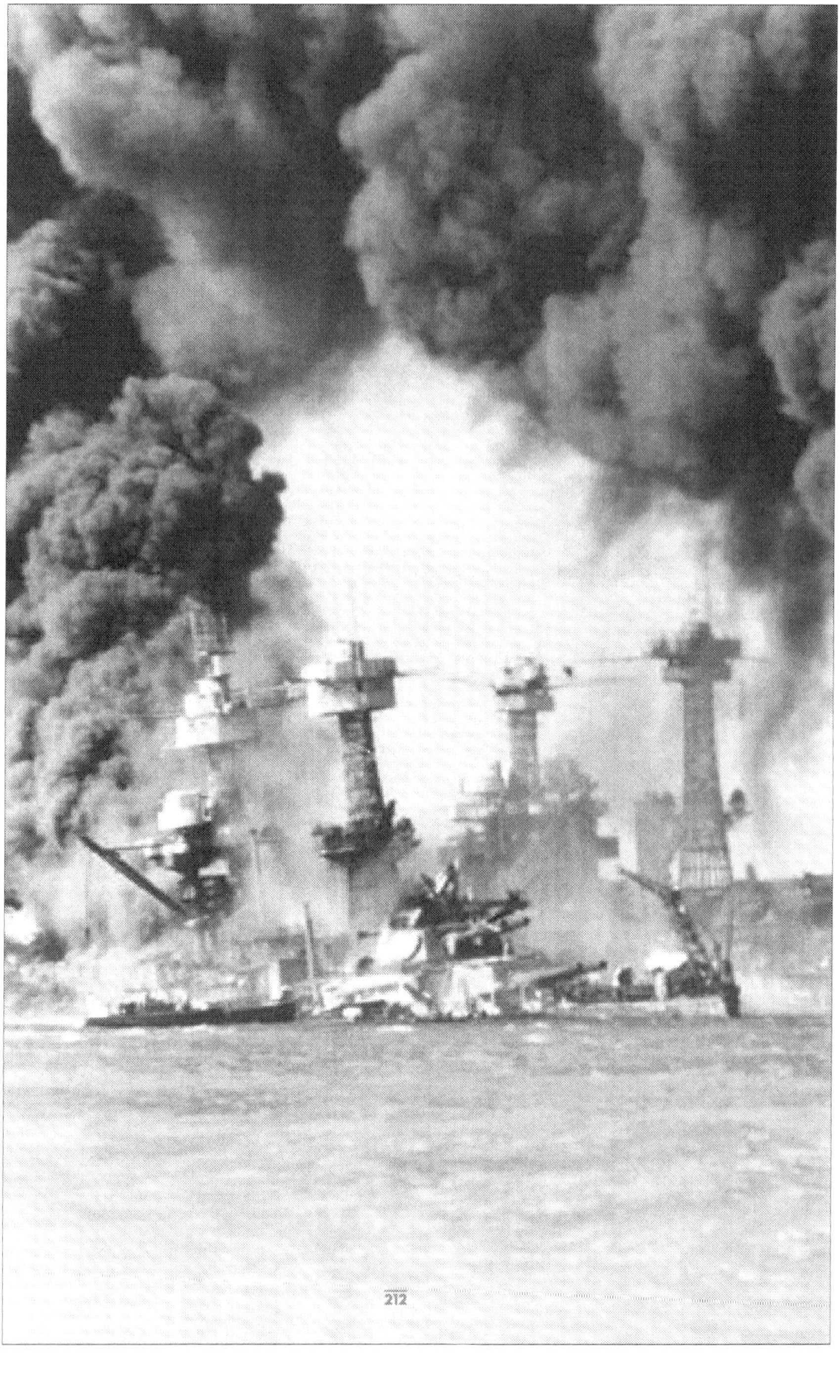

CHAPTER 11

THE NEW DEAL AND WORLD WAR II

U.S. battleships *West Virginia* and *Tennessee*, following the Japanese attack on Pearl Harbor, December 7, 1941.

"We must be the great arsenal of democracy."

President Franklin D. Roosevelt, 1941

ROOSEVELT AND THE NEW DEAL

In 1933 the new president, Franklin D. Roosevelt, brought an air of confidence and optimism that quickly rallied the people to the banner of his program, known as the New Deal. "The only thing we have to fear is fear itself," the president declared in his inaugural address to the nation.

In one sense, the New Deal merely introduced social and economic reforms familiar to many Europeans for more than a generation. Moreover, the New Deal represented the culmination of a long-range trend toward abandonment of "laissez-faire" capitalism, going back to the regulation of the railroads in the 1880s, and the flood of state and national reform legislation introduced in the Progressive era of Theodore Roosevelt and Woodrow Wilson.

What was truly novel about the New Deal, however, was the speed with which it accomplished what previously had taken generations. Many of its reforms were hastily drawn and weakly administered; some actually contradicted others. Moreover, it never succeeded in restoring prosperity. Yet its actions provided tangible help for millions of Americans, laid the basis for a powerful new political coalition, and brought to the individual citizen a sharp revival of interest in government.

THE FIRST NEW DEAL

Banking and Finance. When Roosevelt took the presidential oath, the banking and credit system of the nation was in a state of paralysis. With astonishing rapidity the nation's banks were first closed — and then reopened only if they were solvent. The administration adopted a policy of moderate currency inflation to start an upward movement in commodity prices and to afford some relief to debtors. New governmental agencies brought generous credit facilities to industry and agriculture. The Federal Deposit Insurance Corporation (FDIC) insured savings-bank deposits up to $5,000. Federal regulations were imposed upon the sale of securities on the stock exchange.

Unemployment. Roosevelt faced unprecedented mass unemployment. By the time he took office, as many as 13 million Americans — more than a quarter of the labor force — were out of work. Bread lines were a common sight in most cities. Hundreds of thousands roamed the country in search of food, work, and shelter. "Brother, can you spare a dime?" was the refrain of a popular song.

An early step for the unemployed came in the form of the Civilian Conservation Corps (CCC), a program that brought relief to young men between 18 and 25 years of age. CCC enrollees worked in camps administered by the army. About two million took part during the decade. They participated in a variety of conservation projects: planting trees to combat soil erosion and maintain national forests; eliminating stream pollution; creating fish, game, and bird sanctuaries; and conserving coal, petroleum, shale, gas, sodium, and helium deposits.

A Public Works Administration (PWA) provided employment for skilled construction workers on a wide variety of mostly medium- to large-sized projects. Among the most memorable of its many accomplishments were the Bonneville and Grand Coulee Dams in the Pacific Northwest, a new Chicago sewer system, the Triborough Bridge in New York City, and two aircraft carriers (*Yorktown* and *Enterprise*) for the U.S. Navy.

The Tennessee Valley Authority (TVA), both a work relief program and an exercise in public planning, developed the impoverished Tennessee River valley area through a series of dams built for flood control and hydroelectric power generation. Its provision of cheap electricity for the area stimulated some economic progress, but won it the enmity of private electric companies. New Dealers hailed it as an example of "grassroots democracy."

The Federal Emergency Relief Administration (FERA), in operation from 1933 to 1935, distributed direct relief to hundreds of thousands of people, usually in the form of direct payments. Sometimes, it assumed the salaries of schoolteachers and other local public service workers. It also developed numerous small-scale public works projects, as did the Civil Works Administration (CWA) from late 1933 into the spring of 1934. Criticized as "make work," the jobs funded ranged from ditch digging to highway repairs to teaching. Roosevelt and his key officials worried about costs but continued to favor unemployment programs based on work relief rather than welfare.

Agriculture. In the spring of 1933, the agricultural sector of the economy was in a state of collapse. It thereby provided a laboratory for the New Dealers' belief that greater regulation would solve many of the country's problems. In 1933, Congress passed the Agricultural Adjustment Act (AAA) to provide economic relief to farmers. The AAA proposed to raise crop prices by paying farmers a subsidy to compensate for voluntary cutbacks in production. Funds for the payments would be generated by a tax levied on industries that processed crops. By the time the act had become law, however, the growing season was well under way, and the AAA paid farmers to plow under their abundant crops. Crop reduction and further subsidies through the Commodity Credit Corporation, which purchased commodities to be kept in storage, drove output down and farm prices up.

Between 1932 and 1935, farm income increased by more than 50 percent, but only partly because of federal programs. During the same years that farmers were being encouraged to take land out of production — displacing tenants and sharecroppers — a severe drought hit the Plains states. Violent wind and dust storms during the 1930s created what became known as the "Dust Bowl." Crops were destroyed and farms ruined.

By 1940, 2.5 million people had moved out of the Plains states, the largest migration in American history. Of those, 200,000 moved to California. The migrants were not only farmers, but also professionals, retailers, and others whose livelihoods were connected to the health of the farm communities. Many ended up competing for seasonal jobs picking crops at extremely low wages.

The government provided aid in the form of the Soil Conservation Service, established in 1935. Farm practices that damaged the soil had intensified the impact of the drought. The service taught farmers measures to reduce erosion. In addition, almost 30,000 kilometers of trees were planted to break the force of winds.

Although the AAA had been mostly successful, it was abandoned in 1936, when its tax on food processors was ruled unconstitutional by the Supreme Court. Congress quickly passed a farm-relief act, which authorized the government to make payments to farmers who took land out of production for the purpose of soil conservation. In 1938, with a pro-New Deal majority on the Supreme Court, Congress reinstated the AAA.

By 1940 nearly six million farmers were receiving federal subsidies. New Deal programs also provided loans on surplus crops, insurance for wheat, and a system of planned storage to ensure a stable food supply. Economic stability for the farmer was substantially achieved, albeit at great expense and with extraordinary government oversight.

Industry and Labor. The National Recovery Administration (NRA), established in 1933 with the National Industrial Recovery Act (NIRA), attempted to end cutthroat competition by setting codes of fair competitive practice to generate more jobs and thus more buying. Although welcomed initially, the NRA was soon criticized for over-regulation and was unable to achieve industrial recovery. It was declared unconstitutional in 1935.

The NIRA had guaranteed to labor the right of collective bargaining through labor unions representing individual workers, but the NRA had failed to overcome strong business opposition to independent unionism. After its demise in 1935, Congress passed the National Labor Relations Act, which restated that guarantee and prohibited employers from unfairly interfering with union activities. It also created the National Labor Relations Board (NLRB) to supervise collective bargaining, administer elections, and ensure workers the right to choose the organization that should represent them in dealing with employers.

The great progress made in labor organization brought working people a growing sense of common interests, and labor's power increased not only in industry but also in politics. Roosevelt's Democratic Party benefited enormously from these developments.

THE SECOND NEW DEAL

In its early years, the New Deal sponsored a remarkable series of legislative initiatives and achieved significant increases in production and prices — but it did not bring an end to the Depression. As the sense of immediate crisis eased, new demands emerged. Businessmen mourned the end of "laissez-faire" and chafed under the regulations of the NIRA. Vocal attacks also mounted from the political left and right as dreamers, schemers, and politicians alike emerged with economic panaceas that drew wide audiences. Dr. Francis E. Townsend advocated generous old-age pensions. Father Charles Coughlin, the "radio priest," called for inflationary policies and blamed international bankers in speeches increasingly peppered with anti-Semitic imagery. Most formidably, Senator Huey P. Long of Louisiana, an eloquent and ruthless spokesman for the displaced, advocated a radical redistribution of wealth. (If he had not been assassinated in September 1935, Long very likely would have launched a presidential challenge to Franklin Roosevelt in 1936.)

In the face of these pressures, President Roosevelt backed a new set of economic and social measures. Prominent among them were measures to fight poverty, create more work for the unemployed, and provide a social safety net.

The Works Progress Administration (WPA), the principal relief agency of the so-called second New Deal, was the biggest public works agency yet. It pursued small-scale projects throughout the country, constructing buildings, roads, airports, and schools. Actors, painters, musicians, and writers were employed through the Federal Theater Project, the Federal Art Project, and the Federal Writers Project. The National Youth Administration gave part-time employment to students, established training programs, and provided aid to unemployed youth. The WPA only included about three million jobless at a time; when it was abandoned in 1943, it had helped a total of nine million people.

The New Deal's cornerstone, according to Roosevelt, was the Social Security Act of 1935. Social Security created a system of state-administered welfare payments for the poor, unemployed, and disabled based on matching state and federal contributions. It also established a national system of retirement benefits drawing on a "trust fund" created by employer and employee contributions. Many other industrialized nations had already enacted such programs, but calls for such an initiative in the United States had gone unheeded. Social Security today is the largest domestic program administered by the U.S. government.

To these, Roosevelt added the National Labor Relations Act, the "Wealth Tax Act" that increased taxes on the wealthy, the Public Utility Holding Company Act to break up large electrical utility conglomerates, and a Banking Act that greatly expanded the power of the Federal Reserve Board over the large private banks. Also notable was the establishment of the Rural Electrification Administration, which extended electricity into farming areas throughout the country.

A NEW COALITION

In the 1936 election, Roosevelt won a decisive victory over his Republican opponent, Alf Landon of Kansas. He was personally popular, and the economy seemed near recovery. He took 60 percent of the vote and carried all but two states. A broad new coalition aligned with the Democratic Party emerged, consisting of labor, most farmers, most urban ethnic groups, African Americans, and the traditionally Democratic South. The Republican Party received the support of business as well as middle-class members of small towns and suburbs. This political alliance, with some variation and shifting, remained intact for several decades.

Roosevelt's second term was a time of consolidation. The president made two serious political missteps: an ill-advised, unsuccessful attempt to enlarge the Supreme Court and a failed effort to "purge" increasingly recalcitrant Southern conservatives from the Democratic Party. When he cut high government spending, moreover, the economy collapsed. These events led to the rise of a conservative coalition in Congress that was unreceptive to new initiatives.

From 1932 to 1938 there was widespread public debate on the meaning of New Deal policies to the nation's political and economic life. Americans clearly wanted the government to take greater responsibility for the welfare of ordinary people, however uneasy they might be about big government in general. The New Deal established the foundations of the modern welfare state in the United States. Roosevelt, perhaps the most imposing of the 20th-century presidents, had established a new standard of mass leadership.

No American leader, then or since, used the radio so effectively. In a radio address in 1938, Roosevelt declared: "Democracy has disappeared in several other great nations, not because the people of those nations disliked democracy, but because they had grown tired of unemployment and insecurity, of seeing their children hungry while they sat helpless in the face of government confusion and government weakness through lack of leadership." Americans, he concluded, wanted to defend their liberties at any cost and understood that "the first line of the defense lies in the protection of economic security."

WAR AND UNEASY NEUTRALITY

Before Roosevelt's second term was well under way, his domestic program was overshadowed by the expansionist designs of totalitarian regimes in Japan, Italy, and Germany. In 1931 Japan had invaded Manchuria, crushed Chinese resistance, and set up the puppet state of Manchukuo. Italy, under Benito Mussolini, enlarged its boundaries in Libya and in 1935 conquered Ethiopia. Germany, under Nazi leader Adolf Hitler, militarized its economy and reoccupied the Rhineland (demilitarized by the Treaty of Versailles) in 1936. In 1938, Hitler incorporated Austria into the German Reich and demanded cession of the German-speaking Sudetenland from Czechoslovakia. By then, war seemed imminent.

The United States, disillusioned by the failure of the crusade for democracy in World War I, announced that in no circumstances could any country involved in the conflict look to it for aid. Neutrality legislation, enacted piecemeal from 1935 to 1937, prohibited trade in arms with any warring nations, required cash for all other commodities, and forbade American flag merchant ships from carrying those goods. The objective was to prevent, at almost any cost, the involvement of the United States in a foreign war.

With the Nazi conquest of Poland in 1939 and the outbreak of

World War II, isolationist sentiment increased, even though Americans clearly favored the victims of Hitler's aggression and supported the Allied democracies, Britain and France. Roosevelt could only wait until public opinion regarding U.S. involvement was altered by events.

After the fall of France and the beginning of the German air war against Britain in mid-1940, the debate intensified between those in the United States who favored aiding the democracies and the antiwar faction known as the isolationists. Roosevelt did what he could to nudge public opinion toward intervention. The United States joined Canada in a Mutual Board of Defense, and aligned with the Latin American republics in extending collective protection to the nations in the Western Hemisphere.

Congress, confronted with the mounting crisis, voted immense sums for rearmament, and in September 1940 passed the first peacetime conscription bill ever enacted in the United States. In that month also, Roosevelt concluded a daring executive agreement with British Prime Minister Winston Churchill. The United States gave the British Navy 50 "overage" destroyers in return for British air and naval bases in Newfoundland and the North Atlantic.

The 1940 presidential election campaign demonstrated that the isolationists, while vocal, were a minority. Roosevelt's Republican opponent, Wendell Wilkie, leaned toward intervention. Thus the November election yielded another majority for the president, making Roosevelt the first, and last, U.S. chief executive to be elected to a third term.

In early 1941, Roosevelt got Congress to approve the Lend-Lease Program, which enabled him to transfer arms and equipment to any nation (notably Great Britain, later the Soviet Union and China) deemed vital to the defense of the United States. Total Lend-Lease aid by war's end would amount to more than $50,000 million.

Most remarkably, in August, he met with Prime Minister Churchill off the coast of Newfoundland. The two leaders issued a "joint statement of war aims," which they called the Atlantic Charter. Bearing a remarkable resemblance to Woodrow Wilson's Fourteen Points, it called for these objectives: no territorial aggrandizement; no territorial changes without the consent of the people concerned; the right of all people to choose their own form of government; the restoration of self-government to those deprived of it; economic collaboration between all nations; freedom from war, from fear, and from want for all peoples; freedom of the seas; and the abandonment of the use of force as an instrument of international policy.

America was now neutral in name only.

JAPAN, PEARL HARBOR, AND WAR

While most Americans anxiously watched the course of the European war, tension mounted in Asia. Taking advantage of an opportunity to improve its strategic position, Japan boldly announced a "new order" in which it would exercise hegemony over all of the Pacific. Battling for survival against Nazi Germany, Britain was unable to resist, abandoning its concession in Shanghai and temporarily closing the Chinese supply route from Burma. In the summer of 1940, Japan won permission from the weak Vichy government in France to use airfields in northern Indochina (North Vietnam). That September the Japanese formally joined the Rome-Berlin Axis. The United States countered with an embargo on the export of scrap iron to Japan.

In July 1941 the Japanese occupied southern Indochina (South Vietnam), signaling a probable move southward toward the oil, tin, and rubber of British Malaya and the Dutch East Indies. The United States, in response, froze Japanese assets and initiated an embargo on the one commodity Japan needed above all others — oil.

General Hideki Tojo became prime minister of Japan that October. In mid-November, he sent a special envoy to the United States to meet with Secretary of State Cordell Hull. Among other things, Japan demanded that the United States release Japanese assets and stop U.S. naval expansion in the Pacific. Hull countered with a proposal for Japanese withdrawal from all its conquests. The swift Japanese rejection on December 1 left the talks stalemated.

On the morning of December 7, Japanese carrier-based planes executed a devastating surprise attack against the U.S. Pacific Fleet at Pearl Harbor, Hawaii.

Twenty-one ships were destroyed or temporarily disabled; 323 aircraft were destroyed or damaged; 2,388 soldiers, sailors, and civilians were killed. However, the U.S. aircraft carriers that would play such a critical role in the ensuing naval war in the Pacific were at sea and not anchored at Pearl Harbor.

American opinion, still divided about the war in Europe, was unified overnight by what President Roosevelt called "a day that will live in infamy." On December 8, Congress declared a state of war with Japan; three days later Germany and Italy declared war on the United States.

MOBILIZATION FOR TOTAL WAR

The nation rapidly geared itself for mobilization of its people and its entire industrial capacity. Over the next three-and-a-half years, war industry achieved staggering production goals — 300,000 aircraft, 5,000 cargo ships, 60,000 landing craft, 86,000 tanks. Women workers, exemplified by "Rosie the Riveter," played a bigger part in industrial production than ever before. Total strength of the U.S. armed forces at the end of the war was more than 12 million. All the nation's activities — farming, manufacturing, mining, trade, labor, investment, communications, even education and cultural undertakings — were in some fashion brought under new and enlarged controls.

As a result of Pearl Harbor and the fear of Asian espionage, Americans also committed what was later recognized as an act of intolerance: the internment of Japanese Americans. In February 1942, nearly 120,000 Japanese Americans residing in California were removed from their homes and interned behind barbed wire in 10 wretched temporary camps, later to be moved to "relocation centers" outside isolated Southwestern towns.

Nearly 63 percent of these Japanese Americans were American-born U.S. citizens. A few were Japanese sympathizers, but no evidence of espionage ever surfaced. Others volunteered for the U.S. Army and fought with distinction and valor in two infantry units on the Italian front. Some served as interpreters and translators in the Pacific.

In 1983 the U.S. government acknowledged the injustice of internment with limited payments to those Japanese-Americans of that era who were still living.

THE WAR IN NORTH AFRICA AND EUROPE

Soon after the United States entered the war, the United States, Britain, and the Soviet Union (at war with Germany since June 22, 1941) decided that their primary military effort was to be concentrated in Europe.

Throughout 1942, British and German forces fought inconclusive back-and-forth battles across Libya and Egypt for control of the Suez Canal. But on October 23, British forces commanded by General Sir Bernard Montgomery struck at the Germans from El Alamein. Equipped with a thousand tanks, many made in America, they defeated General Erwin Rommel's army in a grinding two-week campaign. On November 7, American and British armed forces landed in French North Africa. Squeezed between forces advancing from east and west, the Germans were pushed back and, after fierce resistance, surrendered in May 1943.

The year 1942 was also the turning point on the Eastern Front. The Soviet Union, suffering immense losses, stopped the Nazi invasion at the gates of Leningrad and Moscow. In the winter of 1942-43, the Red Army defeated the Germans at Stalingrad (Volgograd) and began the long offensive that would take them to Berlin in 1945.

In July 1943 British and American forces invaded Sicily and won control of the island in a month.

During that time, Benito Mussolini fell from power in Italy. His successors began negotiations with the Allies and surrendered immediately after the invasion of the Italian mainland in September. However, the German Army had by then taken control of the peninsula. The fight against Nazi forces in Italy was bitter and protracted. Rome was not liberated until June 4, 1944. As the Allies slowly moved north, they built airfields from which they made devastating air raids against railroads, factories, and weapon emplacements in southern Germany and central Europe, including the oil installations at Ploesti, Romania.

Late in 1943 the Allies, after much debate over strategy, decided to open a front in France to compel the Germans to divert far larger forces from the Soviet Union.

U.S. General Dwight D. Eisenhower was appointed Supreme Commander of the Allied Forces in Europe. After immense preparations, on June 6, 1944, a U.S., British, and Canadian invasion army, protected by a greatly superior air force, landed on five beaches in Normandy. With the beachheads established after heavy fighting, more troops poured in, and pushed the Germans back in one bloody engagement after another. On August 25 Paris was liberated.

The Allied offensive stalled that fall, then suffered a setback in eastern Belgium during the winter, but in March, the Americans and British were across the Rhine and the Russians advancing irresistibly from the East. On May 7, Germany surrendered unconditionally.

THE WAR IN THE PACIFIC

U.S. troops were forced to surrender in the Philippines in early 1942, but the Americans rallied in the following months. General James "Jimmy" Doolittle led U.S. Army bombers on a raid over Tokyo in April; it had little actual military significance, but gave Americans an immense psychological boost.

In May, at the Battle of the Coral Sea — the first naval engagement in history in which all the fighting was done by carrier-based planes — a Japanese naval invasion fleet sent to strike at southern New Guinea and Australia was turned back by a U.S. task force in a close battle. A few weeks later, the naval Battle of Midway in the central Pacific resulted in the first major defeat of the Japanese Navy, which lost four aircraft carriers. Ending the Japanese advance across the central Pacific, Midway was the turning point.

Other battles also contributed to Allied success. The six-month land and sea battle for the island of Guadalcanal (August 1942-February 1943) was the first major U.S. ground victory in the Pacific. For most of the next two years, American and Australian troops fought their way northward from the South Pacific and westward from the Central Pacific, capturing the Solomons, the Gilberts, the Marshalls, and the Marianas in a series of amphibious assaults.

THE POLITICS OF WAR

Allied military efforts were accompanied by a series of important international meetings on the political objectives of the war. In January 1943 at Casablanca, Morocco, an Anglo-American conference decided that no peace would be concluded with the Axis and its Balkan satellites except on the basis of "unconditional surrender." This term, insisted upon by Roosevelt, sought to assure the people of all the fighting nations that no separate peace negotiations would be carried on with representatives of Fascism and Nazism and there would be no compromise of the war's idealistic objectives. Axis propagandists, of course, used it to assert that the Allies were engaged in a war of extermination.

At Cairo, in November 1943, Roosevelt and Churchill met with Nationalist Chinese leader Chiang Kai-shek to agree on terms for Japan, including the relinquishment of gains from past aggression. At Tehran, shortly afterward, Roosevelt, Churchill, and Soviet leader Joseph Stalin made basic agreements on the postwar occupation of Germany and the establishment of a new international organization, the United Nations.

In February 1945, the three Allied leaders met again at Yalta (now in Ukraine), with victory seemingly secure. There, the Soviet Union secretly agreed to enter the war against Japan three months after the surrender of Germany. In return, the USSR would gain effective control of Manchuria and receive the Japanese Kurile Islands as well as the southern half of Sakhalin Island. The eastern boundary of Poland was set roughly at the Curzon line of 1919, thus giving the USSR half its prewar territory. Discussion of reparations to be collected from Germany — payment demanded by Stalin and opposed by Roosevelt and Churchill — was inconclusive. Specific arrangements were made concerning Allied occupation in Germany and the trial and punishment of war criminals. Also at Yalta it was agreed that the great powers in the Security Council of the proposed United Nations should have the right of veto in matters affecting their security.

Two months after his return from Yalta, Franklin Roosevelt died of a cerebral hemorrhage while vacationing in Georgia. Few figures in U.S. history have been so deeply mourned, and for a time the American people suffered from a numbing sense of irreparable loss. Vice President Harry Truman, former senator from Missouri, succeeded him.

WAR, VICTORY, AND THE BOMB

The final battles in the Pacific were among the war's bloodiest. In June 1944, the Battle of the Philippine Sea effectively destroyed Japanese naval air power, forcing the resignation of

Japanese Prime Minister Tojo. General Douglas MacArthur — who had reluctantly left the Philippines two years before to escape Japanese capture — returned to the islands in October. The accompanying Battle of Leyte Gulf, the largest naval engagement ever fought, was the final decisive defeat of the Japanese Navy. By February 1945, U.S. forces had taken Manila.

Next, the United States set its sight on the strategic island of Iwo Jima in the Bonin Islands, about halfway between the Marianas and Japan. The Japanese, trained to die fighting for the Emperor, made suicidal use of natural caves and rocky terrain. U.S. forces took the island by mid-March, but not before losing the lives of some 6,000 U.S. Marines. Nearly all the Japanese defenders perished. By now the United States was undertaking extensive air attacks on Japanese shipping and airfields and wave after wave of incendiary bombing attacks against Japanese cities.

At Okinawa (April 1-June 21, 1945), the Americans met even fiercer resistance. With few of the defenders surrendering, the U.S. Army and Marines were forced to wage a war of annihilation. Waves of Kamikaze suicide planes pounded the offshore Allied fleet, inflicting more damage than at Leyte Gulf. Japan lost 90-100,000 troops and probably as many Okinawan civilians. U.S. losses were more than 11,000 killed and nearly 34,000 wounded. Most Americans saw the fighting as a preview of what they would face in a planned invasion of Japan.

The heads of the U.S., British, and Soviet governments met at Potsdam, a suburb outside Berlin, from July 17 to August 2, 1945, to discuss operations against Japan, the peace settlement in Europe, and a policy for the future of Germany. Perhaps presaging the coming end of the alliance, they had no trouble on vague matters of principle or the practical issues of military occupation, but reached no agreement on many tangible issues, including reparations.

The day before the Potsdam Conference began, U.S. nuclear scientists engaged in the secret Manhattan Project exploded an atomic bomb near Alamogordo, New Mexico. The test was the culmination of three years of intensive research in laboratories across the United States. It lay behind the Potsdam Declaration, issued on July 26 by the United States and Britain, promising that Japan would neither be destroyed nor enslaved if it surrendered. If Japan continued the war, however, it would meet "prompt and utter destruction." President Truman, calculating that an atomic bomb might be used to gain Japan's surrender more quickly and with fewer casualties than an invasion of the mainland, ordered that the bomb be used if the Japanese did not surrender by August 3.

A committee of U.S. military and political officials and scientists had considered the question of targets for the new weapon. Secretary of

War Henry L. Stimson argued successfully that Kyoto, Japan's ancient capital and a repository of many national and religious treasures, be taken out of consideration. Hiroshima, a center of war industries and military operations, became the first objective.

On August 6, a U.S. plane, the *Enola Gay*, dropped an atomic bomb on the city of Hiroshima. On August 9, a second atomic bomb was dropped, this time on Nagasaki. The bombs destroyed large sections of both cities, with massive loss of life. On August 8, the USSR declared war on Japan and attacked Japanese forces in Manchuria. On August 14, Japan agreed to the terms set at Potsdam. On September 2, 1945, Japan formally surrendered. Americans were relieved that the bomb hastened the end of the war. The realization of the full implications of nuclear weapons' awesome destructiveness would come later.

Within a month, on October 24, the United Nations came into existence following the meeting of representatives of 50 nations in San Francisco, California. The constitution they drafted outlined a world organization in which international differences could be discussed peacefully and common cause made against hunger and disease. In contrast to its rejection of U.S. membership in the League of Nations after World War I, the U.S. Senate promptly ratified the U.N. Charter by an 89 to 2 vote. This action confirmed the end of the spirit of isolationism as a dominating element in American foreign policy.

In November 1945 at Nuremberg, Germany, the criminal trials of 22 Nazi leaders, provided for at Potsdam, took place. Before a group of distinguished jurists from Britain, France, the Soviet Union, and the United States, the Nazis were accused not only of plotting and waging aggressive war but also of violating the laws of war and of humanity in the systematic genocide, known as the Holocaust, of European Jews and other peoples. The trials lasted more than 10 months. Twenty-two defendants were convicted, 12 of them sentenced to death. Similar proceedings would be held against Japanese war leaders. ◇

THE RISE OF INDUSTRIAL UNIONS

While the 1920s were years of relative prosperity in the United States, the workers in industries such as steel, automobiles, rubber, and textiles benefited less than they would later in the years after World War II. Working conditions in many of these industries did improve. Some companies in the 1920s began to institute "welfare capitalism" by offering workers various pension, profit-sharing, stock option, and health plans to ensure their loyalty. Still, shop floor environments were often hard and authoritarian.

The 1920s saw the mass production industries redouble their efforts to prevent the growth of unions, which under the American Federation of Labor (AFL) had enjoyed some success during World War I. They did so by using spies and armed strikebreakers and by firing those suspected of union sympathies. Independent unions were often accused of being Communist. At the same time, many companies formed their own compliant employee organizations, often called "company unions."

Traditionally, state legislatures, reflecting the views of the American middle class, supported the concept of the "open shop," which prevented a union from being the exclusive representative of all workers. This made it easier for companies to deny unions the right to collective bargaining and block unionization through court enforcement.

Between 1920 and 1929, union membership in the United States dropped from about five million to three-and-a-half million. The large unskilled or semi-skilled industries remained unorganized.

The onset of the Great Depression led to widespread unemployment. By 1933 there were over 12 million Americans out of work. In the automobile industry, for example, the work force was cut in half between 1929 and 1933. At the same time, wages dropped by two-thirds.

The election of Franklin Roosevelt, however, was to change the status of the American industrial worker forever. The first indication that Roosevelt was interested in the well-being of workers came with the appointment of Frances Perkins, a prominent social welfare advocate, to be his secretary of labor. (Perkins was also the first woman to hold a Cabinet-level position.) The far-reaching National Industrial Recovery Act sought to raise industrial wages, limit the hours in a work week, and eliminate child labor. Most importantly, the law recognized the right of employees "to organize and bargain collectively through representatives of their own choosing."

John L. Lewis, the feisty and articulate head of the United Mine Workers (UMW), understood more than any other labor leader what the New Deal meant for workers. Stressing Roosevelt's support, Lewis engineered a major unionizing campaign, rebuilding the UMW's declining membership from 150,000 to over 500,000 within a year.

Lewis was eager to get the AFL, where he was a member of the Executive Council, to launch a similar drive in the mass production industries. But the AFL, with its historic focus on the skilled trade worker, was unwilling to do so. After a bitter internal feud, Lewis and a few others broke with the AFL to set up the Committee for Industrial Organization (CIO), later the Congress of Industrial Organizations. The passage of the National Labor Relations Act (NLRA) in 1935 and the friendly attitude of the National Labor Relations Board put the power and authority of the federal government behind the CIO.

Its first targets were the notoriously anti-union auto and steel industries. In late 1936 a series of sit-down strikes, orchestrated by the fledgling United Auto Workers union under Walter Reuther, erupted at General Motors plants in Cleveland, Ohio, and Flint, Michigan. Soon 135,000 workers were involved and GM production ground to a halt.

With the sympathetic governor of Michigan refusing to evict the strikers, a settlement was reached in early 1937. By September of that year, the United Auto Workers had contracts with 400 companies involved in the automobile industry, assuring workers a minimum wage of 75 cents per hour and a 40-hour work week.

In the first six months of its existence, the Steel Workers Organizing Committee (SWOC), headed by Lewis lieutenant Philip Murray, picked up 125,000 members. The major American steel company, U.S. Steel, realizing that times had changed, also came to terms in 1937. That same year the Supreme Court upheld the constitutionality of the NLRA. Subsequently, smaller companies, traditionally even more anti-union than the large corporations, gave in. One by one, other industries — rubber, oil, electronics, and textiles — also followed suit.

The rise of big labor had two major long-term impacts. It became the organizational core of the national Democratic Party, and it gained material benefits for its members that all but erased the economic distinction between working-class and middle-class America. ◆

In the depths of the Great Depression, March 1933, anxious depositors line up outside of a New York bank. The new president, Franklin D. Roosevelt, had just temporarily closed the nation's banks to end the drain on the banks' reserves. Only those banks that were still solvent were permitted to reopen after a four-day "bank holiday."

TURMOIL AND CHANGE

A PICTURE PROFILE

For the United States, the 20th century was a period of extraordinary turmoil and change. In these decades, the nation endured the worst economic depression in its history; emerged triumphant, with the Allies, in World War II; assumed a role of global leadership in the century's twilight conflict known as the Cold War; and underwent a remarkable social, economic, and political transition at home. Where once the United States transformed itself over the slow march of centuries, it now seemed to reinvent itself almost by decades.

Men and women strikers dance the time away on March 11, 1937, during a strike at the Chevrolet Fisher Body Plants in St. Louis, Missouri. Strikes such as these succeeded in winning union recognition for industrial workers throughout the country in the 1930s.

President Franklin D. Roosevelt signs perhaps the most far-reaching legislation of the New Deal: the Social Security Act of 1935. Today, Social Security, one of the largest government programs in the United States, provides retirement and disability income to millions of Americans.

World War II in the Pacific was characterized by large-scale naval and air battles. Here, a Japanese plane plunges in flames during an attack on a U.S. carrier fleet in the Mariana Islands, June 1944. U.S. Army and Marine forces' "island hopping" campaign began at Guadalcanal in August 1942 and ended with the assault on Okinawa in April 1945.

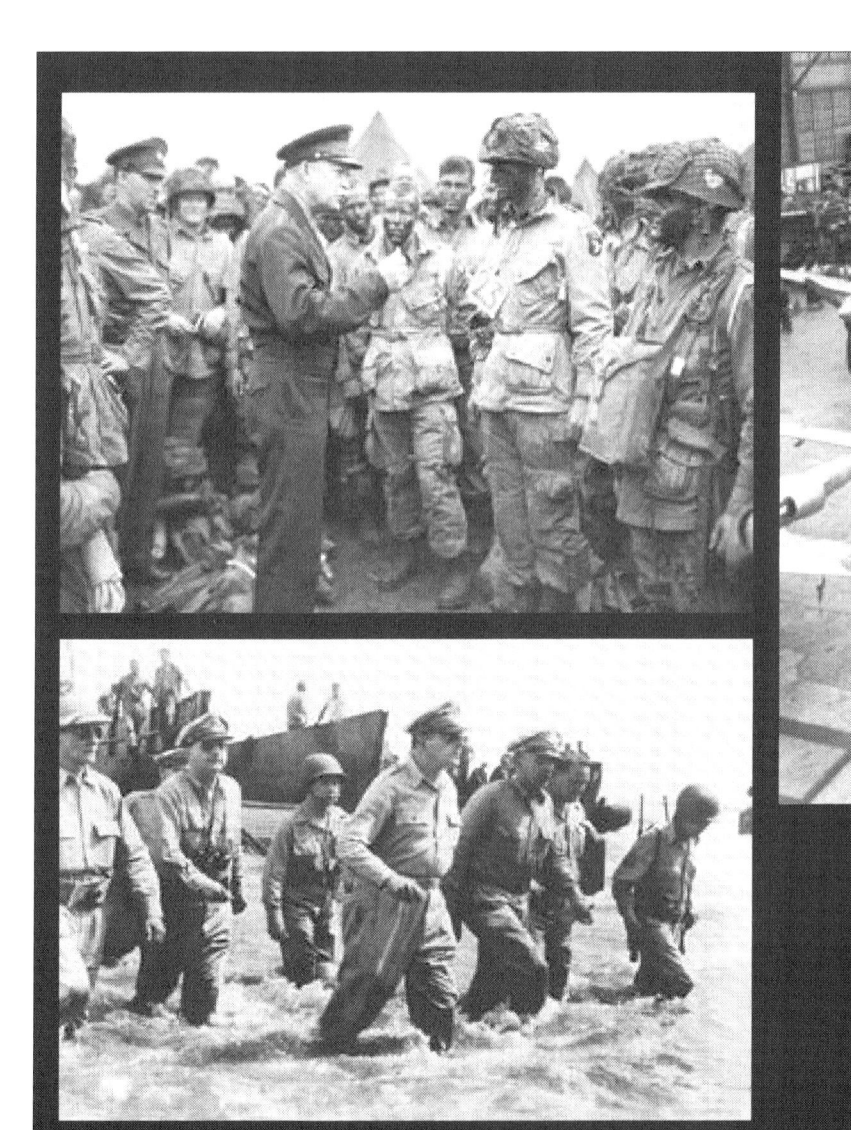

Top, General Dwight Eisenhower, Supreme Commander in Europe, talks with paratroopers shortly before the Normandy invasion, June 6, 1944.
Above, General Douglas MacArthur (center) had declared, "I shall return," when he escaped from advancing Japanese forces in the Philippines in 1942. Two years later, he made good on his promise and waded ashore at Leyte as American forces began the liberation of the Philippines.

Assembly line of P-38 *Lightning* fighter planes during World War II. With its massive output of war materiel, the United States became, in the words of President Roosevelt, "the arsenal of democracy."

Japanese Americans await relocation to internment camps in the worst violation of human rights that occurred inside the United States during World War II.

Meeting of British Prime Minister Winston Churchill, President Roosevelt, and Soviet leader Josef Stalin at Yalta in February 1945. Disagreements over the future of Europe anticipated the division of the European continent that remained a fixture of the Cold War.

U.S. troops witness a nuclear test in the Nevada desert in 1951. The threat of nuclear weapons remained a constant and ominous fact of life throughout the Cold War era.

In perhaps the most famous photograph in American political history, President Harry Truman holds aloft a newspaper wrongly announcing his defeat by Republican nominee Thomas Dewey in the 1948 presidential election. Truman's come-from-behind victory surprised all political experts that day.

U.S. infantry fire against North Korean forces invading South Korea in 1951, in a conflict that lasted three painful years.

At a congressional hearing in 1954, Senator Joseph McCarthy points to a map purportedly showing Communist Party influence in the United States in 1950. His chief antagonist at the hearing, lawyer Joseph Welch, sits at left. Welch successfully discredited McCarthy at these hearings, which were among the first to be televised across the country.

Portrait of President Dwight Eisenhower, whose genial, reassuring personality dominated the decade of the 1950s.

Jackie Robinson, sliding home in a 1948 baseball game. Robinson broke the color barrier against black professional baseball players when he joined the Brooklyn Dodgers and became one of the stars of the game.

America's first star of rock and roll, Elvis Presley, performing on television's "Ed Sullivan Show," September 9, 1956. Today, years after his death, he is still revered by legions of his fans as "The King."

Lucille Ball (second from left) with her supporting cast, including husband Desi Arnaz (standing), on one of the most popular television comedy shows of the 1950s, *I Love Lucy*. The show established many of the techniques and conventions shared by hundreds of the televised "situation comedies" that followed.

Above, Rosa Parks sits in one of the front seats of a city bus following the successful boycott of the bus system in 1955-56 by African-American citizens of Montgomery, Alabama. The boycott was organized to protest the practice of segregation in which African Americans were forced to sit in the back of the bus. The Supreme Court agreed that this practice was a constitutional violation a year after the boycott began. The great leader of the civil rights movement in America, Martin Luther King Jr., gained national prominence through the Montgomery bus boycott.

Opposite page, right, Martin Luther King Jr. escorts children to a previously all-white public school in Grenada, Mississippi, in 1966. Although school segregation was outlawed in the landmark *Brown v. Board of Education* decision of the Supreme Court in 1954, it took decades of protest, political pressure, and additional court decisions to enforce school desegregation across the country.

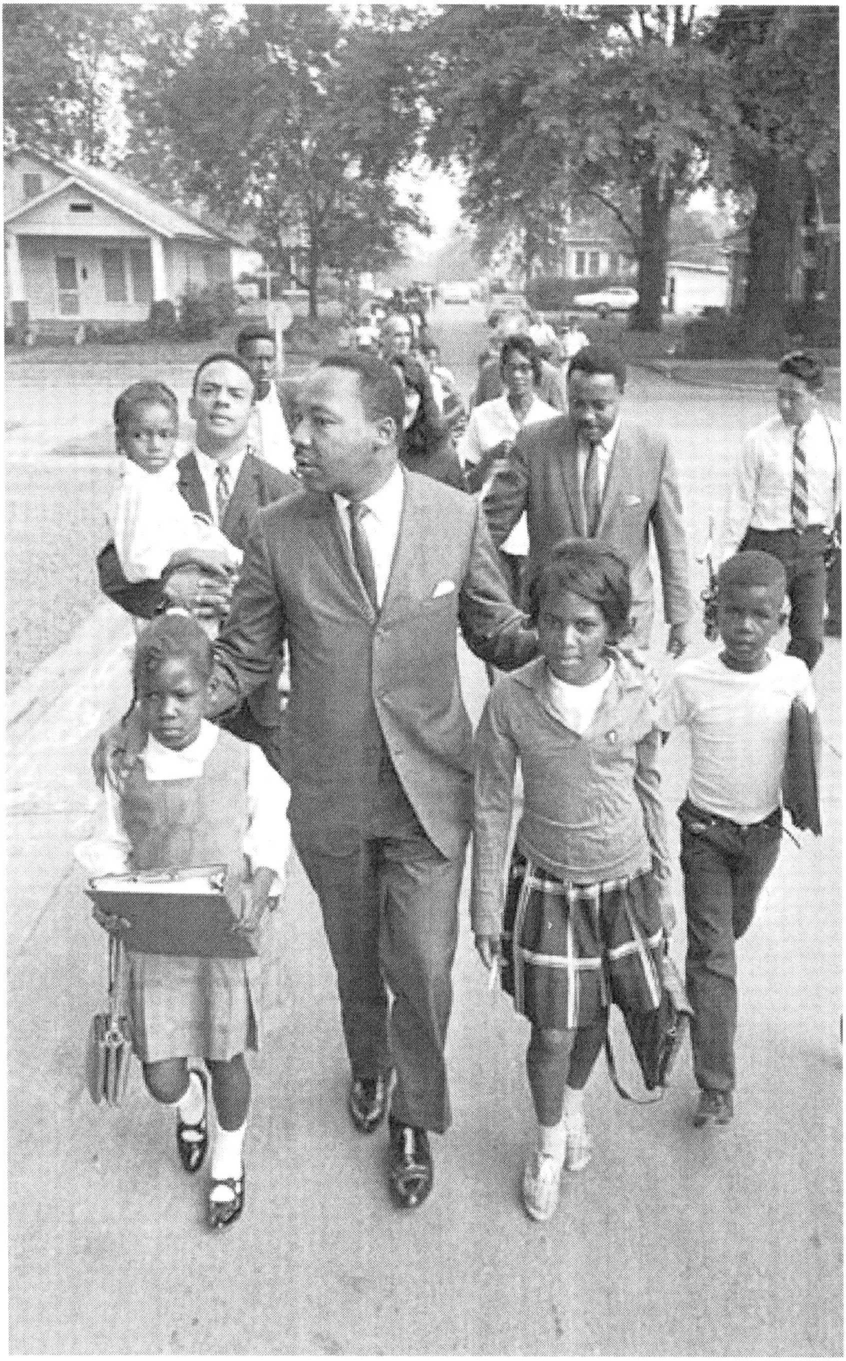

President John F. Kennedy addresses nearly a quarter of a million Germans in West Berlin in June 1963. Honoring the courage of those living in one of the flash points of the Cold War, he said, "All free men, wherever they may live, are citizens of Berlin, and therefore, as a free man, I take pride in the words, 'Ich bin ein Berliner' (I am a Berliner)."

Ratification document for the 1963 Limited Nuclear Test Ban Treaty, one of the first arms control agreements between the West and the Soviet bloc, which ended atmospheric nuclear testing.

Thurgood Marshall, one of the champions of equal rights for all Americans. As a counsel for the National Association for the Advancement of Colored People (NAACP), Marshall successfully argued the landmark 1954 *Brown v. Board of Education* case before the Supreme Court, which outlawed segregation in public schools. He later served a distinguished career as a justice of the Supreme Court.

President Lyndon B. Johnson, born in Texas, was Senate majority leader in the Eisenhower years and vice president under John F. Kennedy before becoming president. One of the most powerful political personalities to serve in Washington, Johnson engineered the most ambitious domestic legislative agenda through Congress since Roosevelt's New Deal. The Vietnam War ended his presidency, however, since it divided the nation.

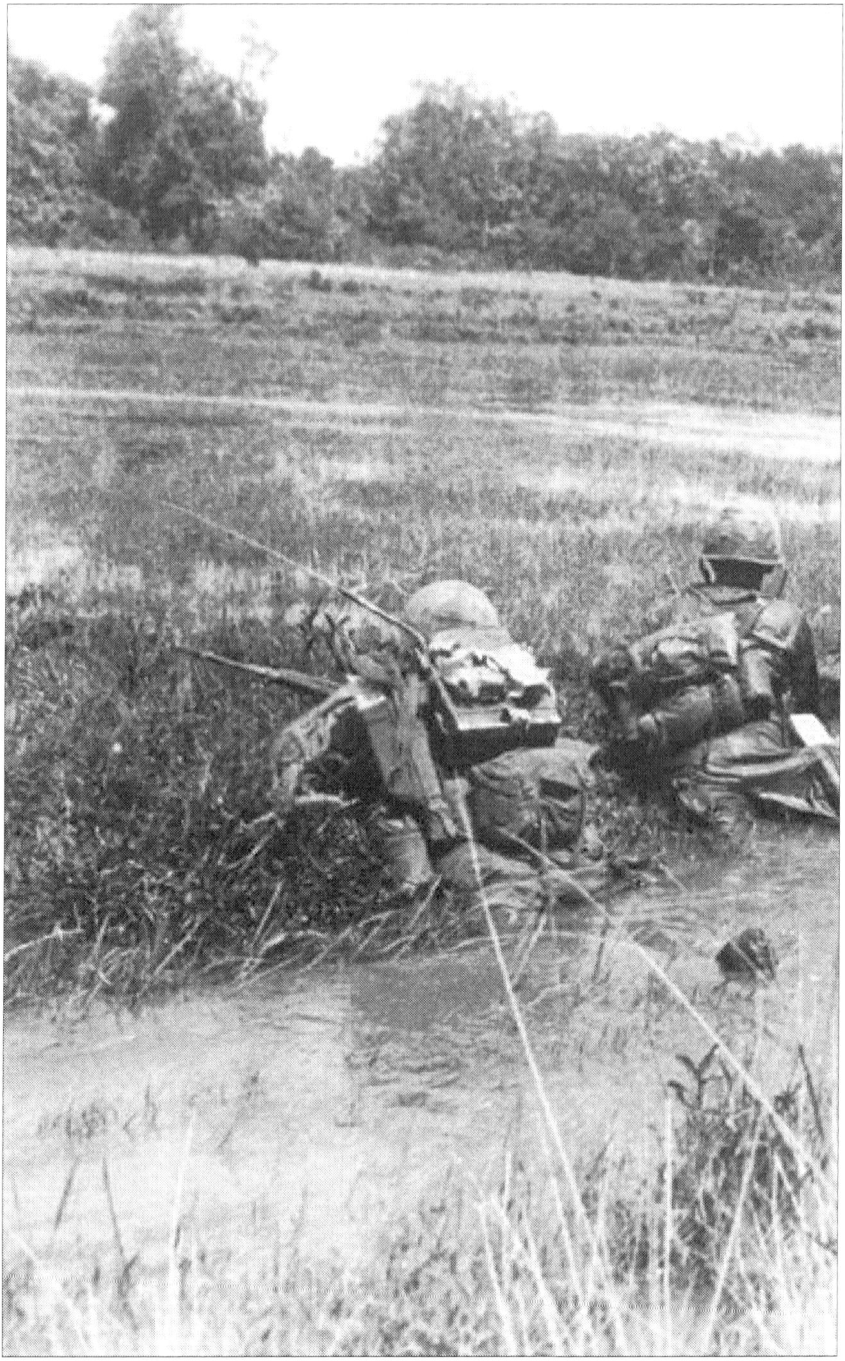

A U.S. Army unit searches for snipers while on patrol in South Vietnam in 1965. From 60,000 troops in 1965, U.S. forces grew to more than 540,000 by 1969, in a conflict that divided the nation more bitterly than any other in the 20th century. The last U.S. combat forces left Vietnam in 1973.

Antiwar demonstrators and police clash during violent protests at the 1968 Democratic National Convention in Chicago, Illinois. Antiwar candidates at the convention lost the presidential nomination to Lyndon Johnson's vice president, Hubert Humphrey.

Two of the leaders of the women's movement in the 1960s: Kate Millett (left), author of a controversial book of the time, *Sexual Politics*, and journalist and activist Gloria Steinem.

The crest of the counterculture wave in the United States: the three-day 1969 outdoor rock concert and gathering known as Woodstock.

Mexican-American labor activist César Chávez (center) talking with grape pickers in the field in 1968. Head of the United Farm Workers Union in California, Chávez was a leading voice for the rights of migrant farm workers, focusing national attention on their terrible working conditions.

President Richard M. Nixon, with his wife Pat Nixon and Secretary of State William Rogers (far right), walks along a portion of the Great Wall of China. Nixon's 1972 opening to the People's Republic of China was a major diplomatic triumph at a time when U.S. forces were slowly withdrawing from South Vietnam.

Participant in a demonstration by Native Americans in Washington, D.C., in 1978. They also have sought to assert their rights and identity in recent decades.

Oil fires burn behind a destroyed Iraqi tank at the conclusion of the Gulf War in February 1991. The United States led a coalition of more than 30 nations in an air and ground campaign called Desert Storm that ended Iraq's occupation of Kuwait.

Civil rights leader and political activist Jesse Jackson at a political rally in 1984. For more than four decades, Jackson has remained among the most prominent, politically active, and eloquent representatives of what he has termed a "Rainbow Coalition" of the poor, African Americans, and other minorities.

A launch of a space shuttle, the first reusable space vehicle. The versatile shuttle, which has been used to place satellites in orbit and conduct wide-ranging experiments, is indispensable in the assemblage (beginning June 1998) and running of the International Space Station.

President George H.W. Bush with Poland's Lech Walesa (center) and First Lady Barbara Bush in Warsaw, July 1989. That remarkable year saw the end of the Cold War, as well as the end to the 40-year division of Europe into hostile East and West blocs.

President William (Bill) J. Clinton, delivering his inaugural address to the nation, January 21, 1993. During his administration, the United States enjoyed more peace and economic well-being than at any time in its history. He was the second U.S. president to be impeached and found not guilty.

PAN AMERICAN VAN
STORAGE
McCallson
VAN & STORAGE CO.
MOVING STORAGE
SHIPPING CRATING
PAN
AND

CHAPTER 12

POSTWAR AMERICA

Moving day in a newly opened suburban community, 1953.

> "We must build a new world,
> a far better world —
> one in which the
> eternal dignity of man
> is respected."
>
> President Harry S. Truman, 1945

CONSENSUS AND CHANGE

The United States dominated global affairs in the years immediately after World War II. Victorious in that great struggle, its homeland undamaged from the ravages of war, the nation was confident of its mission at home and abroad. U.S. leaders wanted to maintain the democratic structure they had defended at tremendous cost and to share the benefits of prosperity as widely as possible. For them, as for publisher Henry Luce of *Time* magazine, this was the "American Century."

For 20 years most Americans remained sure of this confident approach. They accepted the need for a strong stance against the Soviet Union in the Cold War that unfolded after 1945. They endorsed the growth of government authority and accepted the outlines of the rudimentary welfare state first formulated during the New Deal. They enjoyed a postwar prosperity that created new levels of affluence.

But gradually some began to question dominant assumptions. Challenges on a variety of fronts shattered the consensus. In the 1950s, African Americans launched a crusade, joined later by other minority groups and women, for a larger share of the American dream. In the 1960s, politically active students protested the nation's role abroad, particularly in the corrosive war in Vietnam. A youth counterculture emerged to challenge the status quo. Americans from many walks of life sought to establish a new social and political equilibrium.

COLD WAR AIMS

The Cold War was the most important political and diplomatic issue of the early postwar period. It grew out of longstanding disagreements between the Soviet Union and the United States that developed after the Russian Revolution of 1917. The Soviet Communist Party under V.I. Lenin considered itself the spearhead of an international movement that would replace the existing political orders in the West, and indeed throughout the world. In 1918 American troops participated in the Allied intervention in Russia on behalf of anti-Bolshevik forces. American diplomatic recognition of the Soviet Union did not come until 1933. Even then, suspicions persisted. During World War II, however, the two countries found themselves allied and downplayed their differences to counter the Nazi threat.

At the war's end, antagonisms surfaced again. The United States hoped to share with other countries its conception of liberty, equality, and democracy. It sought also to learn from the perceived mistakes of the post-WWI era, when American political disengagement and economic protectionism were thought to have contributed to the rise of dictatorships in Europe and elsewhere. Faced again with a postwar world of civil wars and disintegrating empires, the nation hoped to provide the stability to make peaceful reconstruction possible. Recalling the specter of the Great Depression (1929-40), America now advocated open trade for two reasons: to create markets for American agricultural and industrial products, and to ensure the ability of Western European nations to export as a means of rebuilding their economies. Reduced trade barriers, American policy makers believed, would promote economic growth at home and abroad, bolstering U.S. friends and allies in the process.

The Soviet Union had its own agenda. The Russian historical tradition of centralized, autocratic government contrasted with the American emphasis on democracy. Marxist-Leninist ideology had been downplayed during the war but still guided Soviet policy. Devastated by the struggle in which 20 million Soviet citizens had died, the Soviet Union was intent on rebuilding and on protecting itself from another such terrible conflict. The Soviets were particularly concerned about another invasion of their territory from the west. Having repelled Hitler's thrust, they were determined to preclude another such attack. They demanded "defensible" borders and "friendly" regimes in Eastern Europe and seemingly equated both with the spread of Communism, regardless of the wishes of native populations. However, the United States had declared that one of its war aims was the restoration of independence and self-government to Poland, Czechoslovakia, and the other countries of Central and Eastern Europe.

HARRY TRUMAN'S LEADERSHIP

The nation's new chief executive, Harry S. Truman, succeeded Franklin D. Roosevelt as president before the end of the war. An unpretentious man who had previously served as Democratic senator from Missouri, then as vice president, Truman initially felt ill-prepared to govern. Roosevelt had not discussed complex postwar issues with him, and he had little experience in international affairs. "I'm not big enough for this job," he told a former colleague.

Still, Truman responded quickly to new challenges. Sometimes impulsive on small matters, he proved willing to make hard and carefully considered decisions on large ones. A small sign on his White House desk declared, "The Buck Stops Here." His judgments about how to respond to the Soviet Union ultimately determined the shape of the early Cold War.

ORIGINS OF THE COLD WAR

The Cold War developed as differences about the shape of the postwar world created suspicion and distrust between the United States and the Soviet Union. The first — and most difficult — test case was Poland, the eastern half of which had been invaded and occupied by the USSR in 1939. Moscow demanded a government subject to Soviet influence; Washington wanted a more independent, representative government following the Western model. The Yalta Conference of February 1945 had produced an agreement on Eastern Europe open to different interpretations. It included a promise of "free and unfettered" elections.

Meeting with Soviet Minister of Foreign Affairs Vyacheslav Molotov less than two weeks after becoming president, Truman stood firm on Polish self-determination, lecturing the Soviet diplomat about the need to implement the Yalta accords. When Molotov protested, "I have never been talked to like that in my life," Truman retorted, "Carry out your agreements and you won't get talked to like that." Relations deteriorated from that point onward.

During the closing months of World War II, Soviet military forces occupied all of Central and Eastern Europe. Moscow used its military power to support the efforts of the Communist parties in Eastern Europe and crush the democratic parties. Communists took over one nation after another. The process concluded with a shocking coup d'etat in Czechoslovakia in 1948.

Public statements defined the beginning of the Cold War. In 1946 Stalin declared that international peace was impossible "under the present capitalist development of the world economy." Former British Prime Minister Winston Churchill delivered a dramatic speech in Fulton, Missouri, with Truman sitting on the platform. "From Stettin in the Baltic to Trieste in the Adriatic," Churchill said, "an iron curtain has descended across the Continent." Britain and the United States, he declared, had to work together to counter the Soviet threat.

CONTAINMENT

Containment of the Soviet Union became American policy in the postwar years. George Kennan, a top official at the U.S. embassy in Moscow, defined the new approach in the Long Telegram he sent to the State Department in 1946. He extended his analysis in an article under the signature "X" in the prestigious journal *Foreign Affairs*. Pointing to Russia's traditional sense of insecurity, Kennan argued that the Soviet Union would not soften its stance under any circumstances. Moscow, he wrote, was "committed fanatically to the belief that with the United States there can be no permanent *modus vivendi*, that it is desirable and necessary that the internal harmony of our society be disrupted." Moscow's pressure to expand its power had to be stopped through "firm and vigilant containment of Russian expansive tendencies. ..."

The first significant application of the containment doctrine came in the Middle East and eastern Mediterranean. In early 1946, the United States demanded, and obtained, a full Soviet withdrawal from Iran, the northern half of which it had occupied during the war. That summer, the United States pointedly supported Turkey against Soviet demands for control of the Turkish straits between the Black Sea and the Mediterranean. In early 1947, American policy crystallized when Britain told the United States that it could no longer afford to support the government of Greece against a strong Communist insurgency.

In a strongly worded speech to Congress, Truman declared, "I believe that it must be the policy of the United States to support free peoples who are resisting attempted subjugation by armed minorities or by outside pressures." Journalists quickly dubbed this statement the "Truman Doctrine." The president asked Congress to provide $400 million for economic and military aid, mostly to Greece but also to Turkey. After an emotional debate that resembled the one between interventionists and isolationists before World War II, the money was appropriated.

Critics from the left later charged that to whip up American support for the policy of containment, Truman overstated the Soviet threat to the United States. In turn, his statements inspired a wave of hysterical anti-Communism throughout the country. Perhaps so. Others, however, would counter that this argument ignores the backlash that likely would have occurred if Greece, Turkey, and other countries had fallen within the Soviet orbit with no opposition from the United States.

Containment also called for extensive economic aid to assist the recovery of war-torn Western Europe. With many of the region's nations economically and politically unstable, the United States feared that local Communist parties, directed by Moscow, would capitalize on their wartime record of resistance to the Nazis and come to power. "The patient is sinking while the doctors deliberate," declared Secretary of State George C. Marshall. In mid-1947 Marshall asked troubled European nations to draw up a program "directed not against any country or doctrine but against hunger, poverty, desperation, and chaos."

The Soviets participated in the first planning meeting, then departed rather than share economic data and submit to Western controls on the expenditure of the aid. The remaining 16 nations hammered out a request that finally came to $17,000 million for a four-year period. In early 1948 Congress voted to fund the "Marshall Plan," which helped underwrite the economic resurgence of Western Europe. It is generally regarded as one of the most successful foreign policy initiatives in U.S. history.

Postwar Germany was a special problem. It had been divided into U.S., Soviet, British, and French zones of occupation, with the former German capital of Berlin (itself divided into four zones), near the center of the Soviet zone. When the Western powers announced their intention to create a consolidated federal state from their zones, Stalin responded. On June 24, 1948, Soviet forces blockaded Berlin, cutting off all road and rail access from the West.

American leaders feared that losing Berlin would be a prelude to losing Germany and subsequently all of Europe. Therefore, in a successful demonstration of Western resolve known as the Berlin Airlift, Allied air forces took to the sky, flying supplies into Berlin. U.S., French, and British planes delivered nearly 2,250,000 tons of goods, including food and coal. Stalin lifted the blockade after 231 days and 277,264 flights.

By then, Soviet domination of Eastern Europe, and especially the Czech coup, had alarmed the Western Europeans. The result, initiated by the Europeans, was a military alliance to complement economic efforts at containment. The Norwegian historian Geir Lundestad has called it "empire by invitation." In 1949 the United States and 11 other countries established the North Atlantic Treaty Organization (NATO). An attack against one was to be considered an attack against all, to be met by appropriate force. NATO was the first peacetime "entangling alliance" with powers outside the Western hemisphere in American history.

The next year, the United States defined its defense aims clearly. The National Security Council (NSC) — the forum where the President, Cabinet officers, and other executive branch members consider national security and foreign affairs issues — undertook a full-fledged review of American foreign and defense policy. The resulting document, known as NSC-68, signaled a new direction in American security policy. Based on the assumption that "the Soviet Union was engaged in a fanatical effort to seize control of all governments wherever possible," the document committed America to assist allied nations anywhere in the world that seemed threatened by Soviet aggression. After the start of the Korean War, a reluctant Truman approved the document. The United States proceeded to increase defense spending dramatically.

THE COLD WAR IN ASIA AND THE MIDDLE EAST

While seeking to prevent Communist ideology from gaining further adherents in Europe, the United States also responded to challenges elsewhere. In China, Americans worried about the advances of Mao Zedong and his Communist Party. During World War II, the Nationalist government under Chiang Kai-shek and the Communist forces waged a civil war even as they fought the Japanese. Chiang had been a war-time ally, but his government was hopelessly inefficient and corrupt. American policy makers had little hope of saving his regime and considered Europe vastly more important. With most American aid moving across the Atlantic, Mao's forces seized power in 1949. Chiang's government fled to the island of Taiwan. When China's new ruler announced that he would support the Soviet Union against the "imperialist" United States, it appeared that Communism was spreading out of control, at least in Asia.

The Korean War brought armed conflict between the United States and China. The United States and the Soviet Union had divided Korea along the 38th parallel after liberating it from Japan at the end of World War II. Originally a matter of military convenience, the dividing line became more rigid as both major powers set up governments in their respective occupation zones and continued to support them even after departing.

In June 1950, after consultations with and having obtained the assent of the Soviet Union, North Korean leader Kim Il-sung dispatched his Soviet-supplied army across the 38th parallel and attacked southward, overrunning Seoul. Truman, perceiving the North Koreans as Soviet pawns in the global struggle, readied American forces and ordered World War II hero General Douglas MacArthur to Korea. Meanwhile, the United States was able to secure a U.N. resolution branding North Korea as an aggressor. (The Soviet Union, which could have vetoed any action had it been occupying its seat on the Security Council, was boycotting the United Nations to protest a decision not to admit Mao's new Chinese regime.)

The war seesawed back and forth. U.S. and Korean forces were initially pushed into an enclave far to the south around the city of Pusan. A daring amphibious landing at Inchon, the port for the city of Seoul, drove the North Koreans back and threatened to occupy the entire peninsula. In November, China entered the war, sending massive forces across the Yalu River. U.N. forces, largely American, retreated once again in bitter fighting. Commanded by General Matthew B. Ridgway, they stopped the overextended Chinese, and slowly fought their way back to the 38th parallel. MacArthur meanwhile challenged Truman's authority by attempting to orchestrate public support for bombing China and assisting an invasion of the mainland by Chiang Kai-shek's forces. In April 1951, Truman relieved him of his duties and replaced him with Ridgway.

The Cold War stakes were high. Mindful of the European priority, the U.S. government decided against sending more troops to Korea and was ready to settle for the prewar status quo. The result was frustration among many Americans who could not understand the need for restraint. Truman's popularity plunged to a 24-percent approval rating, the lowest to that time of any president since pollsters had begun to measure presidential popularity. Truce talks began in July 1951. The two sides finally reached an agreement in July 1953, during the first term of Truman's successor, Dwight Eisenhower.

Cold War struggles also occurred in the Middle East. The region's strategic importance as a supplier of oil had provided much of the impetus for pushing the Soviets out of Iran in 1946. But two years later, the United States officially recognized the new state of Israel 15 minutes after it was proclaimed — a decision Truman made over strong resistance from Marshall and the State Department. The result was an enduring dilemma — how to maintain ties with Israel while keeping good relations with bitterly anti-Israeli (and oil-rich) Arab states.

EISENHOWER AND THE COLD WAR

In 1953, Dwight D. Eisenhower became the first Republican president in 20 years. A war hero rather than a career politician, he had a natural, common touch that made him widely popular. "I like Ike" was the campaign slogan of the time. After serving as Supreme Commander of Allied Forces in Western Europe during World War II, Eisenhower had been army chief of staff, president of Columbia University, and military head of NATO before seeking the Republican presidential nomination. Skillful at getting people to work together, he functioned as a strong public spokesman and an executive manager somewhat removed from detailed policy making.

Despite disagreements on detail, he shared Truman's basic view of American foreign policy. He, too, perceived Communism as a monolithic force struggling for world supremacy. In his first inaugural address, he declared, "Forces of good and evil are massed and armed and opposed as rarely before in history.

Freedom is pitted against slavery, lightness against dark."

The new president and his secretary of state, John Foster Dulles, had argued that containment did not go far enough to stop Soviet expansion. Rather, a more aggressive policy of liberation was necessary, to free those subjugated by Communism. But when a democratic rebellion broke out in Hungary in 1956, the United States stood back as Soviet forces suppressed it.

Eisenhower's basic commitment to contain Communism remained, and to that end he increased American reliance on a nuclear shield. The United States had created the first atomic bombs. In 1950 Truman had authorized the development of a new and more powerful hydrogen bomb. Eisenhower, fearful that defense spending was out of control, reversed Truman's NSC-68 policy of a large conventional military buildup. Relying on what Dulles called "massive retaliation," the administration signaled it would use nuclear weapons if the nation or its vital interests were attacked.

In practice, however, the nuclear option could be used only against extremely critical attacks. Real Communist threats were generally peripheral. Eisenhower rejected the use of nuclear weapons in Indochina, when the French were ousted by Vietnamese Communist forces in 1954. In 1956, British and French forces attacked Egypt following Egyptian nationalization of the Suez Canal and Israel invaded the Egyptian Sinai. The president exerted heavy pressure on all three countries to withdraw. Still, the nuclear threat may have been taken seriously by Communist China, which refrained not only from attacking Taiwan, but from occupying small islands held by Nationalist Chinese just off the mainland. It may also have deterred Soviet occupation of Berlin, which reemerged as a festering problem during Eisenhower's last two years in office.

THE COLD WAR AT HOME

Not only did the Cold War shape U.S. foreign policy, it also had a profound effect on domestic affairs. Americans had long feared radical subversion. These fears could at times be overdrawn, and used to justify otherwise unacceptable political restrictions, but it also was true that individuals under Communist Party discipline and many "fellow traveler" hangers-on gave their political allegiance not to the United States, but to the international Communist movement, or, practically speaking, to Moscow. During the Red Scare of 1919-1920, the government had attempted to remove perceived threats to American society. After World War II, it made strong efforts against Communism within the United States. Foreign events, espionage scandals, and politics created an anti-Communist hysteria.

When Republicans were victorious in the midterm congressional elections of 1946 and appeared ready to investigate subversive activity, President Truman established a Federal Employee Loyalty Program. It had little impact on the lives of most civil servants, but a few hundred were dismissed, some unfairly.

In 1947 the House Committee on Un-American Activities investigated the motion-picture industry to determine whether Communist sentiments were being reflected in popular films. When some writers (who happened to be secret members of the Communist Party) refused to testify, they were cited for contempt and sent to prison. After that, the film companies refused to hire anyone with a marginally questionable past.

In 1948, Alger Hiss, who had been an assistant secretary of state and an adviser to Roosevelt at Yalta, was publicly accused of being a Communist spy by Whittaker Chambers, a former Soviet agent. Hiss denied the accusation, but in 1950 he was convicted of perjury. Subsequent evidence indicates that he was indeed guilty.

In 1949 the Soviet Union shocked Americans by testing its own atomic bomb. In 1950, the government uncovered a British-American spy network that transferred to the Soviet Union materials about the development of the atomic bomb. Two of its operatives, Julius Rosenberg and his wife Ethel, were sentenced to death. Attorney General J. Howard McGrath declared there were many American Communists, each bearing "the germ of death for society."

The most vigorous anti-Communist warrior was Senator Joseph R. McCarthy, a Republican from Wisconsin. He gained national attention in 1950 by claiming that he had a list of 205 known Communists in the State Department. Though McCarthy subsequently changed this figure several times and failed to substantiate any of his charges, he struck a responsive public chord.

McCarthy gained power when the Republican Party won control of the Senate in 1952. As a committee chairman, he now had a forum for his crusade. Relying on extensive press and television coverage, he continued to search for treachery among second-level officials in the Eisenhower administration. Enjoying the role of a tough guy doing dirty but necessary work, he pursued presumed Communists with vigor.

McCarthy overstepped himself by challenging the U.S. Army when one of his assistants was drafted. Television brought the hearings into millions of homes. Many Americans saw McCarthy's savage tactics for the first time, and public support began to wane. The Republican Party, which had found McCarthy useful in challenging a Democratic administration when Truman was president, began to see him as an embarrassment. The Senate finally condemned him for his conduct.

McCarthy in many ways represented the worst domestic excesses of the Cold War. As Americans repudiated him, it became natural for many to assume that the Communist threat at home and abroad had been grossly overblown. As the country moved into the 1960s, anti-Communism became increasingly suspect, especially among intellectuals and opinion-shapers.

THE POSTWAR ECONOMY: 1945-1960

In the decade and a half after World War II, the United States experienced phenomenal economic growth and consolidated its position as the world's richest country. Gross national product (GNP), a measure of all goods and services produced in the United States, jumped from about $200,000-million in 1940 to $300,000-million in 1950 to more than $500,000-million in 1960. More and more Americans now considered themselves part of the middle class.

The growth had different sources. The economic stimulus provided by large-scale public spending for World War II helped get it started. Two basic middle-class needs did much to keep it going. The number of automobiles produced annually quadrupled between 1946 and 1955. A housing boom, stimulated in part by easily affordable mortgages for returning servicemen, fueled the expansion. The rise in defense spending as the Cold War escalated also played a part.

After 1945 the major corporations in America grew even larger. There had been earlier waves of mergers in the 1890s and in the 1920s; in the 1950s another wave occurred. Franchise operations like McDonald's fast-food restaurants allowed small entrepreneurs to make themselves part of large, efficient enterprises. Big American corporations also developed holdings overseas, where labor costs were often lower.

Workers found their own lives changing as industrial America changed. Fewer workers produced goods; more provided services. As early as 1956 a majority of employees held white-collar jobs, working as managers, teachers, salespersons, and office operatives. Some firms granted a guaranteed annual wage, long-term employment contracts, and other benefits. With such changes, labor militancy was undermined and some class distinctions began to fade.

Farmers — at least those with small operations — faced tough times. Gains in productivity led to agricultural consolidation, and farming became a big business. More and more family farmers left the land.

Other Americans moved too. The West and the Southwest grew with increasing rapidity, a trend that would continue through the end of the century. Sun Belt cities like Houston, Texas; Miami, Florida; Albuquerque, New Mexico; and Phoenix, Arizona, expanded rapidly. Los Angeles, California, moved ahead of Philadelphia, Pennsylvania, as the third largest U.S. city and then surpassed Chicago, metropolis of the Midwest. The 1970 census showed that California had displaced New York as the nation's largest state. By 2000, Texas had moved ahead of New York into second place.

An even more important form of movement led Americans out of inner cities into new suburbs, where they hoped to find affordable housing for the larger families spawned by the postwar baby boom. Developers like William J. Levitt built new communities — with homes that all looked alike — using the techniques of mass production. Levitt's houses were prefabricated — partly assembled in a factory rather than on the final location — and modest, but Levitt's methods cut costs and allowed new owners to possess a part of the American dream.

As suburbs grew, businesses moved into the new areas. Large shopping centers containing a great variety of stores changed consumer patterns. The number of these centers rose from eight at the end of World War II to 3,840 in 1960. With easy parking and convenient evening hours, customers could avoid city shopping entirely. An unfortunate by-product was the "hollowing-out" of formerly busy urban cores.

New highways created better access to the suburbs and its shops. The Highway Act of 1956 provided $26,000-million, the largest public works expenditure in U.S. history, to build more than 64,000 kilometers of limited access interstate highways to link the country together.

Television, too, had a powerful impact on social and economic patterns. Developed in the 1930s, it was not widely marketed until after the war. In 1946 the country had fewer than 17,000 television sets. Three years later consumers were buying 250,000 sets a month, and by 1960 three-quarters of all families owned at least one set. In the middle of the decade, the average family watched television four to five hours a day. Popular shows for children included *Howdy Doody Time* and *The Mickey Mouse Club*; older viewers preferred situation comedies like *I Love Lucy* and *Father Knows Best*. Americans of all ages became exposed to increasingly sophisticated advertisements for products said to be necessary for the good life.

THE FAIR DEAL

The Fair Deal was the name given to President Harry Truman's domestic program. Building on Roosevelt's New Deal, Truman believed that the federal government should guarantee economic opportunity and social stability. He struggled to achieve those ends in the face of fierce political opposition from legislators determined to reduce the role of government.

Truman's first priority in the immediate postwar period was to make the transition to a peacetime economy. Servicemen wanted to come home quickly, but once they arrived they faced competition for housing and employment. The G.I. Bill, passed before the end of the war, helped ease servicemen back into civilian life by providing benefits such as guaranteed loans for home-buying and financial aid for industrial training and university education.

More troubling was labor unrest. As war production ceased, many workers found themselves without jobs. Others wanted pay increases they felt were long overdue. In 1946, 4.6 million workers went on strike, more than ever before in American history. They challenged the automobile, steel, and electrical industries. When they took on the railroads and soft-coal mines, Truman intervened to stop union excesses, but in so doing he alienated many workers.

While dealing with immediately pressing issues, Truman also provided a broader agenda for action. Less than a week after the war ended, he presented Congress with a 21-point program, which provided for protection against unfair employment practices, a higher minimum wage, greater unemployment compensation, and housing assistance. In the next several months, he added proposals for health insurance and atomic energy legislation. But this scattershot approach often left Truman's priorities unclear.

Republicans were quick to attack. In the 1946 congressional elections they asked, "Had enough?" and voters responded that they had. Republicans, with majorities in both houses of Congress for the first time since 1928, were determined to reverse the liberal direction of the Roosevelt years.

Truman fought with the Congress as it cut spending and reduced taxes. In 1948 he sought reelection, despite polls indicating that he had little chance. After a vigorous campaign, Truman scored one of the great upsets in American politics, defeating the Republican nominee, Thomas Dewey, governor of New York. Reviving the old New Deal coalition, Truman held on to labor, farmers, and African-American voters.

When Truman finally left office in 1953, his Fair Deal was but a mixed success. In July 1948 he banned racial discrimination in federal government hiring practices and ordered an end to segregation in the military. The minimum wage had risen, and social security programs had expanded. A housing program brought some gains but left many needs unmet. National health insurance, aid-to-education measures, reformed agricultural subsidies, and his legislative civil rights agenda never made it through Congress. The president's pursuit of the Cold War, ultimately his most important objective, made it especially difficult to develop support for social reform in the face of intense opposition.

EISENHOWER'S APPROACH

When Dwight Eisenhower succeeded Truman as president, he accepted the basic framework of government responsibility established by the New Deal, but sought to hold the line on programs and expenditures. He termed his approach "dynamic conservatism" or "modern Republicanism," which meant, he explained, "conservative when it comes to money, liberal when it comes to human beings." A critic countered that Eisenhower appeared to argue that he would "strongly recommend the building of a great many schools ... but not provide the money."

Eisenhower's first priority was to balance the budget after years of deficits. He wanted to cut spending and taxes and maintain the value of the dollar. Republicans were willing to risk unemployment to keep inflation in check. Reluctant to stimulate the economy too much, they saw the country suffer three economic recessions in the eight years of the Eisenhower presidency, but none was very severe.

In other areas, the administration transferred control of offshore oil lands from the federal government to the states. It also favored private development of electrical power rather than the public approach the Democrats had initiated. In general, its orientation was sympathetic to business.

Compared to Truman, Eisenhower had only a modest domestic program. When he was active in promoting a bill, it likely was to trim the New Deal legacy a bit — as in reducing agricultural subsidies or placing mild restrictions on labor unions. His disinclination to push fundamental change in either direction was in keeping with the spirit of the generally prosperous Fifties. He was one of the few presidents who left office as popular as when he entered it.

THE CULTURE OF THE 1950s

During the 1950s, many cultural commentators pointed out that a sense of uniformity pervaded American society. Conformity, they asserted, was numbingly common. Though men and women had been forced into new employment patterns during World War II, once the war was over, traditional roles were reaffirmed. Men expected to be the breadwinners in each family; women, even when they worked, assumed their proper place was at home. In his influential book, *The Lonely Crowd*, sociologist David Riesman called this new society "other-directed," characterized by conformity, but also by stability. Television, still very limited in the choices it gave its viewers, contributed to the homogenizing cultural trend by providing young and old with a shared experience reflecting accepted social patterns.

Yet beneath this seemingly bland surface, important segments of American society seethed with rebellion. A number of writers, collectively known as the "Beat Generation," went out of their way to challenge the patterns of respectability and shock the rest of the culture. Stressing spontaneity and spirituality, they preferred intuition over reason, Eastern mysticism over Western institutionalized religion.

The literary work of the beats displayed their sense of alienation and quest for self-realization. Jack Kerouac typed his best-selling novel *On the Road* on a 75-meter roll of paper. Lacking traditional punctuation and paragraph structure, the book glorified the possibilities of the free life. Poet Allen Ginsberg gained similar notoriety for his poem "Howl," a scathing critique of modern, mechanized civilization. When police charged that it was obscene and seized the published version, Ginsberg successfully challenged the ruling in court.

Musicians and artists rebelled as well. Tennessee singer Elvis Presley was the most successful of several white performers who popularized a sensual and pulsating style of African-American music, which began to be called "rock and roll." At first, he outraged middle-class Americans with his ducktail haircut and undulating hips. But in a few years his performances would seem relatively tame alongside the antics of later performers such as the British Rolling Stones. Similarly, it was in the 1950s that painters like Jackson Pollock discarded easels and laid out gigantic canvases on the floor, then applied paint, sand, and other materials in wild splashes of color. All of these artists and authors, whatever the medium, provided models for the wider and more deeply felt social revolution of the 1960s.

ORIGINS OF THE CIVIL RIGHTS MOVEMENT

African Americans became increasingly restive in the postwar years. During the war they had challenged discrimination in the military services and in the work force, and they had made limited gains. Millions of African Americans had left Southern farms for Northern cities, where they hoped to find better jobs. They found instead crowded conditions in urban slums. Now, African-American servicemen returned home, many intent on rejecting second-class citizenship.

Jackie Robinson dramatized the racial question in 1947 when he broke baseball's color line and began playing in the major leagues. A member of the Brooklyn Dodgers, he often faced trouble with opponents and teammates as well. But an outstanding first season led to his acceptance and eased the way for other African-American players, who now left the Negro leagues to which they had been confined.

Government officials, and many other Americans, discovered the connection between racial problems and Cold War politics. As the leader of the free world, the United States sought support in Africa and Asia. Discrimination at home impeded the effort to win friends in other parts of the world.

Harry Truman supported the early civil rights movement. He personally believed in political equality, though not in social equality, and recognized the growing importance of the African-American urban vote. When apprised in 1946 of a spate of lynchings and anti-black violence in the South, he appointed a committee on civil rights to investigate discrimination. Its report, *To Secure*

These Rights, issued the next year, documented African Americans' second-class status in American life and recommended numerous federal measures to secure the rights guaranteed to all citizens.

Truman responded by sending a 10-point civil rights program to Congress. Southern Democrats in Congress were able to block its enactment. A number of the angriest, led by Governor Strom Thurmond of South Carolina, formed a States Rights Party to oppose the president in 1948. Truman thereupon issued an executive order barring discrimination in federal employment, ordered equal treatment in the armed forces, and appointed a committee to work toward an end to military segregation, which was largely ended during the Korean War.

African Americans in the South in the 1950s still enjoyed few, if any, civil and political rights. In general, they could not vote. Those who tried to register faced the likelihood of beatings, loss of job, loss of credit, or eviction from their land. Occasional lynchings still occurred. Jim Crow laws enforced segregation of the races in streetcars, trains, hotels, restaurants, hospitals, recreational facilities, and employment.

DESEGREGATION

The National Association for the Advancement of Colored People (NAACP) took the lead in efforts to overturn the judicial doctrine, established in the Supreme Court case *Plessy v. Ferguson* in 1896, that segregation of African-American and white students was constitutional if facilities were "separate but equal." That decree had been used for decades to sanction rigid segregation in all aspects of Southern life, where facilities were seldom, if ever, equal.

African Americans achieved their goal of overturning *Plessy* in 1954 when the Supreme Court — presided over by an Eisenhower appointee, Chief Justice Earl Warren — handed down its *Brown v. Board of Education* ruling. The Court declared unanimously that "separate facilities are inherently unequal," and decreed that the "separate but equal" doctrine could no longer be used in public schools. A year later, the Supreme Court demanded that local school boards move "with all deliberate speed" to implement the decision.

Eisenhower, although sympathetic to the needs of the South as it faced a major transition, nonetheless acted to see that the law was upheld in the face of massive resistance from much of the South. He faced a major crisis in Little Rock, Arkansas, in 1957, when Governor Orval Faubus attempted to block a desegregation plan calling for the admission of nine black students to the city's previously all-white Central High School. After futile efforts at negotiation, the president sent federal troops to Little Rock to enforce the plan.

Governor Faubus responded by ordering the Little Rock high schools closed down for the 1958-59 school year. However, a federal court ordered them reopened the following year. They did so in a tense atmosphere with a tiny number of African-American students. Thus, school desegregation proceeded at a slow and uncertain pace throughout much of the South.

Another milestone in the civil rights movement occurred in 1955 in Montgomery, Alabama. Rosa Parks, a 42-year-old African-American seamstress who was also secretary of the state chapter of the NAACP, sat down in the front of a bus in a section reserved by law and custom for whites. Ordered to move to the back, she refused. Police came and arrested her for violating the segregation statutes. African-American leaders, who had been waiting for just such a case, organized a boycott of the bus system.

Martin Luther King Jr., a young minister of the Baptist church where the African Americans met, became a spokesman for the protest. "There comes a time," he said, "when people get tired ... of being kicked about by the brutal feet of oppression." King was arrested, as he would be again and again; a bomb damaged the front of his house. But African Americans in Montgomery sustained the boycott. About a year later, the Supreme Court affirmed that bus segregation, like school segregation, was unconstitutional. The boycott ended. The civil rights movement had won an important victory — and discovered its most powerful, thoughtful, and eloquent leader in Martin Luther King Jr.

African Americans also sought to secure their voting rights. Although the 15th Amendment to the U.S. Constitution guaranteed the right to vote, many states had found ways to circumvent the law. The states would impose a poll ("head") tax or a literacy test — typically much more stringently interpreted for African Americans — to prevent poor African Americans with little education from voting. Eisenhower, working with Senate majority leader Lyndon B. Johnson, lent his support to a congressional effort to guarantee the vote. The Civil Rights Act of 1957, the first such measure in 82 years, marked a step forward, as it authorized federal intervention in cases where African Americans were denied the chance to vote. Yet loopholes remained, and so activists pushed successfully for the Civil Rights Act of 1960, which provided stiffer penalties for interfering with voting, but still stopped short of authorizing federal officials to register African Americans.

Relying on the efforts of African Americans themselves, the civil rights movement gained momentum in the postwar years. Working through the Supreme Court and through Congress, civil rights supporters had created the groundwork for a dramatic yet peaceful "revolution" in American race relations in the 1960s.

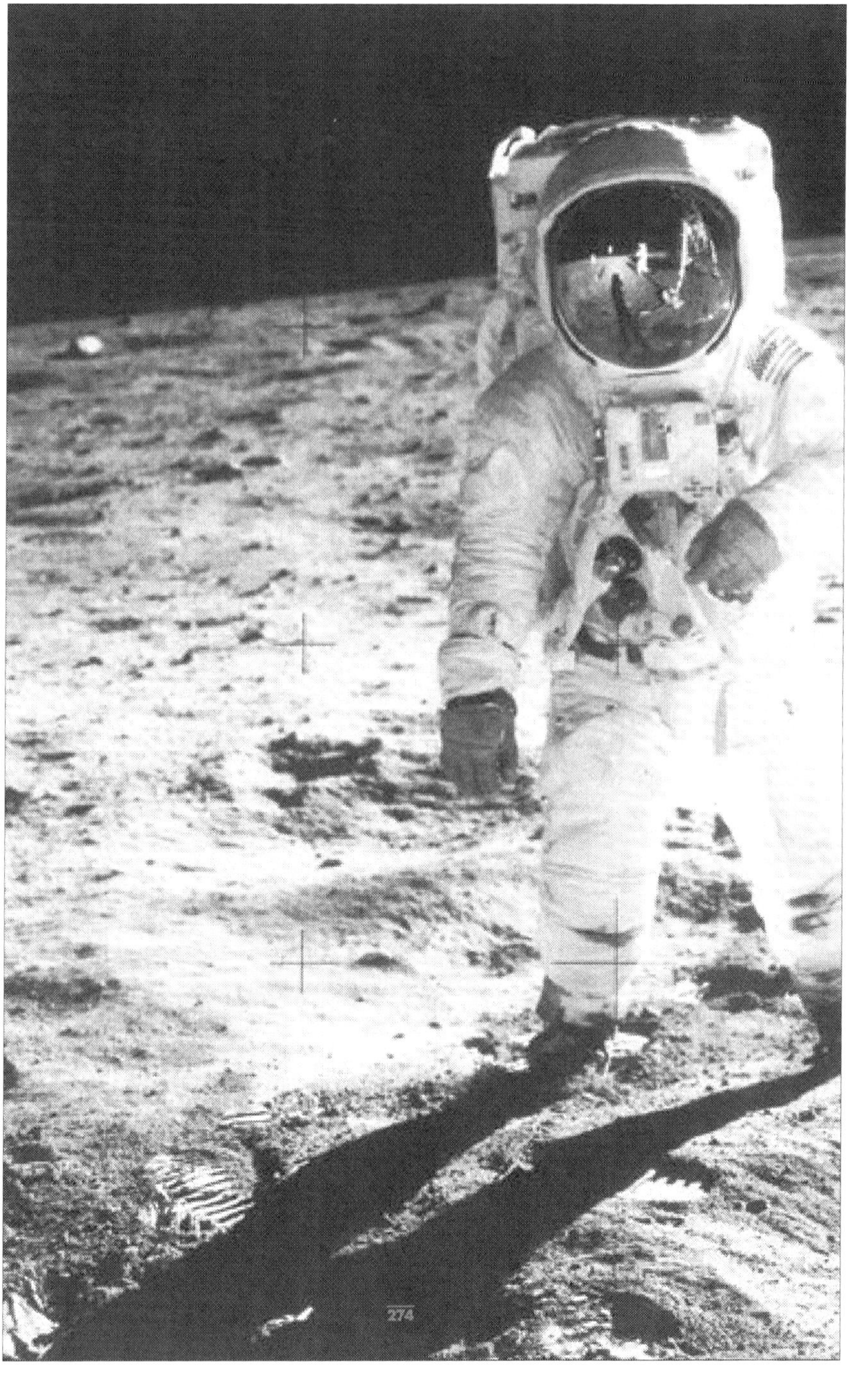

CHAPTER

13

DECADES OF CHANGE: 1960-1980

Module Pilot Edwin Aldrin Jr. on the moon, July 20, 1969.

> "I have a dream that one day on the red hills of Georgia, sons of former slaves and the sons of former slave owners will be able to sit down together at the table of brotherhood."
>
> Martin Luther King Jr., 1963

By 1960, the United States was on the verge of a major social change. American society had always been more open and fluid than that of the nations in most of the rest of the world. Still, it had been dominated primarily by old-stock, white males. During the 1960s, groups that previously had been submerged or subordinate began more forcefully and successfully to assert themselves: African Americans, Native Americans, women, the white ethnic offspring of the "new immigration," and Latinos. Much of the support they received came from a young population larger than ever, making its way through a college and university system that was expanding at an unprecedented pace. Frequently embracing "countercultural" lifestyles and radical politics, many of the offspring of the World War II generation emerged as advocates of a new America characterized by a cultural and ethnic pluralism that their parents often viewed with unease.

THE CIVIL RIGHTS MOVEMENT 1960-1980

The struggle of African Americans for equality reached its peak in the mid-1960s. After progressive victories in the 1950s, African Americans became even more committed to nonviolent direct action. Groups like the Southern Christian Leadership Conference (SCLC), made up of African-American clergy, and the Student Nonviolent Coordinating Committee (SNCC), composed of younger activists, sought reform through peaceful confrontation.

In 1960 African-American college students sat down at a segregated Woolworth's lunch counter in North Carolina and refused to leave. Their sit-in captured media attention and led to similar demonstrations throughout the South. The next year, civil rights workers organized "freedom rides," in which African Americans and whites boarded buses heading south toward segregated terminals, where confrontations might capture media attention and lead to change.

They also organized rallies, the largest of which was the "March on Washington" in 1963. More than 200,000 people gathered in the nation's capital to demonstrate their commitment to equality for all. The high point of a day of songs and speeches came with the address of Martin Luther King Jr., who had emerged as the preeminent spokesman for civil rights. "I have a dream that one day on the red hills of Georgia the sons of former slaves and the sons of former slave owners will be able to sit down together at the table of brotherhood," King proclaimed. Each time he used the refrain "I have a dream," the crowd roared.

The level of progress initially achieved did not match the rhetoric of the civil rights movement. President Kennedy was initially reluctant to press white Southerners for support on civil rights because he needed their votes on other issues. Events, driven by African Americans themselves, forced his hand. When James Meredith was denied admission to the University of Mississippi in 1962 because of his race, Kennedy sent federal troops to uphold the law. After protests aimed at the desegregation of Birmingham, Alabama, prompted a violent response by the police, he sent Congress a new civil rights bill mandating the integration of public places. Not even the March on Washington, however, could extricate the measure from a congressional committee, where it was still bottled up when Kennedy was assassinated in 1963.

President Lyndon B. Johnson was more successful. Displaying negotiating skills he had so frequently employed during his years as Senate majority leader, Johnson persuaded the Senate to limit delaying tactics preventing a final vote on the sweeping Civil Rights Act of 1964, which outlawed discrimination in all public accommodations. The next year's Voting Rights Act of 1965 authorized the federal government to register voters where local officials had prevented African Americans from doing so. By 1968 a million African Americans were registered in the deep South. Nationwide, the number of African-American elected officials increased substantially. In 1968, the Congress passed legislation banning discrimination in housing.

Once unleashed, however, the civil rights revolution produced leaders impatient with both the pace of change and the goal of channeling African Americans into mainstream white society. Malcolm X, an eloquent activist, was the most prominent figure arguing for African-American separation from the white race. Stokely Carmichael, a student leader, became similarly disillusioned by the notions of nonviolence and interracial cooperation. He popularized the slogan "black power," to be achieved by "whatever means necessary," in the words of Malcolm X.

Violence accompanied militant calls for reform. Riots broke out in several big cities in 1966 and 1967. In the spring of 1968, Martin Luther King Jr. fell before an assassin's bullet. Several months later, Senator Robert Kennedy, a spokesman for the disadvantaged, an opponent of the Vietnam War, and the brother of the slain president, met the same fate. To many these two assassinations marked the end of an era of innocence and idealism. The growing militancy on the left, coupled with an inevitable conservative backlash, opened a rift in the nation's psyche that took years to heal.

By then, however, a civil rights movement supported by court decisions, congressional enactments, and federal administrative regulations was irreversibly woven into the fabric of American life. The major issues were about implementation of equality and access, not about the legality of segregation or disenfranchisement. The arguments of the 1970s and thereafter were over matters such as busing children out of their neighborhoods to achieve racial balance in metropolitan schools or about the use of "affirmative action." These policies and programs were viewed by some as active measures to ensure equal opportunity, as in education and employment, and by others as reverse discrimination.

The courts worked their way through these problems with decisions that were often inconsistent. In the meantime, the steady march of African Americans into the ranks of the middle class and once largely white suburbs quietly reflected a profound demographic change.

THE WOMEN'S MOVEMENT

During the 1950s and 1960s, increasing numbers of married women entered the labor force, but in 1963 the average working woman earned only 63 percent of what a man made. That year Betty Friedan published *The Feminine Mystique*, an explosive critique of middle-class living patterns that articulated a pervasive sense of discontent that Friedan contended was felt by many women. Arguing that women often had no outlets for expression other than "finding a husband and bearing children," Friedan encouraged her readers to seek new roles and responsibilities and to find their own personal and professional identities, rather than have them defined by a male-dominated society.

The women's movement of the 1960s and 1970s drew inspiration from the civil rights movement. It was made up mainly of members of the middle class, and thus partook of the spirit of rebellion that affected large segments of middle-class youth in the 1960s.

Reform legislation also prompted change. During debate on the 1964 Civil Rights bill, opponents hoped to defeat the entire measure by proposing an amendment to outlaw discrimination on the basis of gender as well as race. First the amendment, then the bill itself, passed, giving women a valuable legal tool.

In 1966, 28 professional women, including Friedan, established the National Organization for Women (NOW) "to take action to bring American women into full participation in the mainstream of American society now." While NOW and similar feminist organizations boast of substantial memberships today, arguably they attained their greatest influence in the early 1970s, a time that also saw the journalist Gloria Steinem and several other women found *Ms.* magazine. They also spurred the formation of counter-feminist groups, often led by women, including most prominently the political activist Phyllis Schlafly. These groups typically argued for more "traditional" gender roles and opposed the proposed "Equal Rights" constitutional amendment.

Passed by Congress in 1972, that amendment declared in part, "Equality of rights under the law shall not be denied or abridged by the United States or by any State on account of sex." Over the next several years, 35 of the necessary 38 states ratified it. The courts also moved to expand women's rights. In 1973 the Supreme Court in *Roe v. Wade* sanctioned women's right to obtain an abortion during the early months of pregnancy — seen as a significant victory for the women's movement — but *Roe* also spurred the growth of an anti-abortion movement.

In the mid- to late-1970s, however, the women's movement seemed to stagnate. It failed to broaden its appeal beyond the middle class. Divisions arose between moderate and radical feminists. Conservative opponents mounted a campaign against the Equal Rights Amendment, and it died in 1982 without gaining the approval of the 38 states needed for ratification.

THE LATINO MOVEMENT

In post-World War II America, Americans of Mexican and Puerto Rican descent had faced discrimination. New immigrants, coming from Cuba, Mexico, and Central America — often unskilled and unable to speak English — suffered from discrimination as well. Some Hispanics worked as farm laborers and at times were cruelly exploited while harvesting crops; others gravitated to the cities, where, like earlier immigrant groups, they encountered difficulties in their quest for a better life.

Chicanos, or Mexican-Americans, mobilized in organizations like the radical Asociación Nacional Mexico-Americana, yet did not become confrontational until the 1960s. Hoping that Lyndon Johnson's poverty program would expand opportunities for them, they found that bureaucrats failed to respond to less vocal groups. The example of black activism in particular taught Hispanics the importance of pressure politics in a pluralistic society.

The National Labor Relations Act of 1935 had excluded agricultural workers from its guarantee of the right to organize and bargain collectively. But César Chávez, founder of the overwhelmingly Hispanic United Farm Workers, demonstrated that direct action could achieve employer recognition for his union. California grape growers agreed to bargain with the union after Chávez led a nationwide consumer boycott. Similar boycotts of lettuce and other products were also successful. Though farm interests continued to try to obstruct Chávez's organization, the legal foundation had been laid for representation to secure higher wages and improved working conditions.

Hispanics became politically active as well. In 1961 Henry B. González won election to Congress from Texas. Three years later Eligio ("Kika") de la Garza, another Texan, followed him, and Joseph Montoya of New Mexico went to the Senate. Both González and de la Garza later rose to positions of power as committee chairmen in the House. In the 1970s and 1980s, the pace of Hispanic political involvement increased. Several prominent Hispanics have served in the Bill Clinton and George W. Bush cabinets.

THE NATIVE-AMERICAN MOVEMENT

In the 1950s, Native Americans struggled with the government's policy of moving them off reservations and into cities where they might assimilate into mainstream America. Many of the uprooted often had difficulties adjusting to urban life. In 1961, when the policy was discontinued, the U.S. Commission on Civil Rights noted that, for Native Americans, "poverty and deprivation are common."

In the 1960s and 1970s, watching both the development of Third World nationalism and the progress of the civil rights movement, Native Americans became more aggressive in pressing for their own rights. A new generation of leaders went to court to protect what was left of tribal lands or to recover those which had been taken, often illegally, in previous times. In state after state, they challenged treaty violations, and in 1967 won the first of many victories guaranteeing long-abused land and water rights. The American Indian Movement (AIM), founded in 1968, helped channel government funds to Native-American-controlled organizations and assisted neglected Native Americans in the cities.

Confrontations became more common. In 1969 a landing party of 78 Native Americans seized Alcatraz Island in San Francisco Bay and held it until federal officials removed them in 1971. In 1973 AIM took over the South Dakota village of Wounded Knee, where soldiers in the late 19th century had massacred a Sioux encampment. Militants hoped to dramatize the poverty and alcoholism in the reservation surrounding the town. The episode ended after one Native American was killed and another wounded, with a government agreement to re-examine treaty rights.

Still, Native-American activism brought results. Other Americans became more aware of Native-American needs. Government officials responded with measures including the Education Assistance Act of 1975 and the 1996 Native-American Housing and Self-Determination Act. The Senate's first Native-American member, Ben Nighthorse Campbell of Colorado, was elected in 1992.

THE COUNTERCULTURE

The agitation for equal opportunity sparked other forms of upheaval. Young people in particular rejected the stable patterns of middle-class life their parents had created in the decades after World War II. Some plunged into radical political activity; many more embraced new standards of dress and sexual behavior.

The visible signs of the counterculture spread through parts of American society in the late 1960s and early 1970s. Hair grew longer and beards became common. Blue jeans and tee shirts took the place of slacks, jackets, and ties. The use of illegal drugs increased. Rock and roll grew, proliferated, and transformed into many musical variations. The Beatles, the Rolling Stones, and other British groups took the country by storm. "Hard rock" grew popular, and songs with a political or social commentary, such as those by singer-songwriter Bob Dylan, became common. The youth counterculture reached its apogee in August 1969 at Woodstock, a three-day music festival in rural New York State attended by almost half-a-million persons. The festival, mythologized in films and record albums, gave its name to the era, the Woodstock Generation.

A parallel manifestation of the new sensibility of the young was the rise of the New Left, a group of young, college-age radicals. The New Leftists, who had close counterparts in Western Europe, were in many instances the children of the older generation of radicals. Nonetheless, they rejected old-style Marxist rhetoric. Instead, they depicted university students as themselves an oppressed class that possessed special insights into the struggle of other oppressed groups in American society.

New Leftists participated in the civil rights movement and the struggle against poverty. Their greatest success — and the one instance in which they developed a mass following — was in opposing the Vietnam War, an issue of emotional interest to their draft-age contemporaries. By the late 1970s, the student New Left had disappeared, but many of its activists made their way into mainstream politics.

ENVIRONMENTALISM

The energy and sensibility that fueled the civil rights movement, the counterculture, and the New Left also stimulated an environmental movement in the mid-1960s. Many were aroused by the publication in 1962 of Rachel Carson's book *Silent Spring*, which alleged that chemical pesticides, particularly DDT, caused cancer, among other ills. Public concern about the environment continued to increase throughout the 1960s as many became aware of other pollutants surrounding them — automobile emissions, industrial wastes, oil spills — that threatened their health and the beauty of their surroundings. On April 22, 1970, schools and communities across the United States celebrated Earth Day for the first time. "Teach-ins" educated Americans about the dangers of environmental pollution.

Few denied that pollution was a problem, but the proposed solutions involved expense and inconvenience. Many believed these would reduce the economic growth upon which many Americans' standard of living depended. Nevertheless, in 1970, Congress amended the Clean Air Act of 1967 to develop uniform national air-quality standards. It also passed the Water Quality Improvement Act, which assigned to the polluter the responsibility of cleaning up off-shore oil spills. Also, in 1970, the Environmental Protection Agency (EPA) was created as an independent federal agency to spearhead the effort to bring abuses under control. During the next three decades, the EPA, bolstered by legislation that increased its authority, became one of the most active agencies in the government, issuing strong regulations covering air and water quality.

KENNEDY AND THE RESURGENCE OF BIG GOVERNMENT LIBERALISM

By 1960 government had become an increasingly powerful force in people's lives. During the Great Depression of the 1930s, new executive agencies were created to deal with many aspects of American life. During World War II, the number of civilians employed by the federal government rose from one million to 3.8 million, then stabilized at 2.5 million in the 1950s. Federal expenditures, which had stood at $3,100-million in 1929, increased to $75,000-million in 1953 and passed $150,000-million in the 1960s.

Most Americans accepted government's expanded role, even as they disagreed about how far that expansion should continue. Democrats generally wanted the government to ensure growth and stability. They wanted to extend federal benefits for education, health, and welfare. Many Republicans accepted a level of government responsibility, but hoped to cap spending and restore a larger measure of individual initiative. The presidential election of 1960 revealed a nation almost evenly divided between these visions.

John F. Kennedy, the Democratic victor by a narrow margin, was at 43 the youngest man ever to win the presidency. On television, in a series of debates with opponent Richard Nixon, he appeared able, articulate, and energetic. In the campaign, he spoke of moving aggressively into the new decade, for "the New Frontier is here whether we seek it or not." In his first inaugural address, he concluded with an eloquent plea: "Ask not what your country can do for you — ask what you can do for your country." Throughout his brief presidency, Kennedy's special combination of grace, wit, and style — far more than his specific legislative agenda — sustained his popularity and influenced generations of politicians to come.

Kennedy wanted to exert strong leadership to extend economic benefits to all citizens, but a razor-thin margin of victory limited his mandate. Even though the Democratic Party controlled both houses of Congress, conservative Southern Democrats often sided with the Republicans on issues involving the scope of governmental intervention in the economy. They resisted plans to increase federal aid to education, provide health insurance for the elderly, and create a new Department of Urban Affairs. And so, despite his lofty rhetoric, Kennedy's policies were often limited and restrained.

One priority was to end the recession, in progress when Kennedy took office, and restore economic growth. But Kennedy lost the confidence of business leaders in 1962, when he succeeded in rolling back what the administration regarded as an excessive price increase in the steel industry. Though the president achieved his immediate goal, he alienated an important source of support. Persuaded by his economic advisers that a large tax cut would stimulate the economy, Kennedy backed a bill providing for one. Conservative opposition in Congress, however, appeared to destroy any hopes of passing a bill most congressmen thought would widen the budget deficit.

The overall legislative record of the Kennedy administration was meager. The president made some gestures toward civil rights leaders but did not embrace the goals of the civil rights movement until demonstrations led by Martin Luther King Jr. forced his hand in 1963. Like Truman before him, he could not secure congressional passage of federal aid to public education or for a medical care program limited to the elderly. He gained only a modest increase in the minimum wage. Still, he did secure funding for a space program, and established the Peace Corps to send men and women overseas to assist developing countries in meeting their own needs.

KENNEDY AND THE COLD WAR

President Kennedy came into office pledging to carry on the Cold War vigorously, but he also hoped for accommodation and was reluctant to commit American power. During his first year-and-a-half in office, he rejected American intervention after the CIA-guided Cuban exile invasion at the Bay of Pigs failed, effectively ceded the landlocked Southeast Asian nation of Laos to Communist control, and acquiesced in the building of the Berlin Wall. Kennedy's decisions reinforced impressions of weakness that Soviet Premier Nikita Khrushchev had formed in their only personal meeting, a summit meeting at Vienna in June 1961.

It was against this backdrop that Kennedy faced the most serious event of the Cold War, the Cuban missile crisis.

In the fall of 1962, the administration learned that the Soviet Union was secretly installing offensive nuclear missiles in Cuba. After considering different options, Kennedy decided on a quarantine to prevent Soviet ships from bringing additional supplies to Cuba. He demanded publicly that the Soviets remove the weapons and warned that an attack from that island would bring retaliation against the USSR. After several days of tension, during which the world was closer than ever before to nuclear war, the Soviets agreed to remove the missiles. Critics charged that Kennedy had risked nuclear disaster when quiet diplomacy might have been effective. But most Americans and much of the non-Communist world applauded his decisiveness. The missile crisis made him for the first time the acknowledged leader of the democratic West.

In retrospect, the Cuban missile crisis marked a turning point in U.S.-Soviet relations. Both sides saw the need to defuse tensions that could lead to direct military conflict. The following year, the United States, the Soviet Union, and Great Britain signed a landmark Limited Test Ban Treaty prohibiting nuclear weapons tests in the atmosphere.

Indochina (Vietnam, Laos, Cambodia), a French possession before World War II, was still another Cold War battlefield. The French effort to reassert colonial control there was opposed by Ho Chi Minh, a Vietnamese Communist, whose Viet Minh movement engaged in a guerrilla war with the French army.

Both Truman and Eisenhower, eager to maintain French support for the policy of containment in Europe, provided France with economic aid that freed resources for the struggle in Vietnam. But the French suffered a decisive defeat in Dien Bien Phu in May 1954. At an international conference in Geneva, Laos and Cambodia were given their independence. Vietnam was divided, with Ho in power in the North and Ngo Dinh Diem, a Roman Catholic anti-Communist in a largely Buddhist population, heading the government in the South.

Elections were to be held two years later to unify the country. Persuaded that the fall of Vietnam could lead to the fall of Burma, Thailand, and Indonesia, Eisenhower backed Diem's refusal to hold elections in 1956 and effectively established South Vietnam as an American client state.

Kennedy increased assistance, and sent small numbers of military advisers, but a new guerrilla struggle between North and South continued. Diem's unpopularity grew and the military situation worsened. In late 1963, Kennedy secretly assented to a coup d'etat. To the president's surprise, Diem and his powerful brother-in-law, Ngo Dien Nu, were killed. It was at this uncertain juncture that Kennedy's presidency ended three weeks later.

THE SPACE PROGRAM

During Eisenhower's second term, outer space had become an arena for U.S.-Soviet competition. In 1957, the Soviet Union launched *Sputnik* — an artificial satellite — thereby demonstrating it could build more powerful rockets than the United States. The United States launched its first satellite, *Explorer I*, in 1958. But three months after Kennedy became president, the USSR put the first man in orbit. Kennedy responded by committing the United States to land a man on the moon and bring him back "before this decade is out." With Project Mercury in 1962, John Glenn became the first U.S. astronaut to orbit the Earth.

After Kennedy's death, President Lyndon Johnson enthusiastically supported the space program. In the mid-1960s, U.S. scientists developed the two-person *Gemini* spacecraft. *Gemini* achieved several firsts, including an eight-day mission in August 1965 — the longest space flight at that time — and in November 1966, the first automatically controlled reentry into the Earth's atmosphere. *Gemini* also accomplished the first manned linkup of two spacecraft in flight as well as the first U.S. walks in space.

The three-person *Apollo* spacecraft achieved Kennedy's goal and demonstrated to the world that the United States had surpassed Soviet capabilities in space. On July 20, 1969, with hundreds of millions of television viewers watching around the world, Neil Armstrong became the first human to walk on the surface of the moon.

Other *Apollo* flights followed, but many Americans began to question the value of manned space flight. In the early 1970s, as other priorities became more pressing, the United States scaled down the space program. Some *Apollo* missions were scrapped; only one of two proposed *Skylab* space stations was built.

DEATH OF A PRESIDENT

John Kennedy had gained world prestige by his management of the Cuban missile crisis and had won great popularity at home. Many believed he would win re-election easily in 1964. But on November 22, 1963, he was assassinated while riding in an open car during a visit to Dallas, Texas. His death, amplified by television coverage, was a traumatic event, just as Roosevelt's had been 18 years earlier.

In retrospect, it is clear that Kennedy's reputation stems more from his style and eloquently stated ideals than from the implementation of his policies. He had laid out an impressive agenda but at his death much remained blocked in Congress. It was largely because of the political skill and legislative victories of his successor that Kennedy would be seen as a force for progressive change.

LYNDON JOHNSON AND THE GREAT SOCIETY

Lyndon Johnson, a Texan who was majority leader in the Senate before becoming Kennedy's vice president, was a masterful politician. He had been schooled in Congress, where he developed an extraordinary ability to get things done. He excelled at pleading, cajoling, or threatening as necessary to achieve his ends. His liberal idealism was probably deeper than Kennedy's. As president, he wanted to use his power aggressively to eliminate poverty and spread the benefits of prosperity to all.

Johnson took office determined to secure the passage of Kennedy's legislative agenda. His immediate priorities were his predecessor's bills to reduce taxes and guarantee civil rights. Using his skills of persuasion and calling on the legislators' respect for the slain president, Johnson succeeded in gaining passage of both during his first year in office. The tax cuts stimulated the economy. The Civil Rights Act of 1964 was the most far-reaching such legislation since Reconstruction.

Johnson addressed other issues as well. By the spring of 1964, he had begun to use the name "Great Society" to describe his socio-economic program. That summer he secured passage of a federal jobs program for impoverished young people. It was the first step in what he called the "War on Poverty." In the presidential election that November, he won a landslide victory over conservative Republican Barry Goldwater. Significantly, the 1964 election gave liberal Democrats firm control of Congress for the first time since 1938. This would enable them to pass legislation over the combined opposition of Republicans and conservative Southern Democrats.

The War on Poverty became the centerpiece of the administration's Great Society program. The Office of Economic Opportunity, established in 1964, provided training for the poor and established various community-action agencies, guided by an ethic of "participatory democracy" that aimed to give the poor themselves a voice in housing, health, and education programs.

Medical care came next. Under Johnson's leadership, Congress enacted Medicare, a health insurance program for the elderly, and Medicaid, a program providing healthcare assistance for the poor.

Johnson succeeded in the effort to provide more federal aid for elementary and secondary schooling, traditionally a state and local function. The measure that was enacted gave money to the states based on the number of their children from low-income families. Funds could be used to assist public- and private-school children alike.

Convinced the United States confronted an "urban crisis" characterized by declining inner cities, the Great Society architects devised a new housing act that provided rent supplements for the poor and established a Department of Housing and Urban Development.

Other legislation had an impact on many aspects of American life. Federal assistance went to artists and scholars to encourage their work. In September 1966, Johnson signed into law two transportation bills. The first provided funds to state and local governments for developing safety programs, while the other set up federal safety standards for cars and tires. The latter program reflected the efforts of a crusading young radical, Ralph Nader. In his 1965 book, *Unsafe at Any Speed: The Designed-In Dangers of the American Automobile*, Nader argued that automobile manufacturers were sacrificing safety features for style, and charged that faulty engineering contributed to highway fatalities.

In 1965, Congress abolished the discriminatory 1924 national-origin immigration quotas. This triggered a new wave of immigration, much of it from South and East Asia and Latin America.

The Great Society was the largest burst of legislative activity since the New Deal. But support weakened as early as 1966. Some of Johnson's programs did not live up to expectations; many went underfunded. The urban crisis seemed, if anything, to worsen. Still, whether because of the Great Society spending or because of a strong economic upsurge, poverty did decline at least marginally during the Johnson administration.

THE WAR IN VIETNAM

Dissatisfaction with the Great Society came to be more than matched by unhappiness with the situation in Vietnam. A series of South Vietnamese strong men proved little more successful than Diem in mobilizing their country. The Viet Cong, insurgents supplied and coordinated from North Vietnam, gained ground in the countryside.

Determined to halt Communist advances in South Vietnam, Johnson made the Vietnam War his own. After a North Vietnamese naval attack on two American destroyers, Johnson won from Congress on August 7, 1964, passage of the Gulf of Tonkin Resolution, which allowed the president to "take all necessary measures to repel any armed attack against the forces of the United States and to prevent further aggression." After his re-election in November 1964, he embarked on a policy of escalation. From 25,000 troops at the start of 1965, the number of soldiers — both volunteers and draftees — rose to 500,000 by 1968. A bombing campaign wrought havoc in both North and South Vietnam.

Grisly television coverage with a critical edge dampened support for the war. Some Americans thought it immoral; others watched in dismay as the massive military campaign seemed to be ineffective. Large protests, especially among the young, and a mounting general public dissatisfaction pressured Johnson to begin negotiating for peace.

THE ELECTION OF 1968

By 1968 the country was in turmoil over both the Vietnam War and civil disorder, expressed in urban riots that reflected African-American anger. On March 31, 1968, the president renounced any intention of seeking another term. Just a week later, Martin Luther King Jr. was shot and killed in Memphis, Tennessee. John Kennedy's younger brother, Robert, made an emotional anti-war campaign for the Democratic nomination, only to be assassinated in June.

At the Democratic National Convention in Chicago, Illinois, protesters fought street battles with police. A divided Democratic Party nominated Vice President Hubert Humphrey, once the hero of the liberals but now seen as a Johnson loyalist. White opposition to the civil rights measures of the 1960s galvanized the third-party candidacy of Alabama Governor George Wallace, a Democrat who captured his home state, Mississippi, and Arkansas, Louisiana, and Georgia, states typically carried in that era by the Democratic nominee. Republican Richard Nixon, who ran on a plan to extricate the United States from the war and to increase "law and order" at home, scored a narrow victory.

NIXON, VIETNAM, AND THE COLD WAR

Determined to achieve "peace with honor," Nixon slowly withdrew American troops while redoubling efforts to equip the South Vietnamese army to carry on the fight. He also ordered strong American offensive actions. The most important of these was an invasion of Cambodia in 1970 to cut off North Vietnamese supply lines to South Vietnam. This led to another round of protests and demonstrations. Students in many universities took to the streets. At Kent State in Ohio, the National Guard troops who had been called in to restore order panicked and killed four students.

By the fall of 1972, however, troop strength in Vietnam was below 50,000 and the military draft, which had caused so much campus discontent, was all but dead. A cease-fire, negotiated for the United States by Nixon's national security adviser, Henry Kissinger, was signed in 1973. Although American troops departed, the war lingered on into the spring of 1975, when Congress cut off assistance to South Vietnam and North Vietnam consolidated its control over the entire country.

The war left Vietnam devastated, with millions maimed or killed. It also left the United States traumatized. The nation had spent over $150,000-million in a losing effort that cost more than 58,000 American lives. Americans were no longer united by a widely held Cold War consensus, and became wary of further foreign entanglements.

Yet as Vietnam wound down, the Nixon administration took historic steps toward closer ties with the major Communist powers. The most dramatic move was a new relationship with the People's Republic of China. In the two decades since Mao Zedong's victory, the United States had argued that the Nationalist government on Taiwan represented all of China. In 1971 and 1972, Nixon softened the American stance, eased trading restrictions, and became the first U.S. president ever to visit Beijing. The "Shanghai Communique" signed during that visit established a new U.S. policy: that there was one China, that Taiwan was a part of China, and that a peaceful settlement of the dispute of the question by the Chinese themselves was a U.S. interest.

With the Soviet Union, Nixon was equally successful in pursuing the policy he and his Secretary of State Henry Kissinger called détente. He held several cordial meetings with Soviet leader Leonid Brezhnev in which they agreed to limit stockpiles of missiles, cooperate in space, and ease trading restrictions. The Strategic Arms Limitation Talks (SALT) culminated in 1972 in an arms control agreement limiting the growth of nuclear arsenals and restricting anti-ballistic missile systems.

NIXON'S ACCOMPLISHMENTS AND DEFEATS

Vice president under Eisenhower before his unsuccessful run for the presidency in 1960, Nixon was seen as among the shrewdest of American politicians. Although Nixon subscribed to the Republican value of fiscal responsibility, he accepted a need for government's expanded role and did not oppose the basic contours of the welfare state. He simply wanted to manage its programs better. Not opposed to African-American civil rights on principle, he was wary of large federal civil rights bureaucracies. Nonetheless, his administration vigorously enforced court orders on school desegregation even as it courted Southern white voters.

Perhaps his biggest domestic problem was the economy. He inherited both a slowdown from its Vietnam peak under Johnson, and a continuing inflationary surge that had been a by-product of the war. He dealt with the first by becoming the first Republican president to endorse deficit spending as a way to stimulate the economy; the second by imposing wage and price controls, a policy in which the Right had no long-term faith, in 1971. In the short run, these decisions stabilized the economy and established favorable conditions for Nixon's re-election in 1972. He won an overwhelming victory over peace-minded Democratic Senator George McGovern.

Things began to sour very quickly into the president's second term. Very early on, he faced charges that his re-election committee had managed a break-in at the Watergate building headquarters of the Democratic National Committee and that he had participated in a cover-up. Special prosecutors and congressional committees dogged his presidency thereafter.

Factors beyond Nixon's control undermined his economic policies. In 1973 the war between Israel and Egypt and Syria prompted Saudi Arabia to embargo oil shipments to Israel's ally, the United States. Other member nations of the Organization of the Petroleum Exporting Countries (OPEC) quadrupled their prices. Americans faced both shortages, exacerbated in the view of many by over-regulation of distribution, and rapidly rising prices. Even when the embargo ended the next year, prices remained high and affected all areas of American economic life: In 1974, inflation reached 12 percent, causing disruptions that led to even higher unemployment rates. The unprecedented economic boom America had enjoyed since 1948 was grinding to a halt.

Nixon's rhetoric about the need for "law and order" in the face of rising crime rates, increased drug use, and more permissive views about sex resonated with more Americans than not. But this concern was insufficient to quell concerns about the Watergate break-in and the economy. Seeking to energize and enlarge his own political constituency, Nixon lashed out at demonstrators, attacked the press for distorted coverage, and sought to silence his opponents. Instead, he left an unfavorable impression with many who saw him on television and perceived him as unstable. Adding to Nixon's troubles, Vice President Spiro Agnew, his outspoken point man against the media and liberals, was forced to resign in 1973, pleading "no contest" to a criminal charge of tax evasion.

Nixon probably had not known in advance of the Watergate burglary, but he had tried to cover it up, and had lied to the American people about it. Evidence of his involvement mounted. On July 27, 1974, the House Judiciary Committee voted to recommend his impeachment. Facing certain ouster from office, he resigned on August 9, 1974.

THE FORD INTERLUDE

Nixon's vice president, Gerald Ford (appointed to replace Agnew), was an unpretentious man who had spent most of his public life in Congress. His first priority was to restore trust in the government. However, feeling it necessary to head off the spectacle of a possible prosecution of Nixon, he issued a blanket pardon to his predecessor. Although it was perhaps necessary, the move was nonetheless unpopular.

In public policy, Ford followed the course Nixon had set. Economic problems remained serious, as inflation and unemployment continued to rise. Ford first tried to reassure the public, much as Herbert Hoover had done in 1929. When that failed, he imposed measures to curb inflation, which sent unemployment above 8 percent. A tax cut, coupled with higher unemployment benefits, helped a bit but the economy remained weak.

In foreign policy, Ford adopted Nixon's strategy of détente. Perhaps its major manifestation was the Helsinki Accords of 1975, in which the United States and Western European nations effectively recognized Soviet hegemony in Eastern Europe in return for Soviet affirmation of human rights. The agreement had little immediate significance, but over the long run may have made maintenance of the Soviet empire more difficult. Western nations effectively used periodic "Helsinki review meetings" to call attention to various abuses of human rights by Communist regimes of the Eastern bloc.

THE CARTER YEARS

Jimmy Carter, former Democratic governor of Georgia, won the presidency in 1976. Portraying himself during the campaign as an outsider to Washington politics, he promised a fresh approach to governing, but his lack of experience at the national level complicated his tenure from the start. A naval officer and engineer by training, he often appeared to be a technocrat, when Americans wanted someone more visionary to lead them through troubled times.

In economic affairs, Carter at first permitted a policy of deficit spending. Inflation rose to 10 percent a year when the Federal Reserve Board, responsible for setting monetary policy, increased the money supply to cover deficits. Carter responded by cutting the budget, but cuts affected social programs at the heart of Democratic domestic policy. In mid-1979, anger in the financial community practically forced him to appoint Paul Volcker as chairman of the Federal Reserve. Volcker was an "inflation hawk" who increased interest rates in an attempt to halt price increases, at the cost of negative consequences for the economy.

Carter also faced criticism for his failure to secure passage of an effective energy policy. He presented a comprehensive program, aimed at reducing dependence on foreign oil, that he called the "moral equivalent of war." Opponents thwarted it in Congress.

Though Carter called himself a populist, his political priorities were never wholly clear. He endorsed government's protective role, but then began the process of deregulation, the removal of governmental controls in economic life. Arguing that some restrictions over the course of the past century limited competition and increased consumer costs, he favored decontrol in the oil, airline, railroad, and trucking industries.

Carter's political efforts failed to gain either public or congressional support. By the end of his term, his disapproval rating reached 77 percent, and Americans began to look toward the Republican Party again.

Carter's greatest foreign policy accomplishment was the negotiation of a peace settlement between Egypt, under President Anwar al-Sadat, and Israel, under Prime Minister Menachem Begin. Acting as both mediator and participant, he persuaded the two leaders to end a 30-year state of war. The subsequent peace treaty was signed at the White House in March 1979.

After protracted and often emotional debate, Carter also secured Senate ratification of treaties ceding the Panama Canal to Panama by the year 2000. Going a step farther than Nixon, he extended formal diplomatic recognition to the People's Republic of China.

But Carter enjoyed less success with the Soviet Union. Though he assumed office with détente at high tide and declared that the United States had escaped its "inordinate fear of Communism," his insistence that "our commitment to human rights must be absolute" antagonized the Soviet government. A SALT II agreement further limiting nuclear stockpiles was signed, but not ratified by the U.S. Senate, many of whose members felt the treaty was unbalanced. The 1979 Soviet invasion of Afghanistan killed the treaty and triggered a Carter defense build-up that paved the way for the huge expenditures of the 1980s.

Carter's most serious foreign policy challenge came in Iran. After an Islamic fundamentalist revolution led by Shiite Muslim leader Ayatollah Ruhollah Khomeini replaced a corrupt but friendly regime, Carter admitted the deposed shah to the United States for medical treatment. Angry Iranian militants, supported by the Islamic regime, seized the American embassy in Tehran and held 53 American hostages for more than a year. The long-running hostage crisis dominated the final year of his presidency and greatly damaged his chances for re-election. >

The digital revolution of the past decade has transformed the economy and the way Americans live, influencing work; interactions with colleagues, family, and friends; access to information; even shopping and leisure-time habits.

21ST CENTURY
NATION
A PICTURE PROFILE

The first years of the new century unleashed a new threat to peace and democracy: international terrorist attacks that killed and maimed thousands in the United States and around the world. Just as it has with earlier dangers, the United States took up this formidable challenge in unison with its allies. At the same time, it coped with changes sparked by globalization, fast-paced technological developments, and new waves of immigration that have made American society more diverse than in the past. The country sought to build upon the achievements of its history, and to honor those who have sacrificed for its cause.

Malalai Joya, one of about 100 women delegates to the constitutional council in Afghanistan, speaks to the council in Kabul, December 17, 2003. Afghanistan has its first democratically elected government as a result of the U.S., allied, and Northern Alliance military action in 2001 that toppled the Taliban for sheltering Osama bin Laden, mastermind of the September 11, 2001, terrorist attacks against the United States.

President George W. Bush (center) meets with British Prime Minister Tony Blair (left), National Security Adviser Condoleezza Rice, and Secretary of State Colin Powell (right) at the White House during his first term. Great Britain has been a key U.S. ally in the fight against terrorism.

President Barack Obama and first lady Michelle Obama wave goodbye from Gardermoen Airport outside Oslo, Norway. President Obama was in Oslo to receive the Nobel Peace Prize on December 10, 2009.

Top, Microsoft chairman Bill Gates talks with Antwoinette Hayes, a participant in a Microsoft initiative to provide technology access to children and teens. Above, Apple founder and chief executive officer Steve Jobs with his company's iPod mini. Gates and Jobs are seen as the most powerful symbols of the creative and commercial talent that shaped the digital era.

Cable News Network (CNN) report from Moscow: The combination of hundreds of cable television channels and 24-hour news services like CNN gives an unprecedented impact and immediacy to news developments around the world.

Combine youth, rock and hip hop music, and 24-hour television, and you get MTV, a television network whose influence extends beyond music videos to fashion, advertising, and sales.

Bales of sorted recyclables are stacked for processing at the Rumpke recycling center in Columbus, Ohio. Growing environmental consciousness in the United States has led to huge recycling efforts for materials such as glass, paper, steel, and aluminum.

The massive AIDS quilt, with each square commemorating an individual who has died of the disease. The United States is a leading contributor to the fight against this global pandemic.

Americans' love affair with the automobile continues, resulting in increased traffic congestion as well as considerable efforts by government and industry to reduce air pollution.

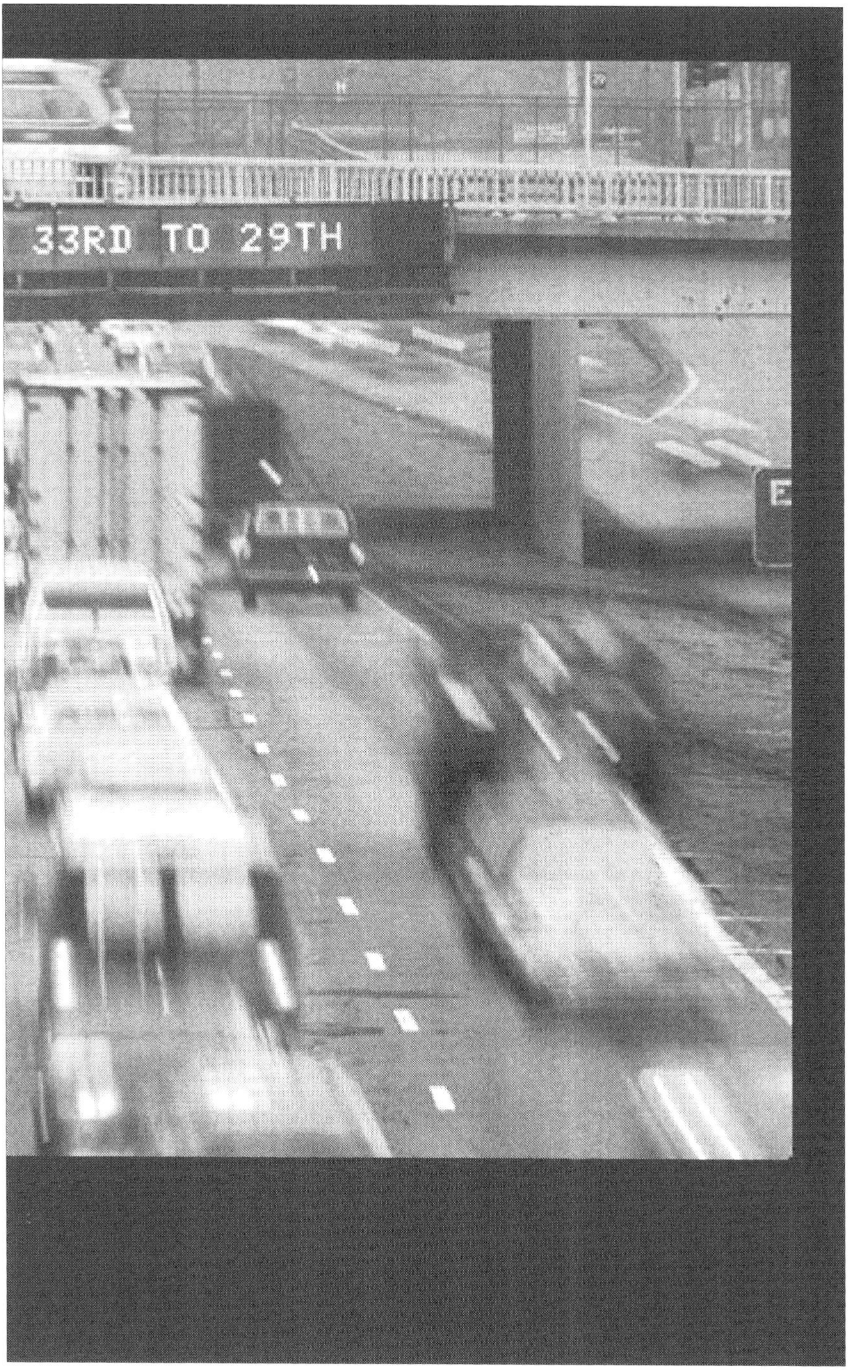
33RD TO 29TH

Iraqis queuing to vote for a Transitional National Assembly at a polling station in the center of Az Zubayr, Iraq, January 30, 2005. More than 8.5 million Iraqis braved threats of violence and terrorist attacks to participate in the elections. The vote followed the 2003 war, led by the United States and other coalition members, which rid Iraq of dictator Saddam Hussein.

With husbands and wives in the typical family both working outside the home, daycare centers for children are commonplace throughout the United States.

A new generation peers into its future.

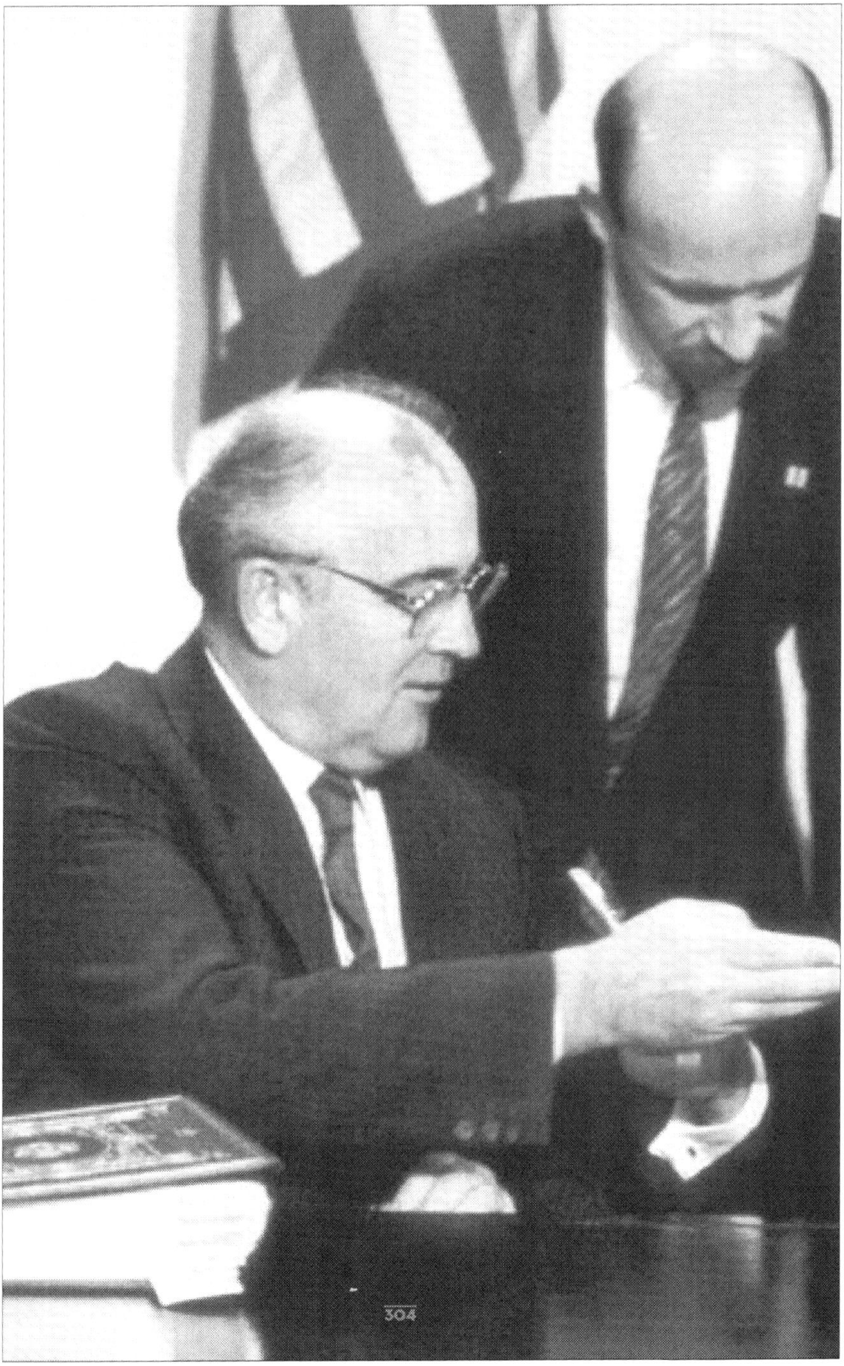

CHAPTER 14

THE NEW CONSERVATISM AND A NEW WORLD ORDER

President Ronald Reagan and USSR President Mikhail Gorbachev after signing the Intermediate-Range Nuclear Forces (INF) Treaty, December 1987.

> "I have always believed that there was some divine plan that placed this great continent between two oceans to be sought out by those who were possessed of an abiding love of freedom and a special kind of courage."
>
> California Governor **Ronald Reagan**, 1974

A SOCIETY IN TRANSITION

Shifts in the structure of American society, begun years or even decades earlier, had become apparent by the time the 1980s arrived. The composition of the population and the most important jobs and skills in American society had undergone major changes.

The dominance of service jobs in the economy became undeniable. By the mid-1980s, nearly three-fourths of all employees worked in the service sector, for instance, as retail clerks, office workers, teachers, physicians, and government employees.

Service-sector activity benefited from the availability and increased use of the computer. The information age arrived, with hardware and software that could aggregate previously unimagined amounts of data about economic and social trends. The federal government had made significant investments in computer technology in the 1950s and 1960s for its military and space programs.

In 1976, two young California entrepreneurs, working out of a garage, assembled the first widely marketed computer for home use, named it the Apple, and ignited a revolution. By the early 1980s, millions of microcomputers had found their way into U.S. businesses and homes, and in 1982, *Time* magazine dubbed the computer its "Machine of the Year."

Meanwhile, America's "smokestack industries" were in decline. The U.S. automobile industry reeled under competition from highly efficient Japanese carmakers. By 1980 Japanese companies already manufactured a fifth of the vehicles sold in the United States. American manufacturers struggled with some success to match the cost efficiencies and engineering standards of their Japanese rivals, but their former dominance of the domestic car market was gone forever. The giant old-line steel companies shrank to relative insignificance as foreign steel makers adopted new technologies more readily.

Consumers were the beneficiaries of this ferocious competition in the manufacturing industries, but the painful struggle to cut costs meant the permanent loss of hundreds of thousands of blue-collar jobs. Those who could made the switch to the service sector; others became unfortunate statistics.

Population patterns shifted as well. After the end of the postwar "baby boom" (1946 to 1964), the overall rate of population growth declined and the population grew older. Household composition also changed. In 1980 the percentage of family households dropped; a quarter of all groups were now classified as "nonfamily households," in which two or more unrelated persons lived together.

New immigrants changed the character of American society in other ways. The 1965 reform in immigration policy shifted the focus away from Western Europe, facilitating a dramatic increase in new arrivals from Asia and Latin America. In 1980, 808,000 immigrants arrived, the highest number in 60 years, as the country once more became a haven for people from around the world.

Additional groups became active participants in the struggle for equal opportunity. Homosexuals, using the tactics and rhetoric of the civil rights movement, depicted themselves as an oppressed group seeking recognition of basic rights. In 1975, the U.S. Civil Service Commission lifted its ban on employment of homosexuals. Many states enacted anti-discrimination laws.

Then, in 1981, came the discovery of AIDS (Acquired Immune Deficiency Syndrome). Transmitted sexually or through blood transfusions, it struck homosexual men and intravenous drug users with particular virulence, although the general population proved vulnerable as well. By 1992, over 220,000 Americans had died of AIDS. The AIDS epidemic has by no means been limited to the United States, and the effort to treat the disease now encompasses physicians and medical researchers throughout the world.

CONSERVATISM AND THE RISE OF RONALD REAGAN

For many Americans, the economic, social, and political trends of the previous two decades — crime and racial polarization in many urban centers, challenges to traditional values, the economic downturn and inflation of the Carter years — engendered a mood of disillusionment.

It also strengthened a renewed suspicion of government and its ability to deal effectively with the country's social and political problems.

Conservatives, long out of power at the national level, were well positioned politically in the context of this new mood. Many Americans were receptive to their message of limited government, strong national defense, and the protection of traditional values.

This conservative upsurge had many sources. A large group of fundamentalist Christians were particularly concerned about crime and sexual immorality. They hoped to return religion or the moral precepts often associated with it to a central place in American life. One of the most politically effective groups in the early 1980s, the Moral Majority, was led by a Baptist minister, Jerry Falwell. Another, led by the Reverend Pat Robertson, built an organization, the Christian Coalition, that by the 1990s was a significant force in the Republican Party. Using television to spread their messages, Falwell, Robertson, and others like them developed substantial followings.

Another galvanizing issue for conservatives was divisive and emotional: abortion. Opposition to the 1973 Supreme Court decision, *Roe v. Wade*, which upheld a woman's right to an abortion in the early months of pregnancy, brought together a wide array of organizations and individuals. They included, but were not limited to, Catholics, political conservatives, and religious evangelicals, most of whom regarded abortion under virtually any circumstances as tantamount to murder. Pro-choice and pro-life (that is, pro- and anti-abortion rights) demonstrations became a fixture of the political landscape.

Within the Republican Party, the conservative wing grew dominant once again. They had briefly seized control of the Republican Party in 1964 with its presidential candidate, Barry Goldwater, then faded from the spotlight. By 1980, however, with the apparent failure of liberalism under Carter, a "New Right" was poised to return to dominance.

Using modern direct mail techniques as well as the power of mass communications to spread their message and raise funds, drawing on the ideas of conservatives like economist Milton Friedman, journalists William F. Buckley and George Will, and research institutions like the Heritage Foundation, the New Right played a significant role in defining the issues of the 1980s.

The "Old" Goldwater Right had favored strict limits on government intervention in the economy. This tendency was reinforced by a significant group of "New Right" "libertarian conservatives" who distrusted government in general and opposed state interference in personal behavior. But the New Right also encompassed a stronger, often evangelical faction determined to wield state power to encourage its views. The New Right favored tough measures against crime, a strong national defense, a constitutional amendment to permit prayer in public schools, and opposition to abortion.

The figure that drew all these disparate strands together was Ronald Reagan. Reagan, born in Illinois, achieved stardom as an actor in Hollywood movies and television before turning to politics. He first achieved political prominence with a nationwide televised speech in 1964 in support of Barry Goldwater. In 1966 Reagan won the governorship of California and served until 1975. He narrowly missed winning the Republican nomination for president in 1976 before succeeding in 1980 and going on to win the presidency from the incumbent, Jimmy Carter.

President Reagan's unflagging optimism and his ability to celebrate the achievements and aspirations of the American people persisted throughout his two terms in office. He was a figure of reassurance and stability for many Americans. Wholly at ease before the microphone and the television camera, Reagan was called the "Great Communicator."

Taking a phrase from the 17th-century Puritan John Winthrop, he told the nation that the United States was a "shining city on a hill," invested with a God-given mission to defend the world against the spread of Communist totalitarianism.

Reagan believed that government intruded too deeply into American life. He wanted to cut programs he contended the country did not need, and to eliminate "waste, fraud, and abuse." Reagan accelerated the program of deregulation begun by Jimmy Carter. He sought to abolish many regulations affecting the consumer, the workplace, and the environment. These, he argued, were inefficient, expensive, and detrimental to economic growth.

Reagan also reflected the belief held by many conservatives that the law should be strictly applied against violators. Shortly after becoming president, he faced a nationwide strike by U.S. air transportation controllers. Although the job action was forbidden by law, such strikes had been widely tolerated in the past. When the air controllers refused to return to work, he ordered them all fired. Over the next few years the system was rebuilt with new hires.

THE ECONOMY IN THE 1980s

President Reagan's domestic program was rooted in his belief that the nation would prosper if the power of the private economic sector was unleashed. The guiding theory behind it, "supply side" economics, held that a greater supply of goods and services, made possible by measures to increase business investment, was the swiftest road to economic growth. Accordingly, the Reagan administration argued that a large tax cut would increase capital investment and corporate earnings, so that even lower taxes on these larger earnings would increase government revenues.

Despite only a slim Republican majority in the Senate and a House of Representatives controlled by the Democrats, President Reagan succeeded during his first year in office in enacting the major components of his economic program, including a 25-percent tax cut for individuals to be phased in over three years. The administration also sought and won significant increases in defense spending to modernize the nation's military and counter what it felt was a continual and growing threat from the Soviet Union.

Under Paul Volcker, the Federal Reserve's draconian increases in interest rates squeezed the runaway inflation that had begun in the late 1970s. The recession hit bottom in 1982, with the prime interest rates approaching 20 percent and the economy falling sharply. That year, real gross domestic product (GDP) fell by 2 percent; the unemployment rate rose to nearly 10 percent, and almost one-third of America's industrial plants lay idle. Throughout the Midwest, major firms like General Electric and International Harvester released workers. Stubbornly high petroleum prices contributed to the decline. Economic rivals like Germany and Japan won a greater share of world trade, and U.S. consumption of goods from other countries rose sharply.

Farmers also suffered hard times. During the 1970s, American farmers had helped India, China, the Soviet Union, and other countries suffering from crop shortages, and had borrowed heavily to buy land and increase production. But the rise in oil prices pushed up costs, and a worldwide economic slump in 1980 reduced the demand for agricultural products. Their numbers declined, as production increasingly became concentrated in large operations. Those small farmers who survived had major difficulties making ends meet.

The increased military budget — combined with the tax cuts and the growth in government health spending — resulted in the federal government spending far more than it received in revenues each year. Some analysts charged that the deficits were part of a deliberate administration strategy to prevent further increases in domestic spending sought by the Democrats. However, both Democrats and Republicans in Congress refused to cut such spending. From $74,000-million in 1980, the deficit soared to $221,000-million in 1986 before falling back to $150,000-million in 1987.

The deep recession of the early 1980s successfully curbed the runaway inflation that had started during the Carter years. Fuel prices, moreover, fell sharply, with at least part of the drop attributable to Reagan's decision to abolish controls on the pricing and allocation of gasoline. Conditions began to improve in late 1983. By early 1984, the economy had rebounded. By the fall of 1984, the recovery was well along, allowing Reagan to run for re-election on the slogan, "It's morning again in America." He defeated his Democratic opponent, former Senator and Vice President Walter Mondale, by an overwhelming margin.

The United States entered one of the longest periods of sustained economic growth since World War II. Consumer spending increased in response to the federal tax cut. The stock market climbed as it reflected the optimistic buying spree. Over a five-year period following the start of the recovery, gross national product grew at an annual rate of 4.2 percent. The annual inflation rate remained between 3 and 5 percent from 1983 to 1987, except in 1986 when it fell to just under 2 percent, the lowest level in decades. The nation's GNP grew substantially during the 1980s; from 1982 to 1987, its economy created more than 13 million new jobs.

Steadfast in his commitment to lower taxes, Reagan signed the most sweeping federal tax-reform measure in 75 years during his second term. This measure, which had widespread Democratic as well as Republican support, lowered income tax rates, simplified tax brackets, and closed loopholes.

However, a significant percentage of this growth was based on deficit spending. Moreover, the national debt, far from being stabilized by strong economic growth, nearly tripled. Much of the growth occurred in skilled service and technical areas. Many poor and middle-class families did less well. The administration, although an advocate of free trade, pressured Japan to agree to a voluntary quota on its automobile exports to the United States.

The economy was jolted on October 19, 1987, "Black Monday," when the stock market suffered the greatest one-day crash in its history, 22.6 percent. The causes of the crash included the large U.S. international trade and federal-budget deficits, the high level of corporate and personal debt, and new computerized stock trading techniques that allowed instantaneous selling of stocks and futures. Despite the memories of 1929 it evoked, however, the crash was a transitory event with little impact. In fact, economic growth continued, with the unemployment rate dropping to a 14-year low of 5.2 percent in June 1988.

FOREIGN AFFAIRS

In foreign policy, Reagan sought a more assertive role for the nation, and Central America provided an early test. The United States provided El Salvador with a program of economic aid and military training when a guerrilla insurgency threatened to topple its government. It also actively encouraged the transition to an elected democratic government, but efforts to curb active right-wing death squads were only partly successful. U.S. support helped stabilize the government, but the level of violence there remained undiminished. A peace agreement was finally reached in early 1992.

U.S. policy toward Nicaragua was more controversial. In 1979 revolutionaries calling themselves Sandinistas overthrew the repressive right-wing Somoza regime and established a pro-Cuba, pro-Soviet dictatorship. Regional peace efforts ended in failure, and the focus of administration efforts shifted to support for the anti-Sandinista resistance, known as the contras.

Following intense political debate over this policy, Congress ended all military aid to the contras in October 1984, then, under administration pressure, reversed itself in the fall of 1986, and approved $100 million in military aid. However, a lack of success on the battlefield, charges of human rights abuses, and the revelation that funds from secret arms sales to Iran (see below) had been diverted to the contras undercut congressional support to continue this aid.

Subsequently, the administration of President George H.W. Bush, who succeeded Reagan as president in 1989, abandoned any effort to secure military aid for the contras. The Bush administration also exerted pressure for free elections and supported an opposition political coalition, which won an astonishing upset election in February 1990, ousting the Sandinistas from power.

The Reagan administration was more fortunate in witnessing a return to democracy throughout the rest of Latin America, from Guatemala to Argentina. The emergence of democratically elected governments was not limited to Latin America; in Asia, the "people power" campaign of Corazon Aquino overthrew the dictatorship of Ferdinand Marcos, and elections in South Korea ended decades of military rule.

By contrast, South Africa remained intransigent in the face of U.S. efforts to encourage an end to racial apartheid through the controversial policy of "constructive engagement," quiet diplomacy coupled with public endorsement of reform. In 1986, frustrated at the lack of progress, the U.S. Congress overrode Reagan's veto and imposed a set of economic sanctions on South Africa. In February 1990, South African President F.W. de Klerk announced Nelson Mandela's release and began the slow dismantling of apartheid.

Despite its outspoken anti-Communist rhetoric, the Reagan administration's direct use of military force was restrained. On October 25, 1983, U.S. forces landed on the Caribbean island of Grenada after an urgent appeal for help by neighboring countries. The action followed the assassination of Grenada's leftist prime minister by members of his own Marxist-oriented party. After a brief period of fighting, U.S. troops captured hundreds of Cuban military and construction personnel and seized caches of Soviet-supplied arms. In December 1983, the last American combat troops left Grenada, which held democratic elections a year later.

The Middle East, however, presented a far more difficult situation. A military presence in Lebanon, where the United States was attempting to bolster a weak, but moderate pro-Western government, ended tragically, when 241 U.S. Marines were killed in a terrorist bombing in October 1983. In April 1986, U.S. Navy and Air Force planes struck targets in Tripoli and Benghazi, Libya, in retaliation for Libyan-instigated terrorist attacks on U.S. military personnel in Europe.

In the Persian Gulf, the earlier breakdown in U.S.-Iranian relations and the Iran-Iraq War set the stage for U.S. naval activities in the region. Initially, the United States responded to a request from Kuwait for protection of its tanker fleet; but eventually the United States, along with naval vessels from Western Europe, kept vital shipping lanes open by escorting convoys of tankers and other neutral vessels traveling up and down the Gulf.

In late 1986 Americans learned that the administration had secretly sold arms to Iran in an attempt to resume diplomatic relations with the hostile Islamic government and win freedom for American hostages held in Lebanon by radical organizations that Iran controlled. Investigation also revealed that funds from the arms sales had been diverted to the Nicaraguan contras during a period when Congress had prohibited such military aid.

The ensuing Iran-contra hearings before a joint House-Senate committee examined issues of possible illegality as well as the broader question of defining American foreign policy interests in the Middle East and Central America. In a larger sense, the hearings were a constitutional debate about government secrecy and presidential versus congressional authority in the conduct of foreign relations. Unlike the celebrated Senate Watergate hearings 14 years earlier, they found no grounds for impeaching the president and could reach no definitive conclusion about these perennial issues.

U.S.-SOVIET RELATIONS

In relations with the Soviet Union, President Reagan's declared policy was one of peace through strength. He was determined to stand firm against the country he would in 1983 call an "evil empire." Two early events increased U.S.-Soviet tensions: the suppression of the Solidarity labor movement in Poland in December 1981, and the destruction with 269 fatalities of an off-course civilian airliner, Korean Airlines Flight 007, by a Soviet jet fighter on September 1, 1983. The United States also condemned the continuing Soviet occupation of Afghanistan and continued aid begun by the Carter administration to the mujahedeen resistance there.

During Reagan's first term, the United States spent unprecedented sums for a massive defense build-up, including the placement of intermediate-range nuclear missiles in Europe to counter Soviet deployments of similar missiles. And on March 23, 1983, in one of the most hotly debated policy decisions of his presidency, Reagan announced the Strategic Defense Initiative (SDI) research program to explore advanced technologies, such as lasers and high-energy projectiles, to defend against intercontinental ballistic missiles. Although many scientists questioned the technological feasibility of SDI and economists pointed to the extraordinary sums of money involved, the administration pressed ahead with the project.

After re-election in 1984, Reagan softened his position on arms control. Moscow was amenable to agreement, in part because its economy already expended a far greater proportion of national output on its military than did the United States. Further increases, Soviet leader Mikhail Gorbachev felt, would cripple his plans to liberalize the Soviet economy.

In November 1985, Reagan and Gorbachev agreed in principle to seek 50-percent reductions in strategic offensive nuclear arms as well as an interim agreement on intermediate-range nuclear forces. In December 1987, they signed the Intermediate-Range Nuclear Forces (INF) Treaty providing for the destruction of that entire category of nuclear weapons. By then, the Soviet Union seemed a less menacing adversary. Reagan could take much of the credit for a greatly diminished Cold War, but as his administration ended, almost no one realized just how shaky the USSR had become.

THE PRESIDENCY OF GEORGE H. W. BUSH

President Reagan enjoyed unusually high popularity at the end of his second term in office, but under the terms of the U.S. Constitution he could not run again in 1988. The Republican nomination went to Vice President George Herbert Walker Bush, who was elected the 41st president of the United States.

Bush campaigned by promising voters a continuation of the prosperity Reagan had brought. In addition, he argued that he would support a strong defense for the United States more reliably than the Democratic candidate, Michael Dukakis. He also promised to work for "a kinder, gentler America." Dukakis, the governor of Massachusetts, claimed that less fortunate Americans were hurting economically and that the government had to help them while simultaneously bringing the federal debt and defense spending under control. The public was much more engaged, however, by Bush's economic message: No new taxes. In the balloting, Bush finished with a 54-to-46-percent popular vote margin.

During his first year in office, Bush followed a conservative fiscal program, pursuing policies on taxes, spending, and debt that were faithful to the Reagan administration's economic program. But the new president soon found himself squeezed between a large budget deficit and a deficit-reduction law. Spending cuts seemed necessary, and Bush possessed little leeway to introduce new budget items.

The Bush administration advanced new policy initiatives in areas not requiring major new federal expenditures. Thus, in November 1990, Bush signed sweeping legislation imposing new federal standards on urban smog, automobile exhaust, toxic air pollution, and acid rain, but with industrial polluters bearing most of the costs. He accepted legislation requiring physical access for the disabled, but with no federal assumption of the expense of modifying buildings to accommodate wheelchairs and the like. The president also launched a campaign to encourage volunteerism, which he called, in a memorable phrase, "a thousand points of light."

BUDGETS AND DEFICITS

Bush administration efforts to gain control over the federal budget deficit, however, were more problematic. One source of the difficulty was the savings and loan crisis. Savings banks — formerly tightly regulated, low-interest safe havens for ordinary people — had been deregulated, allowing these institutions to compete more aggressively by paying higher interest rates and by making riskier loans. Increases in the government's deposit insurance guaranteed reduced consumer incentive to shun less-sound institutions. Fraud, mismanagement, and the choppy economy produced widespread insolvencies among these thrifts (the umbrella term for consumer-oriented institutions like savings and loan associations and savings banks). By 1993, the total cost of selling and shuttering failed thrifts was staggering, nearly $525,000-million.

In January 1990, President Bush presented his budget proposal to Congress. Democrats argued that administration budget projections were far too optimistic, and that meeting the deficit-reduction law would require tax increases and sharper cuts in defense spending. That June, after protracted negotiations, the president agreed to a tax increase. All the same, the combination of economic recession, losses from the savings and loan industry rescue operation, and escalating health care costs for Medicare and Medicaid offset all the deficit-reduction measures and produced a shortfall in 1991 at least as large as the previous year's.

END TO THE COLD WAR

When Bush became president, the Soviet empire was on the verge of collapse. Gorbachev's efforts to open up the USSR's economy appeared to be floundering. In 1989, the Communist governments in one Eastern European country after another simply collapsed, after it became clear that Russian troops would not be sent to prop them up. In mid-1991, hard-liners attempted a coup d'etat, only to be foiled by Gorbachev rival Boris Yeltsin, president of the Russian republic. At the end of that year, Yeltsin, now dominant, forced the dissolution of the Soviet Union.

The Bush administration adeptly brokered the end of the Cold War, working closely with Gorbachev and Yeltsin. It led the negotiations that brought the unification of East and West Germany (September 1990), agreement on large arms reductions in Europe (November 1990), and large cuts in nuclear arsenals (July 1991). After the liquidation of the Soviet Union, the United States and the new Russian Federation agreed to phase out all multiple-warhead missiles over a 10-year period.

The disposal of nuclear materials and the ever-present concerns of nuclear proliferation now superseded the threat of nuclear conflict between Washington and Moscow.

THE GULF WAR

The euphoria caused by the drawing down of the Cold War was dramatically overshadowed by the August 2, 1990, invasion of the small nation of Kuwait by Iraq. Iraq, under Saddam Hussein, and Iran, under its Islamic fundamentalist regime, had emerged as the two major military powers in the oil-rich Persian Gulf area. The two countries had fought a long, inconclusive war in the 1980s. Less hostile to the United States than Iran, Iraq had won some support from the Reagan and Bush administrations. The occupation of Kuwait, posing a threat to Saudi Arabia, changed the diplomatic calculation overnight.

President Bush strongly condemned the Iraqi action, called for Iraq's unconditional withdrawal, and sent a major deployment of U.S. troops to the Middle East. He assembled one of the most extraordinary military and political coalitions of modern times, with military forces from Asia, Europe, and Africa, as well as the Middle East.

In the days and weeks following the invasion, the U.N. Security Council passed 12 resolutions condemning the Iraqi invasion and imposing wide-ranging economic sanctions on Iraq. On November 29, it approved the use of force if Iraq did not withdraw from Kuwait by January 15, 1991. Gorbachev's Soviet Union, once Iraq's major arms supplier, made no effort to protect its former client.

Bush also confronted a major constitutional issue. The U.S. Constitution gives the legislative branch the power to declare war. Yet in the second half of the 20th century, the United States had become involved in Korea and Vietnam without an official declaration of war and with only murky legislative authorization. On January 12, 1991, three days before the U.N. deadline, Congress granted President Bush the authority he sought in the most explicit and sweeping war-making power given a president in nearly half a century.

The United States, in coalition with Great Britain, France, Italy, Saudi Arabia, Kuwait, and other countries, succeeded in liberating Kuwait with a devastating, U.S.-led air campaign that lasted slightly more than a month. It was followed by a massive invasion of Kuwait and Iraq by armored and airborne infantry forces. With their superior speed, mobility, and firepower, the allied forces overwhelmed the Iraqi forces in a land campaign lasting only 100 hours.

The victory, however, was incomplete and unsatisfying. The U.N. resolution, which Bush enforced to the letter, called only for the expulsion of Iraq from Kuwait. Saddam Hussein remained in power, savagely repressing the Kurds in the north and the Shiites in the south, both of whom the United States had encouraged to rebel. Hundreds of oil-well fires, deliberately set in Kuwait by the Iraqis, took until November 1991 to extinguish. Saddam's regime also apparently thwarted U.N. inspectors who, operating in accordance with Security Council resolutions, worked to locate and destroy Iraq's weapons of mass destruction, including nuclear facilities more advanced than had previously been suspected and huge stocks of chemical weapons.

The Gulf War enabled the United States to persuade the Arab states, Israel, and a Palestinian delegation to begin direct negotiations aimed at resolving the complex and interlocked issues that could eventually lead to a lasting peace in the region. The talks began in Madrid, Spain, on October 30, 1991. In turn, they set the stage for the secret negotiations in Norway that led to what at the time seemed a historic agreement between Israel and the Palestine Liberation Organization, signed at the White House on September 13, 1993.

PANAMA AND NAFTA

The president also received broad bipartisan congressional backing for the brief U.S. invasion of Panama on December 20, 1989, that deposed dictator General Manuel Antonio Noriega. In the 1980s, addiction to crack cocaine reached epidemic proportions, and President Bush put the "War on Drugs" at the center of his domestic agenda. Moreover, Noriega, an especially brutal dictator, had attempted to maintain himself in power with rather crude displays of anti-Americanism. After seeking refuge in the Vatican embassy, Noriega turned himself over to U.S. authorities. He was later tried and convicted in U.S. federal court in Miami, Florida, of drug trafficking and racketeering.

On the economic front, the Bush administration negotiated the North America Free Trade Agreement (NAFTA) with Mexico and Canada. It would be ratified after an intense debate in the first year of the Clinton administration. >

THIRD-PARTY AND INDEPENDENT CANDIDATES

The United States is often thought of as functioning under a two-party system. In practical effect this is true: Either a Democrat or a Republican has occupied the White House every year since 1852. At the same time, however, the country has produced a plethora of third and minor parties over the years. For example, 58 parties were represented on at least one state ballot during the 1992 presidential elections. Among these were obscure parties such as the Apathy, the Looking Back, the New Mexico Prohibition, the Tish Independent Citizens, and the Vermont Taxpayers.

Third parties organize around a single issue or set of issues. They tend to fare best when they have a charismatic leader. With the presidency out of reach, most seek a platform to publicize their political and social concerns.

Theodore Roosevelt. The most successful third-party candidate of the 20th century was a Republican, Theodore Roosevelt, the former president. His Progressive or Bull Moose Party won 27.4 percent of the vote in the 1912 election. The progressive wing of the Republican Party, having grown disenchanted with President William Howard Taft, whom Roosevelt had hand-picked as his successor, urged Roosevelt to seek the party nomination in 1912. This he did, defeating Taft in a number of primaries. Taft controlled the party machinery, however, and secured the nomination.

Roosevelt's supporters then broke away and formed the Progressive Party. Declaring himself as fit as a bull moose (hence the party's popular name), Roosevelt campaigned on a platform of regulating "big business," women's suffrage, a graduated income tax, the Panama Canal, and conservation. His effort was sufficient to defeat Taft. By splitting the Republican vote, however, he helped ensure the election of the Democrat Woodrow Wilson.

Socialists. The Socialist Party also reached its high point in 1912, attaining 6 percent of the popular vote. Perennial candidate Eugene Debs won nearly 900,000 votes that year, advocating collective ownership of the transportation and communication industries, shorter working hours, and public works projects to spur employment. Convicted of sedition during World War I, Debs campaigned from his cell in 1920.

Robert La Follette. Another Progressive was Senator Robert La Follette, who won more than 16 percent of the vote in the 1924 election. Long a champion of farmers and industrial workers, and an ardent foe of big business, La Follette was a prime mover in the recreation of the Progressive movement following World War I. Backed by the farm and labor vote, as well as by Socialists and remnants of Roosevelt's Bull Moose Party, La Follette ran on a platform of nationalizing railroads and the country's natural resources. He also strongly supported increased taxation on the wealthy and the right of collective bargaining. He carried only his home state of Wisconsin.

Henry Wallace. The Progressive Party reinvented itself in 1948 with the nomination of Henry Wallace, a former secretary of agriculture and vice president under Franklin Roosevelt. Wallace's 1948 platform opposed the Cold War, the Marshall Plan, and big business. He also campaigned to end discrimination against African Americans and women, backed a minimum wage, and called for the elimination of the House Committee on Un-American Activities. His failure to repudiate the U.S. Communist Party, which had endorsed him, undermined his popularity and he wound up with just over 2.4 percent of the popular vote.

Dixiecrats. Like the Progressives, the States Rights or Dixiecrat Party, led by South Carolina Governor Strom Thurmond, emerged in 1948 as a spin-off from the Democratic Party. Its opposition stemmed from Truman's civil rights platform. Although defined in terms of "states' rights," the party's goal was continuing racial segregation and the "Jim Crow" laws that sustained it.

George Wallace. The racial and social upheavals of the 1960s helped bring George Wallace, another segregationist Southern governor, to national attention. Wallace built a following through his colorful attacks against civil rights, liberals, and the federal government. Founding the American Independent Party in 1968, he ran his campaign from the statehouse in Montgomery, Alabama, winning 13.5 percent of the overall presidential vote.

H. Ross Perot. Every third party seeks to capitalize on popular dissatisfaction with the major parties and the federal government. At few times in recent history, however, has this sentiment been as strong as it was during the 1992 election. A hugely wealthy Texas businessman, Perot possessed a knack for getting his message of economic common sense and fiscal responsibility across to a wide spectrum of the people. Lampooning the nation's leaders and reducing his economic message to easily understood formulas, Perot found little difficulty gaining media attention. His campaign organization, United We Stand, was staffed primarily by volunteers and backed by his personal fortune. Far from resenting his wealth, many admired Perot's business success and the freedom it brought him from soliciting campaign funds from special interests. Perot withdrew from the race in July. Re-entering it a month before the election, he won over 19 million votes as the Reform Party standard-bearer, nearly 19 percent of the total cast. This was by far the largest number ever tallied by a third-party candidate and second only to Theodore Roosevelt's 1912 showing as a percentage of the total. ◆

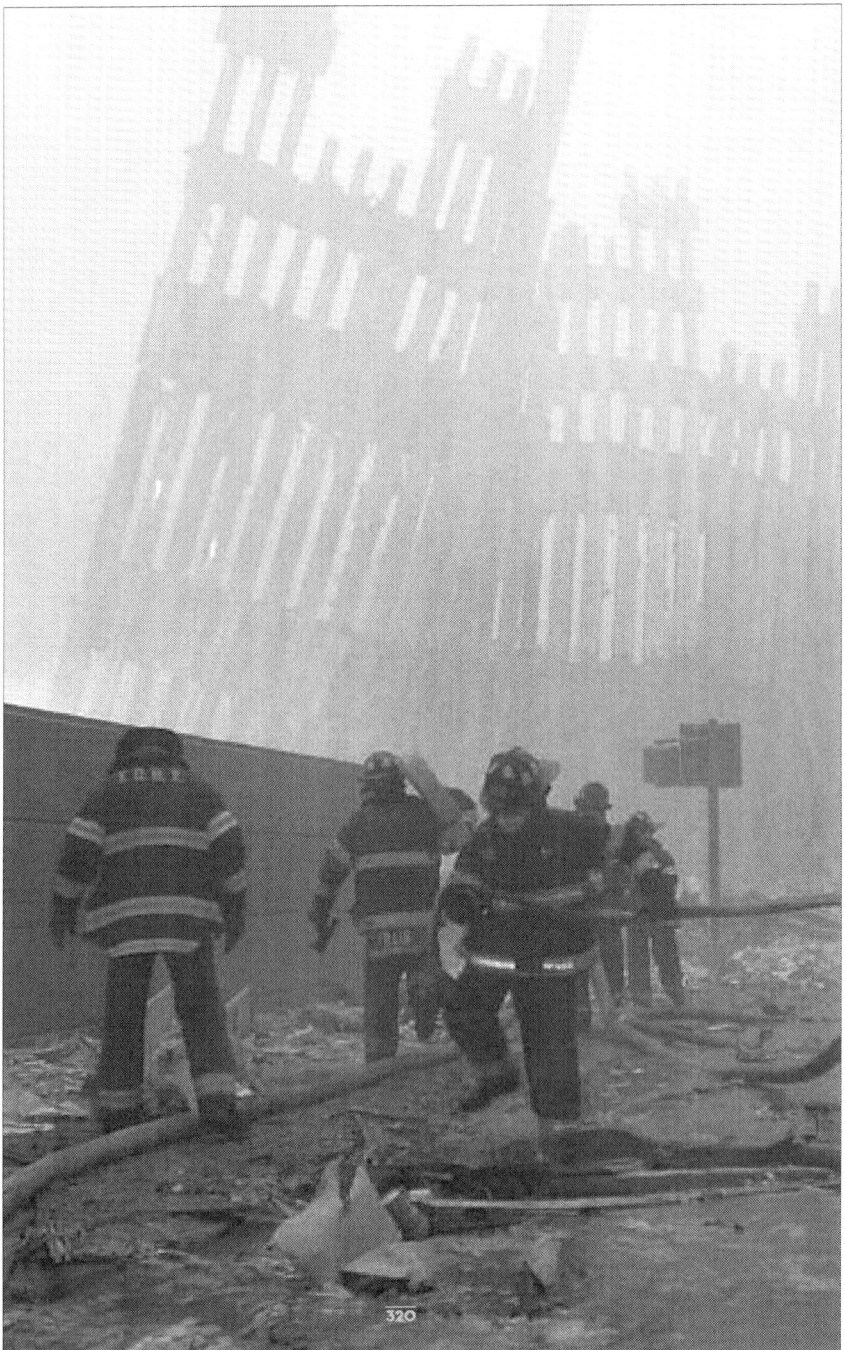
F.D.N.Y.

CHAPTER

15

BRIDGE TO THE 21st CENTURY

Firefighters beneath the destroyed vertical struts of the World Trade Center's twin towers after the September 11, 2001, terrorist attacks in New York and Washington, D.C.

CHAPTER 15: BRIDGE TO THE 21ST CENTURY

> "As we look ahead into the next century, leaders will be those who empower others."
>
> Microsoft co-founder and chairman
> Bill Gates, 2007

For most Americans the 1990s would be a time of peace, prosperity, and rapid technological change. Some attributed this to the "Reagan Revolution" and the end of the Cold War, others to the return of a Democrat to the presidency. During this period, the majority of Americans—political affiliation aside—asserted their support for traditional family values, often grounded in their faiths. *New York Times* columnist David Brooks suggested that the country was experiencing "moral self-repair," as "many of the indicators of social breakdown, which shot upward in the late 1960s and 1970s, and which plateaued at high levels in the 1980s," were now in decline.

Improved crime and other social statistics aside, American politics remained ideological, emotional, and characterized by intense divisions. Shortly after the nation entered the new millennium, moreover, its post-Cold War sense of security was jolted by an unprecedented terrorist attack that launched it on a new and difficult international track.

THE 1992 PRESIDENTIAL ELECTION

As the 1992 presidential election approached, Americans found themselves in a world transformed in ways almost unimaginable four years earlier. The familiar landmarks of the Cold War—from the

Berlin Wall to intercontinental missiles and bombers on constant high alert—were gone. Eastern Europe was independent, the Soviet Union had dissolved, Germany was united, Arabs and Israelis were engaged in direct negotiations, and the threat of nuclear conflict was greatly diminished. It was as though one great history volume had closed and another had opened.

Yet at home, Americans were less sanguine, and they faced some familiar problems. The United States found itself in its deepest recession since the early 1980s. Many of the job losses were occurring among white-collar workers in middle management positions, not solely, as earlier, among blue-collar workers in the manufacturing sector. Even when the economy began recovering in 1992, its growth was virtually imperceptible until late in the year. Moreover, the federal deficit continued to mount, propelled most strikingly by rising expenditures for health care.

President George Bush and Vice President Dan Quayle easily won renomination by the Republican Party. On the Democratic side, Bill Clinton, governor of Arkansas, defeated a crowded field of candidates to win his party's nomination. As his vice presidential nominee, he selected Senator Al Gore of Tennessee, generally acknowledged as one of the Congress's strongest advocates of environmental protection.

The country's deep unease over the direction of the economy also sparked the emergence of a remarkable independent candidate, wealthy Texas entrepreneur H. Ross Perot. Perot tapped into a deep wellspring of frustration over the inability of Washington to deal effectively with economic issues, principally the federal deficit. He possessed a colorful personality and a gift for the telling one-line political quip. He would be the most successful third-party candidate since Theodore Roosevelt in 1912.

The Bush re-election effort was built around a set of ideas traditionally used by incumbents: experience and trust. George Bush, 68, the last of a line of presidents who had served in World War II, faced a young challenger in Bill Clinton who, at age 46, had never served in the military and had participated in protests against the Vietnam War. In emphasizing his experience as president and commander-in-chief, Bush drew attention to Clinton's inexperience at the national level.

Bill Clinton organized his campaign around another of the oldest and most powerful themes in electoral politics: youth and change. As a high school student, Clinton had once met President Kennedy; 30 years later, much of his rhetoric consciously echoed that of Kennedy in the 1960 presidential campaign.

As governor of Arkansas for 12 years, Clinton could point to his experience in wrestling with the very issues of economic growth, education, and health care that were, according to public opinion polls, among President Bush's chief vulnerabilities. Where Bush offered an economic program based on lower taxes and cuts in government spending, Clinton proposed higher taxes on the wealthy and increased spending on investments in education, transportation, and communications that, he believed, would boost the nation's productivity and growth and thereby lower the deficit. Similarly, Clinton's health care proposals called for much heavier involvement by the federal government than Bush's.

Clinton proved to be a highly effective communicator, not least on television, a medium that highlighted his charm and intelligence. The incumbent's very success in handling the end of the Cold War and reversing the Iraqi thrust into Kuwait lent strength to Clinton's implicit argument that foreign affairs had become relatively less important, given pressing social and economic needs at home.

On November 3, Clinton won election as the 42nd president of the United States, with 43 percent of the popular vote against 37 percent for Bush and 19 percent for Perot.

A NEW PRESIDENCY

Clinton was in many respects the perfect leader for a party divided between liberal and moderate wings. He ran as a pragmatic centrist who could moderate the demands of various Democratic Party interest groups without alienating them. Avoiding ideological rhetoric that declared big government to be a positive good, he proposed a number of programs that earned him the label "New Democrat." Control of the federal bureaucracy and judicial appointments provided one means of satisfying political claims of organized labor and civil rights groups. On the ever-controversial abortion issue, Clinton supported the *Roe v. Wade* decision, but also declared that abortion should be "safe, legal, and rare."

President Clinton's closest collaborator was his wife, Hillary Rodham Clinton. In the campaign, he had quipped that those who voted for him "got two for the price of one." As energetic and as activist as her husband, Ms. Clinton assumed a more prominent role in the administration than any first lady before her, even Eleanor Roosevelt. Her first important assignment would be to develop a national health program. In 2000, with her husband's administration coming to a close, she would be elected a U.S. senator from New York.

LAUNCHING A NEW DOMESTIC POLICY

In practice, Clinton's centrism demanded choices that sometimes elicited vehement emotions. The president's first policy initiative was designed to meet the demands of gays, who, claiming a group status as victims of discrimination, had become an important constituency for the Democratic Party.

Immediately after his inauguration, President Clinton issued an executive order rescinding the long-established military policy of dismissing known gays from the service. The order quickly drew furious criticism from the military, most Republicans, and large segments of American society. Clinton quickly modified it with a "don't ask, don't tell" order that effectively restored the old policy but discouraged active investigation of one's sexual practices.

The effort to achieve a national health plan proved to be a far larger setback. The administration set up a large task force, chaired by Hillary Clinton. Composed of prominent policy intellectuals and political activists, it labored in secrecy for months to develop a plan that would provide medical coverage for every American citizen.

The working assumption behind the plan was that a government-managed "single-payer" plan could deliver health services to the entire nation more efficiently than the current decentralized system with its thousands of insurers and disconnected providers. As finally delivered to Congress in September 1993, however, the plan mirrored the complexity of its subject. Most Republicans and some Democrats criticized it as a hopelessly elaborate federal takeover of American medicine. After a year of discussion, it died without a vote in Congress.

President Clinton was more successful on another matter with great repercussions for the domestic economy. The previous president, George Bush, had negotiated the North American Free Trade Agreement (NAFTA) to establish fully open trade between Canada, the United States, and Mexico. Key Democratic constituencies opposed the agreement. Labor unions believed it would encourage the export of jobs and undermine American labor standards. Environmentalists asserted that it would lead American industries to relocate to countries with weak pollution controls. These were the first indications of a growing movement on the left wing of American politics against the vision of an integrated world economic system.

Clinton nonetheless accepted the argument that open trade was ultimately beneficial to all parties because it would lead to a greater flow of more efficiently produced goods and services. His administration not only submitted NAFTA to the Senate, it also backed the establishment of a greatly liberalized international trading system to be administered by the World Trade Organization (WTO). After a vigorous debate, Congress approved NAFTA in 1993. It would approve membership in the WTO a year later.

Although Clinton had talked about a "middle-class tax cut" during the presidential campaign, he submitted to Congress a budget calling for a general tax increase. It originally included a wide tax on energy consumption designed to promote conservation, but that was quickly replaced by a nominal increase in the federal gasoline tax. It also taxed social security benefits for recipients of moderate income and above. The big emphasis, however, was on increasing the income tax for high earners. The subsequent debate amounted to a rerun of the arguments between tax cutters and advocates of "fiscal responsibility" that had marked the Reagan years. In the end, Clinton got his way, but very narrowly. The tax bill passed the House of Representatives by only one vote.

By then, the congressional election campaigns of 1994 were under way. Although the administration already had made numerous foreign policy decisions, issues at home were clearly most important to the voters. The Republicans depicted Clinton and the Democrats as unreformed tax and spenders. Clinton himself was already beleaguered with charges of past financial impropriety in an Arkansas real estate project and new claims of sexual impropriety.

In November, the voters gave the Republicans control of both houses of Congress for the first time since the election of 1952. Many observers believed that Bill Clinton would likely be a one-term president. Apparently making a decision to conform to new political realities, Clinton instead moderated his political course. Policy initiatives for the remainder of his presidency were few. Contrary to Republican predictions of doom, the tax increases of 1993 did not get in the way of a steadily improving economy.

The new Republican leadership in the House of Representatives, by contrast, pressed hard to achieve its policy objectives, a sharp contrast with the administration's new moderate tone. When right-wing extremists bombed an Oklahoma City federal building in April 1995, Clinton responded with a tone of moderation and healing that heightened his stature and implicitly raised some doubts about his conservative opponents. At the end of the year, he vetoed a Republican budget bill, shutting down the government for weeks. Most of the public seemed to blame the Republicans.

The president also co-opted part of the Republican program. In his State of the Union address of January 1996, he ostentatiously declared, "The era of big government is over." That summer, on the eve of the presidential campaign, he signed a major welfare reform bill that was essentially a Republican product. Designed to end permanent support for most welfare recipients and move them to work, it was opposed by many in his own party. By and large, it would prove successful in operation over the next decade.

THE AMERICAN ECONOMY IN THE 1990s

By the mid-1990s, the country had not simply recovered from the brief, but sharp, recession of the Bush presidency. It was entering an era of booming prosperity, and doing so despite the decline of its traditional industrial base. Probably the major force behind this new growth was the blossoming of the personal computer (PC).

Less than 20 years after its introduction, the PC had become a familiar item, not simply in business offices of all types, but in homes throughout America. Vastly more powerful than anyone could have imagined two decades earlier, able to store enormous amounts of data, available at the cost of a good refrigerator, it became a common appliance in American homes.

Employing prepackaged software, people used it for bookkeeping, word processing, or as a depository for music, photos, and video. The rise of the Internet, which grew out of a previously closed defense data network, provided access to information of all sorts, created new shopping opportunities, and established e-mail as a common mode of communication. The popularity of the mobile phone created a huge new industry that cross-fertilized with the PC.

Instant communication and lightning-fast data manipulation speeded up the tempo of many businesses, greatly enhancing productivity and creating new opportunities for profit. Fledgling industries that fed demand for the new equipment became multi-billion-dollar companies almost overnight, creating an enormous new middle class of software technicians, managers, marketers, and publicists.

A final impetus was the turn of the millennium. A huge push to upgrade outdated computing equipment that might not recognize the year 2000 brought data technology spending to a peak.

These developments began to take shape during Clinton's first term. By the end of his second one they were fueling a surging economy. When he had been elected president, unemployment was at 7.4 percent. When he stood for re-election in 1996, it was at 5.4 percent. When voters went to the polls to choose his successor in November 2000, it was 3.9 percent. In many places, the issue was less one of taking care of the jobless than of finding employable workers.

No less a figure than Federal Reserve Chairman Alan Greenspan viewed a rapidly escalating stock market with concern and warned of "irrational exuberance." Investor exuberance, at its greatest since the 1920s, continued in the conviction that ordinary standards of valuation had been rendered obsolete by a "new economy" with unlimited potential. The good times were rolling dangerously fast, but most

Americans were more inclined to enjoy the ride while it lasted than to plan for a coming bust.

THE ELECTION OF 1996 AND THE POLITICAL AFTERMATH

President Clinton undertook his campaign for re-election in 1996 under the most favorable of circumstances. If not an imposing personality in the manner of a Roosevelt, he was a natural campaigner, whom many felt had an infectious charm. He presided over a growing economic recovery. He had positioned himself on the political spectrum in a way that made him appear a man of the center leaning left. His Republican opponent, Senator Robert Dole of Kansas, Republican leader in the upper house, was a formidable legislator but less successful as a presidential candidate.

Clinton, promising to "build a bridge to the 21st century," easily defeated Dole in a three-party race, 49.2 percent to 40.7 percent, with 8.4 percent to Ross Perot. He thus became the second American president to win two consecutive elections with less than a majority of the total vote. (The other was Woodrow Wilson in 1912 and 1916.) The Republicans, however, retained control of both the House of Representatives and the Senate.

Clinton never stated much of a domestic program for his second term. The highlight of its first year was an accord with Congress designed to balance the budget, further reinforcing the president's standing as a fiscally responsible moderate liberal.

In 1998, American politics entered a period of turmoil with the revelation that Clinton had carried on an affair inside the White House with a young intern. At first the president denied this, telling the American people: "I did not have sexual relations with that woman." The president had faced similar charges in the past. In a sexual harassment lawsuit filed by a woman he had known in Arkansas, Clinton denied under oath the White House affair. This fit most Americans' definition of perjury. In October 1998, the House of Representatives began impeachment hearings, focusing on charges of perjury and obstruction of justice.

Whatever the merits of that approach, a majority of Americans seemed to view the matter as a private one to be sorted out with one's family, a significant shift in public attitude. Also significantly, Hillary Clinton continued to support her husband. It surely helped also that the times were good. In the midst of the House impeachment debate, the president announced the largest budget surplus in 30 years. Public opinion polls showed Clinton's approval rating to be the highest of his six years in office.

That November, the Republicans took further losses in the midterm congressional elections, cutting their majorities to razor-thin margins. House Speaker Newt Gingrich resigned, and the party attempted to develop a less strident image. Nevertheless, in December the House voted the first impeachment resolution against a sitting president since Andrew Johnson (1868), thereby handing the case to the Senate for a trial.

Clinton's impeachment trial, presided over by the Chief Justice of the United States, held little suspense. In the midst of it, the president delivered his annual State of the Union address to Congress. He never testified, and no serious observer expected that any of the several charges against him would win the two-thirds vote required for removal from office. In the end, none got even a simple majority. On February 12, 1999, Clinton was acquitted of all charges.

AMERICAN FOREIGN RELATIONS IN THE CLINTON YEARS

Bill Clinton did not expect to be a president who emphasized foreign policy. However, like his immediate predecessors, he quickly discovered that all international crises seemed to take a road that led through Washington.

He had to deal with the messy aftermath of the 1991 Gulf War. Having failed to depose Saddam Hussein, the United States, backed by Britain, attempted to contain him. A United Nations-administered economic sanctions regime, designed to allow Iraq to sell enough oil to meet humanitarian needs, proved relatively ineffective. Saddam funneled much of the proceeds to himself, leaving large masses of his people in misery. Military "no-fly zones," imposed to prevent the Iraqi government from deploying its air power against rebellious Kurds in the north and Shiites in the south, required constant U.S. and British air patrols, which regularly fended off anti-aircraft missiles.

The United States also provided the main backing for U.N. weapons inspection teams, whose mission was to ferret out Iraq's chemical, biological, and nuclear programs, verify the destruction of existing weapons of mass destruction, and suppress ongoing programs to manufacture them. Increasingly obstructed, the U.N. inspectors were finally expelled in 1998. On this, as well as earlier occasions of provocation, the United States responded with limited missile strikes. Saddam, Secretary of State Madeline Albright declared, was still "in his box."

The seemingly endless Israeli-Palestinian dispute inevitably engaged the administration, although neither President Clinton nor former President Bush had much to do with the Oslo agreement of 1993, which established a Palestinian "authority" to govern the Palestinian population within the West Bank and the Gaza Strip and obtained Palestinian recognition of Israel's right to exist.

As with so many past Middle Eastern agreements in principle, however, Oslo eventually fell apart when details were discussed. Palestinian leader Yasser Arafat rejected final offers from peace-minded Israeli leader Ehud Barak in 2000 and January 2001. A full-scale Palestinian insurgency, marked by the use of suicide bombers, erupted. Barak fell from power, to be replaced by the far tougher Ariel Sharon. U.S. identification with Israel was considered by some a major problem in dealing with other issues in the region, but American diplomats could do little more than hope to contain the violence. After Arafat's death in late 2004, new Palestinian leadership appeared more receptive to a peace agreement, and American policy makers resumed efforts to promote a settlement.

President Clinton also became closely engaged with "the troubles" in Northern Ireland. On one side was the violent Irish Republican Army, supported primarily by those Catholic Irish who wanted to incorporate these British counties into the Republic of Ireland. On the other side were Unionists, with equally violent paramilitary forces, supported by most of the Protestant Scots-Irish population, who wanted to remain in the United Kingdom.

Clinton gave the separatists greater recognition than they ever had obtained in the United States, but also worked closely with the British governments of John Major and Tony Blair. The ultimate result, the Good Friday peace accords of 1998, established a political process but left many details to be worked out. Over the next several years, peace and order held better in Northern Ireland than in the Middle East, but remained precarious. The final accord continued to elude negotiators.

The post-Cold War disintegration of Yugoslavia—a state ethnically and religiously divided among Serbs, Croats, Slovenes, Bosnian Muslims, and Albanian Kosovars—also made its way to Washington after European governments failed to impose order. The Bush administration had refused to get involved in the initial violence; the Clinton administration finally did so with great reluctance after being urged to do so by the European allies. In 1995, it negotiated an accord in Dayton, Ohio, to establish a semblance of peace in Bosnia. In 1999, faced with Serbian massacres of Kosovars, it led a three-month NATO bombing campaign against Serbia, which finally forced a settlement.

In 1994, the administration restored ousted President Jean-Bertrand Aristide to power in Haiti, where he would rule for nine years before being ousted again. The intervention was largely a result of Aristide's carefully cultivated support in the United States and American fears of waves of Haitian illegal immigrants.

In sum, the Clinton administration remained primarily inward looking, willing to tackle international problems that could not be

INTIMATIONS OF TERRORISM

Near the close of his administration, George H.W. Bush sent American troops to the chaotic East African nation of Somalia. Their mission was to spearhead a U.N. force that would allow the regular movement of food to a starving population.

Somalia became yet another legacy for the Clinton administration. Efforts to establish a representative government there became a "nation-building" enterprise. In October 1993, American troops sent to arrest a recalcitrant warlord ran into unexpectedly strong resistance, losing an attack helicopter and suffering 18 deaths. The warlord was never arrested. Over the next several months, all American combat units were withdrawn.

From the standpoint of the administration, it seemed prudent enough simply to end a marginal, ill-advised commitment and concentrate on other priorities. It only became clear later that the Somalian warlord had been aided by a shadowy and emerging organization that would become known as al-Qaida, headed by a fundamentalist Muslim named Osama bin Laden. A fanatical enemy of Western civilization, bin Laden reportedly felt confirmed in his belief that Americans would not fight when attacked.

By then the United States had already experienced an attack by Muslim extremists. In February 1993, a huge car bomb was exploded in an underground parking garage beneath one of the twin towers of the World Trade Center in lower Manhattan. The blast killed seven people and injured nearly a thousand, but it failed to bring down the huge building with its thousands of workers. New York and federal authorities treated it as a criminal act, apprehended four of the plotters, and obtained life prison sentences for them. Subsequent plots to blow up traffic tunnels, public buildings, and even the United Nations were all discovered and dealt with in a similar fashion.

Possible foreign terrorism was nonetheless overshadowed by domestic terrorism, primarily the Oklahoma City bombing. The work of right-wing extremists Timothy McVeigh and Terry Nichols, it killed 166 and injured hundreds, a far greater toll than the 1993 Trade Center attack. But on June 25, 1996, another huge bomb exploded at the Khobar Towers U.S. military housing complex in Saudi Arabia, killing 19 and wounding 515. A federal grand jury indicted 13 Saudis and one Lebanese man for the attack, but Saudi Arabia ruled out any extraditions.

Two years later, on August 7, 1998, powerful bombs exploding simultaneously destroyed U.S. embassies in Kenya and Tanzania, killing 301 people and injuring more than 5,000. In retaliation Clinton ordered missile attacks on terrorist training camps run by bin Laden in Afghanistan, but they appear to have been deserted. He also ordered a missile strike to destroy a suspect chemical factory in Sudan, a country which earlier had given sanctuary to bin Laden.

On October 12, 2000, suicide bombers rammed a speedboat into the U.S. Navy destroyer *Cole*, on a courtesy visit to Yemen. Heroic action by the crew kept the ship afloat, but 17 sailors were killed. Bin Laden had pretty clearly been behind the attacks in Saudi Arabia, Africa, and Yemen, but he was beyond reach unless the administration was prepared to invade Afghanistan to search for him.

The Clinton administration was never willing to take such a step. It even shrank from the possibility of assassinating him if others might be killed in the process. The attacks had been remote and widely separated. It was easy to accept them as unwelcome but inevitable costs associated with superpower status. Bin Laden remained a serious nuisance, but not a top priority for an administration that was nearing its end.

THE PRESIDENTIAL ELECTION OF 2000 AND THE WAR ON TERROR

The Democratic Party nominated Vice President Al Gore to head its ticket in 2000. To oppose him, the Republicans chose George W. Bush, the governor of Texas and son of former president George H.W. Bush.

Gore ran as a dedicated liberal, intensely concerned with damage to the environment and determined to seek more assistance for the less privileged sectors of American society. He seemed to position himself to the left of President Clinton.

Bush established a position on the right wing of the Republican Party, closer to the heritage of Ronald Reagan than to that of his father. He softened this image by displaying a special interest in education and calling himself a "compassionate conservative." His embrace of evangelical Christianity, which he declared had changed his life after a misspent youth, was of particular note. It underscored an attachment to traditional cultural values that contrasted sharply to Gore's technocratic modernism. Corporate critic Ralph Nader ran well to Gore's left as the candidate of the Green Party. Conservative Republican Patrick Buchanan mounted an independent candidacy.

The final vote was nearly evenly divided nationally; so were the electoral votes. The pivotal state was Florida, where a razor-thin margin separated Bush and Gore and thousands of ballots were disputed. After a series of court challenges at the state and federal levels, the U.S. Supreme Court handed down a narrow decision that effectively gave the election to Bush. The Republicans maintained control of both houses of Congress by a small margin.

The final totals underscored the tightness of the election: Bush won 271 electoral votes to Gore's 266, but Gore led him in the national popular vote 48.4 percent to 47.9 percent. Nader polled 2.1 percent and Buchanan .4 percent. Gore, his states colored blue in media graphics, swept the Northeast and the West Coast; he also ran well in the Midwestern industrial heartland. Bush, whose states were colored red, beat his opponent in the South, the rest of the Midwest, and the mountain states. Commentators everywhere commented on the vast gap between "red" and "blue" America, a divide characterized by cultural and social, rather than economic, differences, and all the more deep-seated and emotional for that reason. George W. Bush took office in a climate of extreme partisan bitterness.

Bush expected to be a president primarily concerned with domestic policy. He wanted to meld traditional Republican Party belief in private enterprise, low taxation, and small government with a sense of social responsibility for the less fortunate groups in American society. He had talked during his campaign about reforming the Social Security system. Impressed by Reagan's supply-side economics, he advocated lower taxes to stimulate economic growth.

The economy was beginning to slip back from its lofty peak of the late 1990s. This helped Bush secure passage of a tax cut in May 2001. Lower taxes would indeed buoy the economy, but at the cost of an ominously growing federal budget deficit. At the end of the year, Bush also obtained the "No Child Left Behind" Act, which required public schools to test reading and mathematical proficiency on an annual basis; it prescribed penalties for schools unable to achieve a specified standard. Social Security remained unaddressed despite Bush's efforts to make it a priority in his second term.

The Bush presidency changed irrevocably on September 11, 2001, as the United States suffered the most devastating foreign attack ever against its mainland. That morning, Middle Eastern terrorists simultaneously hijacked four passenger airplanes and used two of them as suicide vehicles to destroy the twin towers of the World Trade Center in New York City. A third crashed into the Pentagon building, the Defense Department headquarters just outside of Washington, D.C. The fourth, probably aimed at the U.S. Capitol, dived into the Pennsylvania countryside as passengers fought the hijackers.

The death toll, most of it consisting of civilians at the Trade Center, was approximately 3,000, exceeding that of the Japanese attack on Pearl Harbor. The economic costs were also heavy. Several other buildings near the Trade Center also were destroyed, shutting down the financial markets for several days. The effect was to prolong the already developing recession.

As the nation began to recover from the attack, an unknown person or group sent out letters containing small amounts of anthrax bacteria. Some went to members of Congress and administration officials, others to obscure individuals. No notable person was infected. But five victims died, and several others suffered serious illness. The mailings touched off a wave of national hysteria, then stopped as suddenly as they had begun, and remained a mystery. In 2008, the Federal Bureau of Investigation announced that the likely culprit was a troubled government scientist who had committed suicide.

The administration obtained passage of the USA Patriot Act in October 2001. Designed to fight domestic terrorism, the new law considerably broadened the search, seizure, and detention powers of the federal government. Its opponents argued that it violated constitutionally protected individual rights. Its backers responded that a country at war needed to protect itself.

After initial hesitation, the Bush administration also decided to support the establishment of the Department of Homeland Security. Authorized in November 2002 and designed to coordinate the fight against domestic terrorist attack, the new department consolidated 22 federal agencies.

The administration, like its predecessor, had been unprepared for the unimaginable. However, it retaliated quickly. Determining that the attack had been an al-Qaida operation, it launched a military offensive against Osama bin Laden and the fundamentalist Muslim Taliban government of Afghanistan that had provided him refuge. The United States secured the passive cooperation of the Russian Federation, established relationships with the former Soviet republics that bordered Afghanistan, and, above all, resumed a long-neglected alliance with Pakistan, which provided political support and access to air bases.

Utilizing U.S. Army Special Forces and Central Intelligence Agency paramilitary operatives, the administration allied with long-marginalized Afghan rebels. Given effective air support the coalition ousted the Taliban government in two months. Bin Laden, Taliban leaders, and many of their fighters, however, escaped into remote, semi-autonomous areas of Northeastern Pakistan. From there they would try to regroup and attack the new Afghan government.

In the meantime, the Bush administration was looking elsewhere for sources of enemy terrorism. In his 2002 State of the Union address, the president identified an "axis of evil" that he thought threatened the nation: Iraq, Iran, and North Korea. Of these three, Iraq seemed to him and his advisers the most troublesome and probably easiest to bring down.

Saddam Hussein had ejected United Nations weapons inspectors. The economic sanctions against Iraq were breaking down, and, although the regime was not believed to be involved in the 9/11 attacks, it had engaged in some contacts with al-

Qaida. It was widely believed, not just in the United States but throughout the world, that Iraq had large stockpiles of chemical and biological weapons and might be working to acquire a nuclear capability. Why else throw out the inspection teams and endure continuing sanctions?

Throughout the year, the administration pressed for a United Nations resolution demanding resumption of weapons inspection with full and free access. In October 2002, Iraq declared it would comply. Nonetheless, the new inspectors complained of bad faith. In January, their chief, Hans Blix, presented a report to the UN declaring that Iraq had failed to account for its weapons of mass destruction, although he recommended a resumption of weapons inspections before withdrawing.

Bush in the meantime had received a Senate authorization by a vote of 77–23 for the use of military force. The U.S. military began a buildup of personnel and materiel in Kuwait.

The American plans for war with Iraq encountered unusually strong opposition in much of Europe. France, Russia, and Germany all were against the use of force. Even in those nations whose governments supported the United States, there was strong popular hostility to cooperation. Britain became the major U.S. ally in the war that followed; most of the newly independent Eastern European nations contributed assistance. The governments of Italy and (for a time) Spain also lent their backing. Turkey, long a reliable American ally, declined to do so.

Nevertheless, on March 19, 2003, American and British troops, supported by small contingents from several other countries, began an invasion of Iraq from the South. Groups airlifted into the North coordinated with Kurdish militia. On both fronts, resistance was occasionally fierce, but usually melted away. Baghdad fell on April 8. On April 14, the military campaign in Iraq was declared over.

Taking Iraq turned out to be far easier than administering it. In the first days after the end of major combat, the country experienced pervasive looting. Hit-and-run attacks on allied troops followed and became increasingly organized, despite the capture of Saddam Hussein and the deaths of his two sons and heirs. Different Iraqi factions seemed on the verge of war with each other.

New weapons inspection teams were unable to find the expected stockpiles of chemical and biological weaponry. It became clear that Iraq had never restarted the nuclear program it had been pursuing before the first Gulf War. After his apprehension, Saddam Hussein admitted that he had engaged in a gigantic bluff to forestall attack from abroad or insurrection at home.

In the year and a quarter after the fall of Baghdad, the United States and the United Kingdom, with increasing cooperation from the United Nations, moved ahead with establishment of a provisional government that would assume sovereignty over Iraq. The effort occurred amidst increasing violence that included attacks not only on allied troops, but also on Iraqis connected in any way with the new government. Most of the insurgents appeared to be Saddam loyalists; some were indigenous Muslim sectarians; others likely were foreign fighters.

THE 2004 PRESIDENTIAL ELECTION AND GEORGE W. BUSH'S SECOND TERM

By mid-2004, with the United States facing a violent insurgency in Iraq, considerable foreign opposition to the war there, and increasingly sharp divisions about the conflict at home, the country faced another presidential election. The Democrats nominated Senator John Kerry of Massachusetts, a decorated Vietnam veteran in his fourth Senate term. Kerry's dignified demeanor and speaking skills made him a formidable candidate. A reliable liberal on domestic issues, he was a critic of the Iraq war. Bush, renominated without opposition by the Republicans, portrayed himself as frank and consistent in speech and deed, a man of action willing to take all necessary steps to protect the United States.

Marked by intense feelings on both sides about the war and the cultural conflicts that increasingly defined the differences between the two major parties, the campaign revealed a nation nearly as divided as in 2000. The strong emotions of the race fueled a voter turnout 20 percent higher than four years earlier. Bush won a narrow victory, 51 percent to 48 percent with the remainder of the vote going to Ralph Nader and other independents. The Republicans scored small but important gains in Congress.

George W. Bush began his second term in January 2005, facing challenges aplenty: Iraq, increasing federal budget deficits, a chronic international balance-of-payments shortfall, the escalating cost of social entitlements, and a shaky currency. None were susceptible to quick or easy solutions.

Iraq was the largest and most visible problem. The country had adopted a new constitution and held parliamentary elections in 2005. Saddam Hussein, tried by an Iraqi tribunal, was executed in December 2006. All the same, American forces and the new government faced a mounting insurgency. Composed of antagonistic factions—among them Sunni supporters of Saddam and dissident Shiites aided by Iran—the insurgency could be contained, but not quelled without using harsh tactics that would be unacceptable at home and would alienate the Iraqi population. The constitutional Iraqi government lacked the power and stability needed to impose order, yet the costs—human and financial—of the American occupation eroded support at home.

In January 2007, the president adopted an anti-insurgency strategy advocated by General David Petraeus—one of outreach and support for Sunni leaders willing to accept a new democratic order in Iraq, along with continued backing of the predominantly Shiite government in Baghdad. He accompanied this with a "surge" of additional troops. Over the next year, the strategy appeared to calm the country. The United States began to turn over increased security responsibilities to the Iraqis and negotiated an agreement for complete withdrawal by 2011. Nonetheless, Iraq remained very unstable, its fragile peace regularly disrupted by bombings and assassinations, its Sunni-Shiite conflict complicated by Kurdish separatists. It was not clear whether a liberal-democratic nation could be created out of such chaos, but certain that the United States could not impose one if the Iraqis did not want it.

As Iraq progressed uncertainly toward stability, Afghanistan moved in the other direction. The post-Taliban government of Hamid Karzai proved unable to establish effective control over the historically decentralized country. Operating from the Pakistani tribal areas to which they had escaped in 2001, the Taliban and al-Qaida began to filter back into Afghanistan and establish significant areas of control in the southern provinces. Using remote-controlled drone aircraft equipped with guided missiles, U.S. forces staged attacks against enemy encampments and leaders within Pakistan. In 2009, the new American president, Barack Obama, approved a U.S. military buildup and anti-insurgency effort similar to the Iraq surge. As with Iraq, the outcome remained in doubt.

As the first decade of the 21st century drew to a close, the United States found itself adjusting to a world considerably more complex than that of the Cold War. The bipolar rivalry of that era, for all its dangers and challenges, had imposed an unprecedented simplicity on international affairs. The newer, messier world order (or disorder) featured the rapid rise of China as a major economic force. India and Brazil were not far behind. Post-Soviet Russia re-emerged as an oil and natural gas power seeking to regain lost influence in Eastern Europe. The United States remained the preeminent power in the world, but was now first in a complex multipolar international system.

At home, the nation remained generally prosperous through most of the Bush years. After a weak first year, gross domestic product grew at a relatively steady, if unspectacular, rate and unemployment held at fairly low levels. Yet the prosperity was fragile. Most noticeable was the rapid decline of American manufacturing, a trend that was well along by the time George W. Bush became president and was in sharp contrast to the rise of China as an industrial power. Increasingly, the economy was sustained by consumer spending, finance, and a construction boom led by residential housing. Federal policy, reflecting the American ideal that every person should have an opportunity to own a home, encouraged the extension of mortgage loans to individuals whose prospects for repayment were dim. The financial institutions in turn repackaged these loans into complex securities, represented them as sound investments, and sold them to institutional investors. These ultimately unsustainable investments were fueled to excess by an easy-money policy as the nation's central bank, the Federal Reserve System, held interest rates at low levels. Similar economic currents flowed in much of the rest of the developed Western world, but the United States was the pacesetter.

In line with the theme of compassionate conservatism, Bush proposed a major overhaul of the Social Security system that would allow individuals some discretion in investing the taxes they paid into it. The plan aroused nearly unanimous Democratic opposition, generated little public enthusiasm, and never got to a vote in Congress. Bush's other major project—the enhancement of Medicare by the addition of a voluntary prescription drug program—proved much more popular. It appeased conservative qualms about big government by subsidizing qualified private insurance plans, required fairly large out-of-pocket payments from those who bought into it, but still provided real savings to elderly patients who required multiple medications. Yet, as was the case with already existing Medicare provisions, the costs of the drug program were not fully covered. It added substantially to a federal deficit that seemed uncontrollable.

The growing deficit became a major issue among not simply opposition Democrats but many Republican conservatives, who thought their party was spending too freely. In addition, the difficult war in Iraq was increasingly unpopular. In the 2006 midterm elections, Republicans lost control of Congress to the opposition Democrats, who more than ever looked with confidence to the next presidential election.

President George W. Bush walks down the White House Colonnade with his successor, Barack Obama, on November 10, 2008, six days after Obama's election as 44th president of the United States.

340

CHAPTER

16

POLITICS OF HOPE

Democratic presidential candidate Senator Barack Obama (Illinois) at a campaign rally in Charlotte, North Carolina, September, 2008.

> "The strongest democracies flourish from frequent and lively debate, but they endure when people of every background and belief find a way to set aside smaller differences in service of a greater purpose."
>
> President Barack Obama, 2009

THE ELECTION OF 2008 AND THE EMERGENCE OF BARACK OBAMA

Having served two terms, President George W. Bush was constitutionally prohibited from being elected again to the presidency. After a spirited preconvention campaign, the Republicans chose as their candidate Senator John McCain of Arizona. A Vietnam veteran respected for his heroic resistance as a prisoner of war, McCain possessed strong foreign policy credentials and was a relatively moderate conservative on domestic issues. He chose as his running mate Governor Sarah Palin of Alaska. Much admired by Christian evangelicals and cultural conservatives, she drew almost as much attention as McCain himself.

In late 2007, it seemed nearly certain that the Democratic nomination would go to Senator Hillary Rodham Clinton of New York. The wife of former president Bill Clinton, she had quickly established herself as a leading member of Congress and possessed a strong national constituency among women and liberal Democrats. However, she faced a phenomenon not unusual in democratic societies—a relatively unknown, but charismatic, challenger whose appeal rested not on ideological or programmatic differences but on style and personal background.

Barack Hussein Obama was only in his second year as a U.S. senator from Illinois, but his comparative youth and freshness were assets in a year when the electorate was weary of politics as usual. So was his multicultural background. His father was from Kenya; his mother was a white American sociologist. Born in Hawaii, he had spent his early years in Indonesia, where he attended a Muslim school. After his father left the family and his mother died at an early age, he had been raised by his grandmother. These family crises notwithstanding, he became a successful student at two of the best universities in the United States—Columbia and Harvard. His personal style mixed a rare speaking talent with a hip informality that had great appeal to younger voters. Americans of all ages could consider him an emblematic representative of their society's tradition of providing opportunity for all.

After a close, hard-fought six months of party caucuses and primary elections, Obama eked out a narrow victory over Clinton. He made Senator Joseph Biden of Delaware his vice-presidential selection. Most measures of popular sentiment indicated that the public wanted a change. The two candidates were ahead in many public opinion polls as the fall campaign season began.

Any chance that McCain and Palin could pull ahead was ended by the sharp financial crisis that began in the last half of September and sent the economy crashing. Caused by excessive speculation in risky mortgage-backed securities and other unstable investment vehicles, the crash led to the bankruptcy of the venerable Lehman Brothers investment house and momentarily imperiled the entire financial superstructure of the nation. The Federal Deposit Insurance Corporation (FDIC), created during the New Deal, shut down numerous banks without loss to depositors, but had no jurisdiction over the giant financial investment companies that did not engage in commercial banking. Moreover, it had only limited capabilities to deal with those corporations that did both.

Fearing a general financial meltdown reminiscent of the darkest days of the Great Depression, the U.S. Treasury and the Federal Reserve engineered a Troubled Assets Relief Program (TARP) that was funded by a $700 billion congressional appropriation. The TARP program kept the endangered investment banks afloat. What it could not do was stave off a sharp economic collapse in which millions of Americans lost their jobs.

That November, the voters elected Obama president of the United States, with approximately 53 percent of the vote to McCain's 46.

OBAMA: THE FIRST YEAR

Obama was inaugurated president of the United States on January 20, 2009, in an atmosphere of hope and high expectations. In his inaugural address, he declared: "The time has come to reaffirm our enduring spirit; to choose our better history; to carry forward that precious gift, that noble idea, passed on from generation to generation: the God-given promise that all are equal, all are free, and all deserve a chance to pursue their full measure of happiness." He proclaimed an agenda of "remaking America" by reviving and transforming the economy in ways that would provide better and less-expensive health care for all, foster environmentally friendly energy, and develop an educational system better suited to the needs of a new century.

Speaking to the international community, he pledged U.S. cooperation in facing the problem of global warming. He also delivered a general message of international engagement based on compassion for poorer, developing countries and respect for other cultures. "To the Muslim world," Obama said, "we seek a new way forward, based on mutual interest and mutual respect."

The speech revealed the wide scope of Obama's aspirations. His rhetoric and his strong personal presence won wide approval—so much so that in October, he was awarded the Nobel Peace Prize in recognition of his goals. But, as always in the complex system of American representative government, it was easier to state large ambitions than to realize them.

At home, the administration addressed the mounting economic crisis with a $787 billion stimulus act designed to bring growing unemployment down to manageable levels. The legislation doubtless saved or created many jobs, but it failed to prevent unemployment—officially estimated at 7.7 percent of the labor force when Obama took office—from increasing to a high of 10.1 percent, then receding just a bit. The loans to large investment and commercial banks begun during the Bush administration with the objective of restoring a stable financial system were mostly repaid with a profit to the government, but a few remained outstanding as the president began his second year in office. In addition, the government invested heavily in two giant auto makers—General Motors and Chrysler—shepherding them through bankruptcy and attempting to reestablish them as major manufacturers.

Obama's other major objective—the establishment of a national health care system—had long been a goal of American liberalism. With large Democratic majorities in both houses of Congress, it seemed achievable. However, developing a plan that had to meet the medical needs of more than 300 million Americans proved extraordinarily difficult. The concerns of numerous interests had to be dealt with—insurance companies, hospitals, physicians, pharmaceutical companies, and the large majority of Americans who were already covered and reasonably satisfied. In addition, a comprehensive national plan had to find some way to control skyrocketing costs. In the spring of 2010, the president signed complex legislation that mandated health insurance for every American, with implementation to take place over several years.

In foreign policy, Obama sought to reach out to the non-Western world, and especially to Muslims who might interpret the American military actions in Iraq and Afghanistan as part of a general war on Islam. "America and Islam are not exclusive and need not be in competition," he told an audience at Cairo University. In Tokyo, he reassured Asians that America would remain engaged with the world's fastest-growing region. While hoping to distinguish itself in tone from the Bush administration, the Obama government found itself following the broad outlines of Bush's War on Terror. It affirmed the existing agreement to withdraw American troops from Iraq in 2011 and reluctantly accepted military plans for a surge in Afghanistan. In his Nobel acceptance speech, President Obama quoted the celebrated American theologian Reinhold Niebuhr to the effect that evil existed in the world and could be defeated only by force.

At the conclusion of his first year in office, Obama remained, for many Americans, a compelling personification of their ideals of liberty and equal opportunity.

AFTERWORD

From its origins as a set of obscure colonies hugging the Atlantic coast, the United States has undergone a remarkable transformation into what political analyst Ben Wattenberg has called "the first universal nation," a population of almost 300 million people representing virtually every nationality and ethnic group in the world. It is also a nation where the pace and extent of change—economic, technological, cultural, demographic, and social—is unceasing. The United States is often the harbinger of the modernization and change that inevitably sweep up other nations and societies in an increasingly interdependent, interconnected world.

Yet the United States also maintains a sense of continuity, a set of core values that can be traced to its founding. They include a faith in individual freedom and democratic government, and a commitment to economic opportunity and progress for all. The continuing task of the United States will be to ensure that its values of freedom, democracy, and opportunity—the legacy of a rich and turbulent history—are protected and flourish as the nation, and the world, move through the 21st century. >

BIBLIOGRAPHY

RECENT PRIZE-WINNING BOOKS
The Bancroft Prize for American History
Awarded by the Trustees of Columbia University

2010
Dorothea Lange: A Life Beyond Limits
By Linda Gordon
W.W. Norton & Company

Abigail Adams
By Woody Holton
Free Press

White Mother to a Dark Race: Settler Colonialism, Maternalism, and the Removal of Indigenous Children in the American West and Australia, 1880-1940.
By Margaret D. Jacobs
University of Nebraska Press

2009
Killing for Coal: America's Deadliest Labor War
By Thomas G. Andrews
Harvard University Press

This Republic of Suffering: Death and the American Civil War
By Drew Gilpin Faust
Alfred A. Knopf

The Comanche Empire
By Pekka Hämäläinen
Yale University Press

2008
The Cigarette Century: The Rise, Fall, and Deadly Persistence of the Product That Defined America
By Allan M. Brandt
Basic Books

The Populist Vision
By Charles Postel
Oxford University Press

Our Savage Neighbors: How Indian War Transformed Early America
By Peter Silver
W.W. Norton & Company

2007
Mockingbird Song: Ecological Landscapes of the South
By Jack Temple Kirby
University of North Carolina Press

William James: In the Maelstrom of American Modernism
By Robert D. Richardson
Houghton Mifflin Company

2006
Dwelling Place: A Plantation Epic
By Erskine Clarke
Yale University Press

The Global Cold War: Third World Interventions and the Making of Our Times
By Odd Arne Westad
Cambridge University Press

*The Rise of American Democracy:
Jefferson to Lincoln*
By Sean Wilentz
W.W. Norton & Company

Pulitzer Prize for a distinguished book upon the history of the United States
Awarded by Columbia University Graduate School of Journalism

2010
Lords of Finance: The Bankers Who Broke the World
By Liaquat Ahamed
The Penguin Press

2009
The Hemingses of Monticello: An American Family
By Annette Gordon-Reed
W.W. Norton & Company

2008
What God Hath Wrought: The Transformation of America, 1815-1848
By Daniel Walker Howe
Oxford University Press

2007
The Race Beat: The Press, the Civil Rights Struggle, and the Awakening of a Nation
By Gene Roberts and Hank Klibanoff
Alfred A. Knopf

2006
Polio: An American Story
By David Oshinsky
Oxford University Press

SELECTED INTERNET RESOURCES

American Historical Association
http://www.historians.org

American History: A Documentary Record
1492–Present
http://avalon.law.yale.edu/subject_menus/chrono.asp

The Avalon Project at the Yale Law School: Major Collections
http://avalon.law.yale.edu/subject_menus/major.asp

Biography of America
http://www.learner.org/biographyofamerica/

Digital History
http://www.digitalhistory.uh.edu/

Documents for the Study of American History
http://www.vlib.us/amdocs/

Gilder Lehrman Institute of American History
http://www.gilderlehrman.org

Historicalstatistics.org
http://www.historicalstatistics.org/index2.html

History Matters
http://historymatters.gmu.edu/

The Library of Congress American Memory: Historical Collections for the National Digital Library
http://memory.loc.gov/ammem/

The Library of Congress American Memory: Timeline
http://lcweb2.loc.gov/ammem/ndlpedu/features/timeline/index.html

National Archives and Records Administration
http://www.nara.gov

National Archives and Records Administration: Digital Classroom
http://www.archives.gov/digital_classroom/

National Archives and Records Administration: Our Documents: A National Initiative on American History, Civics, and Service
http://www.ourdocuments.gov/index.php?flash=true&

National Archives and Records Administration: Presidential Libraries
http://www.archives.gov/presidential-libraries

National Atlas of the United States
http://nationalatlas.gov

National Endowment for the Humanities: We the People
http://www.wethepeople.gov

National Park Service: Discover History
http://www.nps.gov/history/

Organization of American Historians
http://www.oah.org/

Smithsonian
http://www.si.edu/

The Historical Society
http://www.bu.edu/historic/

U.S. Department of State Office of the Historian
http://history.state.gov/

WWW Virtual Library History: United States
http://vlib.iue.it/history/USA/

The U.S. Department of State assumes no responsibility for the content and availability of the resources from other agencies and organizations listed above. All Internet links were active as of fall 2010.

INDEX

*Page references in **boldface** type refer to illustrations.*

A

Abolition of slavery
 Brown's raid at Harper's Ferry (1859), 139
 constitutional amendment (13th), 148
 Democratic Party and, 152
 Douglass as abolitionist leader, **91**
 Emancipation Proclamation, 144-145
 Freedmen's Bureau, 148, 151
 Garrison and *The Liberator* on, **91**, 122, 133-134
 Missouri Compromise (1820), 80, 114, 132, 135, 137
 Northwest Ordinance slavery ban, 71, 73, 113, 135
 religious social activism and, 87
 as a sectional conflict/divided nation, 128-139
 as sharecroppers and tenant farmers, 190-191
 southern statesmen on, 113
 Underground Railroad, 91, 134, 136
 See also Slavery
Adams, John, 52, 64, 72, 82-83
Adams, John Quincy, 115, 116, 134
Adams, Samuel, 56-57
Adamson Act, 199
Addams, Jane, 196
Adventures of Huckleberry Finn (Twain), **97**
Afghanistan, U.S. relations, **294**, 334, 345
AFL. *See* American Federation of Labor (AFL)

African Americans
 bus boycott (Montgomery, Alabama), **240**
 civil rights movement, 240, 258, 271-272
 color barrier broken in sports, **237**, 271
 Colored Farmers National Alliance, 191
 culture, 210-211
 Freedmen's Bureau and, 148, 151
 "Harlem Renaissance," 211
 jazz musicians, 211
 labor unions and, 193
 lynchings and violence against, 150, 178, 271
 members of Congress, **96**
 as sharecroppers and tenant farmers, 190-191
 U.S. Colored Troops in Union Army, 145
 See also Abolition of slavery; Civil rights; Racial discrimination; Slavery
Agnew, Spiro, 290
Agricultural Adjustment Act (AAA), 216
Agriculture
 farm-relief act, 216
 Farmers' Alliances, 191
 Grange movement, 191
 land grant and technical colleges, 152, 177
 New Deal programs, 216-217
 Patrons of Husbandry (Grange), 191
 plantation settlements, 26, 28, 113-114, **128-129**
 post-Revolutionary period, 70
 Republican policy, 79, 208
 scientific research, 177

sharecroppers and tenant farmers, 190-191
small farmers and agricultural consolidation, 267
technological revolution, **110-111**, 160, 177
westward expansion and, 125
AIDS (Acquired Immune Deficiency Syndrome)
  epidemic, 307
  quilt (Washington, D.C.), **299**
AIM. *See* American Indian Movement
Alaska
  gold rush, 192
  purchase, known as "Seward's Folly," 182
Albany Plan of Union, 33, 69
Albright, Madeleine, 329
Alien Act, 82, 117
Amalgamated Association of Iron, Steel, and Tin Workers, 194
American Bible Society, 87
American Civil Liberties Union, 209
American Federation of Labor (AFL), 194, 209, 227
American Independent Party, 319
American Indian Movement (AIM), 281
American Philosophical Society, 28
American Railway Union, 194
American Revolution, 50-65
  Boston Tea Party (1773), **50-51**, 57
  British move through the South, 63-64
  colonial declaration of war, 60
  Concord and Lexington battles (1775), 59-60
  economic aftermath, 70
  factors leading to, 50-59
  first shots fired at Lexington, **44-45**, 59
  Franco-American alliance, 62-63
  Long Island, battle of (1776), 61
  Loyalists and, 60, 65
  Olive Branch Petition, 60
  significance of, 65
  Treaty of Paris (1783), **47**, 64
  Yorktown, British surrender at, **47-48**, 64
American Sugar Refining Company, 197
American Telephone and Telegraph (AT&T), 158
American Temperance Union, 121
Amity and Commerce, Treaty of (France-American colonies), 63
Amnesty Act (1872), 150
Anasazi, 8, 20
Andros, Sir Edmund, 31
Anthony, Susan B., **90**, 122
Antifederalists, 76
Antitrust legislation, 160, 187, 196-197, 199
Apache Indians, 180, 181
Aquino, Corazon, 312
Arafat, Yasser, 330
Aristide, Jean-Bertrand, 330
Arlington Cemetery (Virginia), **174**
Armour, Philip, 158
Arms control. *See* Nuclear weapons
Armstrong, Louis, 211
Armstrong, Neil, 285
Arnaz, Desi, **239**
Arnold, Benedict, 62
Articles of the Confederation, 69-70
Asia, Cold War, 263-264
Atlantic Charter (U.S.-Britain), 220
Automobile industry
  auto worker strikes, 228, **230**
  automobile safety crusade, 287
  environmental issues/traffic congestion, 282, **300-301**
  unemployment, 227

B

Babcock, Stephen, 177
Ball, Lucille, **239**
Banking Act, 218

Banking and finance
  currency question and gold standard, 192
  Federal Reserve Board, 199, 218
  Federal Reserve System, 119, 187, 198-199
  financial panic (1893), 192
  First Bank of the United States, 79
  insured savings (FDIC), 215
  national bank, 79-80
  New Deal program reforms, 214-215
  regional and local bank charters, 119
  Second Bank of the United States, 118-119
  state banking system, 119
  stock market crash (1929), 211
Baptists, 87, 88
Barak, Ehud, 330
Beard, Charles, 75
"Beat Generation" (1950s), 270
Begin, Menachim, 292
Bell, Alexander Graham, **107**, 156
Bell, John C., 139
Bell Telephone System, 158
Bellamy, Edward, 160
Biddle, Nicholas, 119
Biden, Joseph, 343
Bill of Rights, 77
bin Laden, Osama, 331, 332, 334
Blaine, James G., 185
Blair, Tony, **294-295**, 330
Blix, Hans, 335
Bolívar, Simon, 114
Booth, John Wilkes, 147
Borglum, Gutzon, 171
Bosnia, 330
Boston Massacre (1770), 56
Boston Tea Party (1773), **50-51**, 57
Breckenridge, John C., 139
Brezhnev, Leonid, 289
British colonization. *See* English colonization
Brooks, David, 322
Brown, John, 139

Brown v. Board of Education (1954), 240, 244, 272
Bryan, William Jennings, 192, 195, 198, 209-210
Buchanan, Pat, 332
Buckley, William F., 308
Bull Moose Party, 318
Burbank, Luther, 177
Burgoyne, John, 62
Bush, George Herbert Walker, **255**
  budgets and deficits, 315
  domestic policy, 314-315
  end of Cold War, 315-316
  foreign policy, 312, 316-317
  presidential election (1998), 314; (1992), 322, 324
  "war on drugs," 317
Bush, George W.
  Afghanistan invasion, 334
  with Barack Obama, **339**
  as a "compassionate conservative," 332
  domestic and foreign policy, 332-336
  on freedom, 322
  Iraq War, 334-336
  on peace, 322
  presidential elections (2000), 333; (2004), 336-337
  with Tony Blair, **294-295**

C

Cable News Network, **297**
Cabot, John, 9
Cady Stanton, Elizabeth, **90**, 122-123
Calhoun, John C., 112, 116, 117, 125
California
  as a free state, 136
  gold rush, 131, 136, 179
  migrant farm workers' unions, 279-280
  territory, 135
Calvinism, 13, 29, 34, 65
Campbell, Ben Nighthorse, 281

INDEX

Capitalism, 187, 193, 214
Carleton, Mark, 177
Carmichael, Stokely, 278
Carnegie, Andrew, **97**, 156-157, 187, 194
Carson, Rachel, 282
Carter, Jimmy, 291-292
Cartier, Jacques, 10
Carver, George Washington, 177
Cattle ranching, 179-180
Central Pacific Railroad, 179
A Century of Dishonor (Jackson), 181
Chambers, Whittaker, 266
Charles I (British king), 12, 13, 15
Charles II (British king), 17, 18, 31
Chase, Salmon P., 138
Chávez, César, **250**, 280
Cherokee Indians, 125
Chiang Kai-shek, 224, 263, 264
Chicanos. *See* Latino movement
Child labor, **102-103**, 177, 193, 196
China, People's Republic of
  Boxer Rebellion (1900), 186
  Taiwan relations, 263, 265, 289
  U.S. diplomatic relations, 186, 289, 292
Christian Coalition, 308
Churchill, Winston
  on the "iron curtain," 260-261
  U.S. support for war effort, 220
  at Yalta, 224, **234**
CIO. *See* Committee for Industrial Organization (CIO); Congress of Industrial Organizations (CIO)
Citizenship, 82, 148-149, 178
Civil rights
  bus boycott (Montgomery, Alabama), 240, 273
  desegregation, 272-273
  desegregation of schools, 240, 241, 244, 272-273, 277
  desegregation of the military, 269, 272
  Jesse Jackson's "Rainbow Coalition," 253
  Truman 10-point civil rights program, 271-272
  See also Civil rights movement; Individual rights; Racial discrimination
Civil Rights Act (1957), 273
Civil Rights Act (1960), 273
Civil Rights Act (1964), 277, 286
Civil rights movement (1960-80), 276-278
  "black power" activists, 277-278
  "freedom rides," 277
  "March on Washington" (1963), 277
  origins of the, 271-272
  riots (1960s), 278
  sit-ins, 277
Civil Service Commission, 307
Civil War (1861-65)
  African Americans in U.S. Colored Troops in Union Army, 145
  Alexandria, Union troop encampment, **94**
  Antietam campaign (1862), 141, 144
  Bull Run (First Manassas), 143
  Bull Run (Second Manassas), 144
  casualties, 92, 144, 145
  Chancellorsville campaign (1863), **92-93**, 145
  Chattanooga and Lookout Mountain campaigns (1863), 146
  Gettysburg address, by Lincoln, 142, 145
  Gettysburg campaign (1863), 92, 145, 146
  Petersburg campaign (1865), 146
  postwar politics, 152-153
  secession from the Union, 142-143
  Sherman's march through the South, 146
  Shiloh campaign, 144
  Spotsylvania (Battle of the Wilderness, 1864), 146
  surrender at Appomattox

Courthouse, 146
Vicksburg campaign (1863), 145, 146
See also Reconstruction Era
Civil Works Administration
(CWA), 215-216
Civilian Conservation Corps (CCC), 215
Clark, William, **47**
Clay, Henry
    compromise agreements, 114, 136
    portrait of, **90**
    presidential elections, 116, 119
    protective tariffs, 112, 117, 118
    Whig Party statesman, 120, 152
Clayton Antitrust Act, 199
Clean Air Act (1967), 282
Clemenceau, Georges, **108**
Clemens, Samuel Langhorne, **97**, 196
Cleveland, Grover, 159, 182, 183, 192, 194
Clinton, Hillary Rodham, 324, 325, 328, 342
Clinton, William "Bill"
    Arkansas real estate investigation, 326
    Cabinet appointments, 280
    domestic policy, 324-326
    foreign policy, 329-331
    impeachment hearings/trial, 328, 329
    presidential election (1992), 322-324; (1996), 328
    presidential inaugural address (1993), **255**
    sexual impropriety/intern scandal, 326, 328
Coercive or Intolerable Acts (England), 57-59
Cold War, 258-267
    in Asia, 263-264
    Eisenhower Administration, 264-265
    end of, 255, 315-316, 324
    in the Middle East, 264
    Kennedy Administration, 284-285

    origins of, 260-261
    Truman Administration, 261, 265
College of William and Mary, 27
Colonial period
    cultural developments, 27-29
    Dutch colonies, 14, 15, 17, 24
    early settlements, 10-12, 24
    English settlers, 10-12, 13-15, 17, 24
    French and Indian Wars, 32-33
    German settlers, 24, 25, 26
    government of the colonies, 29-32
    Jamestown colony (Virginia), 10, 12-13, 16
    Massachusetts colonies, 13-14, 24-25
    middle colonies, 25-26
    Native American relations, 15-17, 18, 39
    New Amsterdam, 14, 15, 26
    New England colonies, 24-25
    New England Confederation, 17
    Pennsylvania colony, 18, 25, 27-28, 30, 39, 69
    rural country daily life, 26-27
    Scots and Scots-Irish settlers, 24, 25, 26
    southern colonies, 26-27
    Swedish colonies, 15, 24
    Virginia colonies, 10, 12-13, 16, 26, 28-30, 68-69
Colored Farmers National Alliance, 191
Columbus, Christopher, 9
Commission on Civil Rights, 280
Committee for Industrial Organization (CIO), 228
Committees of Correspondence, 56-57
Commodity Credit Corporation, 216
Common Sense (Paine), 60
Communism, 206-207
    Cold War and, 258-267, 315-316
    Eisenhower containment policy, 264-265
    Federal Employee Loyalty

INDEX

Program, 266
House Committee on
  Un-American Activities, 266
McCarthy Senate hearings on,
  236, 266
Red Scare (1919-20), 207, 265
spread of, 263
Truman Doctrine of containment,
  261-263
Communist Party, 206, 263, 265, 266
Compromise of 1850, 90, 135-136
Confederation Congress, 71
Congress of Industrial Organizations
  (CIO), 228
Congress, U.S.
  African-American members, 96
  first Native American member, 281
  Hispanic members, 280
  power to make laws, 75
  representation in House and
    Senate, 73
Conservatism, 307-309
Constitution, state constitutions, 68-69
Constitution, U.S.
  amendments
    1st thru 12th, 77
    13th (abolishing slavery), 148
    14th (citizenship rights), 148-
      149, 178
    15th (voting rights), 149, 273
    16th (federal income tax), 198
    17th (direct election of
      senators), 198
    18th (prohibition), 210
    19th (voting rights for women),
      207
  amendments process, 74
  Bill of Rights, 77
  Congressional powers, 75
  debate and compromise, 73-75
  declaration of war powers, 316-317
  on display at National Archives,
    174
  motivations of Founding Fathers, 75

ratification, 75-76
separation of powers principle, 74
signing of, at Constitution Hall
  (Philadelphia), **164**
Constitutional Convention
  (Philadelphia, 1787), **66-67**, 71-77
Constitutional Union Party, 139
Continental Association, 58-59
Continental Congress, First (1774), 58
Continental Congress, Second (1775),
  60, 61, 69, 71
Coolidge, Calvin, 204, 207
Cornwallis, Lord Charles, **46-47**, 64
Coronado, Francisco Vázquez de, 9
Corporations, 158-159
Coughlin, Charles, 217
Counterculture (1960s), 281-282
  New Leftists, 281-282
  Vietnam War demonstrations, 281
  "Woodstock Generation," **249**, 281
Cox, James M., 207
Crawford, William, 116
Crazy Horse (Sioux chief), 180
Creek Indians, 125
Cromwell, Oliver, 12, 17, 31
Cuba, Spanish-American War and,
  182-183
Cuban missile crisis (1962), 284
Cullen, Countee, 211
Culture
  of the 1950s, 270-271
  in the colonies, 27-29
  counterculture of the 1960s, 281-282
  See also Libraries; Literary works;
    Music, American
Currency Act (England, 1764), 53
Custer, George, 98-99, 180

D

Dakota Sioux, 98, 180, 281
Darrow, Clarence, 209-210
Darwinian theory
  Scopes trial, 209-210
  "survival of the fittest," 193

Davis, Jefferson, 142
Dawes (General Allotment) Act (1887), 181
De Soto, Hernando, 9
Declaration of Independence, 61, 68
    burial site for three signers of, **162-163**
Declaratory Act (England), 55
Delaware Indians, 18, **39**
Democracy in America (Tocqueville), 130
Democratic Party, 116, 137, 152, 153, 192, 218-219
Depression. *See* Great Depression
Dewey, George, 183
Dewey, Thomas, 235, 269
Dickens, Charles, 130-131
Dickinson, Emily, **96**
Dickinson, John, 55, 69
Digital revolution, **293**, **296**
    e-mail communication, 327
    mobile phones, 327
    personal computer (PC) growth, 306, 327
Dix, Dorothea, 121
Dixiecrats, 319
Dole, Robert, 328
Doolittle, James "Jimmy," 223
Dorset, Marion, 177
Douglas, Stephen A., 136, 137, 138-139
Douglass, Frederick, **91**, 122, 134, 145
Drake, Francis, 10
Dred Scott decision, 138, 149
Dreiser, Theodore, 196
DuBois, W.E.B., 178, 211
Dukakis, Michael, 314
Dulles, John Foster, 265
Dunmore, Lord, 60
Dutch colonization, 14, 15, 17
    patroon system, 14-15
Dutch East India Company, 14
Dylan, Bob, 281

E
East India Company, 57
Eastman, George, 106, 157
Economic crisis bailout, 344
Edison, Thomas, **106**, 157
Education
    in the colonies, 27-29
    computer technology and, **303**
    day care centers, **303**
    No Child Left Behind Act, 333
    private schools, 27
    private tutors, 28
    public school systems, 121
    school desegregation, 240, 244, 272-273, 277
Edwards, Jonathan, 29
Eisenhower, Dwight David
    civil rights supporter, 272, 273
    Cold War and foreign policy, 264-265
    domestic policy of "dynamic conservatism," 269-270
    portrait of, **236**
    as president of U.S., 264-265, 269-270
    as Supreme Commander of Allied Forces, 223, **232**, 264
Electoral College, 116, 117
Elkins Act (1903), 196
Ellington, Duke, 211
Ellis Island Monument, **102**, 103, 200
Emancipation Proclamation, 144-145
Embargo Act (1807), 84
Emerson, Ralph Waldo, 59
Enforcement Acts (1870 and 1871), 150
English Civil War (1642-49), 31
English colonization
    early settlements, 10-12
    French and Indian War and, 32-33
    map of, **36-37**
    in Maryland, 15
    in Massachusetts, 13-14
    New England Confederation, 17
English common law, 30
Enola Gay (U.S. bomber), attacks on

Hiroshima and Nagasaki, 226
Environmental movement, 282, **298**, 344
Environmental Protection Agency (EPA), 282
Equal Rights Amendment (ERA), 279
Erik the Red, 9

F
Falwell, Jerry, 308
Farragut, David, 143
Faubus, Orval, 272
Federal Aid Road Act (1916), 113
Federal Artists Project, 218
Federal Deposit and Insurance Corporation (FDIC), 215, 343
Federal Emergency Relief Administration (FERA), 215
Federal Employee Loyalty Program, 266
Federal Reserve Act (1913), 198
Federal Reserve Board, 199, 218, 291, 310, 343
Federal Reserve System, 119, 187, 198-199
Federal Theatre Project, 218
Federal Trade Commission, 199
Federal Workingman's Compensation Act (1916), 199
Federal Writers Project, 218
The Federalist Papers, 43, 76
Federalists, 76, 78, 81, 82, 86, 116
The Feminine Mystique (Friedan), 278
The Financier (Dreiser), 196
Finney, Charles, Grandison, 87
Firefighters, **321**
"First universal nation," 345
Fitzgerald, F. Scott, 210
Force Act, 118
Ford, Gerald, 290-291
Ford, Henry, **109**
Fordney-McCumber Tariff (1922), 207
Foreign policy. *See* U.S. foreign policy
France

Louisiana Territory sold to U.S., 83-84
New World exploration, 9-10
U.S. diplomatic relations, 82-83
XYZ Affair, 82
Franco-American Treaty of Alliance (1778), 62-63, 80, 82
Franklin, Benjamin, 28, 33, **43**, 63, 64, 72, 75
Free Soil Party, 136, 137, 138
Freedmen's Bureau, 148, 151
Fremont, John, 138
French and Indian War, 32-33
French exploration, 10
French Huguenots, 24
French Revolution, 34, 79, 80, 81
Friedan, Betty, 278, 279
Friedman, Milton, 308
Fugitive Slave Act, 136, 137
Fundamentalism, religious, 209, 210, 308

G
Gage, Thomas, 59
Gallatin, Albert, 83
Garrison, William Lloyd, **91**, 122, 133-134
Garza, Eligio "Kika" de la, 280
Gates, Bill, **296**
Gates, Horatio, 62, 63-64
Gay rights, 307, 324-325
Genet, Edmond Charles, 80-81
George, Henry, 160
George III (British king), 55, 59
Georgia
  colonial royal government, 31
  early settlement, 18
  Native American tribes relocated, 118
German unification, 316
Germany
  Berlin Airlift, 262
  Kennedy speech in West Berlin, **242-243**

postwar period, 262
reparations, World War I, 224
Germany in World War II
    Holocaust (Jewish genocide), 226
    Nazism, 219, 224, 226
    North African campaign, 222
    Nuremberg war crime trials, 226
    reparations, 206
    submarine warfare, 204-205
Geronimo (Apache chief), 181
Gerry, Elbridge, 72, 73
Ghent, Treaty of (1814), 85
Gilbert, Humphrey, 10
The Gilded Age (Twain), 196
Ginsberg, Allen, 271
Glenn, John, 285
Global warming, 344
Glorious Revolution (1688-89), 31, 32
Goethals, George W., 185
Goldwater, Barry, 286, 308, 309
Gompers, Samuel, 194
González, Henry B., 280
Gorbachev, Mikhail, **304-305**, 314, 315, 316
Gore, Al, 323, 332, 333
Gould, Jay, 194
Grange movement, 191
Grant, Ulysses S.
    as president of U.S., 150, 153
    as Union Army general, 144, 145
    portrait of, **95**
Great Depression (1929-40)
    decline in immigration, 201
    "Dust Bowl" migration, 216
    New Deal programs, 214-218
    soup lines, **202-203**
    stock market crash (1929), 211
"Great Society," 286-287
Greeley, Horace, 112, 124
Green Party, 332
Greenspan, Alan, 327
Grey, Zane, 180
Guadalupe Hidalgo, Treaty of, 135
Guam, U.S. relations, 184

H

Haiti, political situation, 330
Hamilton, Alexander
    and Bank of the United States, 79, 118
    Constitutional Convention delegate, 71, 72
    Federalist Papers and, 43, 76
    as first Secretary of the Treasury (Department of the Treasury), 77
    portrait of, **48**
    and Republican Party, 152
    vs. Jefferson, 48, 78-80
Hamilton, Andrew, 28
Harding, Warren G., 207
Harrison, Benjamin, 160
Harrison, William Henry, 85, 120
Hartford Convention (1814), 117
Harvard College, 27
Hawaii, statehood (1959), 184
Hawaiian Islands, U.S. policy of annexation, 183-184
Hawley-Smoot Tariff Act (1930), 207
Hay, John, 184, 186
Hayes, Rutherford B., 150-151, 153
Haymarket Square incident, 194
Health care, 344
Health insurance, 344-345
Helsinki Accords (1975), 291
Hemingway, Ernest, 109, 210
Henry, Patrick, **42**, 54, 76, 77
Hepburn Act (1906), 197
Hidalgo, Miguel de, 114
Highway Act (1956), 268
Hispanics
    in politics, 280
    See also Latino movement
Hiss, Alger, 266
Hitler, Adolf, 201, 219
Ho Chi Minh, 284
Hohokam settlements, 7
Holy Alliance, 115
Homeland Security Department, 334
Homestead Act (1862), 124, 152,

179, 180
Hoover, Herbert, 185, 211
Hopewellians, 7
Hopi Indians, 8
Housing and Urban Development Department, 287
Houston, Sam, 134
Howe, William, 61-62
Hudson, Henry, 14
Hughes, Langston, 211
Hull, Cordell, 221
Humphrey, Hubert, 288
Hungary, rebellion (1956), 265
Hutchinson, Anne, 14

I

Immigrants and immigration
   diversity of immigrants, 200-201
   Ellis Island Monument, **102**, 103, 200
   illegal immigrants, 201
   immigration quotas, 201, 209
   "Little Italy" in New York City, **104-105**
   Nativists and, 209
   policy reform, 307
   restrictions on immigration, 208-209
Immigration Restriction League, 201
Imperialism, 181-182
Indentured servants, 18-19
Indian Removal Act (1830), 125
Indian Reorganization Act (1934), 181
Indian Wars
   Apache wars, 180, 181
   Custer's Last Stand at Little Bighorn, **98-99**, 180
   French and Indian War, 32-33
   Pequot War (1637), 16
   and westward expansion, 124, 180-181
Indians of North America. *See* Native Americans
Individual rights, 34, 65, 76-77

See also Civil rights
Industrial development. *See under names of industry*
Industrial Workers of the World (IWW), **194**
Interstate Commerce Commission (ICC), 159, 197, 198
Inventions
   adding machine, 157
   airplane, **107**
   cash register, 157
   cotton gin, 114, 133
   light bulb/incandescent lamp, 106, 157
   linotype machine, 157
   motion picture projector, **106**, 157
   reaper (farm machine), 131, 158, 160
   telegraph, 156
   telephone, **107**, 156
   television, 268
   typewriter, 157
Iran, U.S. relations, 292
   Axis of evil, 334
Iraq
   elections (2005), **302**
   provisional government, 335
   U.N. weapons inspections, 329, 334-335
   U.S.-led invasion, 335
Iron and steel industry, 157, 187
   strikes, 194, 228
Iroquois Indians, 14, 16-17, 33
Islam, 345
Isolationism, 78, 206, 220
Israel
   Egypt invasion, 265
   Palestinian relations, 330
   U.S. policy, 264

J

Jacinto, Battle of, 134
Jackson, Andrew
   conflicts with Indians, 125

as general in War of 1812, 86
portrait of, **89**
as president of U.S., 89, 117-118
presidential election (1824), 116
presidential election (1828), 117
Jackson, Helen Hunt, 181
Jackson, Jesse, **253**
Jackson, Thomas J. ("Stonewall"), 144, 145
James I (British king), 12
James II (British king), 31
Jamestown colony (Virginia), 10, 12-13, 16
Japan
attack on Pearl Harbor, **212-213**, 221, 222
Kamikaze suicide missions, 225
surrender (1945), 226
U.S. attacks on Hiroshima and Nagasaki, 226
U.S. relations, 186
Japanese-Americans, internment camps, 222, **233**
Jay, John, 43, 64, 76, 81, 82
Jay Treaty (Britain-U.S.), 81, 82
Jazz Age, 210
Jefferson Memorial (Wash., D.C.), **161**
Jefferson, Thomas
on abolition of slavery, 114
as drafter of Declaration of Independence, 61
face of (Mount Rushmore), **170-171**
as first Secretary of State (U.S. Department of State), 77
portrait of, **46**
as president of U.S., 83
on right of self-government, 68
on slavery, 114
as U.S. minister to France, 72, 79-80
vs. Adams, 82
vs. Hamilton, 48, 78-80
"Jim Crow" laws (separate but equal segregation), 151, 240, 272, 319

Jobs, Steve, **296**
Johnson, Andrew
impeachment trial, 149-150
as president of U.S., 147-149, 153
Johnson, Lyndon B.
civil rights supporter, 273, 277
Great Society programs, 286-287
portrait of, **245**
space program, 285
Vietnam War policy, 287-288
"War on Poverty," 286
Johnson-Reed National Origins Act (1924), 201, 209
The Jungle (Sinclair), 196

K

Kansas
slavery issue and, 138
territory ("bleeding Kansas"), 137, 138
Kansas-Nebraska Act, 137
Kennan, George, 261
Kennedy, John F.
assassination of, 277, 286
Bay of Pigs invasion, 284
civil rights policy, 277, 283
Cold War and, 284-285
Cuban missile crisis, 284
as president of U.S., 282-285
space program, 285-286
Vietnam War policy, 284-285
West Berlin speech during Cold War, **242-243**
Kennedy, Robert, assassination of, 278, 288
Kentucky
Resolutions (1798), 117
statehood (1792), 7-8
Kerouac, Jack, 270
Kerry, John F., 336-337
Khomeini, Ayatollah, 292
Khrushchev, Nikita, 284
Kim Il-sung, 263
King, Martin Luther, Jr.

assassination of, 278, 288
civil rights movement and, 240, **241**, 273, 283
"I have a dream" speech, 276, 277
King, Rufus, 72
Kissinger, Henry, 289
Know-Nothing Party, 120
Korean War, **235**, 263, 264
Kosciusko, Thaddeus, 65
Ku Klux Klan, 150, 201, 209

L

La Follette, Robert, 196, 318-319
Labor unions, 121, 193-195
    air controllers strike, 309
    auto workers strikes, 228
    collective bargaining, 217
    Haymarket Square incident, 194
    membership in U.S., 227-228
    migrant farm workers, 250, 279-280
    mine workers membership/strikes, 194-195, 227-228
    New Deal programs, 217
    post-World War I strikes, 206
    post-World War II strikes, 269
    railway worker strikes, 193, 194
    steel worker strikes, 194, 228
    textile worker strikes, 195
    "Wobblies," 194-195
    See also under names of specific unions
Lafayette, Marquis de, 65
Landon, Alf, 218
Latin America, U.S. intervention, 184-185
Latin American Revolution, 114-116
Latino movement, 279-280
League of Nations, 205-206, 226
Lee, Richard Henry, 61, 64
Lee, Robert E.
    capture of John Brown at Harper's Ferry, 139
    commander of Confederate Army, 144

    declines command of Union Army, 143
    portrait of, **95**
    surrender at Appomattox Courthouse, 146
Leif (son of Erik the Red), 9
Lenin, V.I., 259
Levitt, William J., 268
Lewis and Clark expedition, bicentennial commemorative stamp, **46**
Lewis, John L., 227-228
Lewis, Meriwether, 47
Lewis, Sinclair, 210
The Liberator, 91, 133
Libraries
    American Philosophical Society (Philadelphia), 28
    in the colonies, 27, 28
    public libraries endowed by Carnegie, 97
    subscription, 28
Lincoln, Abraham
    assassination of, 147, 153
    at Civil War Union encampment, **140-141**
    Emancipation Proclamation, 144-145
    face of (Mount Rushmore), **170-171**
    Free-Soil Party and, 138
    Gettysburg address, 142, 145
    on Grant, 95
    as president during Civil War, 142-147
    presidential election (1860), 139
    presidential election (1864), 147, 153
    presidential inaugural address, 142
    senatorial campaign (1858), 138-139
    on slavery and the Union, 130, 138
Lincoln, Benjamin, 63, 70
Lincoln-Douglas debates (1858), 138-139
Literary works

"Beat Generation" (1950s), 270-271
colonial period, 28-29
"Harlem Renaissance," 211
"Lost Generation" (1920s), 109, 211
New Deal programs and, 218
See also names of individual authors or works
Lloyd George, David, **108**
Locke, John, 17, 32, 34, 61, 65, 73
Lodge, Henry Cabot, 181, 184
Logan, James, 28
The Lonely Crowd (Riesman), 270
Long, Huey P., assassination of, 217
"Lost Generation" (1920s), 109, 211
Louis XVI (French king), 64, 80
Louisiana Purchase, 83-84
Lovejoy, Elijah P., 134
Lowell, James Russell, 147
Luce, Henry, 258
Lundestad, Geir, 262

M

MacArthur, Douglas, 225, **232**, 263
Macdonough, Thomas, 85
Madison, James, **43**, 72, 75, 76, 84-86, 113
    as "Father of the Constitution," 72
Mahan, Alfred Thayer, 184
Maine (U.S. warship) incident, 182
Major, John, 330
Malcolm X, 277
Manhattan. *See* New York
Manhattan project (atomic bomb development), 225
Mann, Horace, 121
Mao Zedong, 263, 289
Marbury v. Madison (1803), 113
Marcos, Ferdinand, 312
Marshall, George C., 262
Marshall, John
    as chief justice of the Supreme Court, 49, 113
    funeral of, 168
    portrait of, **49**

Marshall Plan, 262
Marshall, Thurgood, **244**
Martin, Josiah, 60
Maryland
    Calvert family charter, 15, 30
    Catholic settlements, 15
    St. Mary's, first town in, 15
    Toleration Act and religious freedom, 17
Mason, George, 76
Massachusetts
    Boston Massacre (1770), 56
    Boston Port Bill, 57
    Boston Tea Party (1773), **50-51**, 57
    colonial government charter, 30-31
    early settlements, 13-14
    Old Granary Cemetery (Boston), **162-163**
    Salem witch trials, 35
    schools and education, 27
    Shays Rebellion, 70
    trade and economic development, 24-25
Massachusetts Bay Colony, 25, 31
Massachusetts Bay Company, 18
Mather, Cotton, 28, **40**
Mayflower Compact, 13, **22-23**, 30
Mayflower (ship), 13
McCain, John
    (2008) presidential election 342-343
McCarran-Walter Act (1952), 201
McCarthy, Joseph R., **236**, 266
McClellan, George, 144, 147
McCormick, Cyrus, 131, 158, 160
McCulloch v. Maryland (1819), 113
McGovern, George, 290
McGrath, J. Howard, 266
McKinley, William
    assassination of, 195
    Hawaii annexation treaty, 184
    Maine (U.S. warship) incident, 182
    Open Door foreign policy, 195
    as president of U.S., 182, 184, 192, 195

McVeigh, Timothy, 331
Meat Inspection Act, 197
Meat-packing industry, 158, 196, 197
Mellon, Andrew, 207
Mencken, H.L., 210
Menéndez, Pedro, 10
Merchant Marine, 208
Meredith, James, 277
Methodists, 87, 88
Mexican-Americans. *See* Latino movement
Mexican War, 134-135
Mexico
   conquest of, 9
   revolution, 185
   Spanish colonization, 11
Middle colonies, 25-26
Middle East
   Palestinians, 329-330
   peace negotiations, 329-330
   Persian Gulf War, 316-317
   U.S. policy, 264, 292, 313, 329-330
Millet, Kate, **248**
Mining industry strikes, 194-195
Miranda, Francisco, 114
Missouri Compromise (1820), 90, 114, 132, 135, 137
Mohler, George, 177
Molasses Act (England, 1733), 53
Molotov, Vyacheslav, 260
Mondale, Walter, 311
Monetary policy. *See* U.S. monetary policy
Monroe Doctrine, 114-116
Monroe, James, 113, 115, 116
Montgomery, Bernard, 222
Montoya, Joseph, 280
Monuments and memorials, 161-176
   See also under names of individual memorials
Moral Majority, 308
Morgan, John Pierpoint (J.P.), 187
Morrill Land Grant College Act (1862), 152, 177

Morris, Gouverneur, 72
Morse, Samuel F.B., 156
Mott, Lucretia, 122
Mound builders, 7
Mount Rushmore Monument (South Dakota), **170-171**
Mount Vernon (Virginia), Washington's plantation home, **170-171**
Ms. (feminist magazine), 279
MTV, **297**
Murray-Philip, 228
Music, American
   Beatles, 281
   "hard rock," 281
   Jazz Age (1920s), 210
   Jazz musicians, 211
   rock and roll (1950s), 271, 281
   Rolling Stones, 271, 281
   Woodstock (outdoor rock concert, 1969), **249**, 281
Muslims, 344, 345
Mussolini, Benito, 219, 223
Mutual Board of Defense (U.S.-Canada), 220

N

NAACP. *See* National Association for the Advancement of Colored People (NAACP)
Nader, Ralph, 287, 332, 336
NAFTA. *See* North American Free Trade Agreement (NAFTA)
Napoleon, 82, 83, 84
National Association for the Advancement of Colored People (NAACP), 211, 244, 272, 273
National health care system, 344-345
National Industrial Recovery Act (NIRA), 217, 227
National Labor Relations Act (NLRA), 217, 218, 228, 280
National Labor Relations Board (NLRB), 217
National Organization for Women

(NOW), 279
National Recovery Administration (NRA), 217
National Security Council (NSC), NSC-68 security report on Soviet Union, 262-263, 265
National Woman Suffrage Association (NWSA), 123
National Youth Administration, 218
Native-American movement, 280-281
   American Indian Movement (AIM), 281
   Wounded Knee (South Dakota) incident, 180, 281
Native Americans
   cultural groups, map of, **21**
   demonstration in Washington (1978), **252**
   effect of European disease on, 8
   European contact, 9-10
   Great Serpent Mound, Ohio, **168**
   Indian uprisings, 16-17, 180-181
   Mesa Verde cliff dwellings, **4-5**, 8
   migration across Beringia land bridge, 6
   mound builders of Ohio, 7
   Northwest Passage and, 9, 10
   oral tradition, 8
   Pacific Northwest potlatches, 8
   population, 8
   Pueblo Indians, 8, 20
   relations with European settlers, 15-17, 18, 39
   religious beliefs, 8
   slave trade, 18
   Trail of Tears (Cherokee forced relocation), 125
   U.S. policy, 181
   Westward expansion and, 178
   See also Indian Wars; *and see under names of individual tribes*
Nativists, 209
Naturalization Act, 82
Nebraska, territory, 137

New Amsterdam. *See under* New York
New Deal programs, 214-218
New England colonies, 17, 24-25, 30-31
New England Confederation, 17
New Mexico territory, 136
New World exploration, 9-11
New World settlements. *See* Colonial period
New York
   colonial royal government, 31
   Dutch settlers, 14, 15, 25-26
   Manhattan, early settlement, 14, 15, 25-26
   New Amsterdam/New Netherland settlement, 14, 15, 26
   polyglot of early settlers, 25-26
New York Weekly Journal, 28
Ngo Dien Nu, 285
Ngo Dinh Diem, 285
Nichols, Terry, 331
Niebuhr, Reinhold, 345
NIRA. *See* National Industrial Recovery Act (NIRA)
Nixon, Richard M.
   China-U.S. diplomatic relations, 289
   at Great Wall of China, **250-251**
   impeachment and resignation, 290
   as president of U.S., 288-290
   presidential elections (1960, 1968, 1972), 283, 288, 290
   Soviet Union détente policy, 289
   Watergate affair, 290
NLRA. *See* National Labor Relations Act (NLRA)
No Child Left Behind Act, 333
Nobel Peace Prize, 344, 345
Noble Order of the Knights of Labor (1869), 193
Non-Intercourse Act (1809), 84
Noriega, Manuel Antonio, 317
Norris, Frank, 196
North American Free Trade

Agreement (NAFTA), 317, 325
North Atlantic Treaty Organization (NATO), 262
North Carolina colony, 17, 30
Northern Securities Company, 187
Northwest Ordinance (1787), 71, 73, 113, 135
Northwest Passage, 9, 10
Northwest Territory, 71, 113
NOW. *See* National Organization for Women (NOW)
Nuclear weapons
    Intermediate-Range Nuclear Forces (INF) Treaty, **304-305**, 314
    Limited Nuclear Test Ban Treaty (1963), **243**, 284
    Manhattan Project (atomic bomb development), 225
    SALT I (Strategic Arms Limitation Talks), 289
    SALT II agreement, 292
    Soviet atomic bomb testing, 266
    Strategic Defense Initiative (SDI), 313-314
    test bans, 284
    U.S. attacks on Hiroshima and Nagasaki, 226
    U.S. defense buildup, 314
    U.S. military defense buildup, 314
    U.S. nuclear testing, **234**
    U.S. policy during Cold War, 265
Nullification doctrine, 83, 117-118

O

Oath of office, presidential, 77
Obama, Barack H.
    background, 342-343
    at Cairo University, 345
    on democracies, 342
    financial crisis, 343-344
    health care, 344-345
    inaugural address, 343-344
    Nobel Peace Prize, 344-345
    parents, 343
    as presidential candidate, **341**
    presidential campaign (2008), 343
    with George W. Bush, **339**
    with Michelle Obama, **295**
The Octopus (Norris), 196
Office of Economic Opportunity, 286
Oglethorpe, James, 18
Oklahoma Territory, City, homestead claims, **101**
Oliver, King, 211
Olney, Richard, 194
On the Road (Kerouac), 270
Organization of American States (*formerly* Pan American Union), 185
Organization of the Petroleum Exporting Countries (OPEC), 290
Organized labor. *See* Labor unions
Orlando, Vittorio, **108**

P

Pacific Railway Acts (1862-64), 152
Paine, Thomas, 60
Palin, Sarah, 342
Palmer, A. Mitchell, 206-207
Panama, U.S. invasion, 317
Panama Canal
    Gatun locks, **100-101**
    treaties, 101, 184-185, 292
Paris Peace Conference (1919), 108
Paris, Treaty of (1783), 47, 64
Parker, John, 59
Parks, Rosa, **240**, 273
Patroon system, 14-15
Peace Democrats or "Copperheads," 152
Peace of Paris (1763), 33
Penn, William, 18, 25, 30, 39
Pennsylvania colony
    colonial government, 30
    cultural developments, 27-28
    German settlers, 25
    population, 25
    Quakers as early settlers, 18, 25, 27
    relations with Native Americans, 18, 39

schools and education, 27-28
state constitution, 69
See also Philadelphia
Pequot Indian War (1637), 16
Perkins, Frances, 227
Perot, H. Ross, 319, 323, 328
Perry, Oliver Hazard, 85
Pershing, John J., 205
Persian Gulf War, 316-317
   Desert Storm campaign, **252-253**
Philadelphia
   American Philosophical Society, 28
   as "City of Brotherly Love," 18
   colonial period in, 18, 25
   Friends Public School, 27
   Independence Hall, **164-165**
   Liberty Bell, **168**
   private schools, 27
   subscription libraries, 28
Philippine Islands
   elections, 312
   MacArthur's return, **232**
   U.S. relations, 183, 184
   World War II battles, 224-225, 232
Pierce, Franklin, 137
Pilgrims, 13, **22-23**, 30, 65
Pinckney, Charles, 81
The Pit (Norris), 196
Pitcairn, John, 59
Pizarro, Francisco, 9
Plains Indians, 10, 98, 180-181
Plessy v. Ferguson (1896), 178, 272
Political parties
   American Independent, 319
   Bull Moose Party, 318
   Constitutional Union Party, 139
   Democrats, 116, 137, 152, 153, 192, 218-219
   Dixiecrats, 319
   Federalists, 76, 78, 81, 82, 86, 116
   Free Soil Party, 136, 137, 138
   Green Party, 332
   Know-Nothings, 120
   Populists, 191-192
   Progressive, 318-319
   Radical Republicans, 148-151
   Reform Party, 319
   Republicans (or Democratic-Republicans), 78, 81, 138, 139, 152, 153, 218
   Socialists, 206, 318
   Southern Democrats, 139
   States Rights, 272
   third-party and independent candidates, 318-319
   Whigs, 119-121, 137-138, 152, 153
Polk, James K., 134, 135
Ponce de León, Juan, 9
Population growth
   in cities and towns, 159
   household composition, 307
   postwar migrations, 267-268
Population, U.S.
   in 1690, 24
   in 1775, 24
   1790 census, 200
   1812 to 1852, 124
   1860 census, 132
Populist Party, 191-192
Powell, Colin, **294-295**
Presidency, U.S.
   Cabinet, 77-78, 280
   impeachment, 149-150, 290, 328, 329
   oath of office, 77
   role of first lady, 324
   See also names of individual presidents
Presidential elections
   1789 (Washington, first), 77
   1797 (Adams), 82
   1800 (Jefferson), 83
   1824 (Jackson), 116
   1828 (Jackson), 117
   1860 (Lincoln), 139
   1864 (Lincoln), 147, 153
   1868 (Grant), 150
   1884 (Cleveland), 159

1892 (Cleveland), 160
1896 (McKinley), 192
1900 (McKinley), 195
1904 (Roosevelt), 197
1908 (Taft), 197-198
1912 (Wilson), 318, 328
1916 (Wilson), 205, 328
1920 (Harding), 207
1924 (Coolidge), 318-319
1932 (Roosevelt), 211
1936 (Roosevelt), 218
1940 (Roosevelt), 220
1948 (Truman), **235**, 269, 319
1960 (Kennedy), 283
1964 (Johnson), 286, 308, 309
1968 (Nixon), 288, 319
1972 (Nixon), 290
1976 (Carter), 291
1980 (Reagan), 309
1984 (Reagan), 310-311
1988 (Bush), 314
1992 (Clinton), 319, 322-324
1996 (Clinton), 328-329
2000 (Bush), 332-333
2004 (Bush), 336-337
2008 (Obama), 342-343
Presley, Elvis, **238**, 271
Press
   Cable News Network (CNN), 297
   first newspaper, 28
   first printing press in colonies, 27
   freedom of the, 28-29
Progressive Party, 318-319
Progressivism, 195, 196
Prohibition, 121, 210
Protestant religion
   Baptists, 87, 88
   Great Awakening, 29
   Methodists, 87, 88
   revivals in "Burned-Over District," 87
   Second Great Awakening and, 87-88
   See also Pilgrims; Puritans
Public Utility Holding Company Act, 218
Public Works Administration (PWA), 215
Pueblo Indians, 8, 20
Puerto Rico
   ceded to U.S., 182-183
   as U.S. commonwealth, 184
Pulitzer Prize, 347
Pure Food and Drug Act (1906), 197
Puritans, 13-14, 40, **40**, 65

Q

Quakers
   abolition movement and, 133
   and British government relations, 59
   Pennsylvania settlements, 18, 25
   schools and education, 27
Quartering Act (England, 1765), 53-54, 58
Quayle, Dan, 323
Quebec Act (England), 58
Quotations, notable
   "Ask not what your country can do for you — ask what you can do for your country" (Kennedy), 283
   "axis of evil" (Bush), 334
   "The Buck Stops Here," 260
   "city upon a hill" (Winthrop), 13, 309
   "Damn the torpedoes! Full speed ahead" (Farragut), 143
   "a day that will live in infamy" (Roosevelt), 221
   "Give me liberty, or give me death" (Henry), 42
   "Go west, young man" (Greeley), 112, 124
   "A house divided against itself cannot stand" (Lincoln), 130, 138
   "I have a dream..." (King, Jr.), 276
   "I shall return" (MacArthur), 232
   "Ich bin ein Berliner" (I am a Berliner) (Kennedy), 242
   "iron curtain" (Churchill), 260-261
   "shot heard round the world"

(Emerson), 59
"thousand points of light" (Bush), 315
"tyranny over the mind of man" (Jefferson), 161
"With malice towards none" (Lincoln), 147

R
Race riots, 152, 206
Racial discrimination
  bus segregation, 240, 273
  color barrier broken by Jackie Robinson, 237, 271
  in federal government employment, 269, 272
  "Jim Crow" laws (segregation), 151, 272, 319
  lynchings and violence against African Americans, 150, 178, 271
  military segregation, 269, 272
  school segregation, 240, 244
  separate but equal accommodations, 178, 240, 272
  South African apartheid, 312
  white supremacy and belief in black inferiority, 178
Radical Republicans, 148-151
Railroad industry, 131-132
  Great Rail Strike (1877), 194
  nationalization of, 192
  Pullman Company, 194
  regulation, 159, 197
  transcontinental link at Promontory Point (1869), 179
  transcontinental railroad, **154-155**
  westward expansion and, 179
  workers' hours, 199
  workers' strikes, 193, 194
Raleigh, Walter, 10
Reagan, Ronald
  conservatism and, 307-309
  economic policy, 309-311
  foreign policy, 311-313

  as "Great Communicator," 309
  Grenada invasion, 312-313
  Iran-Contra affair, 312-313
  with Mikhail Gorbachev, **304-305**
Reconstruction Act (1867), 148
Reconstruction Era, 148-151
  African-American members in Congress during, **96**
  Lincoln's program, 147-148
Reconstruction Finance Corporation, 211
Red Cloud (Sioux chief), 180
Reform Party, 319
Refugee Act (1980), 201
Religion
  camp meetings and revivals, 87-88
  Christian Coalition, 308
  Christian evangelicals, 332, 336
  circuit riders, 88
  fundamentalism, 209, 210, 308
  Great Awakening, 29
  Moral Majority, 308
  Salem witch trials, 35
  Second Great Awakening, 87-88
Religious freedom
  Coercive or Intolerable Acts and, 58
  freedom of worship, 32
  and tolerance, 17, 29, 32
"Remaking America," 344
Republicanism, 65, 68
Republicans (or Democratic-Republicans), 78, 81, 138, 139, 152, 153, 218
Reuther, Walter, 228
Revels, H.R., **96**
Revolution. *See* American Revolution; French Revolution; Latin American Revolution
Revolutionary War. *See* American Revolution
Rhode Island colony, 14, 31, 41
Rice, Condoleeza, **295**
Ridgway, Matthew B., 264
Riesman, David, 270

"Roaring Twenties," 109, 210
Robertson, Pat, 308
Robinson, Jackie, **237**, 271
Rochambeau, Comte Jean de, 64
Rockefeller, John D., 158
Roe v. Wade (1973), 279, 308, 324
Rogers, William, **251**
Rolfe, John, 12
Rommel, Erwin, 222
Roosevelt, Eleanor, 324
Roosevelt, Franklin D.
   death of, 224
   on democracy, 214, 219
   foreign policy, 185
   Good Neighbor Policy, 185
   labor unions and, 227
   New Deal programs, 214-218
   presidential elections (1932, 1936, 1940), 207, 211, 218, 220
   Social Security Act, signing of, **230**
   Social Security program, 218, 230
   World War II and, 219-220
   World War II peace negotiations, 224
   at Yalta (1945), 224, **234**
Roosevelt, Theodore
   accession to the presidency, 195
   on democracy, 190
   face of (Mount Rushmore), **170-171**
   foreign policy, 181, 184, 186
   Nobel Peace Prize recipient (1906), 186
   Panama Canal treaty, 184-185
   presidential election (1912), 318
   "Rough Riders" in the Spanish-American War, 183
   "Square Deal," 196
   as "trust-buster" and antitrust laws, 160, 187, 196-197
Root, Elihu, 181
Rose, Ernestine, 122
Rosenberg, Julius and Ethel, 266
"Rosie the Riveter," 222

Royal Proclamation (England, 1763), 53
Rural Electrification Administration, 218
Russian Revolution (1917), 206, 259
Russo-Japanese War (1904-05), 186

S
Sadat, Anwar al-, 292
Saddam Hussein, 316, 317, 329, 334-335
San Martin, José de, 114
Santa Anna, Antonio López de, 134
Scopes, John, 209
Scopes trial, 209-210
Scott, Dred, 138
Scott, Winfield, 135
Seamen's Act (1915), 199
Second Treatise on Government (Locke), 32, 61
Sectionalism, and slavery issue, 128-139
Sedition Act, 82, 117
Seminole Indians, 125
Separation of church and state, 14
Separation of powers principle, 74
Separatists, 13
Seven Years' War, 33, 63, 83
Seventh Day Adventists, 87
Seward, William, 138, 182
Seymour, Horatio, 152
The Shame of the Cities (Steffens), 196
Sharon, Ariel, 330
Shays, Daniel, 70
Shays's Rebellion (1787), 70, 73
Sherman Antitrust Act (1890), 160, 187
Sherman, Roger, 72, 73
Sherman, William T., 146
Silent Spring (Carson), 282
Sinclair, Upton, 196
Sioux Indians, 98, 180, 281
Sitting Bull (Sioux chief), **98**
Slave family, **128-129**
Slave owners, 132
Slave population, 132

Slave trade, 19, 25, 133, 136
Slavery
    African slaves, 19, 24
    constitutional amendment (13th) abolishing, 148
    Dred Scott decision, 138, 149
    Emancipation Proclamation, 144-145
    equal rights and, 69
    extension of, 113-114
    free vs. slave states, 114, 123
    Fugitive Slave Laws, 136, 137
    Indian slaves, 17-18
    Missouri Compromise (1820), 90, 114, 132, 135, 137
    Northwest Ordinance ban on, 71, 73, 113, 135
    as the "peculiar institution," 132
    plantations in the south and, 113-114, **128-129**
    revolt in Haiti, 83
    as a sectional conflict/divided nation, 128-139
    in the territories, 71, 73, 113, 135, 136-138
    See also Abolition of slavery
Smith, Capt. John, 6, 12, **36**
Smith-Lever Act (1914), 199
Social activism, 87
Social-contract (theory of government), 61
Social liberalism, 34
Social reforms, 121-122, 195-196
    Great Society programs, 286-287
    Medicaid program, 287
    Medicare program, 286
    mental health care, 121-122
    New Deal programs, 214-218
    prison reform, 121
    progressivism, 195
    prohibition and the temperance movement, 121, 210
    Social Security, 218
    Truman Fair Deal programs, 268-269
    War on Poverty, 286
    welfare state and, 219
Social Security Act (1935), 218, 230
Socialist Party, 206, 318
Society for the Promotion of Temperance, 87, 121
Soil Conservation Service, 216
Somalia, 331
Sons of Liberty, 54
Soule, John, 124
South Africa, racial apartheid, 312
South Carolina
    colonial government, 30
    during American Revolution, 63-64
    early settlements, 17, 26
    French Huguenots, 24
    nullification crisis, 117-118
    protective tariffs, 117
    secession from the Union, 142
Southern Christian Leadership Conference (SCLC), 276
Southern colonies, 26-27
Southern Democrats, 139
Soviet Union
    Cold War, 258-265
    Sputnik and the space program, 285
    U.S. containment doctrine, 261-263
    U.S. détente policy, 289, 291, 292
    U.S. relations, 284, 313-314
Space program, **254**, **274-275**, 285
Spain, and American Revolution, 63
Spanish-American War (1898), 182, 183
Spanish exploration
    European settlement, 9, 11, **169**
    missions in California, **169**
    Seven Cities of Cibola and, 9
    St. Augustine (Florida), first St. John de Crèvecoeur, J. Hector, 24
St. Mary's (Maryland), 15
Stalin, Joseph, at Yalta, 224, **234**
Stamp Act (England), 54, 55
Standard Oil Company, 158, 196, 197

INDEX

Stanton, Edwin, 153
State constitutions, 68-69
Statehood, 78
States' rights, 79, 80
    nullification doctrine, 83, 117-118
States Rights Party, 272
Statue of Liberty (New York City), **167**, 201
Steel industry. *See* Iron and steel industry
Steel Workers Organizing Committee (SWOC), 228
Steffens, Lincoln, 196
Steinem, Gloria, **248**, 279
Steuben, Friedrich von, 65
Stevens, Thaddeus, 148
Stowe, Harriet Beecher, 137
Student Nonviolent Coordinating Committee (SNCC), 276
Sugar Act (England, 1764), 53, 55
Sunday, Billy, 209
Supreme Court Building (Wash., D.C.), **166**
Supreme Court, U.S.
    cases
        Brown v. Board of Education, 241, 244, 272
        Marbury v. Madison, 113
        McCulloch v. Maryland, 113
        Plessy v. Ferguson, 178, 272
        Roe v. Wade, 279, 308, 324
    decisions, 113
        Court's right of judicial review, 49
        Dred Scott, 138, 149
    enlargement proposal, 218-219
    See also Marshall, John; Marshall, Thurgood
Swedish colonization, 15, 200
Swift, Gustavus, 158

T

Taft, William Howard, 197-198, 318
Taiwan, 263, 265, 289
Talleyrand, Charles Maurice de, 82
Tarbell, Ida M., 196
TARP, see Troubled Assets Relief Program
Taxation
    Boston Tea Party (1773), **50-51**, 57
    British right to tax colonies (Declaratory Act), 55
    colonial period, 33, 53-59
    Committees of Correspondence, 56-57
    "without representation," 53, 54-55
    See also names of individual acts
Taylor, Zachary, 135
Technology. *See* Inventions
Television
    Cable News Network (CNN), **297**
    growth of, 268
    impact of, 268, 297
    MTV, **297**
    programming, 239, 268
Temperance movement, 87, 121
Tennessee, statehood (1796), 78
Tennessee Valley Authority (TVA), 215
Tenure of Office Act, 149
Terrorism
    anthrax poisoning scare, 333-334
    Cole (U.S. Navy destroyer) bombing (Yemen), 332
    Khobar Towers U.S. military housing (Saudi Arabia, 1996), 331
    Oklahoma City bombing (1995), 326, 331
    Palestinian suicide bombings, 330
    September 11, 2001 attacks on U.S., **320-321**, 333
    U.S. embassies (Kenya and Tanzania, 1998), 331-332
    World Trade Center bombings (1993), 331
Texas
    Alamo, battle of, 134
    Battle of San Jacinto, 134
    territory of, 134
    and War with Mexico, 134-135

Textile industry strikes, 195
Thorpe, Jim, 181
Thurmond, Strom, 272, 319
The Titan (Dreiser), 196
To Secure These Rights, 271-272
Tocqueville, Alexis de, 126, 130
Tojo, Hideki, 221, 225
Toleration Act (England, 1689), 31
Toleration Act (Maryland), 17
Townsend, Francis E., 217
Townshend Acts (England), 55-56
Townshend, Charles, 55
Trade policy. *See* U.S. trade policy
Transportation Act (1920), 208
Treaties. *See under name of individual treaty*
Troubled Assets Relief Program (TARP), 343
Truman Doctrine, 261
Truman, Harry S.
   accession to the presidency, 224
   civil rights program, 271-272
   Fair Deal domestic program, 268-269
   Hiroshima and Nagasaki atomic bomb attacks, 226
   labor unions and, 269
   NSC-68 defense policy, 262, 265
   as president of U.S., 258, 260
   presidential election (1948), **235**, 269
Trusts, 158
Tubman, Harriet, **91**
Turner, Frederick Jackson, 126
Twain, Mark. *See* Clemens, Samuel Langhorne
Tyler, John, 120

U

Uncle Tom's Cabin (Stowe), 137
Underground Railroad, 91, 134, 136
Unemployment, 344-345
Union Army of the Potomac, 145
Union Pacific Railroad, 179
United Auto Workers, 228
United Mine Workers (UMW), 227-228
United Nations, 224, 226
United States Steel Corporation, 157-158, 187
U.S. economy
   in the 1980s, 309-311
   in the 1990s, 327-328
   in the 2000s, 344-345
   "Black Monday" (stock market crash, 1987), 311
   federal budget deficits, 310-311, 315
   migration patterns in U.S., 267
   post-World War II period, 267-268
   stock market crash (1929), 211
   suburban development and, 268
   "supply side" economics, 309
   unemployment, 215-216, 227, 327
   See also Banking and finance; Great Depression
U.S. foreign policy, 80-82, 181-186
   in Asia, 185-186
   Bush (George W.) Administration, 332-337
   Clinton Administration, 328-331
   Cold War and, 258-267
   imperialism and "Manifest Destiny," 181-182
   Iran-Contra affair, 312-313
   isolationism, 78, 206, 220
   Jay Treaty with Britain, 81
   in Latin America, 185
   Monroe Doctrine, 115-116
   Obama administration, 345
   Open Door policy, 186, 195
   in the Pacific area, 183-184
   Panama Canal treaty, 184-185
   Reagan Administration, 313-314
   Truman Doctrine of containment, 261-263
   XYZ Affair with France, 82
U.S. monetary policy, 79-80, 343
   currency question, 192
   gold standard, 192

INDEX

  See also Banking and finance;
    Federal Reserve Board
U.S. trade policy
  economic impact of War of 1812, 86
  Embargo Act (1807), 84
  Fordney-McCumber Tariff
    (1922), 207
  Hawley-Smoot Tariff (1930), 207
  Massachusetts Bay Company
    "triangular U.S. trade policy," 25
  McKinley tariff, 160, 191
  Native Americans with European
    settlers, 15-16
  Non-Intercourse Act (1809), 84
  North American Free Trade
    Agreement, 317, 325
  protective tariffs, 112, 117, 152, 159
  slave trade, 19, 25, 133
  Underwood Tariff (1913), 198
  World Trade Organization
    (WTO), 325
U.S. Treasury (Department of), 343
USA Patriot Act, 334
Utah territory, 136

V

Van Buren, Martin, 120
Vanderbilt, Cornelius, 158
Vermont, statehood (1791), 78
Verrazano, Giovanni da, 10
Versailles, Treaty of, 206
Vespucci, Amerigo, 9
Vietnam
  French involvement, 284-285
  U.S. involvement, 285
  Viet Minh movement, 284
Vietnam Veterans Memorial (Wash.,
  D.C.), **172-173**
Vietnam War
  antiwar demonstrations, **248**, 258,
    281, 288-289
  Gulf of Tonkin Resolution, 287
  Kent State (Ohio) student
    demonstration, 288

military draft, 288
U.S. forces in, **246-247**
Villa, Francisco "Pancho," 185
Virginia
  Antifederalists, 76
  colonial government, 29-30
  Declaration of Rights, 77
  education by private tutors, 28
  Jamestown colony, 10, 12-13, 16
  Resolutions (1798), 117
  secession from the Union, 142-143
  state constitution, 68-69
  Tidewater region plantation
    settlements, 26, 28
Virginia Company, 12, 18, 29-30
Volcker, Paul, 291, 310
Voting rights
  for African Americans, 273, 277
  church membership requirement, 14
  Pennsylvania constitution, 69
  for women, 122
Voting Rights Act (1965), 277

W

Wallace, George, 288, 319
Wallace, Henry, 319
Wampanoag Indians, 13
War of 1812, 85-86, 112
War on terror, 345
Warren, Earl, 272
Washington, Booker T., 178
Washington, George
  on abolition of slavery, 113
  as commander in American
    Revolution, 60-62
  Constitutional Convention
    presiding officer (1787), **66-67**, 71
  crossing the Delaware (1776), 62
  face of (Mount Rushmore), **170-171**
  as first U.S. president, 77-78
  Long Island, battle of (1776), 61
  Mount Vernon plantation, home of,
    170-171

presidential oath of office, 77
retirement from presidency, 82
at Valley Forge (Pennsylvania), 62
as Virginia militia commander, 33
Yorktown, British surrender, **46-47**
Washington Monument (Wash., D.C.), **175**
Water Quality Improvement Act, 282
Wattenberg, Ben, 337, 345
Webster, Daniel, 120, 136
Welch, Joseph, **236**
Weld, Theodore Dwight, 134
Welfare state. See Social reforms
Welles, Gideon, 143
"The West." See Westward expansion
West, Benjamin, 39
Western Union, 158
Westward expansion
   cowboy life and "The Wild West," 180
   frontier settlers' life, 123-124
   Homestead Act (1862), 124, 152, 179, 180
   homesteading in the last frontier/ "The West," 126, 179-180
   Louisiana Purchase and, 83-84
   map of, **127**
   Northwest Ordinance (1787), 71, 73, 135
   in Oklahoma Territory, 101
   problems of, 53, 70-71
Whig Party, 119-121, 137-138, 152, 153
Whitefield, George, 29
Whitney, Eli, 114
Wigglesworth, Rev. Michael, 28
Will, George, 308
Williams, Roger, 14, **41**
Wilson, James, 72
Wilson, Woodrow
   Fourteen Points for WWI armistice, 205
   League of Nations and, 205-206
   portrait of, **108**
   as president of U.S., 198-199, 204-206
   presidential elections (1912 and 1916), 205, 328
   relations with Mexico, 185
   U.S. neutrality policy, 204-205
Winthrop, John, 13, 309
"Witch hunt," origin of the term, 35
Women
   constitutional council (Afghanistan) delegates, **294**
   education in the home arts, 27, 122
   labor unions and, 193
   no political rights, 69
   role of first lady, 324
   role of Native American, 8
   workers in war production ("Rosie the Riveter"), 222
   working conditions, 193
Women's rights, 122-123
   abortion issue, 308
   Equal Rights Amendment (ERA), 279
   feminism and, 278-279
   Married Women's Property Act, 122
   in Pennsylvania colony, 18
   state constitutions and, 69
Women's rights movement, 90, 248, 278-279
Women's suffrage, 90, 122
   march on Washington (1913), **188-189**
"Woodstock Generation" (1960s), **249**, 281
Works Progress Administration (WPA), 218
World Trade Center Memorial (New York City), **176**
World Trade Organization (WTO), 325
World War I
   American infantry forces, **108**
   "Big Four" at Paris Peace Conference (1919), **108**

INDEX

German submarine warfare, 204-205
  postwar unrest, 206-207
  U.S. involvement, 205
  U.S. neutrality policy, 204-205
  Wilson's Fourteen Points for armistice, 205
World War II
  Atlantic Charter, 220
  Coral Sea, Battle of the (1942), 223
  Doolittle's Tokyo bombing raid, 223
  Eastern Front, 222
  G.I. Bill (veterans benefits), 268-269
  Guadalcanal, Battle of, 223, **231**
  Hiroshima and Nagasaki atomic bomb attacks, 225, 226
  Holocaust (Jewish genocide), 226
  in the Pacific arena, 223-224, 224-225, **231**
  Iwo Jima campaign, 225
  Japanese-American internment camps, 222, **233**
  Japanese Kamikaze suicide missions, 225
  Lend-Lease Program, 220
  Leyte Gulf, Battle of, 225
  Manhattan Project, 225
  Midway, Battle of, 223
  Normandy allied invasion, 223, **232**
  North African campaign, 222-223
  Nuremberg war crime trials, 226
  Okinawa campaign, 225
  peace-time conscription bill, 220
  Pearl Harbor, Japanese attack on (1941), **212-213**, 221
  politics of, 224
  postwar economy, 267-268
  postwar period, 258
  Potsdam Declaration, 225
  Roosevelt call for "unconditional surrender," 224
  Russian defense of Leningrad and Moscow, 222
  U.S. mobilization, 221-222
  U.S. neutrality policy, 219-220
  World War II Memorial (Wash., D.C.), **176**
Wright, Frances, 122
Wright, Orville (and Wilbur), **107**

X
XYZ Affair, 82

Y
Yale University (formerly Collegiate School of Connecticut), 27
Yalta Conference (1945), 224, **234**, 260
Yeltsin, Boris, 315-316
Yorktown, British surrender at, **46-47**, 64
Yugoslavia, post-Cold War, 330

Z
Zenger, John Peter, 28

ACKNOWLEDGMENTS

Outline of U.S. History is a publication of the U.S. Department of State. The first edition (1949-50) was produced under the editorship of Francis Whitney, first of the State Department Office of International Information and later of the U.S. Information Agency. Richard Hofstadter, professor of history at Columbia University, and Wood Gray, professor of American history at The George Washington University, served as academic consultants. D. Steven Endsley of Berkeley, California, prepared additional material. It has been updated and revised extensively over the years by, among others, Keith W. Olsen, professor of American history at the University of Maryland, and Nathan Glick, writer and former editor of the USIA journal, *Dialogue*. Alan Winkler, professor of history at Miami University (Ohio), wrote the post-World War II chapters for previous editions.

This new edition was completely revised and updated by Alonzo L. Hamby, Distinguished Professor of History at Ohio University in 2005. Chapter 16 was added in 2010-11. Professor Hamby has written extensively on American politics and society. Among his books are *Man of the People: A Life of Harry S. Truman* and *For the Survival of Democracy: Franklin Roosevelt and the World Crisis of the 1930s*. He lives and works in Athens, Ohio.

Executive Editor: Michael Jay Friedman
Editorial Director: Mary T. Chunko
Managing Editor: Chandley McDonald
Cover Design: Lisa Jusino
Photo Research: Maggie Johnson Sliker
Ann Monroe Jacobs

PHOTO CREDITS:

Credits from left to right are separated by semicolons, from top to bottom by dashes.

Cover design: Lisa Jusino. Cover images, left column, from top: Photos 1-2: AP/Wide World Photo. Photo 3: Virginia Museum of Fine Arts, Richmond. Photos 4-5: © Bettmann/CORBIS. Photo 6: LOC. Photo 7: California State Railroad Museum Library. Center photo: Mario Tama/AFP/Getty Images. Right column, from top: Photo 1: AP/Wide World Photo. Photo 2: The American History Slide Collection, © (IRC). Photos 3-4: AP/Wide World Photo. Photo 5: NASA. Photo 6: Dirck Halstead/Time Life Pictures/Getty Images. Photo 7: AP/Wide World Photo.
Pages 4, 5: © Russ Finley/Finley-Holiday Films. 21: National Atlas of the United States. 22-38: Library of Congress (3).
39: Courtesy The Pennsylvania Academy of Fine Arts. 40, 41: USIA Library - Library of Congress (2). 42, 43: Library of Congress (LOC); Time Life Pictures/Getty Images - The American History Slide Collection, © Instructional Resources Corporation (IRC). 44, 45: Painting by Don Troiani, www.historicalprints.com. 46, 47: AP/Wide World Photo; LOC - courtesy www.texasphilatelic.org. 48: National Portrait Gallery, Smithsonian Institution. 49: AP/Wide World Photo. 50, 51: LOC. 66, 67: Virginia Museum of Fine Arts, Richmond. Gift of Edgar William and Bernice Chrysler Garbisch.
89, 90: LOC (3). 91-93: The National Archives (NARA) - LOC (3). 94, 95: American History Slide Collection, © IRC (2), top right, LOC. 96: LOC - Amherst College Archives and Special Collections, by permission of the Trustees of Amherst College. 97: LOC - AP/Wide World Photo. 98, 99: LOC; NARA. 100, 101: courtesy Oklahoma Historical Society - AP/Wide World Photo. 102, 103: Culver - LOC. 104, 105: LOC. 106, 107: Edison Birthday Committee; © Bettmann/CORBIS - Fox Photos/Getty Images. 108: The National Archives (2). 109: Hulton Archive/Getty Images - AP/Wide World Photo. 110, 111: © Bettmann/CORBIS. 127: Courtesy Bureau of Census, Perry-Castaneda Library Map Collection, University of Texas. 128, 129: © Bettmann/CORBIS. 140, 141: LOC. 154, 155: California State Railroad Museum Library. 161-166: © Robert Llewellyn. 167: © James Casserly. 168: Mark C. Burnett/Photo Researchers, Inc. - Interior Department/National Park Service. 169: © Miles Ertman/Masterfile - © Chuck Place. 170, 171: AP/Wide World Photo - Cameron Davidson/FOLIO, Inc. 172, 173: Shawn Thew/AFP/Getty Images. 174: PhotoSpin, Inc. - Michael Ventura/FOLIO, Inc. 175: Mario Tama/AFP/Getty Images. 176: Joe Raedle/Getty Images - AP/Wide World Photo. 188, 189: LOC. 202, 203: The American History Slide Collection, © (IRC). 212, 213: The National Archives. 229: New York Daily News. 230: AP/Wide World (2). 231: The National Archives. 232: U.S. Army - The National Archives. 233: Lockheed - American History Slide Collection, © IRC. 234: U.S. Army - LOC. 235: © Bettmann/CORBIS - U.S. Army. 236: © Bettmann/CORBIS - Yousuf Karsh. 237: AP/Wide World Photo. 238: AP/Wide World Photo. 239: Culver. 240: © Bettmann/CORBIS. 241: AP/Wide World Photo. 242, 243: USIS Berlin - © Bettmann/CORBIS. 244: Ebony Magazine. 245: AP/Wide World Photo. 246, 247: U.S. Army. 248, 249: CORBIS - AP/Wide World Photo; Culver. 250, 251: Arthur Schatz/Time Life Pictures/Getty Images; © Bettmann/CORBIS. 252, 253: Barbara Ann Richards; Carol Hightower - John Wicart. 254: National Aeronautics and Space Administration (NASA). 255: David Valdez/The White House - Dwight Somers. 256, 257: J.R. Eyerman/Time Life Pictures/Getty Images. 274, 275: NASA. 293: Chris Honduras/Newsmakers/Getty Images. 294: AP/Wide World Photo (2). 295: © AP Images/Heiko Junge. 296: Jeff Christensen/AFP/Getty Images - AP/Wide World Photos. 297: Courtesy CNN - Courtesy MTV. 298, 299: AP/Wide World Photo; © John Harrington/Black Star. 300, 301: Kevin Horan. 302: AP/Wide World Photo. 303: Ken White - © Steve Krongard. 304, 305: Dirck Halstead/Time Life Pictures/Getty Images. 320, 321: AP/Wide World Photo. 339: © AP Images/Gerald Herber. 340, 341: © AP Images/Chris Carlson.

Made in the USA
Lexington, KY
27 May 2015